INTRINSIC TO
UNIVERSE

INTRINSIC TO
UNIVERSE

Tan Kheng Yeang

Order this book online at www.trafford.com
or email orders@trafford.com

Most Trafford titles are also available at major online book retailers.

Printed in the United States of America.

ISBN: 978-1-4269-5574-7 (sc)
ISBN: 978-1-4269-5575-4 (hc)
ISBN: 978-1-4269-5576-1 (e)

Library of Congress Control Number: 2011902475

Trafford rev. 04/12/2011

 www.trafford.com

North America & International
toll-free: 1 888 232 4444 (USA & Canada)
phone: 250 383 6864 ♦ fax: 812 355 4082

Acknowledgement

"The author wishes to thank Ms. Valerie Cameron for her invaluable assistance in preparing the manuscript of this book for publication."

CONTENTS

Part 3—State (A political, economic, and social system)

Author's Note

Please note that for economy of language, masculine pronouns have been used throughout this text. The author wishes to emphasize that the contents are implicitly and equally applicable to both men and women.

TKY

Preface

Existing civilizations are extrinsic to the scheme of things;
they are experiments on the road of progress and are
destined to be swept away in the course of evolution ...

Civilization is a uniquely human creation that has been fraught with war, strife, and iniquity. Past mistakes have been repeated again and again; and after several thousand years of experimentation, we still haven't gotten it right.

This book is not intended to depict a utopian world order, an unattainable ideal. Rather, it presents a serious system for creating a new civilization, designed to be realized in practice. Of course, there is no valid reason why even an ostensible utopia should evoke scorn in this age of cynicism; it is better to strive for an ideal than to passively accept injustice or, worse, to be so psychologically subjugated that wrong is deemed right. However, an ideal that cannot be effectively put into practice is still only a dream.

As the opening quotation states, existing civilizations are extrinsic to the scheme of things; they are experiments on the road of progress, and are destined to be swept away in the course of evolution.

The synthetic nature of the universe requires the eventual emergence of a civilization that is intrinsic to the universe. Intrinsicalism propounds the principles of a new civilization, which, unlike the idealized societies of Plato, More, Rousseau, and Locke, recognizes the innate foibles of human beings and works with—or in spite of—our faults to create a new world order.

Part 1

Civilization

Chapter 1
What Is Civilization?

When we study any group of people living together, we find certain rules and ways that constitute their common property. They exist in what is termed *society*, into which is interwoven an intricate network of principles enveloping the lives of its members, a network that may persist for centuries or millennia. This network is often torn in places and mended as the occasion requires, sometimes with threads of a hue absolutely different from that of the rest. Seldom has a new version replaced the old in its entirety, and the inevitable consequence is that society is not a harmonious entity but a thing of shreds and patches.

When a society attains a certain level of development, we say it enjoys civilization, which is associated with cities, refinement, culture, and knowledge. We look down on barbarians as beings who are fundamentally different from us, the civilized; however, as a matter of fact, there is a good deal of resemblance between the two modes of existence. Both have usually been moved by the potent force of religion, and both exhibit some kind of law and order—that is, what we may call state organization; religion and state are the two most significant elements of a society. The principal distinction of a civilized person is supposed to be gentleness of manners, but barbarians cannot be said to behave violently toward their friends and relatives, while many civilized races indulge in crude practices. Some primitive tribes expressed their pleasure by slashing their backs; the Germans, in their extremely refined universities, demonstrated their heroism by slashing one another's faces. The fact is that barbarism and civilization constitute dissimilar forms of organization of society, with the latter higher on the scale of evolution, yet often retaining the characteristics of the former. At various times, a number of distinct civilizations have flourished, and each was apt to regard the rest of the world as barbaric. The Greeks called all other people barbarians, including the Persians, who were every bit as cultured as they; in the nineteenth century, some Western writers referred to Oriental barbarism, while Chinese officials, in their memorials to their emperor, invariably called foreigners barbarians.

The lamentable tendency to confer this opprobrious epithet on members of other forms of social organization is based on a narrow definition of the term *civilization*. Every population possesses a certain standard of values, any deviation from which is stigmatized as barbaric. Because of its predominant position and consequent prestige, Western civilization has come to be the norm by which to measure the quality of other modes of existence. Its chief ingredient is the multiplicity and diversity of material products and inventions, which have steadily increased over the last few centuries, and this standard is used to determine the evolutionary stage of the numerous peoples of the world. This is no less preposterous than Oriental apologists harping on the supposedly spiritual excellence by which they connote their own particular national brand of metaphysical concepts and ethical decrees.

A comprehensive definition of *civilization* may be advanced. The first postulate is that there must be a community of people living in sufficient proximity to allow constant mutual intercourse. A number of hermits, each dwelling within a separate oasis and unknown to the rest, could not properly be said to constitute a society, much less a civilization. This does not mean, of course, that the individuals may not be highly cultivated and lead laudable lives; they may indeed be extremely civilized, yet, paradoxical though it sounds, they do not dwell in civilization. There must be a closely knit society whose size, beyond a minimum of a few thousand persons, is not greatly material, though a high population is one advantage.

The presence or absence of community organization is notable, and some common denominators are a prerequisite. Owing to the imitative nature of human beings, wherever people congregate, certain notions and practices automatically emerge and envelop the majority. If there are to be security and understanding, if life is to run its course on a plane of peace and prosperity, if a person is to believe that the man with whom he is amicably conversing will not abruptly draw out a dagger and swiftly dispatch him and that he can with reasonable certainty awake the next morning safe and sound, then there must be at least a minimal pattern of behavior in force and working smoothly. Food could not be well prepared, clothing comfortable, architecture a fine art, books stocked in libraries, poetry a delight, and science a marvel were there no society in which they could develop. I would not possess the paper on which I am writing had the Han Dynasty not ruled over an assemblage of mutually dependent humanity; nor would that sweating group outside my window be struggling to throw a ball into a basket if their minds had not been trained to adhere to rules.

In their primitive stage, humans were at the mercy of their environment, with few tools and little knowledge of how to fabricate any product. Beyond devouring wild flesh and satisfying their sexual instinct, they experienced no other needs. Little difference existed between these primitive people and the beasts they slew for food and that, in turn, preyed upon them; they were at once hunter and hunted, and this wholesome sport was their *raison d'être*. They retired to their natural caves to pass the horrid hours of night as a tiger crawls into its equally serviceable lair or an eagle flies to its more comfortable and commodious aerie. In their own way, these early people probably lived happy, satisfactory lives. Blessed (or cursed) with no haunting vision of a multiplicity of commodities, they could hardly suffer from the arch begetter of misery, discontent.

Well would it be if a mellifluous stream of joy could spontaneously generate in a person's heart and be pumped along with oxygen-carrying blood to the multitude of tiny cells that constitute his complex organs. Unfortunately, he has to depend on external aids, and the more he invents for himself, the more he desires, his appetite growing with its satisfaction. In the last few centuries, humans have stumbled upon the discovery that there is practically no limit to what we can fashion with our brains. We can cause symphonies to travel through space, winged vehicles to transport us from London to Tokyo, and machines to stock our homes with attractive objects created from a collection of crude elements transformed in a strange metamorphosis as wonderful as the emergence of the beautiful butterfly from the ugly caterpillar. What were at first luxuries have, through incessant use, become necessities. People have reached the pathetic stage of finding it difficult to subsist without their numerous crutches; should they sustain any deprivation, they suffer physical and mental pain. Should they lose their fortune and their ability to make purchases, they may even resort to suicide. Perceiving their brethren to be surrounded by the abundance they lack, the denizens of the slums pass their days in tenfold greater misery than the cave dwellers, whose possessions were certainly more exiguous than theirs.

We are captivated by comfort, and, frankly, there is nothing reprehensible in this. After all, pain is a symptom of disease, of derangement of the organism; it is not indicative of good to be desired but of evil to be eschewed. The fanatics who lived "in hope to merit heaven by making earth a hell" were evidently ignorant of the most elementary physiological law; fakirs and monks, with their dirt, fasts, vigils, mortifications, penances, and tortures, were acting in direct contravention of natural imperatives. It is true that too much of anything spells evil; an inordinate profusion of natural props breeds sloth, weakness, and vice, and a sumptuous life often results in intellectual degeneration and the loss of moral fiber. It is clear that spirit is superior to flesh, but, nevertheless, woes are not to be cherished and cultivated. Their mitigation is a proper objective and a minimum standard of well-being is requisite.

Human-created products enrich and beautify life. As the legendary Pan Ku hewed the heavens and earth out of chaos, so must his heirs mold their environment and, by the sweat of their brows, produce tools and appliances, buildings and furniture, statues and paintings and books. They must work relentlessly with their hands and strive with their brains to raise their standard of production and fill their homes and towns with amenities that distinguish them from the beasts. It may be taken as axiomatic that they would not have been endowed with their fertile faculty of invention had it not been intended to make the world a finer and more congenial place in which to live.

Civilization is impossible without refinement, the elaborate alteration of matter, and though exclusive concentration on this process is narrow and pernicious, it is not derogatory to give it its due place. How could civilization have come into existence if crude caves had continued to serve as abodes and jungle trails as lines of communication? Expecting life to be urbane and satisfactory amid filth and a diet of raw meat is irrational; if gentle behavior alone sufficed, then a flock of sheep or a flight of swallows could be considered a civilized community. Most writers are apt to stress some specific mental trait, but some primitive people did indeed display this capacity. The greatest visible distinction of an enlightened people lies in its skilled contrivances and conveniences.

Homo sapiens is the only species that possesses intelligence. While animals live by instinct, the paramount faculty of humans is reason, though, unfortunately, we are not always, or even usually, rational. With our puny bodies, we would have been quickly and easily exterminated by powerful quadrupeds if we had not relied on our supreme weapon. We are now rulers of the earth, monarchs of all we survey, though we emerged last in the lengthy drama of evolution, and we owe this triumph to our superior knowledge.

Primitive humans were endowed with all the faculties their posterity are proud to possess, they were not destitute of reason or imagination, and their capacity for invention is not to be denigrated. Their achievements were varied: they founded villages and built shacks, domesticated animals and originated agriculture, played on drums and pipes, sailed in boats, and fabricated axes and other tools. They practiced magic, which is fumbling science; they endeavored to solve the riddle of the universe, and the mere fact that they could evolve religious theories, however farfetched and ludicrous they might seem today, demonstrates their intellectual curiosity. The Cro-Magnon paintings reveal the presence of an artistic sense. Civilization did not spring into being all at once but was the product of gradual, laborious growth. Who were the contributors—the long succession of the forgotten great who added a noble idea here and created a utilitarian article there? Paradoxical as it may seem, civilization was the handiwork of barbarians, the product of their hands and brains, for they were gifted with that most sublime of attributes—genius, the natural power of origination.

If the cranial contents of the first humans did not essentially differ from ours, what then is the distinction between the barbarous and the civilized? In what way is life today superior to that which flourished a hundred centuries ago? Quantity of knowledge is the answer. The conception of a new idea is an ungrateful task, but its retention is a facile accomplishment. The body of learning, meager at first, gradually accumulated, eventually achieving goodly proportions and far exceeding what was understood in the past. After eons of continual use, the intellect has become keener; it has not changed in kind but in degree. Mind, the tool, and knowledge, its product, have advanced so considerably that there is justification in categorically averring that early cave dwellers were doltish; excellence in anything is purely a matter of comparison. Knowledge has come to be the principal ingredient of civilization, and rightly so. The term *knowledge* must be employed in its broadest sense, not confined to pedants; it must embrace philosophy, concepts of the essence of the universe, science, nature, poetry, literature, music, art, engineering, medicine, ceramics, and agriculture. A people has crossed the Rubicon, dividing barbarism from civilization, when its accumulated knowledge is more than elementary and its ranking on the scale of evolution varies as directly as its culture. Latent intelligence must blossom and bear fruit before we pass our judgment.

There are various types of knowledge, the highest and noblest being the ability to comprehend the universe as a whole. Immense is the totality of things and small is the quantity of gray matter, and it is surely cause for wonder that the unlimited cultivation of the spirit has been justifiably held in boundless esteem and that the mind has been viewed as superior to matter; common sense is all well and good, but it cannot be credited with that genuine grandeur pertaining to reflective science. The exercise of reason is the goal of life, and pure thought marks the greatest advance; a society devoted to pleasure and devoid of sages cuts a sorry figure. The aim of culture is the liberation of mind, and what promotes this most is best.

An ingredient of paramount importance in every society is an ethical system, which tends to harden into painful rigidity. Though in some communities it gives wide latitude to freedom, in most it is inflexibly severe and remorselessly punishes its transgressors. Its primary aim is the preservation of the race, and as such it is unobjectionable; but its methods differ from place to place and from age to age, inviting ample adverse criticism. Very often the precepts of an ethical system, originally embodying a grain of truth and necessity, become meaningless and are maintained from sheer inertia; however, priests cannot take all the blame, as they can do little without general acquiescence.

In spite of easily discernible divergences and variations, the deliverances of the conscience always bear a certain resemblance, the reason being that human nature is one at the core. No discovery is more difficult than that of a new moral truth: the contempt poured on what are termed *platitudes* is almost unjustifiable, as the impugners are not themselves enunciating anything new; all they do is reverse the maxims in their conduct and adopt practices just as ancient. Hedonists champion in theory what libertines did long ago, and Nietzsche only adopted what primitive people knew; such is not the way of progress.

There is no doubt whatsoever that a moral system is essential to civilization, though this, more than anything else, is common to barbarism, its difference consisting in its higher degree of rationality and coherence, nobility and gentleness. Without a substratum of common behavior, mutual understanding would not be attainable nor life secure. Intercourse could not be cultivated, so no society could possibly come into existence. It was no accident that so many of the world's greatest thinkers, even one like Kant, who was zealous in the quest for pure knowledge, placed such emphasis on proper conduct and ranked it above all other acquisitions. Sickened with hypocrisy, one is apt to turn away from long-winded moralists and talk of law as the real restraint on crime, but law is nothing more than the forceful embodiment of ethics.

We may therefore sum up by stating that civilization is organized society, rich in material productions, irradiated with knowledge, and inspired by lofty moral principles. The three attributes of organization—material development, knowledge, and goodness—are not specific to it, for in elementary form they are found in barbarism; the distinction is only in degree and quantity, not in kind. In judgment, values are seldom absolute, only relative; the swift hare and the slow tortoise are both dowered with motion, and it's just a question of more or less. The human race, throughout history, has changed and developed, but it would be strange if it has completely shed all the general characteristics of its earlier days; if it were to do so, it would have to evolve into a new species. Physically, it has remained much the same, while mentally it has gone forward by leaps and bounds. Civilization is the flower grown by the mind in *toto*.

Chapter 2
History of Civilization

Space teems with billions of throbbing bodies, of which the earth is an inconsiderable one, comparatively recent in origin and not to be credited with any particular significance, although to us it is of the greatest concern—it is our abode, whereon we exist. A rushing mass of incandescent gas, it cooled, solidified, and took shape in some dim, remote past and for untold ages rotated and revolved in its maelstrom of a dance, apparently with no vestige of organic life. It is composed of a series of shells, of a core, mantle, and crust; but it is the last, the hard, rocky surface, that interests humanity. In the geological record, the earliest rocks, in the Azoic Era, reveal no evidence of any life form. Scientifically, it is not certain whether plants or animals made the first appearance, and the Paleozoic era contains early specimens of both kingdoms of aquatic origin. However, considering that the complex proceeds from the simple, it may be assumed that the credit for precedence should go to plants. As the earth enviably possessed a more uniform climate at that time, types of life were more evenly distributed, with few local peculiarities—ranging from invertebrates like graptolites and mollusks in the first periods, to vertebrates like fish in the middle, and amphibians of an extinct order, the *labyrinthodonts*, comprising species resembling the modern salamander and lizard, in the latest, the Carboniferous and Permian, the former of which has left vast seams of coal.

Coming to the Mesozoic Era, or secondary division, we find a greater variety of life, and we are filled with wonder at extinct reptiles of enormous size that flourished so extensively that the designation, the Age of Reptiles, sounds appropriate. They crawled on land, swam in the sea, and beat the air with their wings. One type of dinosaur, the Brontosaurus, had a small head, short body, lengthy tail, and huge feet; it weighed twenty tons, and its movements were sluggish. Another, the Atlantosaurus, stood a hundred feet long and thirty feet high and was probably the most gigantic beast ever seen on land. The sea lizards, including the Ichthyosaurus and Plesiosaurus, paddled in the seas and rivers, devouring fish. Denizens of the air, the Pterosaurs, like Pterodactyls, presented an odd, fearful appearance with monstrous heads and a curiously long finger in each front foot; they resembled bats with hollow bones enclosing air.

The next great division in geological history, the Cenozoic Era, or Tertiary Period, produced flora and fauna that look more familiar to us. The seabed rose, and continents assumed much of their present shape; the climate, once warm all over the globe, diversified according to latitude. Mammals emerged to occupy the predominant position, which has been theirs to the present day; then, as now, they were chiefly terrestrial animals. Opossums, moles, squirrels, mastodons, tapirs, rhinoceroses, horses, boars, deer, giraffes, oxen, cats, lions, hyenas, wolves, bears, and monkeys flourished. It is curious to reflect that we, so apt to imagine ourselves the lords of creation, were for long periods nonexistent; the lowly animals over which we now exercise a colossal tyranny were our predecessors, free to roam and multiply without our interference. The Greek legend of Zeus overthrowing Kronos is not without its lesson: "the old order changeth, yielding place to new."

The last of the great divisions, the Quaternary, is still running its course and is subdivided into the Glacial and Recent Periods. A vast sheet of ice extended far to the south, and the animals of previously warm regions migrated elsewhere or were annihilated, while denizens of cold climates, such as reindeer, Arctic foxes, and musk oxen, arrived to take their place. As time went on, the ice sheet gradually retreated, a fresh series of formations accumulated, and the globe settled into its present topography, with the climatic conditions and the flora and fauna of today. Man came into his own; hence the designation of the Human Age has been given to this period.

The exact date of the appearance of humans is unknown, but we certainly did not spring into existence all of a sudden. We evolved slowly from an early form of ape, the ancestor of such modern apes as the chimpanzee, gorilla, and orangutan. Biologically, we belong to the family *Hominidae*, which comprises all types of man, extinct and modern. The first hominids flourished millions of years ago and in the course of evolution eventually gave rise to *Homo sapiens*, the only living human species. With the advent of *Homo sapiens*, a new phenomenon came into being; unlike all other life forms, they could fashion tools to aid them in their struggle for survival. Though these tools were mainly of stone and rude in the extreme, they were nevertheless of great service. Based on the degree of skill and finish in the construction of their weapons, these early races have been classified under the appellations Paleolithic and Neolithic. Just as the animal kingdom still has representatives of the highest and lowest types, so have entire human tribes, notably those in Central Africa, persisted at this primitive level of existence down to modern times. How painfully slow is change, and how laboriously roll the wheels of progress!

Paleolithic tribes lived in natural limestone caves and subsisted on the raw flesh of creatures of the forest, such as bears, horses, bison, and reindeer. They hunted with crude javelins and arrows of flint or bone. Even in those remote ages, they had already developed an urge to express themselves in painting and carving; they drew on the walls of their caves and incised on reindeer horns and mammoth tusks images of animals like buffaloes and horses, with which they came into habitual contact. Could anything demonstrate more convincingly their possession of that principal human attribute—the capacity for thought? Their life was hard; but who knows if they did not find it satisfactory and happy? They must have been spared at least one curse: they could have had no time for the refined malady of ennui.

With Neolithic people began the long struggle to mold the global environment nearer to the heart's desire. They built wooden houses over lakes; they could spin; they knew the use of domestic articles like pins and pots; and they had learned to tame the pig, goat, dog, and horse. No longer were they exclusively hunters for whom every meal spelled danger; they had developed agriculture, sowing and harvesting various cereals. In contradistinction to their predecessors, their stone implements were more exquisitely designed. Their hammers, celts, knives, and axes exhibit their comparative progress; they skillfully polished their tools of bone and ivory and horn. They had a rudimentary knowledge of metallurgy and started fabricating weapons of bronze, an alloy of copper and tin. Over time, iron appeared, and civilization was well on its way.

When we glance at the pages of history, we are struck by the high level of attainment of an early civilization, the Egyptian, which arose on the fertile banks of the Nile. It is impossible that it could have sprung from scratch in the course of a generation or two; millennia must have gone into its making, with haphazard contributions from many minds. By the time a people can boast a written language that is at least adequate for transmitting records, it is well advanced in the arts and inventions. When historians take up their pens, they are by then no longer cognizant of the real achievements of their forbears but are forced to rely on unreliable traditions and fables. Egypt possessed an organized government, a ruthless despotism in the rule of the Pharaohs, and a religion in the hands of a powerful priesthood. Its written language, evolved from symbolic pictures, was stereotyped in hieroglyphs, adequate for the conveyance of ideas. Arts and crafts were varied, and gigantic pyramids, monolithic obelisks, and inscrutable sphinxes remain as a legacy of this remarkable civilization. Egypt's history was long, and its influence on the Mediterranean peoples, including the Cretans of the long-forgotten Minoan culture and the Greeks, was great. It succumbed and lost its ancient heritage when Alexander the Great, in his meteoric career, blew like a violent gust of wind over its moldering structure. The land could not vanish in a mere two millennia, and the Nile continues to perform its annual inundation. The inhabitants remain mixed with successive waves of conquerors—Greeks, Romans, Arabs, and Turks. But the distinctive historical civilization known as the Egyptian has vanished forever.

In Mesopotamia, there arose a series of cultures—the Sumerian, Akkadian, Babylonian, Assyrian, and Chaldean—contemporaneous with the Egyptian and no less important. The Sumerians, the earliest people to inhabit this fertile region, evolved cuneiform writing and built altars on artificial hills. Beside the Euphrates stood the immense, splendid city of Babylon, for ages the capital of Babylonia; it is in the fertile basins of great rivers that cultures, the products of towns, are most apt to originate. The religion of this ancient country was no more enlightened than the Egyptian, and its deities were definitely hostile to men; since gods are created by their worshippers, ghosts of their minds, the destructive phenomena of floods and storms might account for this conception. Early peoples held strange ideas of the earth's geography, which the Babylonians regarded as the base of a rectangular universe, with an engirdling moat of water and mountains on which reposed the heavenly vault. Chaldean astrologers possessed a certain fund of astronomical knowledge, able to predict eclipses; a lunar calendar was in use with seven-day weeks, and the gnomon served as a clock. Mathematics was cultivated, and a mystic value was attached to special numbers like sixty, a fruit of the decimal and duodecimal systems concurrently in vogue. The government was in the hands of a despotic monarch, like Nebuchadnezzar, who took the Jews into captivity. The Chaldean Empire eventually fell prey to Cyrus the Persian.

Several thousand years ago, a tribe of people living where the Hwang Ho leaves its elbow and runs eastward to the Yellow Sea lifted itself out of the widespread morass of ignorance and continued to mold a better life. What is curious is that for long ages its neighbors never cared to imitate or rival its achievements. The nation developed, and its history is the longest continuous record the world has ever seen, a record that is still unfolding. Its political story is principally a succession of dynasties initiated by a strong, enlightened, ambitious person, often a man of the people, and terminated by a profligate or weakling in revolt and dissolution. But this monarchy, albeit autocratic, was tempered by the democratic tenets of the welfare of the people: equal opportunity for all, a large measure of personal freedom, and a civil service to which appointments were made through formalized examinations and to which the peasant could aspire. Feudalism, the worst form of organization yet evolved, was abolished by the first Chin Emperor about the time of the Punic Wars. The economy was agricultural, with farmers either cultivating their own lands or holding them in tenancy. The Chinese were never very religious and had their interests rooted to the earth; their teacher was Confucius, a moral and political theorizer, and the imported religion of Buddhism served only as an outlet for their superstitions. The language was ideographic, capable of the highest literary manipulation, and the body of *belles lettres* bequeathed by a host of writers is as good as any. Science was not outstanding, though such a practical people might have been expected to devote more attention to it. A few beneficial inventions, such as the compass, paper, and printing, enriched the world. In the nineteenth century, this nation was often said to be given to conservatism and unprogressiveness; as a matter of fact, there had always been changes, though they came slowly and with difficulty. Cut off from fruitful contact with other cultures, China depended on itself and civilized a great section of humanity, and its love of peace was a beacon more important than the *Pax Romana*. If China had perished long ago, its culture, like the Cretan, would be only of antiquarian interest; but by its magnitude, duration, and ceaseless evolution, it has contributed its share to the glorification of life.

The human race is said to have taken its rise in Africa and from there migrated northward. The Aryans, from Central Asia, already possessed the rudiments of the art of living when they trekked westward and southward into Europe and Western Asia. One branch entered India and founded a civilization distinguished by spirituality. India was hardly ever a unified nation, what with the unassimilated aborigines already there and wave after wave of conquerors pouring in through the northwest passages. Its tendency for disintegration is undeniable, and it could never be easy to fuse the utterly dissimilar hodgepodge of races, languages, and religions. The Brahmins have erected a religion spiritually on a high plane but socially very low; saintliness is nothing derogatory, but life contains more aspects than that. The monarchs were unmitigated absolutists, founded on conquest as the dynasties were and carried on by intrigue. India, however, has endured for a lengthy period of time, and its culture has been a hardy plant that its subjugators could not uproot; its achievements cannot be overlooked.

The Greeks were the progenitors of European civilization. Short as their history was, embracing only a few centuries, no race has accomplished more. Their importance must, however, be attributed not so much to any inevitable expansion consequent on their splendid heritage as to their position *vis-à-vis* the environing peoples who were capable of learning and developing it. Rulers, wars, or alterations of political boundaries are not most significant in the story of human evolution; more important are discoveries and inventions, changes that mark an upward trend. Therefore, the Greeks must be invested with a glory all their own. Their specific distinction was their devotion to reason. In spite of their lofty disdain for experimentation, they were the founders of modern science, and Aristotle has put subsequent generations in his debt. Their great thinkers can never be forgotten. Politically, they broke away from all precedent and evolved democracy, with its stress on liberty and the value of the individual. Their deficiency in this realm was their narrow conception of the state; and even that intellectual giant, Plato, with his vision of the universe, could not adumbrate a perfect state transcending the bounds of a single tiny city. In the realms of literature and poetry, art, sculpture, and architecture, they attained a rare level of beauty; what remains is still justly esteemed and still inspires. This classical culture might have perished had Rome not adopted it and, with the vastness of its empire and its gift of organization, established it on an immortal basis. Again, what is significant is cultural achievement; the relative positions of these two peoples emphasize this.

No civilization owed so much to one man as the Arabic. Unlettered, not so sublime as Jesus Christ with his conception of universal love, nor a noble saint like Buddha breathing words of peace, Mohammed was more of a hero than a sage. He was that rare phenomenon, a politician and a prophet, a pragmatic idealist who saw his doctrines realized by himself. He organized a formidable state out of a collection of uncouth tribes, and his Old Testament religion became the basis of a forceful culture extending around the Mediterranean Sea. This civilization is not particularly noteworthy, for it did not produce much that marked an advance over earlier ages. It was militant and sought to destroy others as good or better; it is of significance only in that it has lasted until the present day and embraces a considerable portion of the human race.

Finally, we come to Western European civilization, which grew up only during the last few centuries and is still dominant in the modern world. It is a revival and development of Greco-Roman culture, but as it has progressed so far, suffered a cleavage of a thousand years from its predecessor, and sprung up in a new home, it is a distinct entity. Founded on Christianity, which arose from a small people whose sole distinctive achievement was monotheism, it is complex, muddled, and full of inconsistencies and has grown thoroughly materialistic. The democracy of the Athenians and Romans was resuscitated by the French Revolution of 1789 on a national basis. Initiated by the invention of the steam engine, the Industrial Revolution brought on a great expansion of capitalism and a rather new social theory, socialism, which in its fullest implications is hostile to democracy. The great glory of Europe is science, which developed to such proportions and achieved such remarkable results that it might well be regarded as Europe's peculiar contribution. The universe was explored in astronomy, physics, chemistry, geology, and biology; a host of new facts entered into the realm of knowledge, along with their train of revolutionary theories; and inventions serving daily needs, catering to comfort, bridging space, and destroying life multiplied incredibly. Science has realized man's perennial urge to dominate his environment and made the earth a cozier abode, not so alien and terrifying. Western culture possesses excessive variety, and every art is well developed; its literature, for example, is more diversified than any other. While every other civilization was predominantly associated with one or two countries, this is not so with the Occidental. There is one culture but many nations, each speaking a distinct though cognate language; the lack of homogeneity is apparent. In this culture, man has attained the highest level of evolution so far. The culture spread into other lands, notably the Americas; the United States, created by the revolution of 1776, epitomizes the fullest development of its typical traits, with its overgrown capitalism, industrial production, and vitality. Communism, often regarded as a new phenomenon in revolt against Western civilization, was only its offshoot, produced by concentrating on two of its peculiar tenets—materialism and egalitarianism. Establishing itself in Russia in the October Revolution of 1917, it brought forth a narrow, lopsided society, so nihilistic, destructive, and crude as to give an impression of a return to barbarism.

In describing the history of civilization, it has been necessary to deal with one specimen at a time, for the human race did not change as a whole; rather, communities thrived independently of one another. This was mainly due to lack of communication: people lived for long periods with little interrelationship. Historians like Spengler speak of a number of different cultures that lived out their own lives but which, as a matter of fact, were linked in a general sort of way, exciting mutual influence, a later one getting its start from an earlier. They had a common bond in that they differed from barbarism and bore many resemblances; minor variations appear glaring only because they are more exciting to the imagination. Still, there is no denying the fact that the world contained many peoples and states whose histories did not form an indivisible unity.

Not the least important phenomenon of modern times is the mutual intercourse that knits all races. It is no longer possible for a traveler to return from a strange land with tales of "men whose heads grow beneath their shoulders." The airplane has dwarfed distance, and cell phones and the internet prevent ignorance of events occurring at the other end of the earth. Extant cultures are brought face to face; gone is the time when they could work out their destinies in tranquil isolation. All this has been brought about by the West, with its restless energy, its science, its armaments, and its adventurers: its influence bestrides the earth like a colossus. In erstwhile primitive, poorly populated lands, the West has established its system in full; in the East, Western ideas have been largely adopted. Even though sovereign states should continue to flourish indefinitely, the history of human evolution hereafter will scarcely be tabulated in separate compartments.

This earth, which has existed for eons and will presumably exist for eons more, has seen the slow progression of life from simple forms to complex; for the last few thousand years, man has dominated the scene, and the story has become one of the struggle and survival of races and their comparative advances. Nations rose and fell; wars raged and subsided; political boundaries kept changing; ideologies blossomed and died; but, on the whole, there has been progress. True, one could point to numerous lapses and retrogressions, the outstanding example being the Middle Ages following the catastrophic collapse of the Roman Empire. Physically, *Homo sapiens* have not undergone any alteration and still remain the same species, but our knowledge has accumulated so much that we are far from what we were. Basing our judgment on our past, it can be confidently prognosticated that we will persist in our upward career: much lies ahead for us.

Chapter 3
Critique of Barbarism

Barbarism is a primitive state in which humans, groping through the darkness of abysmal ignorance, fashion the rudiments of life that place them on a slightly higher eminence than the beasts that roam freely around them. They have just commenced to make use of their specific gift, intelligence, and they are still wholly concerned with the preservation of their narrow, sordid existence; to this end, they have fabricated a few clumsy tools, bows and arrows, boomerangs, knives, axes, and spears. They are primarily hunters, cunning and intrepid; they may even have progressed to agriculture, sowing and garnering the grains that they have accidentally found could sustain them. They have some notions of family life and are endowed with the natural instinct to procreate. An embryonic society is formed, with the tribe as the unit; a chieftain, a strong man or one of special ability, rules with an iron fist, keeping his subjects in order and leading them in war, which their depredatory propensities make them undertake with fiendish delight. Beholding the forces of nature, so terrifying and mysterious, the barbarians project their personalities onto them and conceive powerful beings, good and evil, whom they seek to propitiate, even with human sacrifice. The more astute pretend to extraordinary knowledge, and their magic is regarded with awe. Intelligible speech has come into being, but there is no written language. A powerful set of customs, traditions, and taboos chain their actions, severely circumscribing their horizon. Thus they spend their entire lives, probably well contented and self-satisfied, in the dim, flickering light of ignorance.

Weary of cities, chaotic institutions, restraints, and refined hypocrisies, not a few thinkers have looked back to prehistoric times and created from their imagination an exemplary society of idyllic simplicity. Writers have addressed the Golden Age with magnificent and touching eloquence. Laotze stigmatized civilization as pure evil and preached a philosophy of inactivity. Rousseau's return to nature was a movement of this kind; admiring the beauty of picturesque natural phenomena and heedless of the ugly, he called man back to his pristine bliss, telling him that he was created good and that he should relinquish his vain attempts at improvement. It is to be feared that such views are woefully fallacious; far be it from us to say that the present age is not out of joint, but the cure is not traveling backward. From the little we know of antiquity, there is no basis for the belief in a virtuous past. The communities of Central Africa have lived until modern times unencumbered by a superfluity of artificial contrivances, but could they be said to have breathed in an atmosphere of peace and virtue? Our remote ancestors could hardly have been different to any appreciable extent. Even if there were incontestable evidence that a glorious race once flourished, it would still be contradictory to the law of evolution to turn back time. It is inconceivable that the human species attained perfection in its infancy and continued to degenerate afterward. The universe is not static; why should humanity be an exception? The Golden Age is an illusion; such a reactionary outlook can never materialize in practice. As human beings, it is in our nature that once we have tasted a certain novelty, we are unlikely to cast it into oblivion; this is not necessarily due to our degeneracy but rather to a desire for conserving what has been hard-won. As is usual with prophets, Rousseau achieved success in a way not fully in accord with his expectations, for his democratic tenets found only partial fulfillment, the sovereign state ceding control to a new set of seigneurs, namely capitalists. As for the return to primeval simplicity, a vaster assortment of artful contrivances than had ever been seen before sprouted like mushrooms, and nature became merely a theme for poets and novelists.

Karl Marx seriously harkened to the call of the wild; a child of the French Revolution, he was captivated by the new doctrine of equality, and in order to realize this, he would leave the human race with nothing but bread. According to him, society marches on its stomach. He meant to convey that civilization is a sham; in his nihilistic system, existence is reduced to its lowest terms. Of course, the economic problem is fundamental, and it is a misfortune and a reflection on the worth of intelligence that after centuries of general progress, it has not had any semblance of a solution. It is a tragedy that the astronomer, intent on the stars, should fall into a well, but this does not make a well more important than a star; for economics to occupy the center of the stage as it does now is anomalous. Russia proclaimed that it was putting Marx's system into practice, and in the early days of the experiment, it tried to adhere to his tenets as closely as possible, but one after another they had to be discarded or modified. Russia finally emerged with a shadow of a culture, mechanical and narrow, but displaying a desire to recapture some of the old Western ways that it found necessary to fulfill its ambition to play a dominant role in the world.

Barbarism is a thing of the past, and, as such, it should never be revived; its practices are antiquated, and nothing can be gained by resuscitating any of them. It is quite common to find a theory put forward as modern and revolutionary, which on examination is found to resonate strongly with prehistory.

One might refer to nudism and Nietzschean brutality as examples of the ludicrous and the horrible, respectively. Such derogatory tendencies have their basis in atavism. Unable to forge ahead, the misguided wish to turn around and leap over the years that have elapsed. Reactionaries are not revolutionaries, and the worst and most dangerous are those who imagine that by feverishly clutching at some almost forgotten trait from the distant past, they are entitled to be called innovators. It is as if a man, after laboriously scaling a mountain, were to slide rapidly down to its foot and proudly proclaim that he has climbed higher than those who refuse to descend. Innovation is the watchword of the day, but beware of the false.

Incorporated into existing civilization are numerous remnants of its precursor, but, unlike fossils, they are active; they breathe and are potent. Saintliness, extremely admired all through history, undoubtedly is rooted in the human instinct to revert to the mud from which we rose. Now the gentleness of a holy monk is an extremely refined product, but his dirt isn't. It is good to sympathize with the misery of poverty but not to clasp it with frenzied enthusiasm as a divine gift and, like Diogenes, throw away one's only cup. The remedy is to eradicate it altogether and bestow a higher standard of living on the masses. To dwell in a cave is surely to imply that troglodytes touched the acme of perfection. Another remnant, a more baleful relic that sharpened its methods with successive centuries, is war. Early humans were instinctively pugnacious and sedulously sought to slay their kind. With growing intelligence, instead of diminishing, this trait persisted in all its primal vigor and, thanks to more efficient weapons, became more pernicious. Entire codes of glory—chivalry, bushido, Nazism—were even woven around it. The misfortune of science is that its immense power can be used for baleful destruction as well as joyous construction. One of these days, the whole world might explode into ruins, and there will not even be the consolation of a Homer left to sing the magnificent epic.

What are the deficiencies of barbarism that make it unacceptable as a way of life? The first and most transparent fact is that it embodies the tentative sprouting of intelligence and, as such, cannot be taken as final. It is crude, a whisper in the wilderness, a tremulous step in the gloom of night. It has raised humanity just a little above the creatures of the field, with which it still has much in common. Nature being in a perpetual state of flux and having evolution as its law, myriad transformations of life finally saw the emergence of a species with a mind capable of rational thought, and the dawn of a brighter era rose over the horizon. This mind was in its infancy; was its growth to be catastrophically arrested, with maturity forever unattainable?

Nature's plan could not be thus envisaged; more easily might the proverbial mountain labor to bring forth a mouse. The mind was meant to work out its destiny and unfold its powers. Society was not to remain stuck in a morass but to walk and run, dance and leap, falling down in a painful crash occasionally but easing its wounds and continuing its onward journey. Barbarism was the starting point of an arduous journey and not the goal.

Insecurity, the fruit of ignorance, is ineluctable at our present stage of development. How much more so was it in primitive times, when early humans were completely at the mercy of their environment?

Their struggle for existence was difficult, and their meager inventions did little to palliate it; nature was a baffling enigma, coiled in insidious evils and sudden horrors. Our ancestors passed their days amid sordid surroundings, a collection of ramshackle huts situated in a clearing in the sinister jungle, from which resounded the roars of wild beasts and a cacophony of weird sounds. What were their expectations and pleasures? Hunting, warring, uncouth dances and yells, frightful ceremonies, and a speedy, violent death.

The sum total of their achievements could be drowned in a bucket of water, so restricted in scope were they, so lacking in variety, so embryonic and devoid of value. Early humans were not capable of profound reflection, and their ratiocinative processes were but one remove from instinct, which still largely guided their actions. Hence came the paucity of their knowledge, which alone is enough to make antediluvian existence unlovable; though ignorance is bliss, 'tis proper to be wise. Whether these primitive peoples were happy or not is open to question; in any case, happiness *per se* is not the objective of evolution, or the process would have ceased long ago when swallows twittered blithely or gazelles softly ran. Quality is of paramount importance in differentiating between the desirable and the repugnant; the more sublime the objects of pursuit, the better. The barbarian's interests were limited and on a low plane; it could not be otherwise, as a more elevated type of life could not be obtained without heroic labor expended through the ages. Humans were absorbed in the urgent problems of food and sex, which left little opportunity for concerning themselves with less necessary, although more valuable, acquisitions.

In analyzing the defects of barbarism, one can better comprehend the requirements of civilization, whose foundations we seldom examine, regarding them as right and inevitable, being familiar. In this critique, very little has been said so far to the credit of barbarism, though it does not present a picture painted only in black. It behooves us to mention its good points, because it must have had some or there wouldn't have been those who were anxious to recapture it. On the whole, its antithesis, civilization, is by far its superior, but just as some of its evil traits persisted in the new era, others that were good perished. The two forms of society share similar fundamentals to a certain extent, the difference being principally a question of more intense development.

What was good, therefore, should have been perfected and what was bad eliminated; unfortunately, as civilization was not a logical, planned, systematic creation but a haphazard process, opposite effects were not rare.

Barbarism may be said to be comparatively natural in that conscious effort on the part of humans played a minor part, a consequence of the adolescent stage of their faculties. The great peril of civilization is that it tends to depart from universal truth and become a hodgepodge of fanciful creations that, regarded as ornamental, more often than not proceed from a distorted sense of appropriateness and beauty and are really pernicious. Unfortunately, reason is only too liable to err, and imagination is the strongest of mental properties. The little worlds of fiction become all-absorbing, and nature is held in disdain. This preposterous attitude arises from egoism: as humans, we believe that we are the center of the universe. Social values are absurdly twisted, and the curious and artificial are highly prized at the expense of the genuinely valuable, if these are abundant. Nature is open for all to enjoy, while covetousness makes treasures of what are available only to a few. This is not to say that primitive people have a truer sense of value, but they are less exposed to factitious corruptions and vanities.

Primitive life is simpler. Complexity is seldom free from confusion, though in itself there is nothing reprehensible, for it means fullness and variety: nature is by no means simple, but it has order and harmony. An unsophisticated life is devoid of stress and strain, corroding cares, weariness, and bodily distempers; it runs in untrammeled rhythm. The complexity of civilization does not breathe ease and sweetness, light and space, but is perverse, unruly, and oppressive, heavy with warped practices and products. It makes everyday life difficult and tortuous, filling it with perplexity; the emotions are harassed, and nervous tension and breakdowns are frequently a consequence. The simple ways and minds of our primogenitors appear sweet by contrast, especially when one has just experienced a tidal wave of anxiety caused by troubles rooted in vain trifles.

Barbarians are endowed with certain virtues that are sadly lacking in more advanced peoples. They don't hanker after luxuries, and their capacity for enduring hardship and pain is enormous. There can be no question of their bravery, and they certainly wouldn't faint at the sight of a tiger. They are inured to hunger and thirst, long journeys on foot over rough terrain, and the awful gloom and silence of the jungle. Their social behavior is the very essence of directness, and they are not aware of the subtle arts of hypocrisy and deceit; the injunction not to hit below the belt is superfluous to them. They are cruel but not treacherous, their minds not cunning enough to weave base stratagems; if they defeat their enemy, it's by force, not faithlessness. The concept of the "noble savage" is not exactly a fiction. The refinement of civilization popularly conveys the notion of the refinement of manners, which is often nothing more than a gentle exterior wrapped around a cruel mind: appearance becomes more appealing than reality.

It is clear that a return to barbarism could not be accomplished without sacrificing the benefits so laboriously accumulated through the centuries. In the process of change, civilization has retained a few evils and degenerated in some respects, but it has made many developments that are too valuable to lose. In contrasting the earlier and later phases of society, the historical law of general progress with the march of time must always be kept in mind. One is primitive, crude, tentative, restricted, unintellectual, and brutal, while the other is advanced, refined, developed, comprehensive, intelligent, and gentle. Nothing is more unwise and hurtful than the proposal for the resumption of the ancient mode of existence under the alluring misnomer of a return to nature, for nature is constantly changing and never stands still; much less does it suddenly pause and make a violent effort to leap back to a state it has traversed. Nature is a sure guide; however, if a calamity is not to ensue, follow it but understand it properly, and do not mistake the unnatural for the natural.

Chapter 4
Critique of Eastern Civilization

In the East, life first assumed a new bloom, and history as we know it commenced its colorful and variegated career; in this vast region, religion and the arts originated, and empires rose and fell. Though to us a few thousand years is an appalling length of time, the Orient wears an aspect of hoary antiquity. The conception that it is romantic and mysterious is profoundly erroneous, and it is time to dissect it in a cold, critical light, evaluate its achievements, estimate its worth, and consider whether its ways of life are worthy of retention.

The major extant cultures of Asia are the Chinese, Indian, and Arabian, all of which are older than the present European culture. They emerged, spread, and attained their heyday ages ago, when the greater part of the immense continent of Eurasia was mired in barbarism and America was a wilderness, and then declined and spent their force. In those days, the East was synonymous with civilization, and wisdom dwelled in its plains. Its achievements stagnated and, persisting through the sheer force of inertia, formed the heritage of a good segment of the world's population. Chinese culture was adopted by the environing people of Mongolian race, from Japan to Annam. The Arabian faith was forcibly exported to a great expanse of infertile territory stretching from Persia to Morocco. The culture of the Aryans of Hindustan has continued to exist almost wholly within the limits of the Himalayas and the Indian Ocean, its principal export being Buddhism, which influenced the inhabitants of East Asia.

The three Oriental cultures do not differ among themselves as much as they do from Western culture, though they are by no means even remotely identical. They could scarcely be designated sisters, for in their origin and development they were apart, and their destinies blended inconsiderably. China was a self-contained unit enclosed by the Pacific, the Gobi Desert, Turkestan, and the Himalayas; its people dwelt in ideological tranquility, harassed only by wild tribes out for plunder. India passively resisted its conquerors and persisted with its Brahmins, fakirs, castes, and cows. Islam was militant but, deriving its impetus from the Old Testament, was particularly concerned with the overthrow of Christianity and directed its gaze westward. Granted all this, the three still possess enough similarities that they can be described together in contrasting them with the Occident. This is because they belong to the same stage of civilization of which national modes are only species or variants. Humanity progresses by stages, and the peoples of one stage, willy-nilly, possess common denominators that distinguish them from their predecessors and successors.

Before the sixteenth century, Europe thought, lived, and moved on the same plane. In spite of its rationalism and democracy, even Athens, the precursor of London, Paris, and Washington, must be placed in the same category, for experimental science had scarcely developed. In the Middle Ages, all Western countries fell under the autocratic sway of an Eastern religion, and their way of life wore an Asian aspect. It is strange that the mythology, history, and ideology of the children of Israel should have been so completely transplanted from a corner of the Levant to a continent and should have flourished so luxuriantly. Tragically, as is so often the case, the benefactors, the Jews, received no reward for their discoveries but were subjected to pogroms and persecution. Jerusalem was the creator of Christian Europe. Without this solid religious wedge, European civilization would have formed a continuity for the last three thousand years, but then it is doubtful if Western culture would have attained its present standard without the quickening force of the Renaissance.

It is to be understood that this critique refers to Eastern civilization as it stood before the advent of the West. In the twentieth century, the impact of the Occident was tremendous, and changes of varying extent have shaken the different cultures so that they no longer retain their purity. Some countries have been more affected than others; Japan was the first student, and innovations were inevitable in the numerous lands that were occupied and turned into European colonies. What then is the purpose of examining pure Oriental civilization? We have to study it to clear our minds of cobwebs and have a better perception of the needs of the future: it behooves us to review all forms of social organization and ways of life. Even today, there are many people who would like to resurrect an idealized version of the past. They don't seem to realize that should a genuine revival occur, it might not be confined to their few notions, but *in toto*. A still greater number are concerned with the preservation of whatever ancient institutions still remain, especially their religions.

Taking the East as a whole, the characteristic that weaves itself into its very being is its profound religiousness. Spiritual life does not elicit a sneer; gods are not remote beings whose existence is a suitable topic for post-prandial discussion but are warm creatures, close to humanity, ready to lend a hand in everyday affairs. When a Westerner prays, a hint of doubt, of unmanly weakness, likely lurks at the back of his mind; not so with a Muslim, who does not consider it a physically irksome waste of time to kneel down five times a day to Allah. Religion to the Easterner is not merely a matter of interesting marriage and funeral ceremonies and languid church services once a week; it enters into every act of life, however trifling, hallowing it with significance.

Much of the so-called romance of the East has its origin in its strange rituals. Vulgar minds appreciate the concrete much more easily than the abstract, and a visible performance holds greater appeal than an idea. Likewise, symbolic representations possess a sensuous attraction that remote entities don't; a stone image of the Buddha, majestic and serene, is a more fitting object of worship than the vague principle of the dharma, and a soaring pagoda with its odd number of stories stands for the spiritual ascent of the struggling soul toward perfect holiness. Festivals, occasions of communal joy, provide the masses with occasional relaxation from their soul-grinding diurnal labors. Chinese peasants have their New Year, "Clear and Bright," Dragon-Boat, All Souls, and Mid-Autumn and Winter Solstice celebrations, which they scrape and save to keep. Ritual, symbols, festivals, and all the paraphernalia of external religion have their modicum of practical use, but a superabundance makes life complicated and, distracting attention, renders the mind incapable of genuine reflection; it acts as an opiate, dulling the capacity for free thought. The oddest thing about Confucius is his preposterous insistence on the correct, punctilious performance of a tremendous array of political and social rites that are more honored in the breach than in the observance.

Magic, which has wielded great power, is spurious science, the attempt to get benefits from nature without truly comprehending its laws. It is probable that primitive magic was the origin of both science and religion. Our world today is the same world as that of our ancestors, who felt the warmth of the same sun and beheld with awestruck eyes the same phenomena of rain and lightning, hills and rivers. The more curious and astute might have accidentally hit upon a few discoveries and, loath to reveal the secret of their power, set themselves up as miracle workers, pretending to special communication with mysterious agencies to explain their prowess. As the ages rolled on, a more complicated mythology and ritual accumulated, and religion came into being. Inventions that passed into general knowledge paved the way for genuine science. Beneath every existing religion is a core of magic, whose ageless popularity emanates from two human needs: health and prosperity. The magician is principally a healer who, with his pills, prescriptions, and incantations, claims the ability to cure diseases and benefits from accidental recoveries. The last infirmity of a troubled mind is a desire to know future vicissitudes, hence the emergence of a host of geomancers, necromancers, palmists, astrologers, crystal gazers, and augurs. The fortune teller, who is not necessarily associated with any particular religion, makes it easier for irrational faith to maintain its existence by fostering a belief in mysteries. With its highly intellectual doctrines, Taoism would probably have disappeared had its devotees not taken over the earlier magic and woven the two together so that they became inseparable.

Superstition takes the place of reason. Every creed has its supreme deity and its pantheon of very human spirits. Mohammedan houris, Hindu gods, Buddhist bodhisattvas, Taoist fairies—the universe rings with their various attractions. Belief in devils is general; every second person can tell of an encounter with a ghost, though the unpleasant experience has usually happened to a relative or a friend. Haunted houses are not rare, and an individual who encounters a violent death is pretty sure to harass the living with his supernatural visitations. Natural phenomena bear romantic interpretations: firecrackers are vigorously set off during an eclipse to scare away the dragon that is swallowing the sun. Some legends are not alluring but disgusting. To each faith is appended a prolific mythology that some apologists have endeavored to justify on the grounds of its practical value in conveying sublime truths to the simple masses.

As for the intellectual content of religions, their common characteristic is irrationality. The doctrines are not verified by reason but are enunciated by divine beings, prophets, or sages and are accepted as necessarily true. As faith is the test of belief, it is doubtful why a person should cling to one system over another. The whole problem revolves around tradition: faith is placed in what has been instilled from childhood, the creed of one's ancestors. Antiquity *per se* has nothing to justify it and is in fact normally an excuse bred of unprogressiveness and tyranny. Although not true, some of the founders' ideas are sublime, but they have lost their purity and simplicity over time. As evidence of intellectual capacity, abstract concepts are superior to concrete images; the Tao and the dharma are more worthy of a thinker than the anthropomorphic first cause of the Old Testament religions. All ancient faiths initially performed some useful service or they wouldn't have spread, but they are plainly out of harmony with modern science and serve no real purpose, persisting in a moribund condition from sheer inertia. Their defense rests on their spirituality, which, one is asked to believe, is their monopoly. This peculiarly attractive term should properly signify the cultivation of the mind, which can be better attained by rational knowledge than by a medley of mystical verbiage. Wishful thinking won't do any good, and the mere thirst for heaven or nirvana does not prove its existence. The creeds are too morbid, too much concerned with death and too little with life, preoccupied with darkness rather than light.

All religions preach ethical codes that display, in the words of a Chinese expression, "great similarity, small difference." The moral rules are all arbitrary commands, not woven into a system, not informed by a central principle from which the others can be deduced. Virtue is set in sharp opposition to vice. In theory, the rules are very rigorous, while in practice, most are neglected. Only those necessary to the stability of society are observed to any appreciable extent; the ineluctable consequence is that their adherents become hypocrites. Irrespective of the professed doctrines, what actually prevails in every community is a mild code of external, gentlemanly behavior, of which Confucius, who was more interested in social harmony than in metaphysics, was the only thinker to make a queer apotheosis. A proper moral system should have a definite objective with the rules coalescing to form a coherent whole, just as all tributaries join the main stream. It should be rational and practical; it should not, if really applied, conflict with the other valuable phenomena of civilization. If all men were to follow Buddha and his monks in leading unproductive lives and depending on charity, then who would be the producers to supply the recipients? If all persons were to behave like the Christian saints in despising the world and devoting themselves to preparations for the Kingdom of God through penance and self-mortification, then would not all natural knowledge, culture, industrial products, and scientific inventions have to be abandoned and the earth turned into a barren wilderness?

Eastern cultures all developed the concept of monarchical despotism in the administration of the state: the theory is the Divine Right of Kings. Some of these rulers are actually regarded as veritable gods, like the Mikado, descendant of the goddess of the sun, Amaterasu, and the Dalai Lama, the reincarnation of Buddha. An uncontrolled autocrat who can do whatever he pleases is an unmitigated evil. If he has newly come into power or his rule is not secure, then he may attempt to win popular favor by a wise and just administration, leading a life of integrity, enlisting the services of the best advisers, promulgating equitable laws, encouraging the arts, and erecting public works. He will be venerated as a great man and his name will be remembered with gratitude. But as even the very best have enemies and can brook no opposition, they resort to the strong hand, rendering liberty nonexistent. The benevolent despot is a *rara avis*. The usual monarch is an extravagant weakling who squanders wealth and hands over the country to the iniquitous control of favorites, unscrupulous ministers, concubines, and eunuchs or a tyrant for whom the sufferings of a people yield laughter and wars of aggrandizement seem the most sensible exercise of his faculties. The country is regarded as private property, an heirloom.

What goes under the misnomer of history is a dreary catalogue of dynasties; China is the best example, where families rose and fell with such regularity and so similarly that a natural law might be proposed to explain it. There are always aspirants to every throne in every land, and historical records show as many civil wars as external ones. The contending armies laid waste to the fields and pillaged and burned towns; as a rule, the rebels were exterminated, and therefore the dynasties were not more numerous than was the case. A new dynasty was initiated by a more than usually ferocious struggle extending over a longer period of time. In an apparently peaceful period, palace intrigues ran high, and the most awful murders were committed with untroubled mien.

Empires were the products of personal ambition, testimonials to vainglory attained by lavish bloodshed. They were, of course, founded with an eye to permanence, and if they could endure as imperishable monuments—vast masses of people united as real nations with the consequent elimination of recurring wars between trifling states—something might be said for their extenuation. But their fleeting character made them inexcusable; sorrow knew no end, and destruction, not construction, was the normal state of affairs. The great spoilers were the numerous Tartar tribes, Huns, Mongols, and Turks, who rode into the plains of Asia and Europe in search of plunder. These nomads were little more than barbarians, and it would hardly be fair to indict Eastern civilization by citing the acts of Genghis Khan and Tamerlane. But the civilized absolutists only lacked their power, not their will, regarding dynastic ambitions.

The economies associated with Eastern civilization are capitalistic—or, rather, patrician. Vast masses labor from dawn to dusk for the benefit of small classes of appropriators; living in grinding penury, they exist on a material level parted but a hair's breadth from what Neolithic men enjoyed. This is why spirituality is admired, for there is nothing else left to stir enthusiasm. Exploitation, however, is only the lesser cause of this abysmal poverty: the greater factor is technological deficiency. Only when the material basis of society revolves around machinery, industry, and science can production be sufficient to provide a comfortable home for all; handicrafts and primitive agriculture would have to be replaced by factories and scientific farming. Many have condemned the Machine Age; nevertheless, it is undeniable that nothing valuable or spiritual resides in diurnal worries over food and clothing and that there is nothing holy in a tumbled-down hut or broken crockery. Plain living does not connote squalor, and high thinking is not best achieved in the vicinity of a pigsty. Ancient governments paid no attention to invention and did not concern themselves with economic problems. Whatever inventions there were occurred haphazardly, and the names of the Chinese inventors are shrouded in mystery. Kings were avid for luxuries over which slaves wore out their fingers; there is nothing more spiritual in an elaborately embroidered tapestry than in a factory-produced garment.

The village was the unit of population concentration, and there was nothing worse than such a squalid collection of shacks, an eyesore, a thing of ugliness. No remedy was ever considered; it was viewed as the proper abode for a peasant who had to till the fields. It is no wonder that the villager was an uncouth, ignorant creature, a befitting subject of amusement in fiction and on the stage. It is universally supposed that country life breeds a robust character: with this moral apology, the problem is apparently solved! Isn't the acquisition of this one trait an exorbitant price to pay for lack of culture, knowledge, and all material facilities? The elephant is an even more robust personage; would it therefore be desirable to imitate its way of life? To be sure, towns existed—few, straggling, built to no plan, chaotic, filthy—with malodorous, narrow streets and sunless houses. There lodged iniquity; there stalked pestilence!

As progress is the essence of things, it could not be utterly checked, but it was so slow that at first glance it appears nonexistent. Institutions had a way of dying hard for a conservative, ossified intelligentsia; mass stupidity was a serious stumbling block, and whatever changes succeeded in establishing themselves were minor. In spite of its constant contact with another culture, and contact of whatever kind is apt to be invigorating, Islam did not produce much. From the time that the enlightened Harun al-Rashid of *Arabian Nights* fame treasured Greek learning, its scholars were devoted to science, and between the eighth and twelfth centuries they produced a moderate amount of work in medicine, chemistry, mathematics, astronomy, and physics. Theology and scholasticism were impediments; hence, original research was not fruitful. The Oriental cultures did not actually perish but tottered along from inanition. Thinkers tended to look to the past, finding their ideals in a fictitious Golden Age, instead of looking toward the future. Ancestor worship; divine revelations delivered at some arbitrarily chosen period and meant for all time; rigid, doubtful ideologies—such an atmosphere was not conducive to advancement.

We have surveyed the East as a whole because its peoples belong to the same level of evolution; in fact, what we are examining is a particular stage of human development. Nevertheless, it is advisable to note the differences among the diverse cultures. The most religious is the Indian and the least the Chinese. Nowhere else in the world is such veneration accorded to a priestly caste as it is in India to the Brahmins, wiseacres of a curiously jumbled creed of polytheism and pantheism. Unlike in other hierarchies, they practice what they preach and are distinguished by living on a materially lower plane than the classes over whom they hold sway; a pariah, be he ever so well-dressed and wealthy, is still vastly inferior to a lice-infested scion of the sacred nobility. Muslims are also devoted to their creed, but theirs is more an affair of ritual than asceticism. The Chinese are materialists in the sense that their ideal is personal prosperity. They respect and strive to attain good food, a fair reputation, office, longevity, and numerous progeny; their interests are of the earth. Confucianism can hardly be termed a *religion*; free from metaphysics, it is merely a social theory promoting the collective welfare with its eyes glued on sublunary needs. The other two of the so-called "Three Teachings" to which the ordinary person in China subscribed in spite of their contradictory character, Taoism and Buddhism, are cultivated by their sectaries but are despised by the educated; their appeal to the masses is founded on their magical formulas for the production of prosperity and restoration of health.

The supreme authority of the caliphs and sultans was only vaguely controlled by the precepts of the Koran; spiritual as well as political potentates, they were the most despotic of despots. Indian sovereigns came to power by intrigue and cruelty, did whatever they fancied, and constantly faced insurrection. China possessed some democratic tenets, for the welfare of the people was the professed aim of government, and the individual enjoyed a large measure of personal liberty, his contact with the authorities being chiefly in the realm of taxation. Confucius did not preach the inheritance of the Dragon Throne and even provided for legitimate deposition of an evil ruler, though in practice power was vested in a family until it was wrested away by a stranger, a new Son of Heaven. A civil service existed, and every man could aspire to the post of prime minister, while the idea of exclusive castes was absent. The polity was not a democracy or limited monarchy, but it was less oppressive than its contemporaries.

Islam was militant, and while it repeated "Salaam" and made peace with Allah, it sought none with humankind. Chinese thinkers, one and all, were pacifists, and conquerors received stern condemnation. Indian and Mohammedan states were not stable, but China remained a single state from the beginning, a supreme government always coming into authority after a longer or shorter interval of disruption, a phenomenon explainable by the homogeneity of its people in race, language, religion, culture, and customs. The direct antithesis of this is India, where disintegration is more natural than unification. The principal virtue of the Mohammedan is charity, of the Indian self-mortification, and of the Chinese filial piety. The Chinese are practical, relying on common sense; they are cheerful, hardworking, and not given to mystical speculation. All in all, they were more "modern" than other Easterners.

Coming to the good points of Oriental civilization, it is fair to admit that it possessed a certain stability, for though little progress was manifest, there was never a danger of reversion to barbarism. Its capacity for survival was immense: it absorbed and educated savage tribes who came conquering and looting, then stayed to admire. The diverse creeds attained a certain degree of completeness and finality, which gave their separate peoples confidence and equanimity. Only thinkers are forever haunted by the baffling hunger for absolute truth; ordinary mortals are essentially pragmatists for whom reality is of no value, save as means to an end. The systems were wrong, but since no better were discovered, they elicited belief, which, *per se*, contains a motive force for the regulation of life. In every age, the real interests of most people have centered on income and family, and conflicting ideologies serve only to confuse and distress them. The more sensitive are so harassed by doubt that their will to action is paralyzed; a class of unhappy, vacillating neurotics is a symptom of a diseased society. The ancients had a sure code of conduct and were not subject to mental torture.

The spiritual faith of the ancients endowed them with peace of mind and contentment, enabling them to smile even in adversity. One of the oddest facts of the twentieth and twenty-first centuries is modern man's preoccupation with economic problems. Nothing is more erroneous than the arbitrary dictum of Karl Marx that society marches on its stomach. Animals are instinctively devoted to the pursuit of food, and the belief cannot be seriously entertained that the evolution of reason should ultimately lead humanity to the same result. Man has a nobler destiny—food is a necessity, not an ideal; it is a means, not the end, of life. Though the economic problem must be solved, other problems hold greater intrinsic value. The ancients could see life more steadily, more wholly, and found joy and glory unapproachable by mere satisfaction of appetite. Even the humblest peasants attained a certain grandeur from their interest in eternity and their belief in concepts transcending the self; though woefully ignorant, they had the enviable quality of a sage—their happiness did not depend on the size of their larders.

Life was simpler than in the West. The mind was not distracted by a superfluity of material cares, and people didn't fret because they couldn't fill the dark, silent night with rollicking gaiety. They didn't feel jaded from debauchery or exhausted from dancing all night, and they didn't lust after sensation and enjoy vicarious thrills from reading scandal sheets, cheap romances, and detective yarns. The moral virtues were admired, and a life of sexual love was not their ideal. They would not have understood the French version of *l'amour* and would have considered it ridiculous for an individual to run from one escapade to another. Nothing is more curious than the fantastic interest of Europe in the relationship between the sexes; tons of books have been woven around this theme, and some talk of nothing else. From literature and the cinema, one is encouraged to assume that it's love, sexual love, that makes the world go round.

There were wars, but not total wars. Professional soldiers might fight and furiously slay those in their way, but not every man was mobilized to be a butcher. The weapons were limited; the populations who were not in the vicinity of the battlefields pursued life undisturbed, and the damage was not too heavy. The poor sword could do little, and bombs did not rain from the skies. Even with its restricted sphere of operations, neither the thinkers nor the masses glorified war as an art or regarded the soldier as a stupendous subject of admiration. One of the tragic ironies of life is that along with increased capacity for construction, there has developed a great power for destruction and, it might be said, a stronger desire to destroy.

A culture's most beneficial element lies in its creative work, which cannot be false like a philosophic or scientific theory or deleterious like a luxury or a gun. It expresses the desire for beauty, refines and elevates the mind, and gives keen pleasure. Literature, art, music, sculpture, and architecture—without them, a people could not be regarded as possessing a culture. The East had plenty of faults, but its artistic triumphs must be admired. It never achieved as much variety as the restless, experimental West; its literary products are romantic and instructional, but they are good within their limits and surpass European works in the matter of imaginative content. Take, for example, *The Thousand and One Nights*, the most gorgeous tales ever conceived. Not surprisingly, poetry was its best gift; Tang poems will be a joy forever. It strove to impart beauty to everything it did, which is a goal art should embody. Chinese artists were absorbed in a vision of nature, which is a grander and better theme than the human figure.

A culture must be appraised as a whole, not in parts, its merits and demerits weighed in the balance; if the latter preponderate, a painful stricture is ineluctable. In truth, the welfare of populations and the irresistible progress of evolution have left the East behind; its cultures have lasted too long and have outlived their usefulness. To retain them is impossible; to reform them is futile. An ancient tree cannot be rejuvenated by decorating it with paper foliage; it can only be done by nurturing its sapling. Some people are so hypnotized by a few traits that they fear would be lost by changing a fundamental character that they strive to hold onto them by clinging to their culture in its entirety. They might not admit it, but the good was, in all probability, not so much the mere accompaniment as the consequence of the bad; it is common for a virtue to be the fruit of a vice, ironic though this may be. It was inevitable that ancient cultures were riddled with grievous faults, for they had just left barbarism behind; after developing for a short while, they became stereotyped and persisted without changing significantly. It would have been truly wonderful and well-nigh ridiculous if they had achieved perfection with such facility so early in the history of the reflective mind. We do not sneer at them as creations that should never have seen the light of day; we regard them as the temporary products of evolution.

Chapter 5
Critique of Western Civilization

Western culture began at the Renaissance, which dates roughly from 1453, when the Turks under Mohammed II took Constantinople, the capital of the Eastern Roman Empire, and Greek scholars found refuge in Italy. It did not spring up from scratch; it had been evolving very slowly for centuries, from the moment the various Germanic tribes, who overran the western provinces of the Empire of the Caesars, settled down and started to learn from the vanquished. In a way, it was a continuation of Greco-Roman culture, which owed a great deal to the East, and thus it could be said to have grown out of Oriental civilization, which developed from barbarians. From a general view of human evolution, these three can be placed as stages in one process, and history thus becomes a unity. In 323, Constantine the Great decreed that Christianity, a Jewish product, should be the official religion of his far-flung domains; within the confines of this characteristically Oriental system, Westerners grew up for a millennium. Religion extended its tentacles into every part of life, exactly as Hinduism or Mohammedanism did, for Europe was then no different from Asia. The causes of the Renaissance lie in the Crusades, from which men returned with widened mental horizons thanks to the recovery of Greek books and the active life of the free cities of Italy and Germany. The formative factors of New Europe included the introduction of Chinese inventions like paper, printing, gunpowder, and the mariner's compass; the voyages of such explorers as Columbus, Vasco da Gama, and Magellan; and the rise of nation-states and the Reformation, which unwittingly helped pave the way for the triumph of free thought and materialism.

For the last five centuries, Europe has been changing rapidly, and the discoveries and inventions of physical science have transformed it into something quite different from what it was during the Middle Ages. One by one, it has shed its old illusions. Charlemagne and Saint Bernard would have been lost in this world of airplanes, quantum theory, mechanized warfare, and democratic socialism. Western culture is dubbed modern, the only one that is not hoary with age, still changing, always restless. No longer confined to Europe, it extends over the whole world, establishing itself in erstwhile sparsely populated lands of barbarism or semicivilization and profoundly influencing old, deeply rooted cultures. It has been forced onto the defensive against one of its curious products, communism, which is a reversion to primeval times, reinforced by scientific inventions and industrial techniques. What will be its outcome? Is it the last word in evolution, meant to endure for all time, beyond which further progress is impossible, not only a fact but the ultimate ideal? It needs to be examined.

Western civilization is materialistic, devoted to the world, sensual pleasure, bodily comfort, and the things of the hour. The ordinary man is ardently and anxiously concerned with the acquisition of a radio set, refrigerator, automobile, and finely furnished flat or house; he can talk of nothing but girls, dances, movies, and football matches, and he measures his bliss and importance by the number of things he possesses. The constant labor agitations and threats of revolution spring wholly from the craving for a greater share of goods, and the numerous political parties have as their sole task the preservation or attainment of wealth for their constituents. There can be no limit to desire, but even with mechanical mass production, it is improbable that every person will be able to wallow in luxury. The inevitable result is that if interest is entirely fixated on pleasurable products, discontent and, ironically, misery will always be the order of the day. Like so many other words, materialism and spirituality are relative terms. Europe, of course, has its modicum of spiritual interests, and even the most saintly have to eat. In the religious East, a wealthy man usually surrounded himself with luxury and kept a fine table. When a nation is said to be materialistic, the inference is merely that the majority of the population is almost exclusively absorbed in the pursuit of physical sensations. We criticize materialism as we did religiousness, for both are narrow ways of life based on erroneous views of the nature of the universe: there is a lack of a sense of proportion. Human beings are composed of both mind and matter, and though a community should have a sound material foundation, the major segment of its attention should be directed to mental cultivation.

The real practical philosophy of the West is Epicureanism, or its revised version, Utilitarianism, which as a specific system was the property of a small sect, the Benthamites, but in a vague, general way is tacitly accepted by almost everybody. The greatest happiness of the greatest number—happiness denoting corporeal enjoyment—is implied in socialism, which has become the most popular formulation of thought. The trouble is that the holders of these doctrines never look beyond the material world and, having no use for intangible aspirations, vainly imagine that society would be perfectly blissful if only the toys of the rich were distributed among the populace. There is no need for any higher preoccupation; if their arguments were irrefragable, then the wealthy must have already achieved the perfect life.

Matthew Arnold, the apostle of "sweetness and light," deplored the Philistinism of the people of his age, characterized by devotion to wealth—an unfortunate trait even more pronounced today, ruling wherever Western civilization is entrenched. The most admired person is the millionaire, and classes are differentiated on the basis of property. A handsome bank balance is the prime requisite of a gentleman, and the least sensible of all occupations, trade, is the most esteemed, for it is the easiest road to that grand goal, riches. The Philistine derides art and is stricken with admiration only when the artist amasses a fortune. He is not interested in the subject *per se*, as he does not discriminate between the good and the bad and lavishes profuse praise on worthless, ephemeral productions that bring money. The poor scientist is looked at askance, and the opulent actor fulsomely lauded. Absolute value is unknown, for what matters is social value in terms of gold, which is supposed to be a panacea for all headaches.

The greatness of a nation is measured by the external criterion of industry: supplies of coal and iron, access to raw materials, collection of machinery, production of consumer goods, trade balance, effectiveness of its mechanized army, and strength in the air and on the sea. The illusion prevails that this is genuine greatness, and the inhabitants of such a glorious state congratulate themselves on their enviable membership. It is not surprising that such competition should breed jealousy and lead to internecine total war. People have become automatons, life is stiff, and, geared to a portentous system of production, the spirit loses its sweetness and ease. Worship of machinery produces baleful effects: the divorce of beauty from utility, a mechanical attitude toward the universe, and undue importance assigned to economics.

Reliance on external apparatus spells colossal danger for the inner life; the spirit fails to develop, contemplation is unknown, and the introvert is condemned as abnormal, while in reality the only way to grasp and possess the universe is by profound, silent reflection. The mind is the only realm where one is truly and absolutely free; only a very restricted amount of liberty can be enjoyed outside it. An internal harmony is more important than any amount of external property, which easily vanishes, leaving the impoverished in a state of despair. It is strange and wonderful how a small quantity of mind enclosed in an inconsiderable volume of matter could draw the entire universe within its compass; not to make use of this sublime gift is a waste indeed! What is the loss of a million dollars or a bag of jewels compared to this loss? Yet many a person would commit suicide if he had to file for bankruptcy, while he would not care for his own inalienable property, his intellect. External machinery, external clothes, external qualifications, external skills in athletics and histrionics—these are what an external culture prizes, thereby losing the internal glory of sublime thought.

As the greatest of all human endeavors, philosophy is the best criterion of a culture, a race of lofty philosophers ennobling a nation as nothing else could. Western philosophy is technical, hair-splitting, unrelated to life, and far removed from the interests of the common man; its moral doctrines constitute mere topics of discussion, more often than not failing to translate into character by the proponents themselves. All thinkers live an ordinary, gentlemanly life, irrespective of their peculiar tenets. Schopenhauer might preach a Buddhist extinction of self, but he was far from a saint; Nietzsche might formulate a terrible doctrine of ruthless struggle, but he never committed a murder. No system of thought so far has been complete, coherent, and convincing; one metaphysic developed out of another and never approached any semblance of finality. The endless succession of fragmentary theories did not even evince the characteristic of science, to wit, genuine progress, and each thinker was ousted for no sufficient reason, the apparent cause of success being that each age liked to enjoy the egotistical satisfaction of possessing its own particular sage. What is the outcome? Philosophy has fallen into discredit. The scientist scorns it as guesswork; the literary man deprecates it as dry; the man in the street derides it as impractical. To be a philosopher today requires courage, for the name is not at all enviable. There are basically two types: one eschews science as dealing with unreal phenomena and produces fanciful schemes remote from ordinary comprehension; the other rears its systems on the one or two scientific theories that have recently come into fashion, forgetting that they revolve around only a limited set of facts and can be exploded by fresh discoveries. The first, imagining that it is grasping the sum of things, merely weaves shimmering gossamer, mysterious to the point of mysticism; it is no wonder that its influence on practical life is nil. The second degrades philosophy to the status of the handmaid of a particular scientific hypothesis, which, however true or important, surely forms a weak foundation for a total view of the universe. As science is constantly changing, such systems are essentially transitory and possess no value; philosophy is superior to science, and it is odd that the more comprehensive should be dominated by the less. A system should work by reason and its own coherence, its hypotheses not at variance with science as a whole; it will thus avoid the pitfall of mere fancy and at the same time exist in its own right with a nearer approach to permanence. It should be able to influence practical life and not appear remote.

It is not out of place here to make a passing reference to Christianity. Western civilization in the Middle Ages was founded on it, and there are those who assert that this has held good through the twentieth century and into the twenty-first, but this view is clearly erroneous. Philosophy, science, democracy, and socialism have combined to shift it to a corner; it is moribund and persists for the simple reason that once a creed is widespread and has endured for a long time, its demise is apt to be protracted. For how long after it ceased to be a vital force did Roman paganism continue to be the nominal official religion of the Roman Empire? Zoroastrianism vanished ages ago, but a few people still maintain their belief. Christianity is quite incompatible with a materialistic culture, and faith cannot coexist with reason. The Roman Catholic Church, still its most powerful exponent, is an anachronism. Christianity, even in the past, did no real good, partly because of misrepresentation; it has never been put into real practice. Its cherished beliefs are the most irrational ever conceived, morbid fairy tales.

Before the Industrial Revolution, which marked the shift from agriculture to mechanical production, European economic organization was feudal, more oppressive than in any other part of the world, with the fatal quality of birth inordinately stressed. Factories had new techniques for manufacturing goods, and a new class of capitalists, owners of the tools of production, quickly came to the fore. When Rousseau, sympathetic to the oppressed and poverty-stricken, wrote *The Social Contract* and proclaimed the ideas of liberty and equality, he did not envision the rise of another race of seigneurs who would use this theory of democracy not to establish universal happiness but to wrest power from their predecessors in exploitation. Throughout history, many systems have engendered lamentable consequences from deliberate misconception, from partially applying some of its doctrines in the letter and neglecting its spirit. Sometimes, one is strongly tempted to join the respectable company of the pessimists and exclaim irritably that the world will never improve, that the bird of happiness will forever elude human grasp! Strange are the ways of institutions; how is it that an idea so easily withers the moment it is stereotyped?

In the early days of capitalism, its tyrannies were stupendous; under the influence of socialism, a threat to its existence, it has become more humane. But as the system is essentially unsound, no amount of props can make it more defensible. In an atmosphere of unrestricted greed, it contains no check on its malpractices, and external controls only produce perpetual friction. That one man should produce and another enjoy is contrary to the very nature of justice. From the point of view of the general welfare of a community, such an iniquitous system must be condemned. Under it, one's personal interests are best secured by ruining another's. The price of existence is vigilance; envy, the cause of strife and woe, reaches an abysmal depth, and cunning is mistaken for wisdom.

Unregulated competition leads to enormous waste. Overproduction in lucrative fields and underproduction in others imply that ability has not been utilized to the best advantage. Chronic unemployment, besides being demoralizing, means the abandonment of valuable energy stores. What waste is involved in the periodical economic depressions, which relief measures can only palliate, not cure! The forces of capitalist society are destructive, and, instead of working to a common end, they struggle to annihilate one another. No satisfactory solution to the relationship between capital and labor can be found when their interests don't tally, and mutual recrimination is the logical result. With proper regulation, enough for everyone could be secured with mechanical production, but instead the masses are more dissatisfied than they ever were in the agricultural stage.

A capitalist democracy often boasts that liberty is preserved; this is the stock excuse for its retention. Liberty is undoubtedly sacred, but is capitalism its synonym? How can an individual be said to enjoy the blessing of freedom when he is at the mercy of his employer? Direct physical force is not the only form of enslavement—subtler methods are available. As capitalism reinforces itself with the trust system, the worker finds himself less able to maintain his priceless freedom. He cannot do as he pleases, or he would starve. No doubt he enjoys the liberty to go hungry just as his compatriot, the slave, enjoyed the liberty to commit suicide. Personal freedom should be more than a mere shadow, and the right should be equally attainable in the realms of politics, economics, religion, culture, and social conduct. Without security, it cannot blossom—livelihood is the most urgent of necessities. In a genuinely free community, the individual should not be subject to any kind of ineluctable external pressure. The mere prerogative to elect to office a candidate put forward by interested, contending parties does not amount to much. Economic liberty is of prime importance, and this connotes the ability to choose one's occupation on reasonable terms and work without undue compulsion from the state or a private employer. A man should not be involuntarily bound by direct or indirect force to disdainful and oppressive superiors.

If capitalist economy had been rigorously maintained in all its original purity, the world might have seen the complete triumph of communism. Capitalism is best defined not as the private ownership of property, for there is nothing wrong in this, but as the exploitation of the many by the few who own the instruments of production. A system cannot endure with such vast inequalities in wealth, with some squandering in luxury and others unable to decently subsist, for the sense of justice is outraged and any desperate expedient may be welcome. Industrial capitalism has had a comparatively short history; yet it has excited more unrest than any other economic system in previous ages. What is the reason? The Roman slave and the medieval serf were no better; indeed, they were much worse off than the modern proletarian, yet they were not so addicted to revolt. The explanation lies in the French Revolution, with its dream of equality and general welfare. Men had come to yearn for a more egalitarian society. The fact is that the existence of a small class of luxurious owners is an anachronism, for the people did not fight in order to free themselves from the nobility of the *ancien régime* and come under the yoke of new oppressors. They had hoped for something more satisfactory and have been hoping ever since; hence capitalism is doomed to eventual extinction.

Western civilization is chaotic; it is not an integral whole, consistent within itself. In a harmonious culture, the constituent elements agree with and supplement one another. Christianity, the religion of faith, must necessarily conflict with science, the child of reason, and they decidedly cannot live comfortably in the same house. A person cannot believe in both without impairing his sense of congruity. The scientist who is a Christian adopts his own version of the religion, and the priest who is a scientist sits precariously on two stools. As for the man in the street, he can, of course, pay lip service to any number of contradictory ideas, for his genuine interest lies elsewhere. And what shall we say of capitalism and socialism, diametrically opposite systems? Is it any wonder that their friction is perpetual? What does the capitalist, the oppressor, have in common with the proletarian, the oppressed? How can the doctrines of the two systems coalesce or work in unison? The mild socialist, with his insurance schemes, pensions, factory supervision, paid vacations, graduated taxation, and whatnot, is vainly endeavoring to create some semblance of order from chaos. Consider again the many philosophies, all engaged in vilifying one another and glorying in imagined triumphs. When even separate systems are not consistent in themselves, still less do they complement one another. Of course, none possess the remotest approach to finality. Turning to literature and the fine arts, what is the strange tug-of-war between realism and romanticism? *Belles lettres* should be the last realm for conflict, yet here it is, with innumerable schools deriding one another.

The resulting attitude is one of vacillation: the honest, perplexed soul finds no rest in reasonable certainty. The person whose ears are fatigued by this perpetual din eschews all the creeds and systems and becomes a pathetic, wistful agnostic or trenchant skeptic, applying both terms not merely to religious speculation but to all the phenomena of life. The ordinary person ceases to be interested in serious things and pursues pleasure as the most sensible of occupations; like Omar Khayyam, he may worship the grape and become impatient for the opening of the tavern. Hedonism is his ideal; he asserts that he doesn't want to hear about the factions and sects and feels superior in what he designates his freedom. The not so frivolous are fed up with their days, which they deem too long, and commit suicide. In either case, life has no real meaning.

Weariness of the spirit is not as rare as it should be; indeed, Western culture is weary at its core in spite of its outward appearance of vitality, its raucous noise of airplanes and voices, and its feverish activity of engines and salesmen. It suffers from disillusionment. It set out to civilize so-called inferior races before putting its own house in order and embroiled the world in its conflicts, disturbing the South Sea Islanders amid their coconut palms and the Berbers beside the minarets of Algiers and Tunis. It is a weariness for which there is no palliative; it is disillusionment, profound and unutterable! A civilization must be sick when its heroes are boxers; its heroines, actresses; and its brain trust, captains of industry.

There is a curious lack of a sense of values. The trifling and ephemeral are eagerly sought after, and the serious and eternal disregarded. Philosophy has become the follower of science, the greater of the lesser. Bodily strength and beauty are more important than meditation and virtue of the mind. Economics—food—is the burning topic, and culture is regarded as an elegant accomplishment, relatively insignificant. Sexual love is for many the sum of existence and for nearly all the meaning of life. Food and sex were practically the only objectives of the earliest humans. They still remain basic needs, but regarding the pursuit of them as the most meritorious of activities does not show much sign of progress. Worth should not be confused with need.

Europe is undoubtedly prone to war, and its history is a lengthy record of interminable conflict. There might be major holocausts involving the entire continent, or there might be only struggles between two nations; at any rate, such conflicts occurred, the intervals between them serving as periods of recuperation and preparation. The passage of time showed little change in attitude, but it brought better-developed weapons of destruction and numerous scientific inventions promising speedy victories. Chivalry was a refinement of the code of homicide, and the nobility was a warrior caste. When democracy struggled into existence, the wars of monarchs underwent a frightful metamorphosis into the wars of peoples. With the development of knowledge, partial massacres became totalitarian. What is the explanation for all this? The comparatively recent emergence from barbarism, the centrifugal tendency to split into smaller nations with touchy pride, the deeply rooted principle of the balance of power, the trifling but important-seeming variations in culture, national ambitions, tradition—all these contributory factors combined to wreak havoc.

Let us now consider the virtues of Occidental civilization. Its most conspicuous product is science, which, though not wholly beneficial with its explosives and materialistic distortions, marks an advance in human evolution. Its store of natural knowledge, high degree of certainty, contribution to human welfare, elimination of superstition, development of reason, achievement in knitting the world into one unit—all these make science an unparalleled blessing. Its evils are the result of human psychology and are not necessary concomitants. Science began at the moment *Homo sapiens* opened their eyes on the world, observed, and wondered, but it is the West that made it systematic and developed its potential to such a great extent that it is fair to regard it as the West's contribution to civilization. Nothing will ever be able to eliminate it, and whatever its detractors may say of various theories, they recognize it by using its facts and inventions. Science is an established entity; it may retrograde or become stationary, but it will remain a force and is more likely to continue its advance. It is the one branch of knowledge that has consistently progressed and will do so for a long time to come. The shape of the future world is determined by it, for it is an inescapable fact, not a literary theory or religion that can be overthrown without leaving much of a trace. The philosopher makes use of it; the literary person writes of it; the ordinary individual enjoys it. It has had a brilliant record and has given humanity more than a hope of arriving at a solution to the riddle of the universe. What can we say of this magnificent gift, save to pour forth a torrent of praise and hope earnestly that it will never be perverted?

The Greek philosophers were the first persons to lay store by pure reason, to consider no belief valid unless it could be proven. Reason is the best faculty of the mind, the finest product of human evolution. Theories created by the imagination and dogmatically asserted, gaining universal credence through repetition and tradition, were the foundations of Oriental cultures. After the Renaissance, more problems came under the acid test of reason, which, though it has its limitations, is the only method that can generate at least a probable certainty. The trouble with this noble human attribute is that the use of reason may often lead to mere sophistry; the numerous philosophies can be explained by the fact that in them reason has not been used systematically and accurately. A greater development is evidently necessary. Nevertheless, the Western attitude of rationality, which has become to a certain degree a habit even among the masses, is a definite, beneficial achievement.

Human beings lived at the mercy of their environment until modern inventions relieved them. Security is no mean achievement. There is nothing good in material misery and no sense in painful drudgery. The higher degree of comfort and convenience secured by a greater number of people was a step in the right direction. Without the ability to avoid endless manual labor, one can hardly cultivate a taste for knowledge and art; without culture, existence is on a low level. It is true that leisure need not necessarily be utilized to the best advantage, but a peasant who must cultivate the land for twelve hours a day will certainly be unable to cultivate his mind. Without machinery, sufficient facilities would be unavailable to everybody; as it is, many an ordinary person enjoys more comfort than a medieval duke. The accelerating tempo of invention during the last century or so is no cause for regret; on the contrary, it augurs well for the future of the race.

The West has made democracy a working system. Though it is riddled with serious defects, including party squabbles, dilatory legislative processes, and plutocratic control, it is endowed with the advantage that it must consider the popular will. Equality before the law, personal liberty, the welfare of the people—these are its aims and results. Individual men and women possess a dignity unknown under autocracy, for they exist in their own right by virtue of their human status. Their political consciousness is deliberately cultivated, and problems are national problems, people's problems, not the exclusive concern of only some persons or cliques. It would be naïve to imagine that representative government has proven to be an unqualified blessing; its roll of unscrupulous or stolid politicians does not constitute an edifying spectacle. The type of democracy that arose from the ideas of eighteenth-century French philosophers can be commended only with reservations. However, in theory, it is more idealistic than autocracy and, in practice, less pernicious.

A social sense is the great gift of the West's political development, a trait contemporaneous with the democratic ideal. In its moral systems, the East preached a man's duty toward his fellows, a duty circumscribed by personal contacts and taking no effective, practical shape in the wide sphere of legislation. Relief of poverty and distress was confined to erratic private philanthropy for the good of one's own soul or reputation. The denizen of a modern state is taught to think in terms of public welfare; he is a citizen and, as such, has duties toward the community. This is not merely vague sentiment but a positive consequence of interest in public problems; because their sympathies are moved, men and women can occupy themselves with affairs that are primarily not their own. Without public spirit, society would be unable to make any general progress.

Human evolution so far has attained its highest stage in Western civilization, which has achieved much; but it is only a step up the ladder of advancement and is by no means final. Civilization is still in the stage of experimentation. An artificial product, not integrated with the universe, Occidental culture is beset with chaos, which is antagonistic to the fundamental cosmic law of harmony. It is ill-balanced, with distorted values. Its partial, mutually contradictory systems of thought and action spell disaster for society and misery for the individual. The world is perpetually in turmoil, on the verge of annihilation or reversion to barbarism. Reason meets with theoretical approval but is little utilized in practice, where self-interest or tradition prevails. Spengler was not wrong in predicting the collapse of Western culture, which is now in its final state of enervation. What will happen on this planet? What will be the destiny of the race? Natural and historical forces point to the emergence of a new way of life.

Chapter 6
The Modern World

The world presents a sorry picture, and chaos is rampant. The conflicts among religions, moral systems, political forms, economic theories, classes, nations, and races are fraught with misery and disaster for both the individual and society. Ceaseless struggle pursues its course without any sign of abatement; ever and anon, its accumulated force reaches a head and bursts into internecine war, which does not solve the problems but, after destroying millions of human lives, relegates exhausted humanity to the status quo. Compromise is not a solution, either, for the diverse parties arrive only at an armed armistice as fragile as it is unsatisfactory. Tragedy stalks abroad, and the situation might easily be considered hopeless.

The influential religions are the same ancient creeds formulated ages ago, when reason was in the chrysalis stage and faith was an indispensable weapon. They were not merely specific ingredients of civilization but its foundation; in their comprehensiveness, they touched every detail of life, embodying natural knowledge and political theories in their arbitrary dogmas. All beliefs and acts were tinged with their hue. Their extensive ramifications made them difficult to overthrow, for all interests were bound up with their maintenance. In the West, Christianity was attacked piecemeal by philosophy, science, politics, and economics; but, as no new religion or complete philosophy arose to replace it, it still persists in spite of its much less influential state in Western countries. In Eastern lands, intellectual slumber allowed the religions to continue their hegemony untroubled until the catastrophic impact of European expansion began to undermine their influence. With their deep roots, it is possible that they will not be completely relinquished in spite of the different forms of attack on the material front. The existing creeds are too concerned with the increasing power of secularism to be engaged in a real struggle among themselves, though their doctrines are divergent and their sects are numerous.

Christianity is most conspicuous for its multiplicity of sects, which in the past engaged in ferocious conflicts. While all the religions cannot be true, it is probable that all are false, based as they are on faith and superstition. Religious freedom should be upheld, but it would be irrational to imagine that any belief would do on the grounds that all creeds are fundamentally similar. This attitude is rooted in indifference, for atheistic Buddhism does not resemble anthropomorphic Mohammedanism. The fact is, spiritual welfare has ceased to be of consuming interest—hence the pathetic spectacle of a horde of sects endeavoring to stand on their tottering legs, mutual dislike in their hearts and stultification in their heads.

Philosophy has often claimed to replace religion, but it is equally impotent to save the world. Its systems are numerous, and it has not produced a single doctrine of universal credence. Its language is abstruse, and its ideas are often fantastic and unrelated to practical life. Its proponents are purblind professors, despising the mob, engaged in technical discussions, not even practicing their own moral doctrines. It is not on the verge of death, for it has never had a vigorous life; it has chosen to dwell in the twilight, somnolent and powerless. Its partial, tentative systems have the unhappy attribute of leaving the ordinary reader cold. A history of philosophy is apt to give one a feeling of mild wonderment, frustration, and vexation, so mild that it soon vanishes under the pressure of diurnal business. The conflicting theories have strange shades, and the variety of systems is achieved by curious admixtures. Chaos may be said to find in philosophy allegedly rational and universal knowledge, the special realm in which to display its genius.

Turning to politics, we find that chaos has found an ally in knavery, for here knowledge is a mere façade for power. The so-called practical individual uses theories insofar as they serve his ambition; his principles are as trustworthy as his character, and ideals are to him unhealthy symptoms of a utopian complex. However, after the fashion set by the French Revolution, governmental control could be obtained only on the heels of ideologies, hence the rise of parties with their programs. Ideas are stereotyped in the form of catchwords supported by insufficient justification and are very often mischievous. Fundamentally, there are only two theories, autocracy and democracy, but by utilizing detailed interpretations, topical problems, and administrative techniques, the numerous parties are able to flaunt separate banners. Each organization is designed to appeal to a definite class or group, and incompatible interests find their expression in clashes. Never before have so many political parties flourished, openly clamoring in electoral politics and working underground in absolutist regimes.

Throughout the twentieth century and into the twenty-first, the focus of interest has been economics, which, having inextricably intertwined itself with politics and superseded religion in importance, may become the foundation of civilization, spreading its tentacles into every department of life. The tendency of economic doctrines to claim the preeminent place in the scheme of things is deplorable, revealing the lack of a sense of balance. The struggle between capitalism and socialism, between management and labor, is the modern epic. Stemming directly or indirectly from Karl Marx, the different schools of socialists agree vaguely in their ultimate aims but disparage one another in their methods. Extremists declare unrelenting war on capitalism, which they seek to overthrow completely; moderates endeavor to alleviate its evils through an illogical admixture of socialist tenets, producing regimes unsatisfactory in practice and in theory. In any case, an ideal society has not attained concrete shape, and industrial unrest is the only positive achievement of the enormous energy of thinkers and agitators. Booms, depressions, strikes, parades, conferences, wholesale massacres, inflation, famine, demonstrations, civil wars—these have been much in evidence.

What is culture? Even this peaceful realm lacks a guiding principle of indubitable validity. One school advocates the pursuit of good old literature and would deny the name of culture to anything but "humanistic studies"; another valiantly champions science, regarding all else as mere trifles and amusement. The artist worships his craft as a religion; according to him, it satisfies his deepest spiritual needs. Indeed, words and colors and sounds harness the secrets of the universe! The ephemeral literary movements do not wreak general havoc, for their influence is restricted, and, as they are expressions of personality and not theories of truth, their disunity need cause no mental disquiet. One can enjoy both realistic and romantic masterpieces without any qualms of conscience and can peruse Ibsen and Tolstoy without disparaging Byron and Hugo. The scientist, with his investigation of a fragment of mechanical nature, can certainly not be said to have attained unimpeachable culture. Scientific theories have lost their certitude, and not even Euclidean geometry, the erstwhile perfect ship sailing majestically on the ocean of doubt, is synonymous with truth. In spite of its shortcomings, science has achieved reasonable unanimity, and there are no belligerent schools of equal prestige. All in all, culture, whether literary or scientific, can give greater harmony to the mind; what is regrettable is its dearth of devotees.

Of all the rivalries, the struggle for existence between nations and races is the most baleful, involving a stupendous amount of effort leading to no genuine solution. Chiefly waged in the political and economic fields, it exhausts its participants and seriously hinders the progress of civilization. The world is divided into a collection of big and small states claiming absolute sovereignty, resulting in a foundation of anarchy. Whereas an individual would be stigmatized as a selfish monster if he did not pay attention to others' rights, a state is not thus vilified. The existing independent states are products of past conflicts; they are not organized on any rational principle. Small groups of people have possessed territorial independence, while larger assemblages have been governed in colonies. Imperialistic powers have sought to maintain their rule; the subjugated races have revolted; militant nations have striven for expansion to the detriment of their neighbors—thus conflict has wielded its fury.

War! War is the last expression of chaos, when the world becomes afflicted with insanity and relapses into barbarism; there are few now who are haunted by its glory, who pretend to see virtues that elevate man and speak of baptism by fire as a blessing. That does not prevent war from erupting, for government policies and the blind support of their peoples lead to it. Mars, the God of War, is not dead and has his subtle ways. An international organization of member states with conflicting aims, invested with no adequate authority of its own, cannot satisfactorily remedy the situation. Pugnacious instincts and irreconcilable interests cannot be eliminated by hypocritical resolution. With the development of the nuclear bomb, the human race might not survive another world war; world wars, in which many nations become embroiled at once, are a peculiar modern phenomenon. Indeed, the outlook is not bright when it is possible for all the forces of chaos to rage at any time, when to moral underdevelopment is added the destructive skill of science.

The ancient moral systems have lost their appeal, and no new system has assumed authority. Ethical canons are spurned as platitudes and pleasure is widely extolled and practiced. The vague term *welfare*, which has many interpretations, is a useful catchword. In the intellectual bankruptcy of the age, the problem of morality is not considered as a whole; but rules of conduct come in confused forms, as appendices to a political or economic theory, social legislation, business, psychological findings, cultivation of beauty or health, sports, and literary visions. In the welter of confusion, each individual behaves according to instincts and traits imbibed from his immediate environment and restraints imposed by the law of the land and society where he seeks to make good. He does not know universal rules and does not pursue a harmonious system founded on natural truth. If anarchism were to succeed, society would immediately disintegrate, not because of the disappearance of the state, but because of the lack of an ethical system.

The various constituents of civilization are at loggerheads with one another. The state's aims are incongruous with those of religion, which is regarded as purely a matter of personal conscience. This may be so, but isn't it obvious that by its coercive decrees and tremendous prestige the government enforces allegiance to behavior destructive of spiritual culture? The unity of life is destroyed when either religion or the state predominates or when their interests are at variance. The state is supposed to be a nonmoral organization, but in practice it confounds morality, making power and office the objects of struggle. The practical politician has no qualms of conscience in pursuing self-aggrandizement.

Religion, philosophy, and science live in hostile camps, deriding one another's beliefs. The first appeals to faith and arrogantly claims unconditional surrender to its divine dogmas; the second upholds pure reason and enunciates dubious doctrines of ultimate truth having little relevance to life; and the last resorts to observation and experiment and brings forward facts and laws that conflict with the idealistic visions of its two predecessors in the realm of knowledge. If one were true, the others must be false; they can exist simultaneously only by dividing humanity into groups, and not everyone is interested in the three subjects together. A person cannot place his belief in one without turning his back on the others; if he professes that all are right, it is only because of unwarrantable inconsistency, a trait as common now as ever.

The prevalent universal confusion arises from the lack of a comprehensive system of thought in which all the elements of civilization are integrated, each existing in its own right yet in harmony with the rest. In bygone ages, a semblance of unity was attained by tracing everything to religion. In Marxist socialism, simplicity was created by violently and arbitrarily suppressing all valuable human achievements as *bourgeois* and unfit for proletarian consumption, and by planning a society based on the single subject of economics. Such unity is attained at the cost of truth and comprehensiveness.

Knowledge has become varied and extensive, hence the almost insurmountable difficulty of founding a harmonious system that is not painfully restricted in scope. Still, harmony is essential and chaos is intolerable if life is to be genuinely happy and if meaningful progress is to ensue. A struggle must be made toward true unity, not by slipshod compromise, not by focusing attention on one part of life, but by creating a system based on reason, where all the constituents have their due place and weight and are complementary. The creation of such a system and civilization is beset with difficulties; but it is not an impossible task, for, after all, nature forms a beautiful unity, and civilization is only the way of life of a part of nature—namely, the human race. Chaos is not the last word, the final destiny, of society; it must give way to harmony.

Chapter 7
Unregulated Course

Civilization has always been dubbed an artificial product, and this indictment has sufficient cause; civilization does not exist by nature but is the work of the human hand and brain. When numerous individuals live in close proximity, they must form ways and means of regulating their intercourse, and hence arise standards. Their minds interact and bring forth new phenomena; environmental stimuli produce responses, and one discovery engenders another. Towns are requisite for great cultural progress. This does not mean that they antedate civilization, for they themselves are products of social life and increasing intellectual consciousness; but, once in existence, they accelerate further advancement. They grow from villages where communities gather. The village was the unit of barbarian society, the primitive form of population concentration. Even the most primitive hamlet contains shacks raised by human hands and does not exist naturally. Barbaric and civilized societies differ only in degree of development, not in kind, for they are both artificial.

Looking back over the past, one is struck by the recentness of civilization, whose bright story of a few thousand years is preceded by an immensely long, dark stretch of time during which the human race dwelled in abysmal ignorance millennium after millennium, illuminated by occasional flashes of discovery and invention. Furthermore, only sections of the human race outgrew their uncultured state, some earlier and some later, while whole races roaming over entire continents continued to live in primitive conditions until their lands were taken by the expanding European peoples who had become civilized comparatively late in history. It is strange that the ideas and techniques we highly prize, which the uncritical are apt to take for granted, arose not long ago. How far has humanity advanced, yet how recent are our achievements! Civilization did not spring up in a day, fully grown as Pallas left the head of Zeus, though recorded history, itself a highly intellectual creation, has only myths regarding its origins. Still, its growth was undoubtedly strangely rapid compared to the slow changes of the eons of barbarism.

What factors were at work in the rise of civilization? Did the innate intelligence of human beings improve? Maybe, but not to any great extent. The same faculties are present in individuals living in the most primitive conditions, and it is possible to take them in childhood and train them, giving them the most up-to-date mental paraphernalia. The mind is extremely malleable, and acquired intelligence is certainly higher than it ever was; molded with certain traits, the brain is ready for "fresh woods and pastures new," as the English poet Milton wrote. When systematic reflection was learned, discoveries became more frequent and civilization grew apace. Acquired character is cumulative and works as though inborn; it makes innovations, and these further its growth.

The environment must have been the prime cause of the original rise of civilization. Mild climate, fertile soil, ease of communication, good mineral supply—these produced a dense population and an easier life, allowing the leisure for curiosity. A large, stable community presented problems of organization; the social sense grew strong; a discovery became common property and could be easily transmitted by imitation. Competition was bound to arise, and it acted as a powerful stimulant to incite fresh efforts. Small as the earth is, its surface conditions are curiously diversified; only a comparatively small area can naturally form the habitat of great masses of humanity. Geography had much to do with the advancement in the arts of life; the first cultures were born in the productive basins of the Nile, Euphrates, Ganges, and Hwang Ho. It would be too much, of course, to imagine that topography was sufficient explanation for the rise of civilization, for no highly advanced civilization grew up along the shores of the

Mississippi, though it was as good as any river. As the causes for any phenomenon are often numerous, doubtless a favorable combination was responsible for the wondrous emergence of civilization.

If we believe in determinism, then we must suppose that civilization was bound to come and that it was no accident. What is really meant when speaking of causes is antecedent events. Human beings are part of the natural scheme of things. The innate faculties of our minds are bound to react to external factors and produce what no lower animal could—we are creators. The first attempts of early humans were tentative and slow; after coming into possession of the requisite mental equipment, they progressed with increasing speed, though not with the regular acceleration of a body falling toward earth. Their intellectual energy was not self-acting but was conditioned by external factors. They molded their environment; their environment molded them.

Unfortunately, the energy of a particular race could evaporate easily, but as compensation, its achievements could be learned and assimilated by another that could develop the heritage. Civilization is not the story of one nation, and its course is fitful. A specific race may remain largely stationary or even retrograde in various ways, but taking into consideration humanity as a whole, it has advanced or, at least, spread. No race, once civilized, has ever really relapsed into barbarism. Dazzled by brilliant creative activity, we tend to confuse an age of enlightenment with the height of civilization, regarding a succeeding, relatively stagnant period as lower on the scale of evolution. This view is true only so far as significance is concerned, for a later century has learned all that its predecessor achieved; from the point of view of knowledge, not originality, it is superior. I suppose the Romans knew whatever the Greeks did and a little more, having learned everything and added something. The China of the Mings was more cultured than the China of the chaotic period of the Chous, for though no Confucius or Laotze arose, it possessed their systems, and the intervening centuries had accumulated a wealth of experience unknown at the time of Confucius or Laotze in the Chou Dynasty. Comparative richness in civilization is to be judged not from original production but from the totality of knowledge; in this sense, a later period is higher on the scale of evolution than an earlier.

The course of civilization has not been shaped by systematic thought but has rolled along haphazardly, with transformations and accretions produced by a variety of circumstances, which from the human point of view might be regarded as accidental. It resembles a runaway horse, uncontrolled. Few people took the trouble to consider it. A renowned thinker, artist, or statesman affected it in a tiny spot with his contribution. It is not directed toward the fulfillment of a definite goal, and comprehending its unplanned chaos requires no sagacity.

A lack of rationalization does not make a culture natural, just as a badly constructed house undertaken by an accidental assortment of builders at different times does not make it less of a factitious product. In the narrow sense of the term, a natural phenomenon is one that comes into existence with no human aid. Though nobody could contend that civilization bears this quality, that it is as natural as a mountain or a star, it is customary for conservatives to oppose a radical change of any kind based on the theory that it interferes with the natural character of society. To them, whatever is already in existence is natural and not to be tampered with. When the French Revolution erupted with its endeavor to erect a new state on preconceived principles, people gaped at the impious and incredible desire of the reformers to abolish the natural work of the ages. Humanity, it would seem, must subject itself to the accidents of fortune and must not take a hand in shaping its destiny; society must remain at the mercy of circumstance. Such a view is profoundly erroneous and indicates the lamentable inertia that unfortunately so readily afflicts the mortal mind. Nature must not be confused with casualness. A casual change is that which comes haphazardly, piecemeal, from diverse hands and causes; it is an accident for humankind, not preconceived and worked out in accordance with theory. It is, nonetheless, artificial.

The evils of an unregulated culture are manifold. It works toward no conscious purpose and rolls heedlessly along until it is extinguished. It is self-contradictory, making strange bedfellows of opposite elements; like a river, it gathers a curious collection of rubbish, which makes it turbid and unwholesome. For a lengthy stretch of time, it makes people stupidly somnolent, bearing their woes with mild despair or pathetic submissiveness; then come some changes that, though limited, shake them to their cores, filling them with exuberance or anguish.

These vicissitudes do not fit in with other constituents that are not questioned, and chaos still reigns supreme. The good and the bad are inextricably intermingled, and one cannot be annihilated without the other; hence arise fatalistic apologies, such as "the best of all possible worlds" and "whatever is, is right."

Trifling reforms are useless in that they palliate specific distresses only to give rise to fresh evils, for the old and the new cannot coalesce, and perpetual friction is engendered. A lengthy string of casual alterations only prolongs misery, keeping the goal of life as far away as ever. Even a small reform can create havoc and bitter opposition. Wars have been waged over the preservation and expropriation of minor interests. The mind can grow as bitter over a petty problem as over an enormous one; there is a limit to all passions, and they are apt to reach it. A fundamental transformation produces no more pain than a superficial alteration, and only the imagination conceives the stupendous difference. In a conservative age, even a minor reform is difficult to carry through, while in a revolutionary period, people are not content to see their days drag along with mere palliatives, which do not really cure their ills. Let us have revolution!

Chapter 8
Fundamental Revolution

The need for a new civilization is incontestable, and a thorough revolution in all the fundamental bases of social existence not only is desirable but grows more imperative over time. Now that people worldwide are accustomed to revolution and the benefits derivable from systematic change, they are no longer afflicted with the stupid attitude of their forbears in vilifying proposed innovations. They want to shape their destiny according to the best scheme they know, as they live in an age of upheaval and are psychologically driven to create, plan, and achieve. This urge, rooted in narrow spheres of activity, continues to extend its horizon until it embraces all of civilization. This tendency should not be deprecated, for it is a sign of growing intelligence. The desire for reform will not be abated until society is reasonably good. Sir Thomas More had the misfortune to have to consider his projects as realizable only in utopia, but today dreams have entered the realm of practicability. The common individual is profoundly stirred and has never before been so ideologically conscious, thanks to successful political and social revolutions, science, the decay of religion, and the rude blow dealt the torpid East. It has become the practice to speak of ages of transition; the present is the greatest of all, for it comprises the entire planet.

It is time to see life steadily and whole. Experiments have become popular, but we must reflect more comprehensively and intensely and consider where they are leading; it will not do if they are engaged in a tug-of-war or if they move in opposite directions. As events succeed one another endlessly, haphazardly, we must establish some control over their course. Rationalization is the order of the day, and this should be extended to include everything. A certain stage of evolution has been reached; transformations have accumulated rapidly into an unwieldy mass; no time is more propitious than the present for reconsidering the bases of civilization. The world may end in destruction or relapse into barbarism if it does not assume a definite shape, and the future is pregnant with destiny, which can be either good or evil. We have left behind an immemorial past, and we stand on the threshold of a new era. The sum of things clamors for a hearing. Stranded amid a welter of moldering cultures and misdirected movements, we are bewildered; we cannot continue in this melancholy impasse; we must recover our equilibrium.

The need for a complete integration of all values is beyond question, for chaos associated with feebleness and stupidity is unsatisfactory and disastrous, and it signifies the triumph of unreason and despair. The universe is a unity, and the laws of nature constitute a harmonious array. Why should humanity exist under the dominion of discord? Why should our creations, a mere fraction of the totality of things, be devoid of the essential principle of harmony? A work of art would not deserve the name if its parts did not present a coherent unity; neither would a culture be esthetically glorious if it were deficient in this trait. The sense of beauty is outraged from contemplating an odd assemblage of objects, and the conscience writhes uneasily when it finds good and evil entangled. Logic, esthetics, and ethics demand the extinction of confusion.

The amount of waste involved in planlessness is enormous, as intellectual and material resources are dissipated in a variety of follies while energy is misdirected. When people perform actions that do not contribute to integrated objectives and their efforts suffer mutual nullification, they might as well fold their hands, sit still like an image of Buddha, and do nothing, for they will inflict less mischief on society and secure for themselves an enviable serenity of mind. If Laotze were alive today, he would have greater cause than ever for proclaiming his message of "do nothing," as the fruits of discord are more bitter than before. One might well exclaim impatiently at the futility of human effort and condemn busyness if it terminated in the shifting, treacherous sands of disorder. Chaos is destruction, irrational and intolerable.

The world has seen revolutions in various fields, and each was mainly devoted to the realization of a theory pertaining to a single subject. In the ages of prehistory, all changes came slowly and randomly, and for some time a people would exist amid an undigested mass of cultural values. Thinkers arose, and attempts at systematization began. But conservatism is such a strong instinct that innovators tend to be looked at askance. There is also the widespread fallacy that a society's unanimous beliefs cannot be wrong, that the ideas of one person, when weighed against the opinions of all his fellows, must be false. Popularity is viewed as synonymous with truth, but clearly this doctrine is untenable. The masses do not initiate ideas but only receive them, and though they may not realize it, their ideas were once the property of individuals. When an innovation starts rolling, it gathers momentum; after a few generations, it comes to be accepted as an incontrovertible fact, as natural as the sun. What is now fashionable was once not so. If general acceptance were truth, then primitive practices that were universal long ago would deserve to be called so. However, in spite of purblind and furious objection, prophets and philosophers did succeed in establishing their systems, and society was forced to undergo some fundamental changes.

The first planned revolutions took place in the realm of religion, the most notable examples being Buddhism, Christianity, and Mohammedanism, which owed their origin to solitary individuals. In the process of expansion, they altered considerably but never lost the impress of their founders' genius. What is significant or interesting about them is not their truth but their character of systematic revolution. To the ancients, it must have seemed presumptuous for individual mortals to endeavor to alter the fabric of society, so it is not surprising that the initiators of the great religious movements were revered as divine personages. The religious systems did not confine themselves to purely metaphysical and ethical problems but extended unwarrantably into other subjects. Life was bound by a set of meticulous rules, their validity founded on dogmatic pronouncements. Once the creeds were established, it was very difficult, if not impossible, to get rid of them, and they obstructed further transformation, both in their proper fields and in all social phenomena. Within them grew numerous sects whose original aim was reformation within limits, though they succeeded only in forming closed corporations, dividing society into diverse bodies at loggerheads with one another. In spite of the ranting of established organizations against heresy, people had learned the possibility of theoretical change in religion.

Political revolution was of more recent origin. In ancient times, movements aimed at transforming state organization on theoretical principles arose only in China. The Chinese thinkers were primarily political and moral philosophers who came forward when feudalism had dissolved into hopeless disorder and war stalked the land. The Taoist, Confucian, Micianist, and Legalist schools struggled for supremacy, though the solution came with the triumph of the sword of the first Chin emperor, whose revolutionary work was momentous. Only administrative technique, however, was new, as the government still remained an absolute monarchy. Later, the conservative Confucianists succeeded in winning prestige for their ideal of benevolent despotism, and thereafter the system of government remained unaltered; only dynasties came and went. The Greek thinkers took little interest in political speculation, and Plato alone formulated a revolutionary system, which was so intertwined with metaphysics and was so like a reverie that it had no influence on practical affairs. The great era of political revolution began with the calling of the states general by Louis XVI, the deputies' meeting at Versailles in 1789; though the nature of the changes did not differ materially from those attempted by the English in 1649 and the Americans in 1776, the efforts were more in accordance with a preconceived theoretical system, and the effect was more startling. Since then, revolutions have been popular, and the governments of one country after another have changed their character overnight. It is now seen as possible for theory to mold a new state, and nobody stares aghast at such an attempt, as it has become reputable.

Economics dominates the scene at present. Russia undertook to create a new economy in accordance with the speculations of Karl Marx, and its experiment was immense in scope. It made economics take the place of religion and arbitrarily connected its dogmas with other subjects in which nothing new had been evolved. Its negative and unenlightened attitudes toward religion and culture, respectively, have shown how dangerous it is to concentrate interest on one subject. Within the bounds of its limited vision, the U.S.S.R. achieved a considerable measure of success in transforming the life of its people to materially surpass that under erstwhile Czarist rule. A horde of other theories exist regarding the organization of industry and the distribution of wealth—anarchism, syndicalism, guild socialism, social democracy, and so on. These have not effected such radical changes as Bolshevism, but the movements are there, and their common aim is systematic rationalization. One may or may not agree with the theories, but few would deny the rightness of economic revolution. Unlike our forebears, we could not seriously hold that wealth and poverty are decreed by heaven and that we must submit unquestionably to our lot.

The scientific revolution has changed the face of the world and more than anything else has demonstrated that the destiny of the human race lies in our own work. True, scientific theories and inventions could not trace their origin to a single source, nor did they begin on the same date. The scientific revolution does not resemble the religious or political, but the achievements of innumerable scientists, great and small, constitute a genuine revolution. All scientists are inspired by the same fundamental principles; they work with the Inductive Method and possess a common criterion. No single person was responsible for the inception of science, though Bacon aspired to the position of herald with his *Novum Organum*. The method of this great thinker has not been closely followed, but we must be impressed by his unified conception. However science arose and progressed, its results form a systematic revolution, as if in accordance with some plan.

We see then that various revolutions have triumphed and that they have been for the good. Why not extend our thinking and make that most sublime and fundamental of revolutions, the revolution of civilization? Reconsider all the elements of existence, let each have its due place, let them be harmoniously blended into a single entity, and create a new civilization! This is the grandest of tasks, and in this alone can life find its complete expression. Innovate and integrate: these are the primary tasks of the future. The world has never witnessed a systematic revolution of civilization; hence, it has never had any really good, complete culture, only confused conglomerations of tentative rules and products. Now that we are accustomed to departmental revolutions, we should be prepared for an inclusive revolution, without which society must forever remain unsatisfactory. Conservatism has reeled under an array of barrages, and it is now time to launch against it a final battering ram. As Omar Khayyam said, let us "grasp this sorry scheme of things entire … shatter it to bits, and then remold it nearer to the heart's desire." This is not a chimerical dream or an evil hope; the world needs to be remolded.

The creation of a new civilization is feasible. If people have been able, as history attests, to establish new states and new religions, then they should be able to initiate a new culture, for the two bases of a culture are state and religion. This task is no more difficult than partial reform, as there are the same vulnerable forces—namely, ignorance and entrenched interests. It is much better to struggle for a comprehensive ideal than a minor affair; and the amount of enthusiasm and effort involved is no greater, for these have a natural limit that we are apt to reach on behalf of any cause, however trivial. In this age, utopias are not remote, intangible conceptions but are genuine possibilities; they do not loom vaguely on the horizon but are close at hand. It is up to us whether we live in the maelstrom of misery or in the serene sea of happiness. Nothing is visionary if it envisages life's possibilities; practical is the new civilization that is reared on truth.

The march of events points to the emergence of fresh values. History is a developing drama, and, like nature, it has never been absolutely static. It is a truism to say that we are the heirs of the ages: it is more important to remember that we are the ancestors of futurity. As heirs, we inherit, but we would not merit the esteem of posterity if we only transmitted and did not produce. How much an age creates depends on conditions; the present is destined to be a tremendous creator. The formative tendencies of previous times have come to a head. The interrelationship among all regions of the earth, the mutual knowledge of once-isolated cultures, rationalism, science, political and economic revolutions, the peril of internecine global wars—all of these point to the need for an integrated civilization. The coming culture is a historical fruit. The Golden Age does not lie in the prehistoric past but exists in the future, the legitimate offspring of countless generations of toil-worn figures. We rejoice, not because we are a little lower than the angels but because we are vastly superior to the apes. The process of continual advance, of development of reason, will naturally lead to a purely rational culture. Hope is reinforced by reality; reality is illuminated by hope. The quintessence of the universe is perfectibility, and on this rest the possibility and inevitability of the new civilization.

Chapter 9
Method

When we formulate a theory in any realm of knowledge, a method of inquiry is a prerequisite, ensuring that the theory rests on a sound foundation and that the pitfalls of guesswork and dogmatism are eliminated. Nothing is more lamentable yet more common than for people, even so-called philosophers, to flaunt fancies as truths; to cling to them passionately; and, if challenged, to produce a random assortment of excuses and reasons in their defense. One curious fact is that a plausible reason can be advanced on behalf of any idea, with the result that contending parties can all claim to have reason on their side. In the bad old days, before the rise of rationalism, the defense of an idea rested on divine inspiration; that age is past, and every theorizer and propagandist now feels compelled to show reason. But a collection of odd, uncoordinated statements, even if each were a genuine proof, still does not constitute a system of reasoning. Without a proper method, such ratiocination is apt to be very misleading, partial and one-sided as it is.

For an integrated, comprehensive theory, a systematic method of proof is needed. This is realized only in metaphysics under the name of methodology, which arose when the French philosopher Descartes propounded his mathematical method. This need is no less imperative in other branches of knowledge, especially when it comes to formulating a general theory, comprehensive in scope and dealing with fundamentals. A revolutionary system that aims to totally reconstruct society must possess as the basis of its ideology a methodology. A mansion wholly harmonized and appearing magnificent would be perilous if it did not rest on a sound foundation. A philosophy might be coherent and imposing yet be only a feat of the imagination unrelated to truth if it were not supported by organized, impregnable reason. A methodology does not necessarily generate truth; but this is either because in itself it is faulty or it has been used to give incorrect conclusions.

The aim of this book is to propose a new civilization, which in its comprehensiveness deals not merely with religion and political concepts but with every aspect of human existence. A civilization is a stupendous subject to discuss, the most tremendous of all themes if it includes a survey of the universe, and for such a subject, a methodology is essential. The aim is not to weave a romance or to discuss one or two problems. It is to construct a serious system that will present a harmony of all human activities. The goal is not to tinker with odds and ends; the objective is more ambitious! The system must be thorough and needs a planned method of elucidation.

The universe is a cosmos, an ordered whole in which things and events are interlinked. The barest experience makes us aware of this fact, and we are struck with the impression of a pattern. We may be unable to explain rifts in the pattern, and we may be confounded by catastrophe, but the general impression of harmony prevails, and we live our lives believing in universal order. The farmer who is somnolent in winter expects spring to return so that he can begin a new cycle of planting and harvesting, and he would be thunderstruck if the trees did not produce fresh foliage. A man moving away from an object would be confounded if it increased in size and revealed itself in greater detail. A methodical universe requires a systematic mode of elucidation.

If it is to form part of a regular universe, a civilization should in itself be a harmony. Therefore, its principles must be arrived at through methodical inquiry, not established haphazardly. Portentous dogmas enunciated by self-styled prophets, excuses cooked up by self-seeking politicians, specious statements addressing specific problems, wishful thinking—these do not constitute an appropriate approach to the subject of civilization. They are travesties of the truth and should be rejected without hesitation.

Reason presupposes method. It is the instrument given to humanity for the attainment of truth, and, in its genuine form, it is methodical. But there is a distinction between reason and methodology: the former is general and diffuse, while the latter is a specific form for the utilization of reason. Without a definite pattern, reason may lead nowhere. Instead of traveling straight to the truth, it may ramble aimlessly and become lost; it may become entangled in a quagmire of ill-assorted statements. It is applicable to any subject, but there must be a specific method of inquiry for each particular branch of study.

Systematization implies method. The aim of a system is to link a number of ideas together into a satisfactory whole, whereas the essence of a method is to enable this process to be executed thoroughly. A system woven haphazardly is unreliable and tends to lose itself in a morass of inconsistencies. Just as in practical life, a well-conceived plan is conducive to a project's eventual success. In the realm of knowledge, a methodology that is an elaboration of reason engenders a more fruitful system. An ideology needs a rational method of inquiry for its starting point.

Matter contains method. The material realm is a cosmos wherein things are interconnected and there is no chaos but sublime order, the law of cause and effect being inviolable. Rain does not fall without a cloud, and a cloud is not formed without water; winds and tides do not behave erratically; the earth does not rotate randomly on its axis, now moving clockwise and now counterclockwise. Because of the order in matter, we are able to have science; if phenomena were not interlinked, if there were no relationship of cause and effect, the sciences of physics, chemistry, astronomy, and geology could not have evolved. What we would have at best would be an elaborate collection of discrete phenomena, difficult to digest and meaningless.

Reason is the only legitimate course for the attainment of truth. It uses facts obtained through observation or elementary axioms formulated by intuition and corroborated by experience and deduces from these new knowledge in ways recognized as valid, logic being the particular subject that deals with proper methods of ratiocination. The supreme value of reason has been established by science.

Of course, the human mind is endowed with other faculties concerned with the acquisition of knowledge and the discovery of truth—sensation, intuition, imagination. Without these, especially sensation, reason could hardly function. Each of them serves some purpose and has its say, but reason must control them and have the final word. Reason is king; the other faculties are its subjects.

Let us examine the nature of reason. It works by joining one thing to another, by deducing an effect from a cause, by proving how a thing has come to be what it is. Its essence is connection, and it does not need any profound discernment to recognize this elementary truth. Through the instrumentality of connection, things are woven into a harmonious pattern. One fact is linked to another fact, one idea to another idea.

The Connective Method is opposed to the Dialectical Method, which aims to discover truth by setting up one idea in antithesis to another and which is contradictory to the very nature of reason. It is ridiculous to employ a method based on disputation and opposition to create a system of harmonizing concepts. Argumentation normally ends as it begins—in argumentation. No exercise is more futile than a debate where both sides adduce arguments that suit them, ignore those that are unpalatable, distort or suppress facts, and use fallacious modes of reasoning. The Hegelian and Marxian methods of setting up a thesis, producing its antithesis, and subsuming both under a third concept presuppose that the universe is made up of contradictions—a doubtful proposition.

Reason can be deductive or inductive. Via deductive reasoning, an idea is derived from another idea; in the last analysis, one arrives at certain *a priori* principles that are true in themselves and cannot be obtained through reasoning—truths such as "two and two make four" or the geometrical axiom that when equals are added to equals, the results are equal. We are unable to prove the truth of the statements; our minds are so constituted that we cannot understand how they could be otherwise—they are self-evident. The principles can, however, be verified by experience, but the fact that we have never encountered a contradictory case does not warrant the assumption that there can never be such an exception.

Inductive reasoning, the method of science, collects facts and evolves a theory to explain them. Because of its remarkable success in the natural sciences, it has been applied to the mental and social sciences, where it has not led to conclusions as incontrovertible as those of the natural sciences. We tend to forget that at no particular time are we able to amass all the facts relating to a problem; those collected may be impressive in number, but they are never exhaustive.

The Connective Method must relate to both ideality and practicality. When it is concerned with formulating what still must come into being, in this case a civilization, it should strive to unfold the ideal but must simultaneously modify its findings to comply with the practicable. The practicable is more extensive than is commonly imagined, and it is a mistake to presume that what did not exist before could not possibly materialize. It is useless to bring into being something pernicious or far short of the ideal; if being practical is evil, then there is nothing to eulogize in the practical individual.

A proper method has for its objective the discovery of the truth and the right. A method that shrouds a subject in mystery and, instead of elucidating a problem, makes it more difficult to comprehend is to be deprecated. One that merely serves the purpose of sophistry and argumentation is poisonous. Truth is an objective entity in the sense that the universe exists in a certain form and the truth is merely the actual nature of the universe. Right indicates that an entity or possible entity is good and is inherent in the scheme of things. Truth and right are not manmade, although a colossal amount of human ideas masquerade as truth and right.

Let us now consider the Connective Method as it applies to the theory of a new civilization. Biology has conclusively shown that all life has evolved from the simple to the complex, and evolution is undoubtedly a principle of the universe. Taking the human race as a whole, we find that primitive society was barbaric; we could say that barbarism is the first stage of evolution in human society. Then came civilization, which is the second stage. But the various civilized societies historically and at present still bear strong vestiges of their barbaric past and are greatly defective. There will come a third stage when a new civilization emerges to envelop the earth. These are the three stages or levels of social evolution.

Each stage necessarily evolves from its predecessor. It is impossible to imagine that human beings would have remained barbaric forever. Although some communities have existed at the primitive level until modern times, civilization would sooner or later have emerged somewhere. As there was physical evolution of species, so was there bound to be social evolution of the human race. We have certainly not reached the acme of civilization, and there is little reason to doubt that social evolution will culminate in a planetary super-civilization.

When we look at history, we see an assortment of events. To bring order from chaos and understand the happenings, we must interpret the data in the light of some criterion. As the events are the actions of human beings who are endowed with mental characteristics, the easiest way to comprehend them would be to fathom the minds of the players; that is, the psychological interpretation of history is the proper path to tread. The history of man is made by man. Through the mere fact of his existence, a human being is driven by the desire to preserve his life and, arising from this, the desire to secure his well-being. The concept of welfare, however, differs from country to country, age to age, and individual to individual; hence the variety of phenomena.

One person desires to secure a throne and found a dynasty, one to conquer a country, one to initiate a republic; one loves capitalism and another communism; one wants to establish a religion, another to unravel the mysteries of the physical world or to make inventions. But the majority just wish to live in peace and happiness and are moved to participate in mass movements only at the instigation, secret or open, of rulers, revolutionaries, and thinkers.

When the human race first emerged, the struggle for existence common to all animals persisted in them. They had the will to live, but since they had the faculty of thought, over time they must have realized that survival was easier if at least some cooperation was introduced in lieu of only conflict, and hence society was born. As their mental attributes unfolded, they made more discoveries and inventions, and society grew in complexity. The desire for power and wealth produced wars, and in the individual was the variant for the struggle for existence.

History as commonly written is a record of the conflicts of individuals, groups, and nations.

But other human desires were powerful, too. The mystery of the universe incited more reflective persons to propound answers, giving rise to religions that gripped large sections of humanity and greatly influenced the course of events. Over time, greater understanding of material phenomena led to the triumph of the human race over its environment. The love of beauty produced works of art, endowing life with a cultural dimension more consonant with the genius of humankind. Eventually, the human mind, which is one whole, will find expression in an integrated civilization.

The universe consists of material and mental phenomena. Ordinarily, the physical realm is more impressive for its seeming substantiality, its magnitude, and its enormous variety of phenomena. We see stars, clouds, rain, land, water, minerals, and the physical forms of plants and animals. At the common-sense level, these phenomena may seem unrelated to one another, but they appear to fit into a pattern and do not evince any great disharmony among themselves. But through science, we find that they are interconnected, and we understand their causes and effects; we discover a harmonious whole, an admirable synthesis of parts. In the mental realm, we are mainly aware of the phenomena associated with human beings. By using scientific methods, psychology has shown that such phenomena are susceptible to rational explanation. Just as the universe constitutes a synthesis of parts, every single object in it is a synthesis of parts, though we may forget or ignore this and think of it only as a unitary, distinctive entity. Together, all entities constitute the great synthesis, the harmonious scheme of things.

The synthetic nature of the universe furnishes us with a criterion for determining the character of civilization. Civilization is a product of humanity but is based on natural things. It is reasonable to expect that a civilization should partake of the nature of the universe, that it should not be alien to or in conflict with it. It should make a unified whole and as a single entity should then be an integral part of the great synthesis. The eventual civilization of the world will be a proper compound of its elements and fit harmoniously into the universe.

Chapter 10
Intrinsicalism

The civilization envisaged is intrinsic to the universe: an integral part of it. It is not an extraneous, factitious something that has come into existence out of tune with its environment. Though associated with humanity, it does not *ipso facto* cease to be natural; it partakes of the essence of the universe and is as natural as clouds and birds. The notion of intrinsicality means that human beliefs, institutions, and products are consequent on natural processes. The various constituents of the civilization form a harmonious entity that is intrinsic to the universe.

The philosophy of the Intrinsic Civilization is designated *Intrinsicalism*, a term that defines the essential characteristic of the system. The Intrinsic Civilization is contradistinguished from the extrinsic civilizations, the civilizations that have existed in the world hitherto. These are artificial, out of harmony with the universe, not forming consistent wholes in themselves, immature and defective experiments in the art of living. The fact that their ingredients arose haphazardly over time does not make them lose their factitious character. It has been the fashion and a serious mistake to regard a human product as natural because it did not issue in accordance with a plan. A chance product undergoing alterations and gathering accretions over the ages is liable to be riddled with defects and is no less artificial because it has been shaped by many hands. In fact, the epithet *natural* has been wrongly applied just as so many other words, popular because of their complimentary significance, are used loosely to describe anything a person likes.

Intrinsicalism does not denote what is commonly known as a "return to nature," the resumption of a primitive state of existence. This is not at all attractive, and there is no legitimate reason for resurrecting it. Despite its woes and injustices, the experience of civilization hitherto does not enhance the value of primitive life, whose miseries and cruelties are worse; only the romantic imagination can gloss over filth, ignorance, disease, ugliness, and bestiality. What is there to admire in cannibalism? Of course, Rousseau never conceived of a return to nature as a return to cannibalism. It is, however, irrational and unrealistic to envision what one considers an ideal society and categorically state that it actually existed once upon a time or that it was due to nature, not human contrivance.

It is doubtful that nature intends a person to look after sheep. Even in the most primitive society, practices and products existed that were not natural in the sense that they had to be learned and made. Is it natural to use fire? Is it natural to make a stone implement? When we talk of a return to nature, what do we really mean? Presumably, animals live in a state of nature, though this is not wholly true of domesticated ones. If the idea behind a return to nature is the elimination of the artificial, then, strictly speaking, it would be a reversion to a time when humans made nothing. Such a situation did not exist, for when *Homo sapiens* arose, they knew how to make tools and even ornaments like necklaces. Their predecessors, the Neanderthals, made weapons of stone flakes. It is not quite correct to assert that prehistoric people lived in a state of nature because their products were few and crude compared to modern man and his multiplicity of goods; primitive society had a lesser degree of artificiality, but it was not natural.

Nature is not perfect. It is subject to the law of evolution and keeps changing. A return to nature does not make for perfection and runs counter to progress. Reverting to the primitive natural is unnatural. It is preposterous that thousands of years after the human race left the slime of savagery we should blithely go back to it. It is incomprehensible why dwelling in a cave, rolling in dirt, or walking about naked should be admirable. The story of Diogenes throwing away his cup when he saw a boy use his hands to hold water is not edifying. Primitive existence has nothing to recommend it.

The faculty of invention is a glorious gift. It makes us creative and endows us with a power that distinguishes us from the other animals. With it we can become master of our own fate instead of being the mere sport of circumstance. We can control our environment and mold it to suit our well-being. It is strange that such a faculty should be condemned; that is what it amounts to when we advocate a return to nature and discard all the artifacts consequent on its exercise. The inventive spirit is the essence of human nature and was operative since the species emerged. Suppressing it would not only be a criminal folly but would be impossible, for this would entail a fundamental change in the characteristics of the human mind.

The Intrinsic Civilization is natural, not in the sense that it condemns human products but because it is in harmony with nature. Its institutions are based on universal truths, not on mere human fancies. An arbitrary dogma not derived from investigation into the principles of nature and not in harmony with them is artificial. An ethical precept accepted merely at the behest of some authority is unnatural. A custom or practice that has grown up over time and is maintained on the pretext of tradition has no claim to be called natural. A belief, custom, or institution is only natural if it follows the principles of the universe.

Material products can be deemed natural only if they are derived from the application of scientific laws or serve human needs in accordance with the principles of nature. The radio is an apparatus made by man, but it is natural in that its operation follows the laws governing the transmission of sound. A painting is a human product, but it is natural if it depicts actual phenomena or the reactions of the artist toward the universe. On the other hand, headgear of fantastic designs, ranging from that worn by early Native Americans to that sported by the fashion-conscious of today, is unnatural.

Human beings are part of nature, and our products should therefore be regarded as an expression of natural activity, just like a bird's nest building. The fact that our work is conscious and deliberate, not merely instinctive, makes no difference. Our intelligence is a natural force and is intended to be exercised. It is in the plan of evolution that we should influence our own growth and control our environment. This process is as natural as the action of waves on rocks. The works of humankind should not all be categorically stigmatized as artificial in the sense that they are made by us, but, if they are the results of the proper use of our faculties, they can be said to have a natural origin.

Intrinsicalism is a comprehensive system of principles constituting the new civilization. Its basic tenets weave its diverse aspects into a harmonious unity. It is a philosophy about civilization, a term used to denote the totality of activities, the complex of humanity's cultural values. Although civilization signifies merely the organized life of humanity, Intrinsicalism has for its scope the entire universe; it also concerns itself with subjects like religion, philosophy, and science, which constitute part of civilized activities and deal with all existence.

The essence of the Intrinsic Civilization is that it is intrinsic to the universe in the sense that its principles are in harmony with those of the universe. It is not alien to it, not in conflict with it; it is not devised by humans for their own comfort and at variance with their environment. That it was not originally existent does not invalidate its intrinsic character. The universe is not static; new things emerge in the course of evolution, and they constitute just as much a part of it as though they existed from the beginning of time. We are a product of nature, and, if through our agency certain phenomena arise to form part of the scheme of things, they must be regarded as being on the same level as what are called natural entities.

The Intrinsic Civilization is good. Evil in whatever form is condemned. Maltreatment of one person by another destroys the value of social life and should be eradicated, whether practiced by individuals, organizations, or states. The Machiavellian justification of corrupt ways is deplorable. A peaceable, just, and happy society, with individuals given to the promotion of public welfare—such a society may be deemed good.

The Intrinsic Civilization is enlightened. Its constituents are rational, and ignorance and superstition have no place. Informed by wisdom, it is not encumbered by the dark fancies of a faith religion; it has no use for tradition as such, for customs and practices that have been proven wrong. All prejudice is discarded in favor of a critical attitude. A benighted civilization is as undesirable as barbarism and in some respects may even be worse, for its pretentious artificialities can be more obnoxious than plain crudities. The superstitions and cruelties of the Middle Ages disgrace the name of civilization and are indefensible on any grounds whatsoever.

The Intrinsic Civilization enshrines an ideal. It is imperative to cherish excellence, for only this can satisfy the human mind. A culture far below perfection is worthless and might as well disappear. It is absurd to aver that only what is villainous or faulty is attainable and that we should be content with what actually exists and not strive for what is supposedly impracticable. The politician who prides himself on being practical—in the sense that all he cares about is achieving power by nefarious methods, while being unconcerned with the good—is a pestilence. An ideal civilization is worth the struggle.

The Intrinsic Civilization is practical. It is true that an ideal may not be capable of realization, as circumstance and human nature may be obstructive factors. The way to implement an ideal is not to postulate that human beings are born good and to imagine that it is only necessary to make an impassioned or pathetic appeal to the human will. An ideal must be in accord with natural truth or it will not come to fruition. Like a scientific invention such as the camera or the radio, an ideal is the development of a natural potentiality, not a contradiction of a law of the universe. It may need modification to suit actual exigencies, this being unexceptionable so long as the main principles are preserved. This kind of practicality is far different from that advanced as an excuse to cover corrupt or incompetent action. The practical ideal is the goal.

Intrinsicalism is founded on the truth and the right. Its principles are not arbitrary dogmas, feats of the fancy, but are derived through due process of ratiocination. It is not a mere academic theory about a particular aspect of civilization but a comprehensive system intended to be put into practice. It is not only true but also right; that is to say, besides being a contribution to knowledge, it is of ethical importance. A vicious or violent society has no justification, and it should not command the allegiance of anyone; it may produce some prosperity for or cater to the vainglory of a section of the populace but is inimical to the genuine welfare of the people. A culture reared on falsehoods is at odds with the intellectual nature of humanity and the essence of the universe.

Intrinsicalism is contradistinguished from all other civilizations that could be collectively dubbed extrinsic civilizations. They are called extrinsic in that they do not conform to the essential nature of the universe. They are random products of human beings, their constituents having come into existence haphazardly at various times. They are no less artificial because they have not been planned. Their elements do not coalesce to form a harmonious whole but are at loggerheads with one another. Their extrinsic character makes it imperative that they be replaced; human society is part of the universe, and if it does not tally with it, it should not endure for good.

A random product can never be truly satisfactory for it is bound to be full of faults. Where the constituents of a complex entity like a culture arise one by one at various times in an uncertain way, they cannot possibly make a harmonious unit; when they themselves are riddled with imperfections, the result must be a chaos of erroneous values. Nothing that has come into being at random can ever be really good, and there is no reason why civilization should be an exception. It is a fallacy to talk of the organic growth of society meaning thereby the lack of a planned system. A haphazard culture can never be in consonance with nature, whose principles must first be explored and understood, then utilized.

Extrinsic civilization is artificial. In a sense, all civilization is unnatural in that it was not originally created by nature and that it is associated with human beings and was produced by them. But we may regard a human product as natural if it is in accordance with natural laws and is in harmony with the universe. The constituents of extrinsic civilization defy this criterion, as they are products of the imagination and serve only human purposes. They have nothing to do with the scheme of things. An extrinsic culture is a chaotic mass of unrelated phenomena, though it tends to be dominated by some religious concept, making it lopsided in its interests. Alien to the universe, it has been artificially contrived to make life more pleasant and as such has been denounced by thinkers like Diogenes.

Extrinsic cultures are experiments in social organization, hence their immaturity. They are the blundering efforts of communities to raise themselves to a more refined level in their evolutionary development and to tame their environment. They were not planned and did not grow in accordance with any system. Their experimental character signifies that they cannot be taken as final and conclusive and explains their hodgepodge of contradictory elements. As human experiments unconsciously undertaken without regard to any method or clear objective, it would be strange if they should harmonize with the fundamental makeup of the universe. Experimentation in civilization was inevitable in the course of evolution, but it would be prudent to recognize this clearly and understand why civilization has been so artificial and alien to the universe.

Since the various cultures are of a tentative character, they could not be ideal. They are made of shreds and patches and are riddled with errors and evils. It would be absurd to regard their muddled, defective structure as a practical necessity, for an evil is an evil, which should not be tolerated as ineluctable. They have fulfilled their purposes and should be relegated to oblivion; they have had a fairly long history, which need not be extended any further.

By virtue of being extrinsic, a civilization can be neither true nor right. Truth is what resides in the universe, and right is the good the universe produces or is capable of producing. What does not accord with nature is therefore false and wrong. Individual constituents of the civilization may not be amiss, but as a whole it is off the mark. Its jumbled assemblage of contradictory ideas and practices manifestly stamps it as misleading.

Not only are civilizations, both extant and extinct, extrinsic to the universe, but the societies deemed uncivilized through the ages have likewise been extrinsic. We tend to consider such societies as existing in a state of nature because of their paucity of human products. But though few in number, they still do not exist naturally; they are artificial, though of a crude character. They are experimental, fabricated out of the imagination, and not in accordance with the laws of nature. The ideas and institutions of prehistoric man were irrational and bore no relationship to reality.

The fundamental principle of the universe is harmony, all its parts being interrelated to form a whole. The essence of the new civilization is harmony; its components constitute a compact entity, and it is in harmony with the universe. Its truths are derived from the verities of nature. It does not advocate a return to nature, for it is progressive, not retrogressive. Its gaze is directed toward the future, not the past. Its oneness with the universe is due to its fulfillment of natural laws, and its way is the way of the cosmos. The human race exists within the universe, and, though we may be able to think and invent, we remain one of its constituents, and our products should not be at loggerheads with it.

Chapter 11
Contents

A civilization consists of many facets. The more advanced it is, the more complex it becomes, and the more numerous and varied its developments. This complexity is probably one of the causes driving some thinkers to advocate a return to nature, to wit, the primitive state of existence with its simple needs. However, there is nothing wrong with complexity, for it enriches life, provided each constituent is necessary or desirable and is not merely a needless encumbrance. It is not right for any aspect of a culture to be suppressed unless it is very objectionable, and even then it is only a variety that might be subject to interdiction, not the entire aspect itself. Plato banished poets from his republic on the grounds that their works were of an imaginative nature and were antagonistic to truth. Apparently he did not consider that poetry could delineate the real. Had this occurred to him, he might have required that poets just produce more sensible work instead of destroying their profession altogether. Poetry would not then completely vanish, although a certain species of it would no longer be available.

A civilization should possess many constituents that should all be developed, each in its own right, variety being a praiseworthy characteristic. It embraces all human activities, and it is unreasonable to elevate one or two of them to supreme importance and treat the remainder with contempt. Each has its place in the scheme of things, and it is best to be broad-minded. If a person cannot cultivate diverse interests because of lack of ability or time, at least he can learn to appreciate their worth. In this age of specialization, when an individual is expected to be proficient in only one occupation, and the narrower the scope of his subject, the cleverer he is supposed to be, there is greater need than ever for a balanced point of view. A specialist may be respected for his professional skill, but it is wrong to let him dominate a nation.

It is objectionable for society to be controlled by a religion. Theocracy, though quite fashionable in history, has proven to be as evil as any other form of government. Even if a priesthood were perfectly good, it doesn't follow that the way of life and mode of thinking of everyone should be directed to the minutest detail by the tenets and practices of a particular religion. Such a phenomenon has not happened hitherto, but it would be just as disastrous to let a particular scientific concept become the focal point of a culture and its practitioners extend its application to every detail of life. In the case of communism, an economic doctrine has been utilized as the criterion for every aspect of existence, thereby engendering a preposterous and distorted society. A culture must pay attention to all its elements, though some may be more important than others.

The components of a civilization are numerous and varied. They include religion and ethics; political, economic, and social organization; material structure; language; fine arts; philosophic and scientific knowledge; recreational activities; and other constituents of lesser import. In dealing with a civilization, we should consider these diverse elements not only from the point of view of civilization as a whole, but also separately so that they can fit into a harmonious pattern and, at the same time, attain independence of action as appropriate to their specific nature and requirements. Before we proceed, we should define and understand each constituent.

Religion is concerned with beliefs about the ultimate nature of the universe and is associated with ethics that attempt to lay down rules of human conduct. A popular religion tends to concern itself with a multitude of issues that should properly fall within the purview of other subjects; this is undesirable and makes for an unbalanced, restricted, and irrational civilization. In a loose sense, the term *religion* has been used to mean a way of life or a pursuit intensely cultivated, but this is a misapplication of the word. Religion, by its proper definition, should be treated as one of the ingredients of civilization, whether it is deemed the most important or not, and it should not subsume everything. A religion should be a combination of knowledge and conduct. There have been many religions in the world and an even greater number of sects. Practically every society, barbaric or civilized, has been governed by some faith. Such a universal social product cannot be lightly dismissed. It is necessary to investigate the problem and decide whether the existing creeds are tenable or whether a new religion is needed. It is desirable to eliminate preconceived ideas of what religion should be—ideas based on existing ones—and begin afresh.

Political, economic, and social organization is of fundamental import; without it, society would disintegrate, and there would be no civilization. The state is the supreme embodiment of force and power. If all human beings were good by nature and always acted rightly, there would be no need for a coercive authority. However, it can engender great tribulations, and in the past it may have wrought more misery than happiness—so much so that many thinkers preferred its total annihilation. But whether there is a state or not, society must have some kind of organization if there is going to be a civilization. Social organization is to be dealt with in all its aspects, including the political and the economic. The term *politician* has a nasty implication, for affairs of state have been mangled by ignoramuses and villains who are actuated solely by the thirst for power. These "practical" people, strangely enough, do come into power, not only by force or fraud, but also through willing election by the people. Perhaps this is not to be wondered at, for the electors in all probability prefer those of the same character and interests as they themselves. The subject of social organization must be studied in two aspects: the ideal and the practical, what should be and what could be.

The material structure shows a community's standard of living and its command over its environment. It denotes the inventions and discoveries made or learned; the type, quality, and quantity of material goods available; the plant for their production; the means of communication; and the works executed to control the environment. The material advances made by the West in the nineteenth and twentieth centuries have far surpassed all that was done in the previous thousands of years, with the result that on a material plane, the world is better off than it has ever been. On the one hand, this material development has made some people equate these advances with greater civilization; on the other hand, it has led some to lament the decay of so-called spiritual civilization. We may take for granted that most people are not likely to act like Diogenes and throw away their tangible possessions. Historically, no invention once made and established was ever lost or ever fell into disuse unless it was superseded by a superior article. Although the materialistic life is not the highest or most desirable, there is no reason why physical necessities and conveniences should be disdained and regarded as evil. The most obvious distinction between a civilized and a barbaric community is the level of its material attainments.

Every community has a language. The most primitive peoples used spoken words. It is axiomatic that without some means of oral communication there could be no society. Owing to the conservative nature of human beings, the language of a people tended to persist; it changed slowly in various ways, but it was never discarded in favor of one systematically produced. However chaotic it might have been, it was preferred because it was familiar. In framing a civilization, it would be well to consider the problem of language.

The fine arts invest a civilization with grace and beauty. The creative activity involved is of the highest order, and the esthetic pursuit results in works designed to give the most lasting and satisfying pleasure. A culture that does not produce great works of art is sadly deficient in value. But art, like everything else, can be decadent, and such stuff does not glorify a culture but debases it. Though art is an end in itself and its primary purpose is pleasure, it is not akin to, say, brandy; it aims to ennoble the mind. If it has no intellectual basis and does not enlarge one's view of life and the universe, it is of little account. More than anything else, it needs freedom of expression; any form of control, whether by the state or some other authority, should be reduced to a minimum. The test of a work of art lies in itself; no extraneous considerations arising from prejudice should influence the judgment. Set rules and fixed notions derived from past practice should not be allowed to operate against originality.

Knowledge is humanity's greatest possession, and the most important kind should be that which deals with the universe. Philosophy and science are committed to understanding the nature of things. While the fine arts constitute that aspect of culture concerned with beauty, knowledge is bound up with truth. A civilization that does not give pride of place to the cultivation of the mind is unsatisfactory and deserves to be destroyed. It is quite evident that knowledge for its own sake has never appealed to most people, but for whatever reason it is cultivated, it is good for its general level to be made fairly high in a community. A state that attempts to keep its citizens ignorant so that they are easy to rule is a tyranny that should not be tolerated. Knowledge as an ingredient of civilization has a twofold aspect: as knowledge *per se* it endows the civilization with a high level of intellectual content, and as a means to an end it regulates the activities of individuals for the enhancement of their welfare. Of course, it can also be used for human destruction, hence the importance of correct education. It is not confined to science and philosophy. Though it largely deals with comparatively trivial matters, it is not to be condemned. No knowledge, pleasant or unpleasant, good or bad, is amiss.

Life is not all seriousness, and a large area is devoted to amusement. Of course, every form of activity, physical and mental, can yield a certain amount of pleasure, but there are pursuits whose aim is either wholly or mainly its production. These recreational activities may be classified as theatrical entertainment or sports. Considering the former, at the moment we find a wide variety of amusement, ranging from the cinema to singing and from the straight drama to dancing. As an ingredient of civilization, the theater has its proper place. In societies dominated by austere religions or puritanical moral codes, theatrical entertainment was viewed harshly as a worthless activity, and the actor occupied a very lowly place in the community. In present-day Western civilization, it is regarded as highly cultural, and the star actor is one over whom the crowd goes wild with enthusiasm. Attitudes and codes of values determine whether an individual is to receive honor or contempt, reward or punishment, for the same performance.

The justification for sports, which are of a physical character, is that they make the body healthy and strong. Their recreational value endows them with great popularity; associated with competition, they appeal to the pugnacious instinct. Their primary aim is for people to take part in them, but they have come to resemble theatrical entertainment in that they provide delight to spectators who may themselves never play them. It is curious to behold an immense concourse gathered at a stadium or playing field to watch a game. The popularity of sporting events lies in the fact that the masses find it easier to appreciate the physical than the mental. This tendency is deplorable, and too much concentration on them is a sign of immaturity and frivolity. It would be well to regard play as play and not elevate it into a fetish and mania. A society where the boxing champion is the idol needs overhauling.

There are other constituents of civilization of lesser import. These miscellaneous concepts and practices include the system of weights and measures, the calendar, clothing, and so on. Most of them serve to cement society, and these may be called *social principles*, which include subjects like education, manners, customs, and crime control. The nature of the social principles of any civilization has been largely dependent on its religion and beliefs. In conformity with Intrinsicalism, each miscellaneous principle is to be judged by its harmony with the other constituents as well as by its own value. The general rule is that it should fit in with the rest of the civilization and should not be at odds with what is natural or rational. Simplicity is a virtue, and what is easy is preferable to what is difficult. Another test is happiness—what promotes pleasure is better than what engenders pain. Each of these miscellaneous ingredients should be carefully considered and accorded its proper place in the scheme of things. It is just as undesirable to stress an ingredient out of all proportion to its importance as to underestimate its significance.

This enumeration and adumbration of the contents of a civilization is meant to point out the subjects we must consider. The scope is tremendous, and we might quail at the formidable problem. But we should not be fainthearted; we should proceed with our task and, undaunted, review every aspect of civilization. This investigation must be undertaken systematically, and we shall proceed from one problem to another in an orderly fashion. Not all topics are of equal importance, but each has its proper place. As the objective is to formulate a new civilization, the various constituents are to be studied in a critical, revolutionary spirit so that they may properly fit into the proposed scheme of things. They must be in harmony with one another and in accordance with the principles of the universe. Rationality is the watchword, and every tenet must be examined in the light of reason. We must not forget to apply the Connective Method of inquiry.

Chapter 12
The Two Bases

Religion signifies a way of life based on a theory of the nature of the universe. There can be nothing more important than this, and it must be a fundamental constituent of a civilization. Note that we are using the term *religion* as defined and that no particular existing creed is being referred to nor any popular concept of religion derived from experience of existing ones. In the minds of many people, the word *religion* immediately conjures belief in an anthropomorphic deity or other ideas familiar to them from childhood, for they equate it with their particular faith. It is a way of life linked to a view of the universe, and there is no reason why it should resemble prevailing ideas and practices. It should be addressed to the individual.

Another subject of the greatest importance to a civilization is the political, economic, and social system. If there were no society, there would be no civilization; the organization of society must accordingly be basic to its establishment. Central to it is the state, a coercive instrument for governing the people. If we use the word *state* to refer not merely to political but also to economic and social phenomena, which concern the organization of a multitude of human beings spread over a certain extent of territory into a society, then we may say that the state is another base of a civilization, religion being the other. Whereas even a hermit may practice a religion, the state deals with individuals as social beings. Since the state is so significant, it is necessary to devise a good one, not only in theory, but in such a way that it is realizable in practice.

Religion and state are the two bases of the Intrinsic Civilization, its most important constituents. What the new religion and political, economic, and social system are like will be delineated in separate parts of this book. Here, we are concerned with a general consideration of the two bases. They are so designated because they are fundamental to the nature of the civilization; without them, it will not merely be different but may not even exist. This does not imply that other ingredients are not important but means only that they are not of such moment as far as the civilization is concerned. The bases occupy a central place, and other constituents are related to them; to understand the civilization, one must be acquainted with them.

The religion has to do with the individual's daily life. It could be practiced by a person without the civilization coming wholly into being. It is, or ought to be, more intimately bound up with one's life than the state or any other constituent. Its value is great, but it need not be the sole concern, nor should every belief and practice be derived from it. It is accessible to everyone and does not resemble a vocation, which calls for a prolonged period of specific training. It is intended to have a popular appeal.

The religion is new and has no connection with any others, extant or defunct. The old creeds that rely on faith and tradition are irrational and ridiculous, and trying to conform them to modern knowledge is a waste of time, for they are fundamentally erroneous. It is strange that people should persist in believing them; nothing shows more forcibly the heavy weight of habit or mental inertia. As a base of the New Civilization, it is natural that the religion be new. A new civilization cannot properly be called such if an important constituent like religion remains unchanged. Newness is, of course, not necessarily right, and it is not advocated for its own sake but because it is appropriate.

Religion has become a decadent force in the world and has lost its glory. In every society it was once the pivot, influencing every domain of activity. The tyranny religion exercised was complete, but was not felt as such by the masses. Of course, the numerous faiths did diverge from one another, and at different times and in different places their power varied, but on the whole they were powerful. Ostensibly, they strove for the good, but in actuality they engendered a tremendous amount of evil. All this has changed, and religion is only a shadow of its former self. In communist countries, it vanished not because it had proven false but because of the irrelevant notion that it was the opium of the people and was inimical to the interests of the workers. In other countries, though it still persists and most people are officially described as adherents of a particular creed, it is in reality of little import. Its persistence is merely the result of old habit, and in most lands its influence is minimal. Its decay is attributable to many factors, chief among which is the progress of science.

A new religion must rest on reason, which will bring it into consonance with the other factors of the proposed civilization. It is ridiculous that after many centuries of development people can still rest content with religions founded on faith and perpetuated by tradition. Faith might have served a purpose in the old days, when the masses were illiterate and the appeal was to the emotions and yearnings, and when fancy was the most developed of all the faculties and knowledge of the facts of nature was restricted. As an instrument for solving the riddle of the universe, it is absolutely unreliable. If it were the criterion of truth, then all religions, though they contradict one another in their beliefs, are equally true; likewise, all legends and fairy tales can be regarded as factual. In this scientific age, it is lamentable even to talk of faith, much less rely on it. Reason is the only mode for the ascertainment of truth, religious or otherwise.

Tradition dies hard. The notions that have grown over centuries around a country's particular religion tend to persist. Though it may not be truly practiced, people still believe in a vague, confused way in its doctrines; or, if they deny its validity, they consider that somehow a religion would not be such if it did not resemble the one to which they are accustomed. Tradition is inimical to progress and, in a modern society, should not be accepted as synonymous with truth. More often than not, it is false and should be relegated to oblivion. Open-minded individuals who are prepared to accept a new religion must get rid of the cobwebs of tradition. Their spirit must be cast in a critical, revolutionary mold. To them, tradition is not sacrosanct but is a useless fossil, a hindrance to progress, and the sooner it is discarded, the better.

Religion is as old as humanity. Primitive societies and barbarians had religious beliefs and practices; it seems that from the moment human beings could think, they began to wonder at the mysterious world around them and started weaving fanciful explanations. Religion fulfilled people's need to believe in something. The trouble is that the beliefs were irrational and erroneous, and the practices were often baneful. Societies came to be governed by priests or sovereigns whose claims to power were derived from ideas furnished by religion; the rulers exploited the masses in its name. In spite of all the evils, however, religion did do some good, for it supplied the people with a corpus of beliefs about nature and an ethical code that helped regulate human relationships. Its more advanced specimens even acted as civilizing agents among wild communities. Its great curse is hypocrisy; if its adherents had all practiced what it preached, the good it did might have far outweighed the evil. But added to their tyrannies, the misconceptions of the old faiths make them untenable in the modern world.

It is necessary that there should be a system of ideas about the universe. It is not right that a person, be he scholar or peasant, should go through life with his mind a vacuum regarding the fundamental principles of existence. Armed with the system to be propounded, he will live a nobler and happier life. Regarding the individual, such an ideology elevates his mind, giving him an interest in the sublime beyond the petty affairs of daily life. Few persons are attracted to philosophy or the pursuit of knowledge for its own sake; only in their religion do they encounter important notions. Regarding society, it would not possess a civilization of real consequence if all it was concerned with were food and material conveniences. A theory of the universe is needed to endow it with a sublime base.

What is needed is a sound religion in tune with the spirit and knowledge of modern times. Adaptation of the old creeds is no solution. A new civilization needs a new religion. In considering which one, it is necessary to get rid of all prejudice and cease thinking along familiar lines. One should not assume that to be designated a religion the ideas must be of a certain kind or the morals of a particular sort. The new religion is one of the two bases of the new civilization.

The state, the other base of the new civilization, implies not merely political but economic and social organization as well. The organization of a people into a durable society is a prerequisite for the emergence of a civilization. Unless the state is good, the civilization will be defective. Through it, measures affecting all its members are easily executed, as without coercive authority there is never any unanimous acceptance of anything. For society to exist as a cohesive unit, organization based on force would seem to be a *sine qua non*.

Today, economics has ousted religion as the center of interest. People, of course, have always been attracted by wealth, but at no time in history has it been of such overwhelming concern as in the twentieth and twenty-first centuries. The French Revolution was a struggle of liberty against monarchic power, while the conflicts of the present century mainly revolve around the distribution of material goods. According to Marxist theory, the kind of economic organization explains all the phenomena of society, including culture and religion. This is absurd. Just because the struggle for wealth is found in every society, it is what it is—just one of the complex phenomena of a culture. However, under the influence of Marx, the economic struggle has come to dominate the world stage.

The state has never been so powerful as the communist state, which controls everything. In olden times, even the most absolutist monarchs did not interfere with many areas of human activity; generally, the efforts of the people to earn their livelihood were not subject to official control. A communist government regulates every detail of an individual's life and effects its orders by brute force. Other states, even so-called democratic countries, have been influenced by socialist ideas to a great extent and rule the lives of their free citizens much more than the ancient Roman or Chinese emperors. The state has, in fact, become a repository of tremendous power. Whether this power is justifiable or not depends on its mode of utilization and its ultimate consequences.

It is usual to classify states by their type of government. Based on the number of rulers, they are called a *monarchy, aristocracy,* or *democracy*. In accordance with the original occupation of the rulers, a state is designated a *theocracy, militocracy, pedantocracy, technocracy,* and so on. Whether a state should be identified with its rulers is a moot point, but it is simple to do so, and undoubtedly it is the rulers who attract attention. A state's quality largely depends on the character of those at the top: good rulers make a good state and happy people; bad rulers, a bad state and wretched people. This being the case, it is imperative to ensure that evil persons do not occupy positions of authority. Unfortunately, no foolproof method has ever been devised, and, in fact, power has fallen more to the ill-disposed than otherwise. In autocratic countries, throughout history the subjects have been taught to revere their sovereigns—this is a great mistake. The rulers are there to perform a job and should be judged like any other worker.

The state is an organization equipped with force to carry out its functions, but though it is not desirable in itself, it is ineluctable, as human nature is by no means good. If human beings were born good, a supposition of many philosophers, and always behaved rightly, then a state based on force would be superfluous. Coercion should be kept to a minimum. Freedom is a precious asset, and the extolling of slavery is absurd, but it must be restricted where it means the infliction of a wrong on others; any limitation should apply equally to all the denizens of a country and should not be a case of one person tyrannizing another. Nothing is more ludicrous than the monarch or dictator who considers freedom inimical to the interests of the state, with which he identifies himself, and who then proceeds to arrogate to himself the right to suppress it.

The state is not necessarily admirable, and most have been detestable in varying degrees. The power acquired by rulers has been used to promote the interests of a section of the populace and to oppress the masses, and it has led to wars of territorial aggrandizement. In the ages when there was no need for a government constantly to justify its existence, oppression was unbridled, and kings behaved as though their subjects were vermin. The very concept of sovereign and subject is obnoxious, for it denotes that the sovereign is not just a person with a job to perform but a grand personage who holds sway over inferior beings. When a government must have a *raison d'être*, it can still come into power through trickery or force and insidiously work for its benefit to the detriment of the people.

Owing to the undoubted evils of the state, thinkers from Laotze to Kropotkin have considered its abolition an ideal. Anarchism would be feasible only if human beings were born good and all continued to tread the right path. That we are born good is doubtful; that everyone always acts in conformity with the right is manifestly not the case. A few villains are sufficient to terrorize a community. Anarchism is not only impracticable but it is inconsistent with the concept of an extensive civilization. Without an organization to spread ideas and promote cooperative enterprise, every little community would exist as an isolated group of barbarians.

Social cohesion needs the organization provided by the state. Unless a society can persist as a harmonious unit, its development will be frustrated. If contentious forces threw it into chaos, its primary purpose, the cultivation of the public welfare, would be nullified. Social cohesion need not, however, be such a fetish that it justifies tyranny. Order is a prerequisite for the arts of civilization to flourish; excessive and perpetual chaos spells the end of culture. Social order cannot exist apart from the state, as it would crumble without control.

Every people in history, if it could, endeavored to expand its territory through war, one consequence being the fluidity of boundaries. One race became subject to another. There was also a centrifugal force whereby part of a country might separate out under a new government, and this was especially the case when chaos and civil war emerged. Over time, the inhabitants of a country tended to subscribe to a common culture and become one people. However, nationalism became more pronounced after the French Revolution, and by now it has become a fetish. Irrespective of the type of government a country has, autocracy or democracy, nationalism is the buttress of its policy. Napoleon failed in his dream of empire against the rising tide of nationalism. The international creed of Marxist communism has floundered on the rock of nationalism, each of the various communist countries being just as anxious to preserve its national identity and territory as any *bourgeois* state. Nationalism is a good thing in that it has been instrumental in freeing one people from the control of another and ending racial exploitation and oppression. But it is less than admirable when, besides leading to jingoism, it splits the world into a multitude of nations with different languages and numerous restrictions ranging from trade to immigration.

The ideal state would cover the whole world. War would then cease to exist, and there would be no threat of the extermination of the human race by scientific means of destruction. The elimination of war is not the only benefit of the planetary state, which would be the foundation of a planetary civilization. There is no particular advantage in the existence of diverse cultures on a territorial basis. What good could there be in a multiplicity of languages? The planetary state is an objective, but it is not necessary for the new state to cover the whole globe for it to be realized in full. Extent of territory need not influence the complete application of the new theory.

The two bases, religion and state, will largely describe the nature of the new civilization. They are called *bases* since they are the most important components of the civilization. The roles they play are complementary. While the religion is directed mainly at the individual, the state is chiefly concerned with the population as a whole. While religion appeals to voluntary effort, the state cannot escape association with force. The state is not primarily actuated by moral considerations; on the other hand, the religion is linked to a moral system. Though as a member of the state an individual has a moral duty, he is not required to do more than a necessary minimum, but in his religious capacity, he should do more than this. Religion and state are not identical. The ideal is not a theocracy in which the state is merely subserving the interests of the religion; nor should the state control the religion altogether. The two should form a harmonious association.

The new religion and the new state must conform to the Intrinsic Civilization. Their importance cannot be overstressed: they are basic to the new civilization. They are in harmony with each other and with the other constituents. They are derived from natural principles and are in accordance with the concept of a civilization intrinsic to the universe. In them, the general principles of the civilization are displayed in detail, and they give it its distinctive character. They are inseparable from the Intrinsic Civilization.

Chapter 13
Material Structure

The main visible difference between a civilized and a barbaric society lies in the material appurtenances—clothing, tools, gadgets, furniture, houses, roads, vehicles, and so on. On the basis of material advancement, the three levels are barbarism, prescientific civilization, and modern civilization. The barbarian's few material possessions were coarse and simple and came into being by accident over long periods of time. The old civilizations saw numerous discoveries and inventions, which arose without much thought, and the products were made with artistic skill. In Western Europe during the last few centuries, science was developed, invention was deliberately pursued, and mass production was undertaken. The multiplicity of commodities has made past achievements pale into insignificance and has spread over the whole world.

The mass of concrete products may be considered as constituting a system. This material system or structure is the material foundation of a civilization, and it can be studied and analyzed to find the best or at least to make improvements where feasible. This subject has never before been pursued. The neglect is a strange phenomenon and is difficult to explain, save for the assumption that the subject is vast and intricate and philosophers have tended to despise material things. This is an inadequate explanation, but it is not particularly significant to probe into the causes. We just accept the fact of omission and set about rectifying it.

Is the material system desirable? It has been the fashion of religious and philosophic thinkers and their followers to disdain material goods as somehow evil. The extreme cases were those of the cynics like Diogenes, who threw away his cup when he learned from a boy that he could use his hands instead, and the saints, who did not wish to have any physical pleasure or comfort. These men and women gained great reputation mainly because in those days goods could be produced only in meager quantities; the masses, without these goods, therefore sympathized with those who lauded poverty. This sounds cynical, but that does not detract from the truth. Now that Marx has shown how the workers can get the world's goods, and now that machinery and mass production have made it feasible for the average person to enjoy material possessions, the ascetic has ceased to receive popular support.

Ordinary people have always admired tangible goods. They might have worshipped the holy folk, but they were more concerned with getting what they could for themselves. Unfortunately, as the supply was extremely restricted, the majority got very little. Governments were not interested in the economic problems of their subjects. Beautiful objects were laboriously fabricated by hand for monarchs and nobles. It is not surprising that the bulk of humanity admires factitious articles, for these are concrete, visible objects that do not require abstract intelligence to appreciate.

But is the material system contemptible? Is it wrong? We should view it dispassionately and objectively without considering the predilections of ordinary and extraordinary individuals. For the most part, it consists of products that do not exist in nature but are fabricated by humans from natural materials. A product first came into being through the ingenuity of an individual. The inventive faculty is a rare gift, but in past ages the innovators seldom revealed their names; at any rate, they were not remembered. Surely it is more meritorious to be able to control our environment than to be ignorant and lie at its mercy.

We live in a world of matter, in which the mind is comparatively shadowy, and there is no valid reason for despising it. It is against sound judgment to regard concrete objects as noxious; from a common-sense point of view, they are more real than abstract ideas, and we cannot just dismiss them as being of no account. Through control of the physical world, we can improve the quality of our life and eliminate a great deal of misery. The advantages of living in a good physical environment are many and include happiness, sound health, esthetic appeal, cleanliness, safety, cultural possibilities, recreational facilities, and a full life. It is preposterous to entertain the notion that it is preferable to have a society of peasants dwelling amid filth and disease, toiling from dawn to dusk, often hungry and steeped in abysmal ignorance.

The branch of study dealing with the material system is not the same as economics, which concerns the production, distribution, and consumption of wealth. The aim is to consider the totality of physical products on which some human effort has been expended, judge the value of its diverse constituents in the promotion of human happiness, and determine their relationship to society and civilization. Economics is primarily concerned with the acquisition of wealth, which is assumed to be desirable, whereas in the present study the important problem is the contribution of the material system to human welfare.

Material products should, in general, combine utility and beauty. They must efficiently serve the purpose for which they are designed and at the same time be of a pleasing appearance. For every article, significant or otherwise, it would be well for science to enter into its fabrication; it could bear some scientific investigation and be made according to scientific principles. If it is made on the basis of the laws of nature, it will have the semblance of a natural product and lose its association with fantasy. With the aid of science, qualities like economy, precision, and safety of execution could be more readily cultivated. Concurrently, the production should be treated as an art. One should not lose sight of artistic qualities. Esthetic appeal by way of a simple beauty of form is desirable, while elaborate and fanciful superfluous ornamentation should, in general, be rejected as unnatural.

In former ages, when production was scanty and the welfare of the people was neglected, most articles were available only to the few. This is reprehensible, and commodities should be as widely distributed as possible. The problem has been solved by mass production in factories with machinery. In the past, it has been the fashion to stigmatize mass-produced goods as shoddy and vulgar in contrast to the beautiful work of the craftsman. In the early days of mechanical production, much imperfection was evident, but things have improved considerably since then, and there are no grounds for assuming that the machine must always remain incapable of displaying artistic qualities in its products. But were this to remain the case, the utility of the machine is nevertheless so great that it would be ridiculous to dream of scrapping it and restoring handicrafts on a large scale. The crafts are to supplement the machine and do what it cannot do, not to displace it altogether. Automation and computerization have made mechanical production more impressive than ever, and doubtless other techniques will develop over time.

The technological revolution of the twentieth and twenty-first centuries has seen amazing advances. It has even enabled man to travel to the moon. The marvels of science seem to know no bounds. With the arrival of the technological age, it has become possible, given proper planning and control, to give every person in the world a decent standard of living—this achievement would be the greatest boon that science could confer on the human race. That this result has not been attained is attributable to the inadequacies of the present social organization. The material system has been transformed by science and must rest on it; its future development depends on science, and this is as it should be, for scientific products follow the laws of nature.

The material structure is not necessarily good and can give rise to baneful effects. One serious problem is the pollution of the environment—the atmosphere and the lakes, rivers, and seas. Noxious fumes from factories and vehicles cloud the air, and poisonous waste clogs the waters. These fumes and waste must go somewhere, and legislation cannot eliminate them. They are the results of scientific exploitation of resources, and greater scientific knowledge should bring them under control. This is an instance of scientific development without regard to consequences.

As the population increases and more land is used for the construction of towns or the exploitation of mineral resources or some other purpose, there will come a time of extinction of forests, wild animals, natural scenery, and even the earth's physical features. This obliteration of natural phenomena is deplorable; for humanity to be in harmony with the universe, we should not be completely deprived of the natural environment. There is no solution to this catastrophe except population control and legislative restriction.

One of the most lamentable consequences of technological development comes from the invention of the motor vehicle. Traffic accidents, in spite of all sorts of measures, still wreak their havoc; this kind of mishap was unknown in former ages. It would appear that accidents are unavoidable unless vehicles can be automatically controlled so that they cannot come into contact with other objects, be these human beings, inanimate obstructions, or other vehicles, and, furthermore, unless the vehicles cannot develop defects that make them skid, overturn, explode, and perform other lethal antics. Another problem is traffic congestion, which makes the streets impassable. It would be desirable to take vehicles off the streets altogether and within a town to make all traffic go underground, but the cost of the tunnels would be prohibitive.

The worst result of scientific progress is the manufacture of destructive weapons of war. With every upward stage in material civilization came more potent instruments of mass annihilation; the sorry catalogue extends from stone weapons and steel swords to artillery and nuclear bombs. At long last in our pugnacious history, we have come into possession of a weapon potent enough to wipe out our species altogether. Maybe that is what humanity wants! Without a doubt, the continual production of more complex and efficient instruments of carnage constitutes progress in the strict sense of the term, but we could well dispense with this kind of advance without any tinge of regret. It is not possible to prevent the manufacture and distribution of offensive weapons, for where a desire exists, means will be found to gratify it. It is not the individual who requires them, but the state; and as the nations are sovereign entities, their actions are uncontrollable. However, the human race does not necessarily face destruction, for fear of mutual annihilation may keep the states from going to extremes, or they may accept control by all of them acting as a body, or they may merge into a single world state.

The material system should be controlled by certain principles. One is simplicity, which is also applicable to every other aspect of civilization. *Caeteris paribus*—what is simple is preferable to what is tortuous. Material objects should be free from ornateness, and they should be made as easy to understand and handle as possible. Another principle is standardization. For ease of operation and use as well as economy, products for a specific purpose should fulfill certain standards; variety is to be restricted but not so as to fall into the other extreme of monotony. It goes without saying that safety is a major consideration and that any potential source of injury should be remedied as much as possible. Beauty is to be cultivated, and what is appealing to the senses promoted. Rationality and orderliness are fine characteristics. It must not be forgotten that an object is designed for a specific purpose, and therefore its effective utility comes first and other considerations are subsidiary.

The material structure can be divided into a number of categories for general consideration, namely, basic requirements, consumer goods, capital goods, communications, and town planning. The basic requirements comprise food, clothing, and housing. Food is of vegetable and animal origin, and large tracts of land have been necessary for its production. With the increase in population and the growth of towns, less land will be available as time goes on. It would be a good idea to further develop synthetic foods that could be from nonliving sources. Moreover, it would be desirable to reduce and eventually eliminate the consumption of meat, for the killing of animals is not a good measure. One of the major benefits of mechanical production has been in regard to textiles, whereby the masses can clothe themselves decently. No one can possibly object to this kind of scientific achievement. It is to be hoped that there will be continual experimentation to make clothing even cheaper, more durable, and easier to keep clean. Housing has never been satisfactory and will remain inadequate unless buildings can be built cheaply and the population does not go on increasing. A home for the ordinary individual is mainly utilitarian, and comfort is what is required, though some elegance in the building is desirable. Great architecture has always been the most visible testimony of a culture's splendor; it is a fine art, but unlike, say, painting, it has a functional value. From the simple home to the architectural splendor, from the useful to the beautiful, buildings are an incomparable product of civilization.

Goods that are produced are mostly intended to be utilized directly by people for their enjoyment. Termed *consumer goods*, these include items like paper, furniture, knives, bags, crockery, soap, mirrors, jewelry, personal computers, and so on. They should be a blend of art and science: they should be based on scientific principles and made to satisfy the artistic sense. Many kinds of products first came into being long ago and were painstakingly made by craftsmen; science was unknown then, and art was supreme. Other commodities arose with the scientific inventiveness of recent times and, made in factories from the start, lacked esthetic merit. It is, however, undesirable to categorize them permanently as scientific and artistic products. What is scientific should be made artistic, and what is artistic scientific. It is to be noted that our esthetic taste may change, and new concepts of beauty could arise. Simple, natural beauty is preferable, while florid decoration is to be eschewed. With scientific control, not only will harmful consequences be studied and eliminated, but fanciful deviations from nature will also be curbed.

Machinery is produced not to be used directly by people but to turn out consumer goods. This class of commodities, which did not exist in prescientific times, may be designated *productive machinery*; in economics, it is called *capital goods*. Productive machinery is purely a means to an end and is totally inartistic in appearance. Possibly it could be made to look less ugly, as beauty need not be completely sacrificed to utility. Mechanization has replaced craftsmanship in the making of goods, and this has meant greater productivity, reduction in cost, and easier labor, but also less beauty and less satisfaction in personal achievement. Valuing art above everything else, some people have deplored the machine age and have advocated a return to craftsmanship. This is a misguided view, for the benefits of mechanical production far outweigh its disadvantages. Capital goods are the preliminary to the mechanical production of consumer goods, and they are necessary, but their relative importance should not be unduly stressed. It would be unreasonable to concentrate on producing mechanical tools in order to build up the resources of a state and for many years neglect consumer goods. This might lead to the worship of the machine for its own sake.

Transportation, or the means of moving from place to place, is intended to cover all types of vehicles operating on land and sea and through air and space. Communication refers to all apparatus designed to transmit sound and images, including the telephone, computer equipment, radio, and television. Transportation and communication by mechanical means, which may be jointly referred to under the term *communications*, are products of science, and they have advanced by leaps and bounds. In former ages, people could move about only slowly and with difficulty, employing carriages pulled by horses and ships propelled by wind. News of events occurring at a distance was provided by messengers or travelers. It was truly a wondrous revolution, this conquest of distance. The earth, which loomed so enormous to the ancients, now appears small, and we are fanning out to other planets. Ease of travel has made tourism an industry, and distant places are no longer mysteries to the person in the street. Cultural barriers have broken down. Rapidity of transport and communication has made it much simpler for the world to have a single civilization.

Town planning aims to provide a pleasant environment. A town consists mainly of buildings and roads, and the layout of the network of roads is the principal concern in its planning. It should possess a definite shape. This should preferably be an ellipse, which is endowed with an esthetic appeal; with varying lengths of the major and minor axes, it is not monotonous, as in the case of the circle or square. Its shape and boundaries are determined by a circumferential road that distributes traffic to other places. A road runs through the major axis, while from one long side to the other is a series of streets forming a zigzag pattern and connected, if they are lengthy, by short roads at suitable intervals. This pattern of streets differs from the usual checkerboard or spider web types. There is no town center, it being undesirable for the most important activities to be concentrated in one spot. The town should not be divided into neighborhood units, for it should be planned as one whole, not as a collection of virtually separate towns. It is surrounded by a belt of park. This layout of streets is the standard for new towns. For existing ones, it would be extremely difficult, economically and otherwise, to replace their patterns in *toto*, and so only modifications are practicable. In planning a town, the points to consider are utility, comfort, and beauty; regard, of course, must be paid to feasibility produced by the nature of the terrain and other factors.

The material structure has advanced greatly in modern times, and colossal quantities of natural resources from timber to minerals have been consumed. There must come a time when irreplaceable raw materials are exhausted. Of course, substitutes can be found, but these would likewise vanish eventually. What then? It would be strange if the outcome of progress were the cessation of production for lack of resources. We are surely not destined to revert to the barbaric level of material culture. The solution has to be making raw materials, and as these cannot be produced from nothing, they could be obtained only by the transformation of matter. They would be derived from other materials and may either resemble the existing types or be new types altogether. The act of recycling, recovering the waste products of consumption, and changing them back to their original state is now being widely practiced in many countries.

One scintillating triumph of the material system is psychological, in that human beings have control over their environment. It is a testimony to our intelligence that, unlike other animals, we are not wholly at the mercy of our surroundings. Understanding the forces of nature and utilizing them for our advantage are achievements of supreme importance. To be able to live in a comfortable house instead of a cave, to know how to avoid and cure disease and prolong life, not to suffer cold and hunger, to flood the dark night with bright lights, to have music at will through elaborate sound systems, to look at a newspaper or to browse the Internet and know what is happening in the world when one sits down to breakfast, to fly from one part of the world to another—such achievements could not be disparaged. But there is still much to do, and fuller control over the environment is possible. The inventive faculty is far from exhausted, and science can be expected to continue rendering meritorious service.

Chapter 14
Creative Culture

Creative culture describes the branch of human activity utilizing thought and imagination to produce works of esthetic appeal that are practically without any utilitarian purpose. The subjects include literature, music, painting, and sculpture. Concrete products serving ordinary needs but of esthetic worth—for example, architecture and porcelain—are excluded. Language is not an esthetic activity, but as it is a creative product and is in the medium of literature, where it attains its highest excellence, it will be treated in this section.

The world has a multitude of languages, both extinct and extant, for in spite of their complicated nature, human beings have found it easy to create them. To be sure, they were not deliberately produced, but came into being slowly and grew haphazardly. For this reason, they are unmethodical, chaotic, and difficult for most people. They are irrational and could hardly be otherwise, as they were initiated in prehistoric times. Just because they evolved unplanned, they have been dubbed natural—a misuse of the term. They are, in fact, highly artificial, more so than any other product, concrete or abstract. A concrete product like a cup is made from natural materials, while an abstract product like a metaphysical theory has reference to the universe.

Language is useful for human purposes, but it is wrong to emphasize its significance to an undue extent; it is more important to have a knowledge of the universe than a knowledge of words. It is significant only as a tool, a means to communicate thought. But after the invention of writing, familiarity with the written language came to be almost an end in itself, and an individual's learning was gauged by the scope of his command of a language. Just as a miser comes to love money for its own sake, so a pedant comes to love grammar on its own account. In modern times, a distinctive tongue is paraded as a symbol of nationalism. People do not mind adopting new ideological systems or assiduously imitating scientific inventions, but in the matter of language, they are conservative.

The Intrinsic Civilization should have its own language, which will harmonize with its character. This must be rational and in consonance with nature. It must be methodical, from its alphabet and writing to its rules and vocabulary. It should be simple and easy to learn, there being no merit in intricacy and difficulty. It is better to invent a language that is genuinely new than to modify an existing one or concoct a potpourri of ingredients from various sources. In this way, the prejudices bound up with a particular tongue resulting from historical associations will be eliminated.

Every civilized people in possession of a written language has evolved a literature. What is literature? It may be defined as the embodiment of thought in appropriate language and in a form calculated to appeal to the esthetic sense. The written word is the vehicle, and mind is the force. A statue is not literature, though it embodies an idea; a prospectus issued by an insurance company is not literature, though it makes use of print. By literature is meant such works as those of Li Po, Goethe, Dickens, and Tolstoy. Its two main divisions are poetry and prose; the genres of prose include fiction, drama, history, biography, and the essay.

In the West, literary standards were set by the ancient Greeks, who prized rationality and restraint. In modern Europe, two great movements arose in departure from the traditional classicism: first romanticism, then realism. The romantic writer stresses imagination and tends to look at the world through rosy spectacles; he is said to distort the truth in his view of life. The realist, who rose in protest against romanticism, declares that he depicts life as it is, his true world being characterized by sordidness. Both of these movements flout classical restraint and are highly emotional. Romanticism is most at home in poetry, while realism, oddly enough, has chosen the novel—the realm of fiction—wherein to display its concept of the truth. Great literature has been produced in the classical tradition as well as in the freer modern styles.

In point of fact, all literature is the expression of the author's personal view of life. Be he classicist, romanticist, or realist, he looks at the universe, selects what he wants in accordance with his temperament, and describes phenomena as colored by his personality. Reaction is a principle of nature, and the mind is not passive in its contact with the external world but molds it. In a sense, any kind of literary work is reactive; that is, it records the reaction of the individual mind to some aspect of life or the universe. Literature is thus contradistinguished from science; its aim is not objective truth, although that is what realistic writers delude themselves into believing they are presenting. A novel of the realist school commonly deals with a tragic theme, which is treated with emotion. A series of events can be looked upon as comic, tragic, beautiful, ugly, admirable, or disgusting, depending on the makeup of one's mind. Even if all human beings considered it tragic, it may still not be so, the unanimous view merely signifying that their minds all work in the same way. The presentation is therefore not a record of unvarnished truth but only of external phenomena as molded by the mind. Literature is not science, and if the realist could engender works accurately delineating things as they are, they would cease to be literature.

In the restricted sense, reactive literature may be contradistinguished from the classical, romantic, and realistic types. Reactivism denotes the principles of this specific literary type, the fundamental tenet being that the aim of literary production is to record the individual writer's reaction to life and the universe. There are two factors to consider: external phenomena and the individual mind. The subject of a piece of writing, be it a poem, a novel, or an essay, is the existing world, which is of interest to us as we are a part of it, and not an imaginary realm as created by romantic authors. A fairy tale would not fall into the category of reactivist literature, which, as the literature of the Intrinsic Civilization, an integral part of the natural universe, should concern itself with actual things.

But literature is not concerned with the external world as objective truth. The mind of the author digests the raw material presented to it, and the result is what is recorded. Phenomena and personality are irrevocably blended. What the reader peruses is not objective but subjective truth; it is reality as envisaged by the writer, not scientific but literary truth. This does not mean that it is false; it is true in its own way. Its nature is creative, and it possesses a profoundly satisfying value and beauty. It must not be forgotten that the external world revealed by science evinces considerable dissimilarity from the world known through the senses. This signifies that sensory phenomena, common to all human beings, are digested stuff. The material realm is devoid of emotion and humor and has no sound or color. The mind experiences them, but, save for pure and simple sensory phenomena, different persons can view the same things in different ways, depending on their mental constitution. When we say that the writer records his reactions, we do not imply that we are interested in his psychological processes; what is wanted is an account of purportedly external phenomena.

What the author depicts is preferably to be ordinary life and common objects, as these stand more for reality than out-of-the-way phenomena. Unlike realistic literature, which is devoted to portraying sordid, unusual aspects of life, reactivism attends mainly to the universal. A writer is unlikely to encounter much of what is rare; if he does and records it, the result would excite curiosity but, without the character of universal truth, would not be significant.

All life is of concern to the writer, and the entire universe is a fit subject for delineation. A comprehensive interest betokens breadth of mind. Every author's knowledge is perforce limited, and he can only write about that with which he is cognizant. All experience is, however, pertinent to literature, and it is absurd for a nation's fiction to be preoccupied with love or sex or its poetry to be devoted to a few themes like drinking and the evanescence of life. When a writer reacts to nature, there is no reason why he should confine himself to purling streams and singing birds; why not typhoons and forests? The nature that is perceived by understanding its laws can evoke just as emotional a response as its visible works. As for human life, the thoughts and actions of all types of people, all forms of behavior, and all kinds of happenings are suitable themes for poetry or prose. Attention need not be concentrated exclusively on visual phenomena; aural, olfactory, gustatory, and tactual experience can very well be described.

Literature should partake of the character of the universe. As nature is not static or peaceful but is subject to change and movement and vibrates with force, so literature is preferably dynamic—it should be active and pulsate with rhythmic power. The writer should adopt a lofty, comprehensive attitude and judge all things with a fearless mind; nothing is too great for him to criticize or too small to escape his notice. In contemplating the universe, he should imbibe its grandeur and impart to his writing width of comprehension and depth of purpose. Literature creates a world in thought compounded of existing phenomena and the responses of the mind. It is not a pedantic exercise in words, a reporter's column in a newspaper, or an amusement for an idle hour.

Literature should be written from the standpoint of a participant in the scheme of things. The author may not actually have experienced what he refers to, but he should write as though the matters concern him and affect his life; an aloof, cold attitude is contrary to reactivism. He should react with his whole being, his reason, intuition, imagination, and emotion. His business is not to portray things as they are or to discover the facts—his *forté* is to create beauty. If he has nothing to contribute, if he can only hold up a mirror to nature, then he is not a creative artist but is no better, probably worse, than a photographer, whose pictures are actually more enlightening than a mass of descriptive verbiage. He should employ reason to impart patterns to phenomena, intuition to grasp things with immediacy, and imagination to fill in the blanks in experience. Above all, it is with the emotions that reactions are most meaningful; all emotions are appropriate—love, hatred, fear, anger, surprise, curiosity, joy, sadness, sympathy. Participation, actual or assumed, is essential to adequate response.

A literary work possesses a certain form depending on the genre. Form constitutes the shell; like style, it is of secondary importance compared to the content. However, technical excellence cannot be neglected; without it, a composition does not confer the degree of esthetic satisfaction that is what art exists to provide. The form should not be unduly restrictive but should allow considerable latitude for individual discretion. Fluid form is ideal—that is, form not rigidly bound to rules and offering ample scope for freedom. The style is up to the writer to cultivate, and there need be no inviolable regulations. The only requisite tenet, which is plain common sense, is that the language should be intelligible and not consist of a farrago of distortions masquerading as profundity.

Let us consider the different categories of literature and how reactivism can operate in them. Poetry may be defined as an emotional reaction to life and the universe expressed in unusual language. It is more intensely reactive than prose and contains the most characteristic element of reaction, emotion, to a more heightened degree. But it is quite possible to express emotional reaction in prose, and it is necessary, if poetry is to be regarded as a distinct literary form, for it to differ from prose in language. Poetry has traditionally been confined to a few themes, but everything should come within its scope. It is the greatest of the arts, as it utilizes all the mental faculties; unfortunately, the medium, language, is an artificial contrivance specific to a particular people. It is impossible to translate it effectively from one tongue to another, and the consequence is that a poem does not generate a direct, universal appeal as does a piece of music.

Prose fiction at first sight appears puerile, an idle pastime; but as serious themes can be dealt with effectively under the guise of entertainment, it has become an important literary genre. The author should react to this material with emotion, humor, or some other quality that shows his active involvement in the story. The reactivist novel does not purport to show life as it is or to weave a happy romance remote from reality, but to record the author's view of life as filtered through his mind. It may also show the reactions of the characters to life as it affects them; for this purpose, the technique of recording their thoughts and describing their environs through their eyes may be adopted.

Other forms of prose composition, such as the essay, are made reactivist in the same way, by utilizing reaction; any composition on any subject becomes a personal critique. The primary aim of a literary composition is beauty rather than knowledge, and using emotion to endow it with warmth and the imagination to make it glow is essential. The writer should not deliberately falsify the truth but should envisage it, not as the scientist should see it, but from the standpoint of his personality and with the aim of creative beauty.

All literature should be unified under the aegis of reactivism. There is no need for a sharp cleavage between poetry and prose or between romanticism and realism. The principles enunciated clearly indicate the nature of reactivism, which, as a literary movement, is of universal applicability. However, since a literary work is written by an individual and freedom to do as one thinks best is essential to creativity, it is not required that all the tenets of reactivism be observed or that no other principles may be introduced for a work to be designated reactivist. In fact, it is of the essence that reactivist literature should be for the individual to express his personality; hence, no rules are to be so stringent that they cannot be broken. Criticism that aims to establish infallible standards leads only to scholastic insipidity and the extinction of the creative impulse. A book is to be termed *reactivist* if it displays some of the essential principles of such literature.

Reactivism is applicable to all the fine arts, which differ from one another mainly in the media of expression; the spirit that informs them can be identical. The aim of every creative art is to produce beauty and pleasure, and an artist should primarily be concerned with expressing his personality. Just as all literature can be harmonized by a unifying movement, so can all the fine arts be united by the same movement to make them part and parcel of the Intrinsic Civilization, wherein each constituent is related to the others. The tenets of reactivism applicable to every species of creative culture come down to this: a work of art is a record of some part of life or the universe as molded by the mind of the individual. The real world, rather than fantasy, is to be dealt with. Common phenomena are preferable to those that are unusual. The standpoint of a participant in the scheme of things is to be adopted, not the detached view of a spectator.

Music is the most highly emotive of the fine arts; it can transmit emotional reaction more intensely than poetry. Extremely popular, it uses sound as the medium of expression, and the process of recording and reproducing sound makes it easily available. It is primarily a stream of mellifluous sounds, but it is imbued with the capacity to evoke a mood. It is a battery charged with emotion. It may convey personal reaction to life with no reference to external entities, but to be reactivist, there should be an objective content. Because it employs language that imparts a definite meaning, vocal music is more than a pattern of sounds. Instrumental music would not convey any specific import, save that on account of conventional association, a certain arrangement of sounds is given a particular interpretation. Like literature, music can be romantic or realistic; but to be consistent with Intrinsicalism, it should be neither this nor that but should fulfill the canons of reactivism.

Painting, if it is to be reactivist, would not be devoted to delineating ideally beautiful scenery or people or to depicting things as they are in order to reveal objective truth. The artist should look at the ordinary world of humans and nature and give his impression of it as shaped by his temperament. Things are not in themselves merry or tragic, humorous or appalling, appealing or disgusting, but he can endow what he paints with any mental or emotional quality that he considers appropriate. If he is a misanthrope, he shows how detestable humankind is; if he is a satirist, he finds much to excite his critical mirth; if he is kind, he would depict gentle scenes. Regarding technique, it is not necessary to distort phenomena, as in cubism; but if the artist can show his reaction to an object best in that way, then it is legitimate for him to do so.

Sculpture is largely but not necessarily concerned with the human figure. Reactivism requires that the statue is intended to represent a person not as he is but as an embodiment of the sculptor's personal reaction to his subject. It is desirable for sculpture to deal with an extensive range of objects, natural or artificial, instead of being obsessed with the human form. A bird, a flower, an airplane—the representation can be made esthetically satisfying. In art, symbolism is not incompatible with the principle of dealing with the real world, though direct imaging is preferable, as it is more expressive of reaction; in sculpture especially, an abstract concept needs to be exhibited symbolically.

The reactivist style is not the only one valid in the fine arts; music, painting, and sculpture may have diverse modes of expression. The creative artist must be free to pursue his own bent and do what he thinks fit. In no sphere of human activity is freedom more essential, and enforced adherence to rules spells the death of art. But reactivism in general is applicable to the majority of artistic efforts, and it is more consonant with the Intrinsic Civilization.

Chapter 15
Knowledge

Knowledge is tremendously extensive in scope, referring in its broadest sense to the entire universe. Of course, after thousands of years it is still extremely limited. We are acquainted with little of the truth of things, and there are large areas of reality of which we are totally ignorant. Nevertheless, with its ever-increasing accumulation and consequent complexity, we tend to lose sight of the forest for the trees, and the individual finds it difficult to have even a general conception of the whole. In fact, we have come to boast of specialization, and with his intimate grasp of a minute section of the sum of things, the specialist is regarded as possessing superior attainments.

Knowledge is desirable. The most important attribute of the mind is thought, which finds its highest expression in comprehending the universe. The mere exercise of mind by way of reflection enhances its quality and gives the most sublime form of happiness. A culture that does not value knowledge for its own sake and is not rich in theoretical learning should not command high regard. In comparing the relative worth of Greek and Roman civilizations, it is on the score of pure knowledge that the world has come to esteem Greece more, although it was conquered by Rome, which in its own day was a greater military power than the captive country had ever been.

Knowledge can also be a means to an end, the end being the furthering of human purposes, such as control over nature, production of material goods, organization of society, and development of various skills. This practical knowledge is inferior to theoretical knowledge, though the average person not only deems it superior, but tends to not to care for the latter. Nevertheless, the former, subservient to its utilitarian fruits, should not be treated with highbrow neglect. It is the creative force of civilization, improves existence, and makes every ordinary mind exercise its thinking faculty. A certain amount of it is essential for survival. Indeed, practical knowledge is a necessity, while theoretical knowledge may be regarded as a luxury.

Knowledge can thus be divided into two broad categories: theoretical or pure knowledge, and practical or instrumental knowledge. The two cannot be absolutely differentiated, for theoretical knowledge can often be turned to practical account; for example, a scientific theory may lead to an invention. However, the distinction is genuine and depends on a person's primary purpose in pursuing a particular branch of learning. We will regard a subject as practical if its cultivation is mainly on account of its utilitarian results, if it serves as an instrument for the attainment of material welfare.

Practical subjects of study are those that concern the crafts and professions, as well as hobbies. They teach one how to acquire the requisite skill. They deal with such pursuits as engineering, law, medicine, accountancy, agriculture, commerce, navigation, stenography, carpentry, plumbing, acting, sports, and stamp collecting. They are concerned with the ordinary, workaday world and carry on the tasks that are part of a civilized society. With their narrow, vocational, specialist character, they do not appear weighty individually, but they are needed for their utility; they may not seem inspiring, but their absence would have serious repercussions on society, especially the material system. Not all practical knowledge is beneficial; a considerable section may be deleterious to human welfare, including that relating to warfare, politics, commerce, pornography, spying, explosives, and trickery. Of course, the knowledge itself is harmless if it is not put into practice; furthermore, even the application need not necessarily be unjustifiable.

But it is pure or theoretical knowledge that should be our primary concern when we discuss knowledge. This knowledge revolves around the universe and all reality. Becoming acquainted with natural entities is the most valuable acquisition of the human race, as we are a part of the scheme of things, and it is proper that we should study our environment. Pure knowledge is good in itself and invaluable for the mind, whose specific attribute is thought. It must be discovered first by somebody before the ordinary person can learn it. It is not at all obvious, and though we imply awareness of the truth when we talk of it, a good deal of human belief actually relates to falsehoods. We can put our trust in erroneous ideas with as much conviction as in facts, for we find it extremely difficult to distinguish between them. When knowledge is referred to in the following paragraphs, pure knowledge or knowledge of the universe and its phenomena, past or present, physical or human, is the understood meaning.

The method for attaining knowledge is the Connective Method, which has been discussed in the realm of formulating a civilization. It is versatile and applicable to all subjects of study. The relative amounts of deduction, induction, synthesis, and analysis to be employed depend on particular requirements of the subjects. Method is the means, and truth is the end. Every inquiry must be conducted in a spirit of cold, detached objectivity; any intrusion of the personality is to be eliminated, and all partisanship shunned.

The various branches of knowledge are to form a harmonious whole in accordance with the structure of the universe. Harmony does not denote similarity, for nature contains tremendous variety. But where there are two contradictory ideas about the same phenomenon, one must be wrong, and both may well be merely a convenience for human purposes. The essential unity of knowledge that has thus been cut up as it were into packages, each bearing a label, is not thereby destroyed, and one should guard against regarding the compartmentalization as natural; it is only a tool devised to suit the limited human intellect.

With the passing of time, the entire body of knowledge has grown in complexity, and no one can master it, but one can learn to grasp it in outline and view it as a whole. The bogy of specialization, currently fashionable, should not deter us from cultivating general knowledge. Specialization may be a necessity for vocational purposes, but a person is not a vocation, although many people consider the person and his vocation as synonymous, it would seem that they are. Knowledge of any kind is beneficial to the mind, and the wider a person's is, the more truly intellectual he is. The tendency to view the specialist as peculiarly brainy is ridiculous. He has merely studied in detail some subdivision of some division of learning, and if his interest and accomplishments are confined to this, then he may actually possess a low order of intelligence, even though he may be useful to his profession.

All pure knowledge can be classified under three groups: philosophy, science, and human studies. Philosophy comprises the subjects dealing with the fundamental principles of the universe or with abstractions like metaphysics, ethics, logic, and esthetics. *Science* here means physical science, which investigates the material world and includes such subjects as mathematics, astronomy, physics, chemistry, geology, and biology. Under human studies, we refer to psychology and history as well as that group of subjects commonly known as social sciences or social philosophy, including political science, economics, and sociology. These subjects concern the mind and the phenomena associated with human action.

Though philosophy utilizes pure reason as its instrument, and reason is the most reliable of our faculties, its conclusions do not spell certitude, with the result that all kinds of conflicting ideas vie for allegiance. A person's philosophy is what he has been brought up to believe or what tallies with his temperament. The problems of philosophy revolve around the fundamental constituents of the universe and are of supreme importance; were they impossible to solve, it would still be good and necessary to tackle them. The word *philosophy* here designates a particular division of knowledge dealt with in a number of subjects. Metaphysics concerns the ultimate nature of the universe; ethics deals with the good to be pursued by humanity; logic sets out the rules of valid reasoning; and esthetics concerns good taste in art and the appreciation of the beautiful.

Loosely used, the word has a meaning that renders it unqualified to be regarded as a branch of learning. *Philosophy* may just signify a set of beliefs about life and behavior in general, and this is what is called a person's philosophy of life. Popularly, philosophers are expected to practice what they preach. Although this should be the case, practice does not make a system true, nor does an idea become false because it does not appear in action. Knowledge as such has no necessary nexus with conduct. Philosophy antedated science, and before knowledge grew more detailed and differentiated into a multitude of separate subjects, it was almost synonymous with knowledge of all aspects. The early Greek philosophers who postulated water, air, earth, or fire as the primordial elements out of which all things were made were referring to the physical world. Philosophers have not all relied on reason; many have been hostile to it and have advocated intuition. Again, many of them have not worked out any systems but have made a miscellaneous collection of statements on various topics. These diverse types of belief and opinion are not, strictly speaking, philosophy.

What is termed *religion* deals with much the same material as philosophy, the difference lying in the mode of apprehending reality. While philosophy purports to use reason, religion rests on authority, its ideas having been delivered by a person deemed divine or invested with some peculiar power. Religion is not a specific division of knowledge, its aim being the conversion of the masses to a particular way of life based on a certain view of the cosmos. The traditional or authoritative religions have exercised immense influence on the diverse civilizations, and, though this has declined, they still hold sway over the inhabitants of many lands.

Science uses inductive reasoning to discover the truth, and it places great stress on facts obtained by observation and experiment. It has proved much more fruitful than philosophy and has evolved an extensive body of knowledge about which there is scarcely any dispute. It is strange that science should have risen later than philosophy; one would have thought it would have been simpler and more natural for human beings to use their observational powers first before indulging in the more intricate process of ratiocination. The explanation, of course, lies in the fact that scientific observation and experimentation involve laborious, systematic work, while the reasoning of many philosophers in past times was unmethodical, slipshod, and largely mingled with fancy. The scientific process is strict reasoning based on facts.

Whether science will eventually deal with the totality of things and will ever be able to solve the riddle of the universe is debatable. So far, it is successful only in explaining a section of the human experience—namely, certain aspects of the physical world. It is concerned with unraveling the structure of material bodies and demonstrating how one phenomenon leads to another. Its method does not enable it to comprehend the *why* of things. It would seem, therefore, that as the problems it attempts to solve are the fundamental ones of existence, it is less important than philosophy. Nevertheless, the role it plays in its restricted sphere is unique in the certainty of the knowledge it uncovers; its progressive accumulation of facts is impressive, especially compared to the dubiousness and apparent unprogressiveness of philosophy.

Science is the dominant force in modern times, and its influence has spread into every realm of human activity. It is always dangerous for any particular thing to have its importance unduly stressed; a society completely subjugated by science is just as lopsided as one under the sway of religion. Science has performed great deeds in its own sphere, but there is no reason to suppose that its method or spirit means anything in the realm of art. Its great gift lies in its extensive accumulation of detailed and accurate knowledge of the physical world. It is not primarily concerned with human aims and aspirations; if it happens to fulfill any of them, it is incidental.

Each branch of science comprises several sub-branches, whose number increases with greater knowledge of details. Mathematics is the basic science, but, unlike the others, its reasoning is purely deductive; there were mathematicians long before there were experimental scientists. Astronomy began as astrology, which is ancient; here we see the difference between pure science devoted to acquiring knowledge for its own sake and a pursuit expressly serving human ends. Physics uses both mathematics and experimentation in a way that no other science does. Chemistry is based on analysis, and Dalton's formulation of the atomic theory originally propounded by Democritus shows how a philosophic concept can become a scientific theory. Geology studies the crust of the earth, but it could very well be part of a larger subject concerned with the earth in all its aspects. Biology deals not with inanimate matter but with living organisms; the Darwinian theory of evolution was cataclysmic in its effects and extended far beyond its original subject even into philosophy, exemplifying how in modern times a scientific theory tends to be utilized to erect a philosophy.

Science as pure knowledge is not necessarily linked to invention. But it likely would not have commanded such universal admiration or influenced civilization so profoundly if it had not initiated a host of inventions, if it had been as unfruitful for practical purposes as philosophy. There are no grounds for assuming that an invention requires less intellectual power than the discovery of a law of nature; like a work of art, it displays greater creativity in that something new is brought into existence. There were many inventions in the world before, but they were made without any scientific investigation. One problem with the inventions of science is that they are not necessarily conducive to human welfare, for bombs and poison gas are also its products; here it becomes plain that we cannot rely on science alone to guide us.

Human studies have been given the name of science, and they attempt to pursue scientific methods in their quest for knowledge. However, they are not as successful as physical science, and their ideas are by no means indubitable. The reason is clear. Material phenomena are comparatively less complicated, and certain general principles cover all instances. Mental and social phenomena are extremely complex, so no general principle is devoid of exceptions, and there is no necessary nexus between cause and effect; the same cause can lead to diametrically opposite effects. We may or may not have free will, but things happen as though we do. It is impossible to predict a future event by surveying the present. From the standpoint of theoretical knowledge, the pursuit of human studies is harmless, but one must maintain a scientific attitude and realize that the knowledge is uncertain. However, the studies tend to lead to conclusions that are used to regulate practical life. This is dangerous. One may forget that these so-called sciences are different from the physical sciences; the principles and precepts are as likely to be false as true. The studies may guide, but no absolute reliance can be placed on them.

Psychology exemplifies the scientific claim at its worst. With its techniques and experiments, it gives the impression of being a real science. One of the most fatuous absurdities is its conception of the normal man, whose behavior is that of the average person living in the psychologist's society. Surely it takes no great intelligence to realize that different communities at different times have different norms of conduct. It is therefore irrational to stigmatize as abnormal and wrong behavior that varies from what the psychologist usually finds. There is no reason whatsoever why the individual who does not conform to the usual behavior pattern should be regarded as mentally sick. The most misleading of the studies is psychoanalysis, with its false findings masquerading as verities and its shibboleths so dear to pretentious novelists. It has still to be seen whether psychology will ever be able to establish principles as sound as those of physical science; in the meantime, its conclusions must be considered exceedingly dubious.

History is an ancient subject and has been treated as a branch of literature. It can scarcely be deemed a science, as it is a record of events that have passed away, of evanescent phenomena. But it purports to deal with actual happenings from which general principles may be extracted, and it is therefore a genuine branch of knowledge, not a literary creation. The trouble is that the facts are hard to discover, and much of history is probably fictitious; furthermore, the events are jumbled. The principles obtained by examining the facts are of doubtful validity, as they do not cover all cases and cannot be used to predict future events. As a literary genre, history will presumably always be interesting, but as a branch of knowledge, its limitations are not easy to overcome.

Political science, economics, and sociology are important subjects and deserve to be pursued vigorously. However, like the other human studies, they cannot be placed on the same footing as the physical sciences. Political science inquires into the principles of government, a manmade institution. Economics deals with wealth or the products of human industry, and its laws are fallible. Sociology studies society, which cannot be compared to a natural organism. Human institutions cannot be treated like natural entities, which are rigorously subject to discoverable laws, as their phenomena are erratic, the laws are uncertain and do not always apply, and fresh institutions can be produced.

Chapter 16
Recreation

Recreational activities are those undertaken for pleasure. Of course, every pursuit, even the most serious, can yield it and does so, at least to some persons; pleasure is subjective, and different people may enjoy different things. On the other hand, a recreation may confer benefits quite apart from pleasure. Nonetheless, it is correct to classify certain pursuits as recreation, judging from the emphasis placed on pleasure.

Some activities are scarcely of any benefit other than giving enjoyment. They are mainly harmful; examples are gambling, alcoholism, smoking tobacco, and taking narcotics. Such habits are among the unfortunate byproducts of civilization and are best avoided. There is no need to discuss them any further, for they have no cultural value.

Recreational activities that are part of civilized life may be divided into two categories: sports and theatrical entertainment. The former produce health and strength, and the latter appeals to the esthetic sense and contributes to culture. It is undesirable to overstress their value; a civilization in its decadent stage tends to concentrate too much attention on them. The right course is to regard them as useful and accord them their proper place in the scheme of human activities.

The term *sports* here denotes all recreational pursuits of a physical nature, including athletics and games. Athletics refers to the development of natural movements, usually without the use of apparatus, including walking, running, jumping, climbing, swimming, boxing, wrestling, calisthenics, cycling, driving, and boating. The movements of calisthenics are not such as one would normally make but are specially designed ones. Cycling, driving, and boating involve skill in the handling of vehicles. The ancient Greeks had great esteem for athletics and instituted the Olympic Games, which have been revived in modern times.

Games are mainly competitive, with two sides taking part, each hoping to emerge the victor. Played with some paraphernalia, they are artificial and can be of as many kinds as human ingenuity can devise. They are bound by rules, which are ordinarily quite simple. They are merely forms of recreation and are of little importance, and skill in playing them does not indicate any kind of superiority, physical or mental. However, since the average person tends to prefer the frivolous to the intellectual, a strange amount of enthusiasm is lavished on games, and the champion players receive a ludicrous degree of renown. Among the games are football, baseball, cricket, badminton, tennis, table tennis, polo, hockey, golf, billiards, basketball, volleyball, chess, and draughts. Games differ in popularity from country to country. Chess and draughts do not involve physical agility and are of an intellectual character.

Note that sports are not necessary for health, though they may promote it. Their ostensible justification is the healthful nature of their physical activity; however, most people undertake such activity to some extent, even those with sedentary occupations, so it is unnecessary to cultivate it artificially. Health is undoubtedly important, but spending an inordinate amount of time on sports on the grounds of its maintenance is irrational, because other factors affecting health are just as significant, if not more so, including cleanliness, sufficient nutritious food, adequate sleep, and fresh air.

Sports have their proper place, some of them being useful skills and all of them having recreational value. It is, however, preposterous to exaggerate their worth and take as serious what are intended to serve merely as recreation. There is no gainsaying the fact that a person can take tremendous pleasure from playing or watching a game, just as he can from watching a theatrical performance. Though as a rule sports are harmless, some are destructive, such as those associated with the chase and involving cruelty to animals and those concerned with fighting, entailing needless physical injury. Sadistic enjoyment in the name of sports or otherwise is not to be tolerated.

Games are nearly all competitive: one side struggles against another, hoping to emerge the victor. A typical example is football, and huge crowds gather to see one team defeat another. Why must games be associated with rivalry? And is this competitive spirit, in what purports to be entertainment, desirable? This competition, of course, appeals to the pugnacious instinct; without it, games might not be as popular as they are. It makes play less innocent and joyous than it would otherwise be. It would be an excellent variation to have games in which the competitive element is absent.

As in everything else, a code of conduct has grown up on the sports field, and this has been employed as the spiritual justification of games. Such codes of behavior are usually pretentious and spurious, and sportsmanship is no exception. The sportsman is supposed to be a person given to fair play who takes defeat with a smile. Why games should breed a sense of justice any more than any other activity is inexplicable. It is doubtful whether anybody loves defeat; if he does not, but is obliged to pretend that he doesn't mind losing, he gets great training in hypocrisy. Anyway, what is so wonderful about taking defeat light-heartedly that it needs to be specifically cultivated?

Sports serve a useful purpose in that they provide entertainment for the masses. As such, they should not be elaborate and costly; the rules of a game should be few and simple and the apparatus cheap. Games are artificial, easy to devise. Life is complicated, and it is pointless to add to its complexity; recreational pursuits may be troublesome if there are too many kinds—it is best to avoid variants of a game. The entertainment value of sports means that they can be enjoyed by spectators who do not participate in the play.

Using animals for the purpose of sport is almost always associated with cruelty. The usual type is to make two beasts fight each other, sometimes to the death. Another is for a man to battle an animal, as in the bullfights of Spain. This sort of sport is thoroughly objectionable and should be suppressed by law.

The gambling associated with certain kinds of sports is to be eradicated, as it is objectionable in any form; the supreme example is horseracing. Whether the players themselves bet on their play or whether the spectators wager which side will win a game, it is all equally reprehensible.

It must be remembered that sports are for recreation and health; any other considerations are extraneous and can only vitiate them. They have a place in a balanced society, but all the claptrap is to be deprecated. For children, sports should not be regarded as their most important activity; for adults it is, of course, ludicrous to advocate that everyone should play or enjoy them or to treat sports figures as heroes. A society that regards play as its principal pursuit is puerile. Recreational activities are to be strictly treated as such, and they are of secondary import.

Another species of recreation revolves around the theater. The forms of entertainment include drama, opera, ballet, musical plays, and variety shows, as well as the circus and the cinema; music, singing, and dancing are popular on the stage. Different cultures have developed their own types and variants of theatrical entertainment, some of which have become obsolete, but there is no need to go into them. It is proposed just to touch on the theater generally as a constituent of civilization.

The appeal of the stage is esthetic. Acting, dancing, and singing are art forms, but as they directly impact the senses and as a rule have little intellectual content, they are much more popular than, say, poetry. Their beauty is visual or auditory. As modes of artistic expression, they are significant. Before the advent of sound and film recordings, the great actors, dancers, and singers had a limited audience. In modern times, their performances can be widely witnessed, and they need not be mere names to those who come after them.

As art, stage performances have a cultural value that can be greatly enhanced by making them more intellectual. Their worth depends, of course, on what they offer; if what they present is slapstick comedy or pornography, they are not conferring any cultural benefit on anybody. Their origin was religious, but since they became secular, they have tended to be associated with lewdness, possibly as a reaction against their pristine purpose. In former ages, they were of ill repute, but today their importance is apt to be overstressed. Since they are essentially entertainment, it is out of place to link them with religion, the feeling for which should not express itself through them. They should be treated in their own right as art forms capable of giving intellectual satisfaction.

Reactivism, which has been discussed in connection with literature and the fine arts, is just as applicable to drama and the other theatrical forms. Instead of dealing with romance and fantasy as in the opera and ballet, it is better to concern oneself with real life. But reactivist art is made up not of life as objectively viewed but life as it has passed through the crucible of the mind. The theater has a cultural and artistic value that should never be overlooked, and so it should be brought into conformity with other forms of creative art.

The theater has a greater popular appeal than literature and other arts, primarily because its appreciation requires no intellectual labor. People like enjoyment in company, and sitting together in a big hall laughing, weeping, or thrilling simultaneously is very much to their taste. Because of its popularity, the theater can exercise tremendous influence on the thoughts, attitudes, and behavior of the masses. They come to admire what they see the majority of people admiring and to dislike what they dislike; in a society given to inordinate admiration of the stage, they even imitate what their favorite actors do. The reverse is also true; that is, a theatrical presentation is more likely to succeed if it follows the prejudices of its audience, and actors can more easily achieve fame if they stand for the type of individual their fans appreciate. This means that in the theater as everywhere else, genuine originality is rare.

The theater has traditionally been associated with sexual laxity. Presumably, this is because in the days when morality was strict and the sexes mixed much less or not at all, the actors and actresses, by virtue of the needs of their work, came into close contact with one another. Furthermore, it was considered that only loose women earned money via their physical attractions. Acting was considered such a disgraceful occupation in imperial China that, whereas peasants could sit for the official examinations and could be appointed mandarins, actors were prohibited from doing so. There is no real connection between the theater and lewdness, the link existing because the audience wants it. The degree of license varies according to the prevailing morality. Pornography on the stage is worse than in books and magazines; when people enjoy it *en masse* instead of singly, they come to regard it with less concern and without any sense of wrongdoing.

The main object of the theater is entertainment, and all other purposes are incidental and secondary, as people do not go to it for instruction. But there are all sorts of entertainment, ranging from buffoonery to wit and from melodrama to tragedy. There is nothing objectionable in innocent enjoyment, even if it is silly; but there is no reason why popular taste cannot be elevated. It is wrong for the theater to be bracketed with vice, and it is deplorable for it to be transformed into a propaganda forum for political purposes. It should first and foremost be a means of recreation and secondarily a cultural medium.

Drama is the form of theatrical entertainment capable of the greatest intellectual content, and it is associated with literature. It can be the vehicle of expression of a poet or prose writer, and it is subject to all the fashions that beset other categories of literature. It can be deadly serious and be used as a medium of propaganda; of course, it can still be entertainment even if it is invested with a serious purpose. Like the novel, it tells a story and is criticized for its plot, characterization, dialogue, portrayal of life, and stylistic merits. However serious they may be, dramatists must regard their art as a species of entertainment, and whatever message they may be preaching, they must convey it indirectly, wrapped up in the story. As a form of literature, a play should preferably be reactivist. Romantic or realistic drama need not cease to be produced, but reactivist drama is more appropriate. A play may be written purely as literature without any thought of theatrical performance, but if it is incapable of being produced on the stage, it can scarcely be regarded as drama.

Opera, which is associated with music, also tells a story, and it provides a grand spectacle. There is no reason why the tale should be of a legendary character and be less appealing if divorced from romance. The ballet is a species of dance, unfolding a story in silence; as in the case of opera, there is no need for it to be linked with legends. Injecting singing and dancing into a straight play to create a musical play endows it with a certain exuberance and romance. The variety show, consisting of an unrelated collection of songs, dances, feats of legerdemain, and sketches, is unsophisticated entertainment; occasionally, it may be worthwhile to impart a certain unity by having the separate items revolve around one central theme. The circus resembles the variety show in exhibiting a collection of unconnected spectacles but relies on animals and acrobatics for its interest; its simple character endears it to children.

Cinematography, a product of modern technology, is another medium for storytelling, the others being the written word and the stage play, and is unequalled for depicting action and scenery. Before its invention, audiences worldwide could not see a show at about the same time. The cinema is a form of art that should not be decried. Highbrow critics might disdain it for its mass appeal and consider it of inferior value. However, if the entertainment it provides is mainly silly, this does not signify any inherent fault but suggests only that the public, which also has a penchant for ridiculous novels and inane stage shows, should cultivate better taste. Television and radio are also media of entertainment, but they serve other purposes as well, including the dissemination of news and propaganda. For storytelling, television does not differ from the cinema. The radio play is unsatisfactory compared to other forms of narrative entertainment; devoid of their features, it doesn't possess any distinctive trait of its own to compensate for them.

Chapter 17
Miscellaneous Constituents

Besides the two bases and the other major constituents of the Intrinsic Civilization, miscellaneous problems must be considered. These minor constituents are mainly social, helping to cement society and contribute to its stability and welfare; their social force would entitle them to be designated *social constituents*. Though they are considered minor, this does not denote that they are of little importance. They are numerous, and we will deal with only some of them. In considering these problems, we must remember the general principles of Intrinsicalism. Each constituent must be in harmony with the universe and with the other parts of the civilization. It should be rational, methodical and as simple as possible. It should be as ideal as it is practicable, and it is to serve human welfare.

Concerning weights and measures, it would be on the side of rationality to relate the different units to one another and make a coherent system. It is best to employ the decimal system on account of its simplicity. Let us start with the unit of time. The day could be divided into twenty hours, ten for daytime and ten for nighttime. It could commence with the break of dawn, the actual point taken to be determined scientifically, and, for the sake of convenience, varied at regular time intervals around the earth in accordance with the meridians. Each hour is to have one hundred minutes and each minute one hundred seconds. The second can be regarded as the unit of time. For the unit of length, take the distance traveled by the earth around the sun in, say, one ten-thousandth of a new second; this measurement must be made as accurately as possible. The units of area and volume are simply the square and the cube of the unit of length, respectively. The unit of weight will be the weight of a unit volume of water under specified conditions. In this way, the units of time, length, area, volume, and weight are linked to one another; other units, such as the scientific ones of force and so on, are derivable from them. In deriving one unit from another, a decimal multiple or measure of the latter may be used; furthermore, different units for different purposes can be established, but each must be a decimal multiple or measure of the basic unit.

The calendar is preferably based on the solar year; save for an occasional adjustment for the odd five hours, forty-eight minutes, and forty-six seconds more than the 365 days it takes the earth to revolve around the sun, the year is of constant duration, and the seasons remain unaltered. The calendar year is divided into twelve months of thirty days each. The extra five days are to be distributed among the even months—that is, the second, fourth, sixth, eighth, and tenth months have thirty-one days each. The intercalary day for leap year necessary to keep the year corresponding to the period of the earth's revolution will be in December. The seven-day week, which is independent of the day of the month, is discarded. If it is desired to name certain days as rest days for most people, the fifth, tenth, fifteenth, twentieth, twenty-fifth, and thirtieth of each month, plus the thirty-first day, where there is one, can be utilized. The first day of the year should coincide with the vernal equinox as experienced in the northern hemisphere, which contains most of the earth's land surface; the day, which would remain the same for all years, would have to be chosen as the most appropriate in accordance with the findings of astronomy.

Education is to have four objectives: to make children conversant with a particular language as a means of expression and communication, to train them in the ways of civilization, to give them a general knowledge of the universe and the arts and sciences, and to fit them for useful employment. Specialized training for a profession or calling is to be given only in universities and vocational institutes after a person has completed his general education in schools. The school curriculum should allow students to enroll in any professional course they like later. Methods of teaching should be devised to suit the course of study. A system that brings suffering to the pupil must be deemed bad, irrespective of what supposed benefits it might confer on society or on the student. Although education aims to produce a good citizen, this should be treated as secondary, the primary concern being to equip students with knowledge that will aid their development. They should not be trained or warped just to fulfill the purpose of the state.

Careers should be as numerous and diversified as society requires. An occupation must serve a social need, or else an individual would not be able to earn anything from exercising it. No person should be prevented from pursuing a vocation he likes, and state control is to be exercised only if ignorance or malpractice endangers society. An obnoxious tendency is to identify the person with the occupation, which should be regarded only as one of his activities and not the whole person. There is no reason why a person should not take up more than one career, either simultaneously or at different times; a wide range of interests is not amiss.

Health is what everyone wants. With the immense increase in knowledge science has brought, the health of people worldwide has improved phenomenally. We may expect medical knowledge to advance, and there is much more to discover, for many ailments and diseases are still incurable. It is preferable for cures to be effected in gentle rather than violent ways, by therapeutics rather than meddling. It is as objectionable in the name of health for every member of a community or a division of it to have part of his physical constitution permanently altered, be it only a mark on his skin, as it is in the name of beauty or religion. Important though health is, it should not be made into a fetish, there being many values in life just as weighty. It is preposterous that a person should do this or not do that because of the off chance that he may catch a certain disease or suffer some injury. Life is hazardous, and little can be absolutely guaranteed not to impair the body in any way.

The manners of a society are based on its moral code. Whereas it is only motives and actions that determine genuine ethical worth, manners, which are merely superficial behavior, influence the pleasantness of social intercourse. It costs nothing to say an obliging word or refrain from uttering a nasty remark, but its effect is significant.

Manners should be natural and not stilted, formal, or exaggerated. Behavior should not be bound by fantastic and finicky rules, which are as annoying as they are senseless. Kindness and not elegance is the quality that should regulate good manners, which can be common to all people; the refined variety peculiar to a certain section of society is laughable.

Customs are not sacrosanct, as they tend to be in most countries at most times. A custom is crystallized practice; it has arisen through the circumstances of the time and may have been of real use at its inception. Preserved and sanctified by tradition, it may have lost all sense and serves no laudable purpose. It should be periodically examined, and, if it does not contribute to human welfare, or, worse, if it does more harm than good, it should be eradicated. There is no excuse for preserving a custom on its own account; the argument of custom is a fallacy. Some customs may seem picturesque, while others are grotesque, but a romantic flavor does not warrant the retention of a futile practice. As a matter of fact, many a custom is so beset with formalities and regulations as to be complex and unnatural. Whatever militates against rationality is wrong and should be discarded; a practice is to be followed not because it is a custom but because it is right. Customs are found in every sphere of human activity, including religion, politics, and social life, but wherever and whatever they are, they must be carefully scrutinized; and the same test of rationality, truth, and utility must be applied to them.

Tradition is no authority; it is allied to custom, and reliance on it is due to mental inertia. A country hidebound by it is lamentably stagnant. However, it is neither necessarily wrong nor necessarily right. It should undergo periodical review, and there is nothing reprehensible in a violent break from the past. There is no merit in mere continuity, and antiquity is not an excuse for retaining any practice. Antiques might be treasured because they are rare, but they are mere objects of curiosity and exercise no influence on life. If they were regarded as the acme of material perfection and people never produced anything new but just copied them, they would be pernicious. It is lamentable when the inhabitants of a country can refer only to tradition as a prop for whatever they do. To have one's eyes riveted on the past is not the way of progress. Incidentally, merely reviving the ways of an earlier generation in order to flout those of the immediate past or resurrecting a previous practice as an innovation does not spell true advancement. What is proclaimed to be new must really be so; what is deemed progress must genuinely be such.

When people are poor, they eat whatever they can afford in order to satisfy their hunger and live, but when they are rich, they eat to satisfy their palates. In the olden days, when nutritional values were little known, the rarer the article of food, the more precious it became; in modern times, in spite of knowledge, the foods most difficult to obtain are still the most coveted. Such is human perversity. The taste for a specific food is cultivated, and there is no dish that somebody doesn't relish. The first and foremost consideration regarding food is nutritional value, but for people to like a particular food on this account, the child must learn to take it early; once a person grows up with a certain preference, no consideration can make him lose his pleasure in it. With greater research, synthetic foods may come to dominate the scene, and this should be welcome if they are wholesome, inexpensive, and easy to produce. It is better on grounds of health, cleanliness, and kindness for people to eat more vegetables and less meat; eventually, it might be possible for the slaughter of animals to cease altogether. We are referring to the feasibility of a general abstention from meat and not to the personal fad of vegetarianism, which has scarcely any effect on humankind or the animal kingdom. Synthetic and vegetable foods could be made attractive and children could be taught early to appreciate them.

Nowhere more than in clothing has the human race shown its capacity for variety. It is astonishing how many different styles of dress have evolved, some of which were ludicrous in the extreme—but their wearers felt nothing of the sort. Clothes should be simple, elegant, and comfortable and serve their intended purposes: protection against the weather and decency. Clothing has grown up with humanity since primitive times. The movement of nudism is a resuscitation of an ancient practice and signifies not progress but retrogression. The beauty of apparel exists in the mind of the beholder and is not inherent in the apparel itself. Oddly, fashion can make one regard as ridiculous what one considered chic not so long ago. A style of clothing need not be embraced for good, as there is no meaningful norm and no harm in change. It is absurd to insist upon a particular mode of dress as the only appropriate one; any suitability it seems to possess is merely a belief rooted in habitual association. This does not mean that clothing fashions should change continually, for this would yield material waste and signify pettiness. But a society may evolve its styles, and occasional change is unobjectionable.

In primitive times, sexual expression was uninhibited. But as civilization advanced, it was considered to be of an animal nature, and people were taught to control it. It is undeniable that human advance should denote intellectual progress. As humanity ascends the ladder of civilization, we should relegate sex to a minor place. Sex has always been the obsession of the worthless libertine. To uphold it in the name of necessity is absurd, for a necessity is not *ipso facto* desirable; to glorify it in the name of art is a misuse of art, which is not a justification for everything. There is no reason why people should not speak of sex; on the other hand, there is no reason why they should refer to it obsessively, introduce it into everything from novels to advertisements, and talk about it seriously, laughingly, libidinously, and so on. It is better to take sex as a fact of life, discuss it if the need arises, and forget about it as a rule. There is no justification for preoccupation, glorification, or sensual devotion. There is nothing to warrant pornography. One of the ridiculous excuses for sexual laxity is that it is modern and a revolt against convention. There is nothing modern about it and nothing unconventional; when it is widespread, it is the convention. The trouble is that society has always accorded sex too much importance, whether in support of it or against it. The severe condemnations meted out against sexual transgressions in former societies are irrational and inhuman, attributable to the undue significance attached to sex.

Gambling is to be prohibited, for it is an illegitimate way of earning money. Unfortunately, it is an instinctive pleasure; it gives one a sense of adventure, a feeling of excitement. However, an evil yearning must be suppressed. It has nothing to commend it, and, pushed to the extreme, it can ruin an individual and wreck society. Like many other activities, it has various forms, some more pernicious than others, but however innocuous they may be, they all militate against the principle that only proper work should be remunerated. It has never been easy to suppress it; it is doubtful whether any species of crime can ever be completely exterminated. But it does not follow that it should be legalized; the excuse that it can then be brought into the open and closely supervised doesn't hold water. Putting it on the right side of the law merely encourages many more people to indulge in it and converts a comparatively rare, clandestine pursuit into a normal, widespread one. If an evil cannot be entirely eliminated, it can still be largely controlled. The argument of legalizing an insuppressible evil like gambling or prostitution would apply to any other kind of misdeed.

A crime is defined as a violation of the law, and punishment is meted out to the criminal. Laws are not natural principles but are made by human beings for their own purposes. The best are designed for the good of the people as a whole, but many are also intended merely to preserve or advance the interests of a particular section of the community. Of all categories of crime, the political is usually chastised with the greatest severity, for it endangers the power of the ruling clique. However, it is often the least reprehensible, for it may be based on just a conflict of ideologies and is often perpetrated by individuals of the highest moral rectitude. The aim of punishment is threefold. First, justice requires that an act should have due retribution; second, there should be a deterrent against future offences; and third, an attempt should be made to reform the criminal. Punishment should not be unduly severe and degrading and should certainly never be brutal. Imprisonment should be the penalty only for crimes involving violence, actual or threatened. For other forms of misbehavior, monetary fines, loss of privileges, or enforced labor in a government institution without confinement unless necessary, should suffice.

Human beings are a late development in the evolution of animal life. The evolutionary process involves the struggle for existence, characterized by cruelty and the eating of animal by animal. As we are animals involved in this process, it is not surprising that we should have been callous toward other creatures and thought nothing of ill-treating and killing them. However, as part of our moral and intellectual advancement, it behooves us to cultivate kindness toward animals. To this end, hunting as a sport is reprehensible; so is the bullfighting of the Spaniards and the staging of fighting matches between creature and creature, as in cockfighting. It may be impossible to make one animal behave kindly toward another, but it is possible not to enjoy their mutual cruelty or give them the opportunity to indulge in it. This does not mean that noxious creatures should be allowed to harm us; it is not wrong to kill a rattlesnake, scorpion, or mosquito. Swift, necessary extermination is defensible, but torture isn't—plucking off a butterfly's wings is not the thing to do. There was a time when forests covered the world and animals roamed and flourished. But as humans cleared the land and developed more effective weapons of destruction, animal life dwindled, especially rapidly in modern times, so much so that it may become extinct. This is deplorable, as animals form a part of nature, and the world should not be devoid of its natural environment. That animals should be preserved for human convenience, to provide a delightful spectacle, or to satisfy scientific curiosity is not exactly amiss, but a better reason is that they have a natural right to exist.

Nature, meaning the natural environment, should not be destroyed. The world would be a poorer place to live in if it were entirely covered with artificial works. We require nature to remind us that we are part of it and to refresh our spirit. The environment that can be easily changed is humanity's habitat. The scenery has been transformed through the clearing of forests, the planting of trees and plants, and the construction of roads and houses. The main physical features—the mountains, plains, deserts, and rivers—have remained practically the same. The oceans and sky have hardly been touched. But it is possible that with the advance of science, sky, sea, and land might have their scenery considerably altered. It is a tribute to the might of humankind that we should be able to shape our environment instead of being at its mercy, but it should remain largely natural. Preservation of wide tracts of land in its original state will always be desirable.

A city is graced by its buildings that house cultural objects: libraries, art galleries, and museums. Every town should have one or more libraries, which would encourage the appreciation of books. Of all human productions, books are the most precious; those that are good can confer benefits as nothing else can, while even those that are bad need not be sneered at, for from them one may still glean something by way of knowledge or amusement. The trouble is that education is a prerequisite to the ability to read and comprehend; furthermore, people more easily appreciate material things than intellectual activities. Reading is a cultivated art. Libraries should not just be places where books are stored and borrowed and where people gather to read, but should also be cultural centers for the diffusion of knowledge about them. Art galleries exhibiting paintings and sculptures vary from the national ones, where masterpieces are permanently placed, to the local ones that display ephemeral productions. But art is a living thing, and there is no reason why comparatively unimportant works should not elicit appreciation. Museums collect all sorts of relics that are just as interesting as they are educational; though it is undesirable to be hypnotized by the past, there is no harm in knowing about it. Museums need not, of course, be concerned only with things defunct; things current can be amassed to give instruction and delight.

Every nation has public holidays other than the regular days of rest. Where a religion predominates, these tend to be festive, dedicated to some deity, historical or legendary personage, or event. In modern times, political occurrences and heroes tend to take the stage. Holidays are phenomenally important for the average person, and, in this respect, he is like a schoolchild. There should not be too many public holidays, just as there should not be an excessive number of regular rest days, for it stands to reason that the service provided to the public at large should be available as much as possible and not be restricted to a few hours for a minimum number of days a year. It would be preferable, in theory, that workers not all take their rest on the same day or all start work and go off at the same time.

Chapter 18
Organization

This book is not intended to depict a utopia, a fanciful dress of the ideal world, but contains a serious system designed for realization in practice. A poetic fantasy may be pleasurable for the dreamer and may make interesting reading, but it doesn't solve the world's problems. Merely lamenting the decadence of the age or thundering against abuses doesn't yield one jot of good. Of course, there is no valid reason why even an ostensible utopia should evoke a sneer, for it is better to dream than to acquiesce to an iniquitous state of affairs or, worse, to be so psychologically subjugated that the wrong is deemed the right. It is better to cherish an ideal, even one that is unattainable, than to get stuck in the wretched bog of so-called reality. However, it would be still better to have an ideal that can be put into practice.

Existing civilizations are extrinsic to the scheme of things; they are experiments on the road of progress and are destined to be swept away in the course of evolution. The predominant civilization of present times is the type that evolved in Western Europe and from there spread to the rest of the world; but Western civilization is decadent and has run its course. Notable for the development of science, it has opened up new vistas and made the world a conglomeration of interrelated countries; but it is essentially experimental and riddled with contradictions and rivalries. Owing to its scientific weapons, it conquered the world, and its values came to be regarded as norms, but admiration or acceptance does not render it the less erroneous.

Communism has often been regarded as a new civilization challenging Western civilization. In truth, it is merely an aberration of Western civilization, a preposterous development of its materialistic aspects combined with a reversion to barbarism. It concentrates on one narrow feature of society, the economic, and is, at best, an experiment in social justice. It has no claim to being thought a new civilization, for a civilization is multifaceted. Its appeal lies in its exploitation of the materialistic, selfish instincts of human beings. By its very nature, it is bound to engender violent power struggles, as it is ridiculous to imagine that a system with no aspiration beyond sufficient food and material goods for the masses under the dictatorship of the proletariat (a masquerade for the masters of the people) can breed anything but unscrupulous strife for personal domination. It is not an advance in civilization.

It has been shown that the new civilization is inevitable; there must come a third stage in the evolution of society. The psychological interpretation of history indicates that the human race will produce an integrated civilization. The synthetic nature of the universe requires the eventual emergence of a civilization intrinsic to the universe. Intrinsicalism propounds the principles characterizing the new civilization that, though inevitable, will not just come of itself but will have to be set up by human endeavor.

The establishment of a new civilization requires a total revolution. A gradual system of reforms is useless and is, in fact, pernicious, for it will yield only a few trifling changes grafted onto the existing system, which will remain but with fresh incongruities added to it. Reforms are desirable only when an existing system is fundamentally sound and only some errors and malpractices need correction. Consistency will soon disappear when only part of a system is altered. Gradual action spread over too many years tends to lose momentum and imperceptibly ceases. A revolution is a *sine qua non* for the foundation of the Intrinsicalist society.

A revolution means that the process of societal transformation is carried out in minimum time. What is important is the speedy establishment of the basic principles of the civilization, for the details can be worked out later. Changes on such a vast scale can be effected only through the machinery of a state's government. Part of the system can be realized apart from governmental action, but this will not bring forth a new civilization. Some people are apt to be frightened by the term *revolution*, as though there were something sinister about it, but this is ridiculous. Revolution is nothing more or less than a radical transformation in the organization of a society or state and there is not the slightest thing culpable about it as such.

To effect a revolution and initiate the new civilization, there must be an organization of persons steeped in the principles of Intrinsicalism and dedicated to the task of their realization in practice. The organization is to be tightly knit. It is not necessary for a member to practice every one of the tenets. Some of these cannot be translated into action until the civilization as a whole is established. Furthermore, one may believe a principle yet find it difficult to put it into practice because one's nature is set and habits are already formed. It must be remembered that the persons who are to make the revolution have been brought up in a different milieu, exposed to the tremendous influence of the multitude and the insistent pressures of the law and society. They must adapt at least partially to their environment if they are to survive or use their talents.

The organization to be known as the *Intrinsicalist Organization* is open to anybody, the only qualification being a willingness to accept the principles of the new civilization. The organization is to be resilient, able to adapt itself to circumstances and not get fixed in a meaningless, ineffective rut. It is not an end in itself but a means to an end. Its rules of operation are to be simple, clear, and practical. It should not be allowed to gather cumbersome paraphernalia, and it should be devoid of weird ritual and ceremonies. The members must always keep in mind the purpose of its existence, its stupendous objective, and not allow this to be deflected by minor issues.

As the Intrinsicalist Organization expands, there will have to arise a system for the appointment of leaders or office bearers to carry out its functions. The mode of appointment will depend on the circumstances prevailing at the time, but, generally speaking, it will utilize both selection and election. The method itself is not of great consequence; what is wanted is effective work of carrying out the revolution. The only criterion is the ability to perform the required tasks.

The function of the organization is to spread the principles of the new civilization and to plan for its establishment. As the system is new, progress will not be easy; people may be less conservative than in former ages, but they do not thereby welcome new ideas, which spread rapidly only after great numbers of individuals have been converted to them. It is a truism that popularity breeds popularity. But whether they meet with success or failure, those earnestly devoted to the principles do not lose heart; they should learn to be unswayed by popular reaction in their own response to the truth.

The Intrinsicalist Organization has a sublime purpose and must not deviate from it. It has been common for a society to start off with one objective and, in the course of time, lose sight of it. It must not become a mere social club or mutual-benefit society. Plenty of associations in the world are devoted to promoting the welfare of their members or performing some minor service to the public. It need not completely rule out mutual aid among its members or service toward the public, but these are not its main function, which it must constantly keep in mind. Its aim is the promotion of a civilization, and this tremendous endeavor is not to be equated with the trifling pursuits of other groups. There is no point pretending to be modest; its work will be incomparably greater than what has ever been performed by any society or party.

Action must depend on circumstance. It is futile to indicate beforehand the plan of action needed, for circumstances are multitudinous, and a rigid scheme will not prevail. For a successful outcome, the organization must be prepared to change rapidly and easily; it should never depart from the fundamental concepts of Intrinsicalism, but its tactics for the practical establishment of the civilization must be fluid. Given a certain set of circumstances, one may prepare a specific plan of action, but even this may have to be varied owing to unexpected difficulties. Flexibility in the mode of attaining the ultimate objective is a necessity.

The aim envisaged is that the Intrinsic Civilization should cover the entire earth, the ideal being a world state, though it can be practiced in each country by itself. The Intrinsicalist Organization can therefore take the form of a single organization with worldwide branches working toward a global revolution, or it can consist of separate national organizations, each operating independently within its own country. As existing states and peoples differ, it might not be feasible to have a simultaneous revolution in all lands. It might be more practical for each country to work out its own revolution in its own time. A world revolution has never occurred; there has never even been a revolution inspired by a single ideal and directed by a single organization occurring in several countries simultaneously.

Some visible symbols to distinguish the Intrinsicalist Organization are not out of place. The ellipse could be a symbol, its meaning being that as the earth revolves around the sun in an elliptical orbit, so the Intrinsic Civilization encompasses society. There could be a new greeting and salute. The greeting is the word *great*, meaning the Intrinsic Civilization is great. The salute is bringing together the tips of the fingers and thumb of the right hand, raising up the arm, and touching the right shoulder with them; the import is that one supports the Intrinsic Civilization.

The principles of Intrinsicalism are as delineated in this book. The two basic concepts are Entitarianism and Exchangism, which deal with religion and state or the life of the individual and the working of society, respectively. For the convenience of the members of the Intrinsicalist Organization well as the public, a simple, easily remembered table of ten principles has been compiled. This is not intended to cover the entire extent of the Civilization but is merely to serve as a program to give an inkling of the nature of the new civilization.

Table of Principles	
1.	Intrinsicalism enshrines the concepts of a new civilization and is a complete system.
2.	The two bases of the Intrinsic Civilization are Entitarianism, a new religion, and Exchangism, a new mode of social organization.
3.	The Primary Substance is the origin of all things.
4.	Matter and mind will ultimately evolve into a collection of Perfect Objects.

5.	Live a life that comprehends the universe.
6.	Free and equal exchange is the basis of society.
7.	The government is the agent of exchange.
8.	The developed town is the proper abode for all persons.
9.	The material structure should combine beauty with utility and be simple, methodical, and rational.
10.	The language of the new culture will be the simple and rational language of Luif.

The new civilization has many aspects, and individuals may be interested more in one than in another. They should endeavor to appreciate all of these aspects but may more closely concentrate on one if they desire. Furthermore, it is feasible for the religion to be put into practice prior to the establishment of the general revolution, for it is a personal code of belief and conduct and requires no action by the state for its foundation. Likewise, some other aspects, such as creative culture, can be implemented at any time. The Intrinsicalist Organization need not, therefore, be concerned wholly with the general revolution but could find room within its fold for the encouragement of activities independent of political action.

In the Organization there may be sections, each dealing with an aspect of the Civilization. It must be emphasized that every member should take an interest in the Civilization as a whole, and it does not mean that, if a person holds a post in or does not belong to a particular section, he should be considered a specialist in or ignorant of the subject, respectively. There should be no conflicts of interests among the diverse sections.

The members of the Organization may practice straightway the tenets of the religion, which is personal rather than social. They should not only know and believe in its principles, but they should try to mold their behavior on them. It should not be subject to much regulation, and the individual is to determine his own conduct. Rites and ceremonies, if introduced for popular convenience, are to be kept to a bare minimum. One of the oddities of many faiths is the preoccupation with death and the resulting weird mummeries—this should be avoided. Death is to be accepted as a sad fact, and the tragic event should not be made worse by arcane rites. The religion is a set of ideas about the nature of the universe and a code of conduct, and the work of the Organization is to enlighten its members and the public regarding them. The religious section of the Organization will spread the Entitarian religion and institute measures to regulate it. As much as possible, it should be developed as an intellectual experience; but for the masses, some regulations and ceremonies are unavoidable. Care must be taken that it should not degenerate into a collection of absurd superstitions and unwholesome rites. Although it is associated with Exchangism and the other components of Intrinsicalism, it should be pursued for its own sake, its utilization for social and other purposes being kept to a minimum.

The main work of the Organization is in connection with the launching of the Exchangist state. Only with political power can the new civilization be thoroughly set up and all its constituents brought to fruition. Political revolution is the immediate objective, the prerequisite to the revolution of civilization. The state is the pivot around which all else revolves. The political section of the Organization is to adopt whatever measures are most suitable to cope with the prevailing circumstances. The capture of power must not be regarded as an end in itself but purely as a means to an end. True Exchangists must not behave like ordinary politicians, office seekers, rulers, and even so-called revolutionaries, who are engaged merely in acquiring power and position. They must be filled with the resolve to realize an ideal, to be the agent for a gigantic social transformation. Unlike the new religion, which can be practiced by the individual immediately without reference to any external factors, the new state is not an ideology for realization by the individual. The individual can only work toward its establishment. While imbued with religious fervor and conscious of the uniqueness of its nature as not being just an ordinary political party, the Organization should be orientated toward the political objective as its primary concern.

The language of the Intrinsic Civilization will be Luif, a simple and rational language. Language is useful principally as the medium of communication, and its importance should not be exaggerated. The language section of the Organization may begin teaching Luif to its members, but the language can be really established only when a country adopts Intrinsicalism in *toto*. Until such time, the members of the Organization may employ for the sake of convenience any existing tongue to which they are accustomed. No matter how simple a language is, a good knowledge of it is beyond the capacity of the average adult tackling it for the first time. It is best learned by habitual use in speaking, reading, and writing, and, when a person already possesses a language, it is laborious for him to utilize another. A specific language does not make as much difference to a civilization as a religion or form of state, although it may make a people consider that it singles it out from other peoples. The language section is to develop Luif for common usage, make it a vehicle for all purposes, and create a literature for the day when it becomes a universal tongue.

Other constituents of the civilization may be dealt with by a miscellaneous section or, employing the term loosely, a *cultural section*. This section will deal with matters relating to material structure, creative culture, knowledge, recreation, and so on. Some of these ideas may be implemented by the members of the Organization readily enough, while others have to wait for the Exchangist state to come into being. In any case, the members could discuss and familiarize themselves with them. Not all subjects are important to everyone; for instance, reactivism is intended for writers and artists and does not much affect others. In matters like creative culture, the widest tolerance and most catholic taste are to be cultivated; there should be no rigid official standards that must be followed to win approval from the state or the Organization. These miscellaneous problems are of the least immediate concern and need not even be dealt with by the Organization in its early stages.

To sum up, the Intrinsicalist Organization is the instrument for the establishment of the new civilization. It is to be conducted along practical lines and be able to adapt itself to circumstances. It will cherish the fundamental ideas of Intrinsicalism but is not to be dogmatic about the modes of action required to establish the civilization. It is to be conscious of the fact that the revolution it seeks to bring about is of colossal dimensions and that this sublime task ought to give its members a profound sense of dedication to a noble cause. Even if it repeatedly fails in its objectives, it should not be disheartened, for it is working in conjunction with the inexorable course of the universe moving toward an inevitable outcome.

PART 2

RELIGION

Chapter 1
Religion and Philosophy

What is religion? The world possesses a number of religions with diverse tenets and practices: what they have in common is that they are organized systems of worship with cosmogonies, moral ideals, rituals, priests, and places of worship. Belief in their doctrines rests on faith, which denotes necessary trust in the dogmatic utterances of some authoritative person invested with mysterious wisdom, usually a special instrument of the divine power and, in the case of the founder of Christianity, God incarnate. A religion is a popular guide for the masses, resting more on feeling than intellect, and is a way of life rather than a body of ideas to gratify the curiosity for knowledge. It is deeply rooted in instinct and prehistory, and the more advanced type is simply a refinement of the beliefs of our primitive ancestors. It appeals to a desire for dependence on agencies that will aid people in their struggle for existence; in times of ignorance and calamity, when they find themselves utterly helpless, faith is strong. Its essence is a theory of life and the universe conceived of as true, for it is doubtful whether anyone would keep up his devotions if he seriously held that its foundations were false. His subconscious yearning to believe may have created his feeling of certitude, but he identifies it with objective truth.

What is philosophy? It is a system of knowledge professedly arrived at through reason, which thinkers hold is the only proper method for separating truth from error. Historically, the East has bred religions and the West philosophies. As a powerful factor in molding the lives of peoples and shaping the course of civilization, philosophy was comparatively uninfluential; Europe was conquered by an Asian religion. It is often accused of being barren, arid, impractical, removed from life, engaged in definitions and hair-splitting distinctions, a pleasant task for pedants but negligible for the masses. The indictment is unfortunately well-merited; hitherto it has been only a branch of learning, not life itself. A philosophy purports to be a theory of the structure of the universe; this is its primary aim, and its incidental effect on behavior is relegated to the background. It satisfies the head, not the heart; the thinker, not the person in the street. It is theory, not practice. It views the universe as an intricate puzzle, the solution of which constitutes the *summum bonum*.

Religion and philosophy, as explained above and as ordinarily understood, are commonly treated as separate subjects; they can, however, be harmonized, since their fundamental basis is a comprehensive view of the universe, a synthesis of experience. They deal with the same problems and may arrive at the same conclusions, their difference lying chiefly in the methods whereby they profess to obtain their knowledge. Philosophy has sometimes claimed to be the champion of religion, though the reverse has never happened. They may be defined as follows: a religion is an earnest way of life and worship based on a conception of the universe; a philosophy is a rational system of knowledge concerning the nature of the universe. One appeals to the masses, the other to the learned few. One deliberately excites emotional enthusiasm; the other is of purely intellectual interest.

When discussing the relative merits of religion and philosophy, we can hardly deny that religion's claim of possessing truth rests on impossible foundations. Faith as an indicator of reality is untenable. The doctrines of the various creeds are dissimilar and, in many cases poles apart. They are all maintained by faith, which, were it to spell actuality, would make every religion true—a palpable absurdity, for two contradictory ideas cannot both represent the real, just as a hill cannot also be a sea and a tree cannot be both tall and short. Faith is just blind belief in notions evolved by the imagination and is associated with tradition, racial vainglory, environment, wishful thinking, and dreams. Intuition, the method of acquiring knowledge claimed by mystics, is most unreliable, being either instinct, whose deliverances are not necessarily right; prejudice absorbed in forgotten ways; or plain guesswork. It is true that human beings have a faculty that makes us apprehend things directly. However, it is so easy to attribute erroneous but ardently maintained convictions to its power that it is a very dangerous criterion. The historical religions rest on a very precarious basis and, largely fiction, should not command belief. Theoretically, the ordinary religion is wrong. What are its benefits? It provides spiritual life, gives the common person a higher interest than preoccupation with wealth, endows society with a moral code, consoles misery, and offers hope of salvation. Its practical assets are genuine, and a society needs them. It supplies a unitary directive, a common way of life; one cannot go about the difficult business of living without a set of ideas. Peasants or artisans do not have the time, energy, and capacity to make a personal system by intensely studying a confused array of books with contradictory notions. They are not in a position to sift them; still less can they originate any ideas from their own reflections. If they are not readily furnished with some ideology, they would dwell in a mental vacuum.

Philosophy uses reason, which is the only legitimate faculty given to us for testing truth and right. It is the sole trustworthy road to reality, its function being to link ideas to form a consistent pattern. Genuine reason has for its foundation the facts knowable through the senses; experience and reason should be companions. The mystery of the universe must rely on philosophy for its solution, though it has not yet evolved any incontestable doctrines. The extant systems fail even though they are supposed to be rational, because their reasonings are faulty and incomplete; still, they clarify the issues. If reason will never penetrate reality, then it can confidently be asserted that until a new faculty is born in us, of which there is not the slightest sign, we shall forever remain in the abyss of ignorance. The activity of philosophy is legitimate and necessary, even though it has not been an effective social force. Natural science, whose interests are limited to the material universe, influences countless lives and makes an important contribution to the advancement of civilization in its accumulation of facts and its brilliant inventions, which have lightened the burden of human hardships. But philosophy, which purports to grasp the totality of things and, as the whole must be superior to the part, ought to be more valuable than science, bears no fruitful results. What a paradox! What is the cause of this lamentable state of affairs? Why does religion, a congeries of ludicrous stories, command more respect and exert immeasurably more authority than philosophy? The reason is clear. Technical philosophy is technical knowledge, and most people are not interested in theories for their own sake; its ideas are not related to the needs of ordinary life. If it is to become a social force, it must discard a purely cold, critical attitude; it must abandon its Olympian aloofness from the workaday world; it must be a way of life. It should be beneficial, intertwining itself into the being of everyone.

It is necessary to colligate religion and philosophy, coalesce their advantages, and eradicate their faults. It is necessary in the interest of life, especially today, when both are perishing. It is necessary so ordinary people may enjoy the intellectual and spiritual part of their being and cease to be dominated by materialism and Philistinism, thus enabling them to realize their full nature and avoid one-sidedness. Life is more than sensual gratification and an abundance of goods. The lamentable trend toward the exclusive pursuit of wealth since the rise of industrialism has brought its nemesis in the form of furious, futile conflict among individuals, classes, and people.

It is possible to integrate philosophy and religion into a single subject under the name of religious philosophy: no distinction is to be made between them when they form a unified theme. A religious philosophy is a rational theory of the universe terminating in a devoted way of life. The knowledge is acquired by a process of strict ratiocination; once firmly implanted in the mind, it should excite enthusiasm and exert beneficial impact on everyday existence. Religion was the precursor of philosophy, just as astrology and alchemy issued in astronomy and chemistry, respectively. However, it had a handsomer destiny, for it was not superseded by its offspring but continued to flourish. It is time to strip away its superstitious and irrational character and endow it with sense. A religious philosophy is called such because, like philosophy, its ideas are derived from reason, and, like religion, its aim is to mold the individual life, offering it hope and a goal. It forms an indissoluble blend of its two components and effects real reconciliation. It includes metaphysics and ethics as its main themes and incidentally touches on psychology and science.

It possesses two aspects: the theoretical and the practical. The theoretical is in line with philosophy, a technical branch of knowledge that has the ultimate nature of the universe as its objective and uses reason as its instrument. It is intellectualistic in the sense that it aims at elucidating and comprehending reality; it is naturalistic in the sense that in establishing its doctrines, it takes into account only processes inherent in nature and makes no use of external divine agencies that can arbitrarily alter the working of the cosmos. Science is invoked to confirm its theories. It proposes to give a picture of truth with a consistent system of general principles within whose framework the specific sciences can take their place. It promotes the resolution of the conflict among religion, philosophy, and science—a proper aspiration, since the real is an indivisible whole. However, this task will not be achieved by eclecticism, the desire not being the reconciliation of existing religions and philosophies; that, besides being impossible, presupposes that they already divide the truth among them, a hypothesis that has no justification. The right procedure is a dispassionate, impartial examination of the universe, not of theories; the inquiry will take its course free of prejudice and convention. Some, but not all, of the results may be new: the primary motive is not to maintain conservatism, as is the case with religious apologists, or to say something startling, as some are accused of doing. It is much more arduous to be original than conventional; the critical thinker should be motivated only by a thirst for truth. The reconciliation of the three subjects will be effected not by incorporating their specific ideas but by considering their spirit and tendencies.

The practical aspect is more closely associated with religion: the ethical code guides action and is designed to be translated into behavior. One of the misfortunes of the Christian and Buddhist codes is that they are at complete variance with human nature, even with the existence of civilization itself, so that they are very successful at producing hypocrisy and a morbid conscience. Rules of conduct should be such that they can be generally followed if they are going to be useful. A moral rule is ostensibly advocated only for the promotion of human welfare; if in practice it breeds chiefly misery or is not observed at all, then it falsifies its aim and loses its value. When philosophy is related to life, it becomes superior to science both in theory and practice: in theory as it probes the entire sum of things and not merely a portion; in practice as it molds our being's end and aim and does not just contribute a few aids to living. The practical part of the system is rightly interlocked with emotion. An idea must be wreathed in feeling, and it must burn with a luminous flame before it can produce energetic action; reason establishes its truth, and emotion makes it work. The presence of emotion gives the system its religious nature.

In stressing the need for practical philosophy, I am not deprecating pure knowledge, which is of the highest good. I do not profess to be a pragmatist who believes that any theory will do so long as it serves his purpose and has a utilitarian result; according to this view, a principle is to be tested by its consequences, not by its relation to absolute truth. This conception is erroneous, for a falsehood has no right to elicit belief no matter what good it achieves. The quest for truth may be futile, but it is legitimate by virtue of humanity's rational nature. For us to segregate ourselves from the universe and live in a world produced by our own imagination is to make ourselves unnatural, running counter to our position as an integral part of nature. The universe is greater than humankind; could we maintain ourselves by flouting it? The advocacy of practical philosophy means merely that philosophy should have both practical and theoretical sides. Truth is required; so is practice. Science illustrates this principle; it creates ideas and inventions, the ideas being true and valuable as pure knowledge, and the inventions making for its importance in ordinary life. Only the naïve would fancy that its concepts are true because they issue in useful appliances. Theory and invention are related. Science would be very insignificant in spite of its material products if its ideas had no connection with reality; it would not be of social importance were it to confine itself to pure knowledge and produce no inventions. Similarly, philosophy ought to seek truth as well as mold life.

In forming this religious philosophy, we must keep in view its possible impact on the life of the ordinary individual, but the importance of truth is not thereby minimized: unless based on reality, a way of life is not legitimate. Truth must be cherished partly for its own sake and partly as the only reliable foundation for a right life. Falsehood is wrong *per se*, and its consequences can never be genuinely good; a right rule from a wrong premise is an inherent contradiction.

By interchanging the words, *religious philosophy* may be alternatively called *philosophical religion*, but the two are not absolutely identical in meaning, the differences being one of emphasis, the substantive indicating the nature. The former stresses the philosophy, the theoretical side, the quest for truth, while the latter may be defined as religion with a philosophical basis. As this system is propounded in the hope that it may be put into practice, it may simply be dubbed a religion. Admittedly, a popular religion connotes more than a body of doctrines; it includes an organization for worship. The system is intended to be the basis of such an organization; the objective is human salvation. The existing creeds are antiquated, not consonant with the spirit of present times; they could not be seriously accepted as truth. They are moribund and have lost their hold on thinkers and ordinary people alike. If they still have adherents, mental inertia is the cause, an unfortunate trait that is as real as physical inertia. However, just as a material body at rest can be made to move by a force, so a habit can be ousted by the force of circumstances; changed conditions call for a change of thought. We are in reality dwelling in a religious vacuum; mere nihilism is not a solution, and we cannot remain long satisfied with the unwarranted affirmation that economics is our only concern. Humanity's destiny must be interpreted in terms of the universe. What is the goal of life? That is the problem of a religious philosophy, the most fundamental and momentous of any question for us.

Chapter 2
The Spherical Method

In the past, philosophers have employed various methods to formulate their systems about the structure of the universe. What they have in common is that they all claim to adhere to reason. These methods range from the dialectics of the Greek thinkers to the mathematical or dogmatic method of the Cartesian school, the psychological method of Locke and his followers and the critical method of Kant. A peculiarity in the methods in use for the last few centuries, from Descartes onward, is that they all start with an examination of mental processes; all are subjective and, in fact, might be labeled psychological. The mind of the individual is a minute fraction of the sum of things. Though the mind may be wonderful, and though knowledge is a property of the mind, undertaking an investigation of the nature of the colossal universe by analyzing the working of the mind seems curious and faulty. Using the mind to reflect on the character of the mind as a starting point for an inquiry into objective reality is calculated to produce pitfalls; it is not surprising that idealism should be so popular, it being the logical consequence of interest in the mind. It is perplexing to understand how, if one begins with the mind, one can go beyond it; it is natural to get bogged down in its confines.

I propose to follow another method, which is objective and is suggested by our sensory experience. When we open our eyes, we directly perceive the world and find that it consists of things that are related to one another in an orderly manner. This perceptual world seems external to us, solid, real, though most thinkers are assured that it is an illusion. But the question of its actual existence would be best solved by dissecting its structure and discovering how it could be misconstrued, instead of immersing ourselves in an examination of our consciousness.

Is the external world real? Consciousness tells us that it is, but this is not necessarily right. *Prima facie*, there is no reason why the universe should be so constructed that a particular species of beings should enjoy the privilege of apprehending it spontaneously; whether or not they can do so is arguable. Certain facts point to the fallibility of common sense. When we behold a tree from a distance, the foliage appears to be one connected mass, but when we approach it, we find that it consists of distinct units separated by empty spaces. Now what is the true nature of the foliage? We cannot just cavalierly affirm what it is when we are near the tree. When we stand beside a railway, we find that, farther on, the parallel lines appear to converge, but we swear that the parallelness is correct, for we can walk on and see whether they ever meet. The first point to be noticed is that our senses can play tricks on us in a disconcerting way by giving us different appearances of the same object; the second is that we cannot arbitrarily conclude that one picture is right and the other wrong. Numerous instances can be cited to confirm the subjectivity of sensory experience; the above two concern the effect of distance. It is a fact that our minds never come into immediate, direct contact with material objects, which we observe only at some distance. Supposing the distance is so great that we never perceive them as they are—what then? Common sense fails as a sure test of truth.

In what way can we be said to know external objects? What we actually experience are only images. Rays of light impinging on the retina set up a motion in the nervous system; somehow, this motion is translated into a percept. We don't genuinely behold the material object but have only a mental sensation. Is the latter a precise replica of the former? Evidently it is not, or there couldn't be more than one appearance of the same object. Is there then any necessary connection between the image and the object? In other words, is the image dependent on the object for its existence? This is the crux of the problem of the objective actuality of matter. Since what we are aware of is only sense data—colors, sounds, shapes, and so on—we can deny the commonsense explanation of their origin and attribute them to some other agency; we may say that the mind generates them as part of its activity or that they are ideas in a supernal mind, called God. This is the position upheld by idealists whose belief is almost a corollary of their initial assumption that the universe should be investigated by first exploring the intellect.

Let us examine this question of objective existence. Logically, there need be no connection between physical object and sense data, but then, also logically, such a relationship need not be ruled out: the problem is whether the weight of evidence inclines to one side or the other. When we examine our beliefs, we find that for some of them we can adduce no proofs whatsoever; we just feel they are right, and we say it is our intuition that makes us know the truth. Some people are more apt to pin their trust to this faculty than others. These individuals attribute many of their notions to it and are quite unmoved, even though these can be disproved by reason. If, however, reason can be thus regarded, then anyone can call his fancy an intuition; any opinion is then possible, and unanimity becomes a mirage. Those who make little use of intuition nevertheless have to fall back on a few elementary ideas taken as axiomatic. One of the laws of thought states that a thing must either be or not be; we are persuaded of it without any proof. Similarly, we are positive that two plus three equals five. Such intuitions are valid, because we can't think how these truths can be false, because they are the necessary foundations of reason itself, because everyone is convinced by them, and lastly—probably the most important consideration—because all our experience confirms and does not contradict them. Among our natural beliefs is the idea that the external world exists, this being the most fundamental and universal of all. Every person, whether child or adult, barbarian or civilized, fool or sage, of whatever place or age, entertains it without being taught, while, after tremendous reflection, only a few philosophers question it. Such an instinctive belief cannot be dismissed without an impressive array of adverse arguments. The behavior of animals indicates that they, too, feel its force. Even the proposition that two plus three equals five is unknown to a child without some instruction, but this is not so with the belief in external reality. As philosophers have a propensity to fall back on ultimate instinctive beliefs, it is strange that they should reject this most elementary of all with such apparent airiness. Common sense bids us to subscribe to such a universal notion; at least it is better to broach a metaphysical inquiry with the seemingly objective. One's quest may lead to strange conclusions, and the real may be found very unlike the visible, which, however, is not cast away without sufficient justification, without showing its relationship to the real.

The method of investigation, which I name the *Spherical Method*, is a species of connection. The method of connection, or the Connective Method, is applicable to all knowledge, is of the very essence of knowledge. We have a natural tendency to connect or link ideas to form a consistent system, to arrange things into a pattern. The ultimate intention of every type of knowledge is to have the data fall into an orderly array. Commonsense knowledge registers a world of objects in space; scientific knowledge binds them together as causes and effects; philosophic knowledge grasps the entire universe in a single view. The historian marshals the events of his subject matter and indicates their relationship in a sequence of time; a novelist depicts a section of life or a group of incidents, keeping in view the problem of unity.

The Connective Method follows the nature of reason. What is reason? It is a faculty by which we infer conclusions from the premises or data; we colligate two ideas in a certain necessary association and show that one follows the other. The goal of reasoning is to obtain derived judgments, judgments consequent on others, strict connection being the mode of operation. It is natural that in an attempt to obtain a rational explanation for all existence, the Connective Method should be resorted to instead of one of doubtful validity. The method of opposition, or the Dialectical Method, is its antithesis; this tries to find truth by contradicting an idea with another. It is an inherent paradox: arriving at harmony through opposition. It is based on the presupposition that every idea has an antithesis or that every entity implies another of diametrically opposite character; whether the universe is of this nature may be questioned. In any case, the method sets out with an assumption not naturally suggested to us by observation, intuition, or reason. It is peculiarly adapted to controversy, quibbling, and sophistry; it is the method of debate, not reflection. Hegel has developed it to the point of absurdity with a single absolute comprising a multitude of contradictories.

The Connective Method rests on the character of the universe, which is a systematic whole, with every part harmonizing with every other. The objection may be raised that this view is false or, at least, that it is only an assumption and that the method therefore begins with a precarious hypothesis about the nature of reality. True, this is only a preliminary supposition, but it is suggested to us by our experience. Though we cannot say at the outset whether it is right or wrong, the method does not thereby become invalid. The universe is either a related whole or it is not. If it is, then the method whose aim is connection is the proper one to adopt; if it is not, then the method will break down, and we shall discover one great truth, that reality is chaos. In this latter eventuality, the method will show us what entities are not related and how. The possibility of chaos is not ruled out, and therefore the method does not rest on a gratuitous, preconceived idea.

The Connective Method is scientific. The Inductive Method, the method of science, is a particular type of connection; it is objective, begins with observation, and has for its purpose generalization. Adapted only to observable phenomena and based on the assumption that an inference from known particulars will apply to all particulars of the same class, it is tested by its results and has been remarkably successful. In philosophy, the Connective Method subsumes the scientific; not erected on it, it includes it since the Connective is the more general method. The Spherical Method is the application of the Connective Method to religious philosophy. The aim is the formulation of a self-enclosed system wherein the principles are linked. The name is obtained by analogy. A sphere gives the impression of a perfect whole; every point in its figure is related to contiguous points and is essential to its wholeness, while from the center run the radii, and the points on the circumference are thus related to one point. The method will be used to secure a philosophy that will give the impression of a distinct whole. The doctrines will not be isolated but interconnected and mutually dependent; they will also relate to one central idea. For its full realization, the method presupposes that the universe is a definite unity, but this assumption is not inflexible; should reality be disjointed, it will show its cracks.

The method works by connection. Truth will be attained by endeavoring to link one idea with another, not by placing them in opposition. For this purpose, use is made of induction and deduction, analysis and synthesis. Starting with the external world as revealed in experience, the method tries to locate its general factors and principles and bind them together into a coherent whole. It is a process of penetration from the visible to the invisible, from the surface to what is below. From one central principle it radiates outward, interweaving all facts in an indissoluble completeness.

The method is objective. It is devoted to an examination of the apparently external universe of objects, which we know through direct perception. The inquiry could proceed no further if perceptual judgments were found to be ultimate truths, if on close observation and critical reflection they did not reveal flaws. This is what makes science possible, which will be called to the aid of metaphysics. Since it is only a piecemeal affair, concerned with only a part of reality, philosophy will have to go beyond it. With an objective attitude, one will consider the totality of existence and find in this the true position of the mind. To investigate one's mind first is to go from the little to the great: egoism is good neither for metaphysics nor ethics. Nature cannot be won by such means. Truth is objective: it is plain that an appropriate method should partake of this character. Isn't the fruitfulness of science assignable to the objectivity of its method?

The method is logical. Based on reason, it deduces conclusions in accordance with the rules of valid inference. Deduction is naturally of more account than induction in metaphysical speculation, which deals with general principles and their mutual relations. Knowledge acquired by deduction is not to be belittled. The hostility of mystics can dismissed, while another class of opponents, those who pride themselves on what they designate common sense, are merely endeavoring to maintain their untenable prejudices. Logic is cold, impartial; it must adhere rigorously to the desire for truth and must not degenerate into sophistry. A *non sequitur* argument violates logic; a rhetorical flourish is not reason. Consistency is the proper consequence of logic and must never be overlooked.

The method is critical. It is the peculiar prerogative of philosophy to examine and criticize our beliefs, however self-evident and indubitable they appear. Nothing is too sacred for its inspection, as every idea, however ancient or popular, may be false. No fear of consequences may be considered; a bold attitude is a *sine qua non*. Many beliefs arise through circumstance and are maintained through tradition—they are not thereby rendered invulnerable. It is time to use pure reason as the only criterion of opinion. Criticism does not necessarily connote destruction: it is a means to an end, understanding. The method is said to be critical, not in the special sense applied by Kant to his epistemology, but in that it follows an attitude of free inquiry, untrammeled by authority or established notions, no idea taken for granted.

The method uses sensation, intuition, and reason as the sources of knowledge, the two former directly supplying ideas that must be tested by reason before acceptance. Without sensory experience, the mind would be a total blank, for sensory experience must exist before intuition and reason can exercise their functions. Some thinkers predicate that it is possible to acquire a picture of the universe by deduction from innate ideas, which are but few and can only indicate certain necessary relationships; they are not in a position to reveal objective facts, a function that appertains only to the senses. We have to start with sense data and examine them critically by means of reason. Intuition does not reveal the existence of external objects but only certain necessary truths that are brought to consciousness by sensory experience; the truths are universal and cannot actually be confirmed by sensation, which is limited, and they are also unprovable by reason, being its foundation.

The method uses induction, deduction, analysis, and synthesis. Induction, the conspicuously successful method of science, proceeds from the particular to the general; a number of facts are collected, and a theory is formulated to account for them. It is scarcely the business of philosophy to marshal a multitude of factual phenomena that can be effectively studied only in detail. Scientific concepts are based on such facts, and, if a philosophy makes use of them, it can be said to resort to induction, since, indirectly, it rests on facts, painstakingly accumulated. Induction can also be utilized in the sense that incontrovertible facts are not contradicted. It is true that not all scientific theories are indisputable; the history of science is strewn with the debris of exploded ideas. Herein lie both the strength and weakness of science, the strength because free inquiry functions unhampered by prejudice, the weakness because induction is not conclusive, dealing as it does with a very limited set of cognizable facts; any new discovery is apt to overturn what has hitherto appeared a sound theory. Scientific ideas are not certainties but probabilities; they wear the air of infallibility only so far as our knowledge extends.

Deduction proceeds from the general to the particular; it may also proceed from one truth to another, the latter being as general as the former or even more so. In philosophy, this second type of deduction is more important. The connection between the two truths is some necessary relationship between them; formal logic will show whether the inferences are trustworthy. Deduction, which is pure reason, forms the principal ingredient of the philosophical method, and its importance is great. However, it is dangerous to rely on it exclusively in an investigation of external reality, the trouble being that, if one step is wrong, the others are untenable. In practice, in ratiocination it is common to make assumptions or choose between alternative hypotheses; if the choice is erroneous, the result is disastrous. The dogmatic method, an application of pure deduction, is beset with pitfalls; the clear ideas of Descartes are not clear, and the deductions are often arbitrary. Only in mathematics has deduction evinced its tremendous triumph, but even here, should the axioms that are taken for granted prove false, the entire superstructure collapses; Euclidean geometry, for ages considered infallible, has at long last proven not to be so. Deduction must be supplemented by induction or reference to experience.

Analysis consists of discovering an entity's constituents. It is of best service in chemistry, where objects are broken down into their elements; in reasoning, a complex idea is dissected into simpler ideas. When trying to understand the universe, we must divide it into its natural sections and consider them one at a time. Analysis must be systematic—it will not do to select arbitrarily only a few points for examination. An analysis can be carried out in several stages: an object is first separated into its main divisions, these again into subdivisions, and so on to greater detail. Philosophy is not concerned with minutiae but general principles. To understand the universe, we must grasp its composition, seeking knowledge of its primary divisions and their nature.

Synthesis is the opposite of analysis. It strives to arrange ideas into a pattern so as to form a systematic whole; thus unity emerges from diversity. History is just a synthesis of events disposed in time. Synthesis is necessary for the construction of a system, and the manifold ideas are shown to either emanate from a single idea or be properly associated with one another; an esthetic feeling of harmony is the consequence. Were the universe a chaos, synthesis would be impossible, and the lack of unity and order would make all knowledge sensory and irrational. Synthesis should not be obtained by leaving out inconvenient facts, rendering the picture false; the selective process, which is unexceptionable in a work of art, is misleading in a system of philosophy. A metaphysic does not set out to create but to apprehend what is already in existence; synthesis is its highest task.

Consistency is of great moment in a system and serves as a test; as, however, it can be displayed in a fairy tale, by itself it does not constitute proof. If in a story the separate ingredients can be definitely proven erroneous, then it must be fiction; if none of them is obviously untrue, while some can be substantiated, then so long as the others tally, there is good reason to presume that they also are true. Only in this way is consistency valuable. Inconsistency plainly demonstrates error, if not of the system as a whole, at least of the parts affected. Some persons claim to despise consistency; their admission evinces only their incapacity or their lack of concern for the attainment of truth, they being content with their fancies and prejudices.

Chapter 3
Theory of Knowledge

What is the connection between knowledge and reality? How is it possible for us to obtain cognizance of truth? Are we just juggling with words, or have our beliefs a solid foundation? What, in brief, is the nature of knowledge? This problem is integral to an examination of the nature of existence, though it is not as important. The two subjects are distinct, but it is possible for a writer to derive his ontology almost automatically from his epistemology. The study of method, which is a means to an end, must not be confused with the theory of knowledge, which deals with a peculiar, significant phenomenon.

Kant prioritized the problem, but his interesting answer is of doubtful validity. Deeming it strange that the results of ratiocination should apparently tally so well with observed facts, he concluded that reality is an inchoate mass that, combining with mental properties, presents us with the universe we know. Events appear rational simply because they are products of reason. Noumena are unknowable; phenomena are unreal. A variety of idealism, Kantian transcendentalism makes mind the creator of its world. Can knowledge be explained away in this fashion? His solution only makes mystery more mysterious. What part is played by noumena in the formation of phenomena? Knowledge can correspond only with that part of phenomena contributed by the categories; it need not tally with that contributed by noumena. That is, knowledge need not show absolute correspondence with phenomena, a correspondence substantiated by experience. "Things in themselves" could not be altogether unknowable, for, as categories and phenomena are both known, it should be possible to subtract the former from the latter and arrive at some idea of the residue. If such mysterious entities as noumena can affect the mind, then physical objects as ordinarily understood could do likewise; a certain relationship subsists between mind and matter, and it is not far-fetched to suppose that a satisfactory relationship implies correspondence.

How then do the inferences of reason accord so closely with physical events? Mind and matter exist in the same world; their mutual influence is undeniable if experience is any guide. Mind has always evolved in conjunction with matter. Is it not natural then that their operations should harmonize? The sharp cleavage imagined to exist between the two substances, a cleavage first enunciated by Descartes, is what makes it impossible to believe that they can ever have anything to do with each other; but the demarcation is unwarranted, and all experience refutes it. Facts are known solely via the senses; much of reason is just induction from them, while the remainder is implanted in the mind, whose specific trait is understanding, in order that it may exercise its function of comprehending the universe. The mind does not create.

The three tools of knowledge are sensation, intuition, and reason. Sensation is the primary and most significant element, without which no form of knowledge would be possible. It is through sight, the most important sense, that we are immediately cognizant of a marvelous world of objects disposed in space. The empiricists hold that the mind is a perfect blank until it is imprinted with images, and they believe that sensation is the only factor in knowledge. This is claiming too much, as there must be a faculty capable of interpreting the sense data; nevertheless, there is no doubt that without sensation, the mind would be inactive and could not begin to have knowledge. How does an object produce sensation? The connecting link between the object and the eye is light; in the nervous system, the physical reaction is transformed into a mental sensation. This stage is mysterious, but interaction is not impossible. Influence is common in the material world; for example, the moon produces tides in the sea. We think there is nothing strange in this, for the same substance is affected. If matter and mind are not absolutely dissimilar substances, the capacity of the former to influence the latter ceases to be incredible.

Intuition is an important fact that is liable to be overstressed by mystics and undervalued by scientists. Descartes, in demolishing the whole universe and reconstructing it from his celebrated dictum, *cognito, ergo sum*, commenced with the praiseworthy determination to doubt everything. He proceeded to say that as he was doubting, he was thinking. How was he so certain that he was doubting? One could easily say, "I doubt that I am doubting," and would then be unable to advance a step. Obviously, his intuition is what informed him of the certainty of his self-imposed skepticism. He did not, as he claimed, engage in universal doubt. Intuition convinces us that when we have sensations, we are actually experiencing them. Its scope is limited to a few elementary truths: it cannot give facts regarding the actual existence of external objects. Its deliverances form the bases of reason. Innate ideas or *a priori* principles undoubtedly exist. Propositions like "two and three make five" and "a thing must either be or not be" are self-evident; their certainty cannot be derived from mere experience, which is restricted. If their source is sensation and intuition is absent, then no matter how many instances we can adduce to support them, they would still lack incontrovertibility, since it would be possible for other instances as yet undiscovered to violate them. The grave defect of intuition is that it is not easy to distinguish its deliverances from other convictions erroneously attributed to it; the irrational tend to maintain that their beliefs are due to its power and even claim that in them the faculty is specially developed. An intuitive belief must be confirmed by experience to remove all doubt, to distinguish it from a false conviction, to separate certain certainty from uncertain certainty. Genuine intuition is universal, simple, and clear and is not at loggerheads with the facts of experience or the deductions of reason.

Reason, the most admirable of human faculties, is the determining factor in the separation of truth from error. Its basis is intuition, and its material is sensation. It starts with a few axioms or self-evident ideas; without the phenomena known through the senses, its scope would be circumscribed. The essence of reason is the interconnection of ideas in an inevitable relationship. One idea, the inference, is deduced from another, the premise; reasoning consists of a collection of premises and inferences relating to a specific topic. The rules of reasoning are formulated in logic, which is divided into deductive and inductive; the former works by deducing one idea from another, while the latter works by generalizing from collections of facts. Theoretically, deductive logic can produce truths of absolute certainty; practically, with the exception of mathematics, which is the perfect example of pure reason, its conclusions are apt to err, for frequently the initial premises are dubious and the inferences are *non sequitur*. On the other hand, inductive logic gives only probable results, as facts are inexhaustible and theories from limited assortments are not strictly irrefragable. However, the scientific method justifies its adoption and proclaims its utility. The fact is, deductive logic works in a vacuum, while its rival revolves around a mass of concrete material—sense data. Though each type of reasoning has its appropriate place in philosophy, deduction is more important, concerned as it is with general principles.

On examining the various branches of knowledge, we find that each contains in different proportions sensation, intuition, and reason; no knowledge is absolutely devoid of any of these components. The importance of sensation goes without saying. Intuition, even in science, is indispensable; the idea that a theory formulated by considering a limited number of specific cases will apply to all similar cases can be corroborated by neither reason nor observation. What about reason? When we refer to rational knowledge, we mean that reason is the determining factor; when we talk of irrational knowledge, we refer to its preponderance of arbitrary statements for which there is some show, however slight, of reason. Even a primitive tribesman who weaves a fairy tale to explain a solar eclipse bases his belief on reason by analogy, which happens to be invalid. It is a mistake to imagine that rationalism was a recent growth, when in fact it has existed ever since the emergence of the human race, though its force was extremely weak at first.

We may classify knowledge into three levels, according to the relative proportions of sensation and reason. The first is perceptual knowledge, which every person possesses, even the child and the primitive human; this direct knowledge, often dubbed *commonsense knowledge*, is the immediate result of sensation. The world reveals itself as a pattern, structurally coherent and esthetically pleasing, so much so that it took millennia before people questioned whether it could spell ultimate reality. For practical life, common sense is all important; so far as action is concerned, it may be regarded as sufficient. Its beauty is that there is little room for divergence of opinion. This is sad for idealists, who are so anxious to prove the fallibility of the senses that all normal eyes see in the same way; for example, one man does not behold a tiger, which another mistakes for an elephant. Unfortunately, perceptual knowledge, in spite of its universal character, has been found to disagree with primary truth; it is a curious illusion produced by the nature of perception. One does not see objects directly but only their representations: strictly speaking, what we are experiencing resembles a "magic shadow show," but common sense identifies the images with solid external objects, making life orderly and comprehensible. To discover actuality, we must begin with the commonsense world.

The next stage is scientific knowledge. Through closer observation, patient experimentation, and logical reasoning, the ingredients of the commonsense world were found not to harmonize, and a new pattern was gradually built up. This second world, below the surface, has been revealed with a good measure of success, mainly in the material scheme of things; moreover, it consists of a vast mass of facts and principles that, though not contradictory, are not shown to emanate from a single entity. Science has proven the most trustworthy branch of knowledge; reason and observation are in balanced proportions. Facts are collected and conclusions drawn; these are labeled *hypotheses, theories,* or *laws* in ascending order of certitude. Superstition has largely vanished, and life has advanced by leaps and bounds in respect to safety and material happiness. The scientific method has extended into subjects not dealing with the physical realm, including psychology, sociology, history, and so on, though the achievements are still controversial and lack finality. Science is indispensable; it can never disappear. Its defects are that it is concerned with specific problems and its method is inapplicable to unraveling the mystery of the universe as a whole.

The third and highest level of knowledge is the philosophical: the aim is to penetrate below the scientific world and discover a single entity pervading the totality of existence, including mind and matter, or at least to unify the sum of things. Reason plays the major role; many thinkers go so far as to spurn observation altogether. That reason should be paramount is inevitable, since the subject matter deals with general principles that are knowable only through deduction. However, it is dangerous to neglect observation in view of the fact that curious fancies can be framed behind a façade of plausible rationalization: just as science is connected with common sense, so philosophy must be connected with science. The three stages of knowledge bear a certain relationship to one another; they are not water-tight compartments. If common sense is wrong, science can demonstrate the how and wherefore of it; if science is in error, philosophy should point out its nature. Philosophic reasoning is stricter than the scientific, more logical, and it revolves around problems of deeper mystery, wider range, and more tremendous import.

What is truth? Plainly it is just knowledge that accords with fact; truth is existence. Error is belief that has no foundation in actuality. It is indefensible to maintain a false opinion on the grounds of its utility; those who say that even if there were no God, it would be expedient to make use of him as a hypothesis run full tilt against the very spirit of philosophy. The universe may be at bottom evil; if so, the fact must be acknowledged. The romanticist who sees a river of gold where there is only mud is as ludicrous and ineffective as Don Quixote. While in fiction it may be no worse than an idle pastime to bemuse oneself with picturesque dreams, in real life, this is fraught with peril. The thinker must be on guard against mesmerization by a beautiful fancy. In the realm of practical affairs, truth is given the cold shoulder from a different motive, self-interest, and the ensuing harm is incalculable; in politics, the sin is most conspicuous. The inveterate foes of truth are laziness, wrong sense of esthetics, prejudice, passion, self-interest, ignorance, malice, false loyalty to nation or group, invalid ratiocination, and irrational methods of approach toward the riddle of the universe.

How is it possible to distinguish truth from error? How can we tell whether a belief is right or wrong? An idea can be known to be right if it can be verified by observation or if it is logically deduced from another idea held to be true. In philosophy, consistency is the chief test; hence the necessity of a complete system that will account for the totality of experience. Such a system must be coherent, and one strong point in favor of the truth of a principle is its harmony with the rest of the system. Several theories can seemingly account for the same set of phenomena, but it will be found that very often facts are distorted or ignored. Consistency, of course, it not by itself a proof of truth, for if an assumption is erroneous, a logical deduction must follow suit. The geometry of Euclid is erected on axioms and postulates that, if they do not accord with reality, would make it an elaborate fiction, of interest only as a beautiful and ingenious exercise in logic. But if consistency is not a sufficient test of truth, inconsistency assuredly spells falsity, perhaps not of the entire system, but of those parts not in agreement with those that are true.

Knowledge, which is its own aim, is the mind's highest function, and in its genuine form it means comprehension of reality. Agnosticism and skepticism are contradictory to the nature of the mind. How should the mind exist if it could not possibly realize its *raison d'être*? One of the oddities of philosophers is that they are prone to reach a Socratic conclusion, such as that all we know is nothing can be known; they don't seem to feel that if such were the case, then they must have wasted their lives in vain pursuit. In spite of their opinion, they do not give up their futile quest and devote themselves to pleasure or business; evidently, they have become bereft of all sense.

One of the great historic controversies is between empiricists, who maintain that all knowledge comes from sensation, and rationalists, who believe in innate ideas or *a priori* principles. Locke regards the mind as a blank tablet on which objects imprint their images; knowledge consists of sense data and the operations of the mind on them. The fact that he is forced to add reflection as a factor in the acquisition of knowledge makes his theory break down. The mind possesses faculties like reason and memory, which enjoy certain powers; as they are not products of sensation, the mind is not therefore a perfect blank at the start. These powers may not be strictly ideas, that is, ideas of external truths, but they must bear some relationship to truth or they could not digest it. *A priori* principles are elementary truths essential to the comprehension of the world, and they cannot be the results of sensation but must precede it. No number of instances can make us feel more convinced that a thing must either be or not be; induction cannot beget unquestionable certitude. The fact that an axiomatic truth is first brought to light by actual experience does not invalidate the claim that the mind already possesses it in latency.

The faculties include intuition, reason, memory, and imagination: they are instruments of mental activity. Memory is the retention of experience; theoretically, no experience should vanish. What a strange thing memory is, what a tremendous storehouse! Imagination is the power of forming images that either have no counterparts in actuality or have counterparts that one has not yet met. It is the only genuinely creative faculty, for its images are pure products of the mind. It is looked at askance—first, because it appears to be more developed than other faculties, and, second, because it is common to mistake its deliverances as enjoying objective truth. As a matter of fact, its contribution to the acquisition of knowledge is not negligible. When a thinker evolves a new idea, be he philosopher or scientist, it is assumed that he discovers it gradually from prolonged ratiocination or observation, but this is far from the case. Reason is not likely to lead anywhere if one has no definite goal. The thinker first imagines an idea, which may not be out of simple imagination but suggested by experience, still not yet known to be a verity, then proceeds to test it by reason. Without this creative imagination, originality is impossible.

Emotion exerts great influence on the acquisition of knowledge. The type of opinion one sports is determined in considerable measure by sympathy and antipathy: for no manifest reason, anger follows when one is confronted with certain notions, which are then not likely to be given due consideration. Much of this emotional reaction is based on prejudice and self-interest; pure truth is seldom pursued for its own sake. As a motivating force, emotion can both aid and hinder the attainment of knowledge. On the whole, it is useful only for putting into practice an idea already established by reason, not for the development of knowledge, for which purpose a dispassionate attitude is best.

Knowledge is humanity's greatest treasure, not to be compared with any other of our possessions; it would not be so if it were unrelated to truth, if it were not the link between diminutive humanity and the colossal universe. It is amazing that, were it not a familiar fact, it would be impossible to give credence to its existence. That it should be difficult to attain, that it should be beset with error, that the ordinary person is indifferent or hostile to it, does not depreciate its paramount importance. It can mirror reality, which need not be unknowable or distorted. It smacks of indolence to predicate that the workings of the universe are so mysterious that they must forever remain a sealed book; it is illogical to use reason to prove that the universe is irrational, to know that truth is unknowable, to be certain that certainty is unattainable. It is as arid to be a skeptic as to repose on an imaginative dogma. It is right to strive to explain the sum of things, and, even if the quest is fruitless now, it may succeed eventually. This is not wishful thinking and groundless optimism; why should reason exist if it were never to fulfill its objectives?

Chapter 4
Experience

The sources of experience are the senses, without which the universe must be a closed book. In trying to apprehend reality, we must commence the investigation with an analysis of experience, which is the most obvious fact to consciousness. To begin with, it is subjective and personal; it is dangerous, however, to examine it on this basis. The first problem is whether it can be given a character of objectivity and universality.

I am conscious: this is an elementary fact. I cannot doubt the existence of my consciousness or I cannot proceed any further. This is not rational proof, for no such vindication is available; but the intuitive conviction can be corroborated indirectly. It is plain that reason cannot disprove it, and the consequences of the assumption do not contradict it. As an illustration of an untenable supposition, assume that fairies exist, beings who are visible and have relationships with people and things. None of us has ever seen them, and no phenomenon is known to be affected by them. The consequences do not confirm the premise, which is therefore false. In the case of consciousness, there is nothing to nullify the proposition: my consciousness is a self-evident fact.

I am aware of sense data; I am conscious of a succession of images. How do I know they exist? I feel certain they do through my awareness; in fact, my conviction arises from intuition. As in the case of consciousness, their existence is not susceptible to direct proof, but in the same way it can be corroborated. Take them away, and what is left? Consciousness becomes a vacuum. My sense data appear to exist. If I assume they do, I meet with no difficulties; if I do not, then I am driven to account for the illusion, an impossible task. This is a case where intuition cannot be refuted.

What are sense data? They are vivid images, in multitude so great that they defy tabulation. Pondering them, certain points emerge:

1. They depend on the condition of the receptive organ, the eye, and the existence of light.

2. They do not present an impression of chaos, unrelated to one another, but fall into groups, the images of each bearing such close resemblance that they are attributed to one object, which has such a degree of permanence that it is capable of eliciting what appears to be the same images at different periods of time.

3. The objects are felt to exist externally, independent of the consciousness, arranged in space.

4. Each object is not a unique specimen; many are extremely similar. Hence they are regarded as belonging to the same class.

5. Each object has a number of qualities. For example, I have before me what is called a book, which I observe is oblong, small, compact, blue, and motionless. All objects possess factors like shape, size, solidity, rest or motion, and color. These qualities display many variations; an object must have a shape, but this may be square, round, cylindrical, elliptical, and so on. Thus we find that though sense data are multitudinous, order is introduced into them by classifying them into objects, which fall into classes and are definable in terms of a few qualities.

Sense data recognized through vision are the most important, though the senses of hearing, smell, taste, and touch provide other varieties that are also allocated to the same objects as known through sight. Through my ears, I find that a sound may be loud or low, shrill or deep, melodious or discordant, and I can associate it with a particular object, such as a piano or violin; door or vehicle; dog, cat, or horse;

and even an individual man. With my nose I can distinguish between fragrance and foulness and can tell the source of an exhalation. My tongue discerns every degree of sweetness, bitterness, sourness, and saltiness. With my fingertips and skin I can note whether an object is soft or hard, smooth or rough, and can feel heat and cold. Sound, smell, taste, and texture are regarded as qualities in the same way as shape and color.

Other kinds of images are of similar character to, but distinguishable from, sense data; they comprise those created by the imagination and existing in dreams. Imaginative pictures are alterable at will, are indistinct, and do not convey the impression of objectivity. Dream pictures are chaotic, fleeting, and seldom repetitious, and they cannot be deliberately experienced. These two types are separated from sense data in that they do not harmonize with the world of sight; neither are they in themselves coherent.

The existence of my sense data is indubitable, for they are directly present to my consciousness. Two problems connected with them need elucidation. First, do they have objective existence? Do they exist only in my consciousness, or do they exist outside me? Second, are they present in other units of consciousness, or am I the only person enjoying them? My instinctive belief is that they are objective facts and that they arise in other persons. These two convictions are not in themselves sense data and, though instinctive, are to be regarded as judgments; hence they cannot be taken as true without additional reflection.

No two sense data are absolutely identical. In actual experience, I never see in one image the whole of an object or one object alone; I see larger or smaller portions of different objects lying in the field of vision, forming a composite picture. From a number of these pictures, I sort out a number of objects with what I believe are their true qualities. It is a fact pointed out by every philosopher that images of the same object may give different accounts of its qualities; for example, a square table appears rhombic when viewed from a corner. Hence, the images must be subjective; were they otherwise, they could not be unlike for the same object.

Though sense data are subjective, do they have any relationship to external entities? Are they pure products of consciousness? Their production is not accompanied by mental effort; they are not alterable at will and are tremendously steady; though the eyes are directed at an object a thousand times, it gives the same impression of identity. The images are extremely distinct, and the objects appear external. The totality of images is coherent; if the pictures were fabricated by the consciousness, then the memory would have to be vastly stronger than it is to retain such an enormous collection. Each fact by itself is not conclusive proof, but all go to show that sense data must be excited by external entities.

The scientific account of vision confirms this. Light traveling from the direction of an object strikes the eye, producing a motion in the nervous system, and an image results. In the formation of the image, the mind is passive. The sum total of physical factors, including the object, light, the eye, and various attendant conditions, is sufficient to explain the nature of the image; the mind makes no contribution whatsoever. The fact that the object does not always appear the same is due to modifying factors that can be explained. If the image were created by the mind, light, the eye, and so on are clearly superfluous, and how they come to give the illusion of existence and association with the image needs explanation, which is a hopeless task.

It is much easier and simpler to assume the actuality of matter, for innumerable facts would become inexplicable otherwise. Take, for example, the phenomenon of recurrence: whenever I return to my house, I find the identical door, and I do not expect to behold a dragon instead. If it were only an idea, I see no reason why it should constantly recur, why at least once or twice it might not be replaced by another. Ideas are notoriously erratic, and they easily vanish, but this is not the case with sense data. Only when I assume that my pen truly exists, irrespective of the number of times I direct my eyes toward it, am I confronted with the same appearance. If we are going to have any knowledge at all, we should not reject a simpler theory that can explain things for a more tortuous one that can't.

The illusions of the senses can be accounted for and the real distinguished from the false by showing the relationships between them. Take the example of the railroad tracks previously cited: their apparent convergence is easily ascribed to distance. If a room has a constant temperature, yet we feel warm when we have just entered it from the cold, and cool when we have just been standing beside a furnace, we know why its heat affects us differently. We behold the sun traveling from east to west, an appearance belied by scientific discovery, which can account for it in a comprehensible way. It is the specific function of science to demonstrate how a particular image does not correspond with its object; it does not just jump to conclusions about reality without showing its connection to appearance. If we think of a physical object and its sense datum as related but with intervening factors, we can understand how they do not exactly tally. We can point to conditions like light, distance, the condition of our receptive organs, and so on, and we can find that the discrepancy between object and image varies proportionally to their influence.

So far, I have been considering only my consciousness and the existence of objects that occasion my sense data. Do other units of consciousness exist? Among the objects I see is my body. I am likewise aware of other bodies that look and behave in much the same way; I hear sounds issuing from them that I associate with certain sense data. I therefore legitimately conclude that inside these bodies are units of consciousness capable of experiencing sense data. From my observation, I infer that there is a horde of other beings possessing consciousness and sensation.

We have now arrived at the conclusion that there are two types of entities: the agent experiencing sensation and the external object; the former is termed *mind* and the latter, *matter*. Matter consists of objects instrumental in the production of sense data; mind comprises a collection of conscious units. For the moment, we will leave out the consideration of their true nature but consider their palpable characteristics. It is obvious that they possess dissimilar properties. Matter is the object; mind is the subject. The mind apprehends matter. Their properties appear so dissimilar that Descartes made a sharp distinction between them, regarding them as absolutely different in nature—a postulate that exercised a cataclysmic effect on all subsequent philosophy, giving rise to its principal systems. Matter is more extensive than mind and gives an impression of greater substantiality.

We will now consider in more detail the contents of experience, assigning the phenomena to their appropriate departments of mind and matter. The first and elementary stage of classification is based on the simple and direct knowledge of common sense: the validity of this knowledge will be determined by successive analyses.

Consciousness reveals sense data supplied through the channels of sight, hearing, smell, taste, and touch; these sense data, which are engendered involuntarily and continuously as long as the senses function, point to a world of external objects. The faculty for the reception of sense data is sensation, by means of which they are combined and interpreted to form objects fitting into a coherent scheme. This cognitive function is spontaneous, direct, and simple. Sensation is of primary import to the mind, which, without it, would cease to have any real function. It is the link between matter and mind, though it does not exist outside the mind or in matter but is part of the mind itself. Through it, matter may be said to have a second existence, duplicated in the mind: a physical object strangely comes to reside in another realm.

Outside sensation, we are aware of certain mental powers; we can produce the ideas comprised in intuition, reason, memory, and imagination. Intuition creates ideas by direct action; reason produces notions by an arduous chain of connection; memory recalls images previously experienced; imagination fashions pictures that may have no counterparts in reality. They sit in the brain and work over the materials furnished by sensation, of which they are not independent. In the absence of these faculties, experience would consist of a succession of transitory images that would not enable us to penetrate into the nature of truth or to obtain any genuine knowledge. They are to sensation what machinery is to the raw materials of production.

A type of experience that has no reference to ideas consists of feelings, emotions, and passions, which, located in the skin and various organs, comprise such feelings as hunger, pleasure, pain, hope, despair, love, hatred, shame, anger, and so on. Pleasure and pain are two principal feelings, so connected with the mind that one or the other accompanies every mental experience to a greater or lesser degree. These phenomena express relationships to objects—conscious reactions indicative of value.

They are not particularly useful in the search for truth but are of great account in practical life, supplying it with its motives and urging us to undertake a diversity of tasks. It is the habit of thinkers to deprecate them, and a philosophy like the Stoic tries to suppress them. However, human existence would be mutilated without them.

Lastly, there is life, which we do not perceive and is not a sense datum but of which we are aware. Found only in a limited section of the material world, in vegetables, animals, and human beings, it cannot be classed along with the physical qualities, since it is not sensible, not universal, and fundamentally different from them; on the other hand, it resembles mental properties that are found only where it abides. Its most obvious differences from other mental phenomena are that it exerts greater influence on matter and can exist apart from them in vegetables. It must be regarded as part of the mind, one of its traits; I believe it is erroneous to hold it as standing by itself, neither mental nor material. Consciousness disappears when it is extinguished; the connection is too intimate for them to be distinct entities. It is not commonly associated with the mind, because this tends to be viewed as the substance that engenders thought, and the vegetable, though it lives, evidently is not capable of thinking. It is also distinct from matter, as, unlike other physical properties, it is not measurable and does not necessarily coexist with them. But there is no reason why the definition of *mind* should not be extended. It is incredible that the animal body should contain two other substances within it; but, if life is not a substance, what is it? In any case, in classifying phenomena it is best to include it under mind as its resemblance to mental properties is indubitable.

To recapitulate, the mind consists of consciousness, sensation, the faculties, the emotions, and life. Its investigation is not strictly susceptible to scientific methods, and it is still largely a mystery; psychology in its present state is untrustworthy.

Turning to the material realm, and for the present considering it from the commonsense point of view, we may divide it into the following divisions:

I	**SKY** Containing the sun, moon, planets, stars, and so on.

II	**EARTH**
	
	1. Inorganic objects
	
	    a. Atmosphere—with clouds, lightning, winds, and so on.
	
	    b. Land—with hills, rocks, minerals, metals, and so on.
	
	    c. Water—with seas, rivers, lakes, springs, and so on.
	
	2. Organic objects
	
	    a. Vegetables
	
	    b. Animals
	
	    c. Human beings

This elementary classification is based on primary sense data and is not subjected to close investigation. The outstanding fact is that, earthly inhabitants as we are, almost all our sensations are derived from the phenomena of this world. What this amounts to is that our sensible knowledge, though extensive, deals with but a tiny fraction of the universe, and when we proceed either in science or philosophy to make judgments deemed true of all existence, we are postulating that terrestrial phenomena are typical of the entire sum of things. This I take to be the boldest of inductive assumptions.

Some facts, discernible by observation, may be noted of matter. Every object is an aggregate of qualities like extension, size, shape, color, smell, and so on. A sensible thing is not changeless, with all its qualities remaining forever the same; what is round may change into square, big into small, yellow into red. Transformation is ceaseless: solid ice melts to form liquid water, which evaporates into gaseous steam. One object may seem to disappear altogether and another rise out of nothing. An object is seldom homogeneous but has different parts; a tree is not identical in every respect throughout its entire extent but is made up of roots, trunk, branches, leaves, and flowers. As matter of fact, an object may be regarded as composed of diverse objects; the more complex it is, the greater the number it contains, the combination being necessary to endow it with its distinctive character.

Two peculiar phenomena do not form part of material bodies, but such bodies exist and move in them: space and time. Space has the three dimensions of length, breadth, and depth and looks more negative than positive, more akin to nothing than something. It is known first through the empty intervals between visual objects. That an object occupies space is immediately recognizable from the fact that when it moves, the position it occupied is found to be space, and what was emptiness is now filled up by its bulk. Space is homogeneous; so is time, which moves in one continuous line. Time is not as obvious as space, for it is not discernible; neither are we directly conscious of it. Belief in its existence involves an elementary commonsense judgment based on change. Because a body alters its character gradually and we experience a succession of days and nights, we conclude that time is accountable. Our memory informs us of past events, our present experiences being different. Time has only one dimension, and we divide it into past, present, and future, purely a relative division, for the future will become the past. All material objects exist in space and move along the road of time.

We have been surveying objects from the commonsense point of view; for practical purposes, the scheme is serviceable, and we can live out our lives without much trouble. Unfortunately, regarding truth, the knowledge is untenable; under close investigation and rational examination, many flaws and inconsistencies appear. Science steps in to remedy this and to present a truer picture; its findings should be accepted unless there are strong reasons they should not be. Philosophy should harmonize with it, though not necessarily with every particular theory. This is possible, for scientific ideas are piecemeal affairs, not sacrosanct or irrefutable, subject to constant revision; by their nature, they are probabilities rather than certainties.

Science divides the universe into groups of phenomena that are studied separately under the headings of mathematics, physics, chemistry, astronomy, geology, biology, and so on. The aim is not the awareness of a mass of individual concrete objects but the unraveling of the laws underlying the behavior of phenomena. Mathematics is invaluable, and measurement constitutes the ideal part of mathematics. Of prime importance is the concept of cause and effect: every event has a predecessor and a successor; no object comes from nothing and passes into nothing. A quantity of matter, irrespective of how it is transformed, remains the same: this fact is embodied in the Law of Conservation of Matter. No factor is taken into account except for what is present in the physical realm.

The most momentous discovery undoubtedly relates to the size of the universe, which comprises an incredible multitude of huge bodies floating in space—the earth becomes insignificant. This immense amount of matter may not be associated with the mind, which appears to be the prerogative of the sublunary world alone. The multitudinous array of objects resolves into about a hundred elements, which are composed of atoms, and these in turn are composed of electrified particles like electrons and protons in violent motion. A single entity, electricity, whose nature is mysterious, appears to be at the basis of matter.

In sensory experience, objects are resolvable into qualities, which in science do not occupy the chief place of interest. Many philosophers distinguished between primary and secondary qualities, a distinction that science has accepted. The former comprise nearly all those perceived by the eye, such as extension, size, shape, solidity, number, and motion, which are held to exist as integral to the objects; while the latter, with the conspicuous exception of color, are those known through the other senses, such as smell, sound, taste, and texture, and are said to reside only in the mind. This differentiation is invalid. Color appears as objective as shape, and the same arguments that claim truth for the one apply equally to the other. Science accepts the distinction because its method is inapplicable to secondary qualities; it is not easy to measure a smell or a taste. In any case, it has not concerned itself much with them. Likewise, it does not consider problems like meaning, value, and beauty; but neglect is not to be confused with nonexistence. Why is color a mental property? The reflection of light rays of different lengths produces varied color sensations, but reflection does not bear the remotest resemblance to color; hence color is deemed subjective. This cannot be the explanation of the origin of color—simply because reflection is not color. The connection must be explained otherwise: color is inherent in the object, and reflection is the mode of transmission.

We now come to the problems of philosophy that are suggested by sensory and scientific experience. What is existence? What is the nature of matter? What is the nature of the mind? What is the relationship between these two substances? Are there any other substances? What is the origin of the universe? What is its end? Does the universe form a harmonious entity? These and other fundamental questions are what make philosophy distinctive; Plato said that the philosopher is the spectator of all time and all existence. From what has been noted of experience, it is variegated, manifold. Science has shown the possibility of reducing it to a number of basic truths and giving it unity; but science is restricted in scope, does not deal with experience as a whole, and does not penetrate to the most basic principles. The task of philosophy is unique, making it the most important of inquiries.

Chapter 5
Entity

The most fundamental problem, which has never received due consideration, is this: "What is the explanation of the existence of entity?" An *entity* is defined as what is really in existence. Using the term in a collective sense, I refer to the entire universe, including everything in being, matter, mind, space and time, substance and quality, the first cause, and so on. This problem is not identical to the common one of the nature of the universe; it is not a question of the origin of things or even of their meaning. About this one crucial fact of existence it asks: "What is existence?" Things exist—this is a momentous truth. They might have lasted from eternity, they might have come from God; in any case, we still insist on wondering why they do not vanish.

The origin of any particular object can be traced. Science does it with the notion of cause and effect, the process of analysis continuing until we ultimately arrive at the beginning of the cosmos. Three possible solutions present themselves:

1. The cosmos is eternal.

2. It proceeded from a first cause, which is eternal.

3. It issued from nothingness.

Irrespective of the answer we adopt, we come upon the problem of existence. If the cosmos is eternal, what makes it so? If there is a first cause, how does it exist? If the cosmos arose from the void, how did it come into being?

It is impossible to assign an extraneous cause of the universe to explain its existence, for the cause itself needs explanation. The reason for existence must be sought within the universe itself. Such being the case, there is only one possible answer: the universe contains a principle of existence. This may be expressed in various ways: the universe exists by virtue of its nature, or the entity exists because it must; or, everything possesses an Existential Principle. The idea that an object has necessary existence does not imply that it persists in the same fashion, changeless; but its components will always exist in some form and will not vanish. An individual lives and after a period dies, but the substance of which he is made does not cease to be; his mode of existence changes, but his substance is not destroyed. Existence must be distinguished from life and from any specific form of being. The proofs for this theory of an Existential Principle may be enumerated.

1. Tracing one entity to another, we are bound to arrive at a First Entity. How does it exist? Not from a cause outside it and logically prior to it, or it would not be the first cause. The cause must lie within itself.

2. Existence *ipso facto* needs an Existential Principle, or the entity could not exist.

3. The hypothesis is necessary to explain existence; there is no other alternative.

4. If there is no Existential Principle, then an entity need not necessarily have existence, which must therefore be an accident. Nothing is known to come into being this way; accident would logically make for a chaotic universe, a notion belied by observation.

5. The characteristic of mind is consciousness; the instinct to live is an incontrovertible fact and is only the Existential Principle become conscious. Life can end; the principle loses consciousness but still exists, for an organism that perishes merely transforms into another form.

6. Were the principle absent, an object could arise from nothing and vanish into nothing, a notion repugnant to sense and falsified by science. Existence is evidently not necessary for a

thing that either emerged from or passes away into emptiness; it is because an entity must necessarily exist that such events do not happen.

This religious philosophy is given the name *Entitarianism*, for it is founded on a doctrine of entity, which assigns the existence of entity to its nature: the basis of all entity is the Existential Principle. This tenet is the point from which the others radiate. The existence of entity is the central problem of philosophy, the most stupendous fact of the universe. The nature or composition of the universe is secondary to the astonishing circumstance that it exists, and understanding why it does not disappear is the most important of tasks. The cause is intrinsic to it, not acting from outside. Entitarianism describes a philosophy whose central idea revolves around the quintessential characteristic of entity.

As no entity can emerge from nothing or terminate in nothing but can only change its form, the total collection of all entities remains constant, a fact that may be designated the *Law of Conservation of Energy*. This subsumes all the scientific laws of conservation, such as those of matter and energy; it embraces everything, including matter and mind. No entity is destructible; the idea of necessity attached to existence produces certain consequences. The origin of the universe must be attributed to an eternal substance, but it could not have sprung out of nothing at the bidding of a god, however omnipotent. Matter and mind might change but cannot vanish into nothing; even a thought must have an antecedent and a consequent.

It behooves us to examine the nature of entity. We have employed the term *mind* to describe the collection of properties internally revealed in consciousness, including sensation, the faculties, and emotions, as distinguished from the other set of phenomena, such as shape, size, and color, which characterize matter. What is a physical object or an individual mind?

All we directly know about an object is its qualities. Does it consist then only of these? A quality is usually conceived of in relation to a base; a shape is not supposed to hang suspended in space by itself but belongs to a solid substratum. An object is composed of substance and quality, the former, which is invisible and mysterious, being regarded as more important and possessing a greater measure of reality.

Material substance, absolutely different from quality and thoroughly incomprehensible, is a pure postulate. It is unimaginable how two completely dissimilar entities could relate to each other so closely. They are not separable; it is impossible to conceive of substance existing alone. What is the relationship between substance and extension? Is it conceivable that the former does not occupy space? If it does, then isn't its possession of a quality, which is defined as occupancy of space, precluded? Size is described as a mode and substance as the substratum; does the mode lie on top of the substratum or permeate it? In truth, substance is very unsubstantial, the profoundest of mysteries.

The same difficulty ensues when the popular conception of mind is considered. All I ever experience of my mind is seemingly transitory ideas and feelings. It is taken for granted that thought cannot float unanchored. A substance is posited as the medium in which it operates; mental substance, for which the word *mind* is used, is said to be totally unlike material substance. Descartes held it as axiomatic that because he could think, he enjoyed the possession of a mind, meaning an indivisible unit of mental substance. What is this substance? Mysterious, unknowable, different from thought, it is a gratuitous assumption; as in the case of matter, the two entities, mental substance and thought, bear no mutual resemblance, and their intimate union is unimaginable.

We find ourselves facing the difficulty of comprehending two dissimilar substances, both equally mysterious, though they elicit belief from the need for providing anchorages for quality and idea. They are regarded as unlike, apparently because their properties are so. This difference has been the principal stumbling block of modern philosophy, leading to the diverse theories of dualism, monism, materialism, idealism, and transcendentalism, each of which presents a respectable array of arguments. Thought and quality differ but not as much as their two substrata, which, as long as they are conceived of as they presently are, will continue to bewilder when we consider the palpable interaction of mind and matter. It is strange to think that sages have postulated two unknown substances and then argued over them for centuries without reaching any solution commanding general assent! Truly we wrangle over words!

There is no reason for maintaining the notion of substance, and a fresh explanation of the nature of entity is feasible. It is evident that if deprived of their common base, the qualities of an object need not maintain any association; for example, motion might be wandering about freely by itself. The same applies to ideas, which arise in a person and have mutual relationships. The difficulty is solved by the concept of the Existential Principle, which maintains the physical object or the conscious unit by binding its qualities or ideas together.

The Existential Principle is not a substance but a property, as shape is. Appertaining to both matter and mind, it possesses the cohesive power of binding other constituents to form a unified whole so that the object might exist as such. Like other properties, it has different forms, one for matter and another for mind. Qualities may be described as material constituents, ideas as mental constituents, and the Existential Principle as the basic constituent. When they possess a common constituent, the mutual influence of mind and matter is intelligible; they are not entities of absolutely opposite character.

The idea of an Existential Principle aligns more with the modern scientific theory of the nature of matter than the old-fashioned notion of substance. Matter is said to consist ultimately of electrons, which, whatever they may be, do not appear very substantial but seem more abstract than concrete.

It may be said by way of animadversion that, unlike other properties, the Existential Principle is not given in sensation. This is wrong, for we do perceive the existence of objects and feel positive that they exist; we could not possibly do so if the principle were not present. Existence itself is the principle. Regarding mind, we are aware of the instinct to live, which is the principle floating into consciousness.

Truth can be said to be existence. An idea is true if it corresponds to something that actually exists in the universe; hence the Existential Principle is the principle of truth. However, the terms *existence* and *truth* are not synonymous: *existence* refers to objective reality, while *truth* is more descriptive of knowledge. It is possible to deduce according to the laws of logic propositions that are true in the sense that they are valid, though they may have no actual existence outside the mind; an ethical concept may be true yet not be a property of reality. Nevertheless, truth and existence are closely related.

It is more rational to substitute the Existential Principle for substance, it being understandable, as we see existence. It is the most important, fundamental constituent, serving as a base for the others; it bonds the various qualities. It may be given the name of substance provided it is not confounded with the ordinary notion of something tangible. The word *substance* can also be used to denote the aggregate of constituents composing an entity and also the primary divisions of the totality of reality, like the material and mental worlds.

The word *entity*, which indicates what has real existence, refers to the universe; a primary division of the universe, such as matter or mind; or a unit of being, such as a planet. To be more specific, the universe or everything that has being, a primary division of the universe, and an individual object may be called the totality of entity, a division of entity, and a unit of entity, respectively.

Constituents have forms that, in turn, are revealed in expressions. They are the fundamental types of phenomena composing entities and are not very numerous; examples are shape and emotion. Forms are the ways in which a constituent manifests itself: shape has forms like the sphere and the cube; and emotion's forms include joy and anger. We experience constituents only in their various forms. Constituent and form are not distinct entities existing apart and arbitrarily associated; the latter is merely a variety of the former. Expressions are the individual cases of a constituent appearing in a certain form and are innumerable: shape may display itself as a sphere of which each example is an expression. Expression is just a name given to signify an instance of a form, not a distinct entity joined to it.

Among the constituents are the three principles of harmony, value, and meaning. It is common to regard harmony as not being a property of substance because it is connected only with the aspirations of humanity. Value is often deemed to signify utility and meaning. An egocentric attitude has always been the bane of *Homo sapiens*: many thinkers have reiterated that man is the measure of all things. There is no less reason for believing in the objectivity of the aforementioned constituents than in the primary qualities, though it is indubitable that they are more subject to interpretation. The diversity of judgments of harmony, value, and meaning rests on the activities of the human mind, which is prone to error, experience being a product of the impact of mind on matter.

The harmony constituent is apprehended through reflection; but in the case of matter, it also shows itself as visible beauty. Though our judgment of beauty is largely subjective, it does not follow that beauty does not possess actual existence; it means only that our judgment may be distorted. This case is a little different from what happens in sensory experience where images are not exact replicas of physical objects.

Value is a constituent that determines the position of an entity in the scheme of things, and it may be referred to as *good*. It is absolute, an actual entity, and not merely a judgment arbitrarily imposed on things by human beings.

Meaning as a constituent endows the universe with its *raison d'être*. It signifies that the universe is pregnant with an inner sense, not existing casually or accidentally. It is incredible that the cosmos is purposeless; the mere fact that we are unable to fathom the meaning is no proof to the contrary. Meaning is not identical with aim but includes it, as aim is associated with an evolutionary process that must ultimately attain fruition so that the aim will eventually cease to operate, whereas meaning is eternal; it is ridiculous to imagine that the universe would ever exist without any meaning. As a constituent, meaning, like value and harmony, is objective and absolute, not a human fancy; but again like them, it can be partially or falsely apprehended.

An entity is an aggregate of constituents, not a compound of substance and quality. Some of the constituents, such as the Existential Principle and value, are common to both matter and mind, while others are specific to either, as, for example, extension and shape are peculiar to matter, thought and emotion to mind.

Chapter 6
Matter

To us, the most obvious existing substance is matter, which is instinctively believed to be directly apprehended by the senses. It appears solid, indubitable—not, as described by Shakespeare, "such stuff as dreams are made of." Yet what we really know of it is only the images it engenders in the mind, and these often conform too little to the original; the moon looks larger than any star, completely belying facts. The great task of science is to demolish the illusions of the senses. Still, it is uncalled for to rush to the conclusion, as most philosophers have tended to do, that matter itself is illusion, that only minds and thoughts exist, that there is nothing to choose between the fancies of the dreamer and the objects seen in broad daylight. If phenomena seem what they are not, science can account satisfactorily for the divergence. It is incredible that the mind is sublime enough to conjure up a coherent world of multitudinous images out of nothing or that God considers it less dignified to create matter than to act the part of a perpetual magician, revealing mellifluous streams of pictures to his creatures and deceiving them with the illusion of solid reality.

Matter is often viewed with lofty contempt, apparently in deference to the mind. What warrant is there for such an attitude? A world of marvelous beauty and order deserves veneration. The vilification is attributable to the religious conception of the flesh as the incarnation of evil, which ignores the fact that appetite is a mental sensation. Mind, with its sorrows and hatreds, is just as imperfect as matter. Another cause is evidently mortality. Science can prove that matter never vanishes, but it is in the dark about the destiny of mind. In any case, should the individual soul enjoy eternal bliss while the body meets with total extinction, it would still be sheer egoism to extol the one and condemn the other.

Does matter exist? Berkeley contended that an idea could resemble nothing but another idea and could have no possible relationship to an inconceivable substance. This is palpably fallacious when we consider a picture: a three-dimensional object is represented by a two-dimensional outline, which is hardly to be regarded as matter itself, even though it is recorded on it. A copy of an object is thus seen to be a possibility. What is more logical and natural than that such a representation could be imprinted on the mind? An idea and a picture are both copies, and they represent an object in the same fashion. When we see a photograph, we experience a copy of a copy; if matter does not exist, how do we come to cherish the illusion that we have an idea of a copy of an object? Clearly, pictures are superfluous. With their evidence, however, we find it easy to believe that ideas are copies of material objects; there is no question of impossibility.

In our experience, mind is always associated with matter, which, on the other hand, can stand alone; and there is no evidence that disembodied spirits exist. Again, according to the facts of evolution, the physical universe existed for untold eons before life appeared; the human race is an upstart. It is inconceivable that what preceded in time and is of greater extent should be less real. If the *esse* of matter were *percipi*, as Berkeley maintained, then history would have to be rewritten. It seems impossible to place the evolution of the physical world, or rather the ideas thereof, after that of mind. It is also impossible to understand why mind always appears to exist in conjunction with matter.

Without an objective reference, thought has no meaning; life with its hopes and fears, struggles and triumphs, horrors and failures would appear to be an unwholesome dream. What could be the notion of death? Apparently, it would mean the disintegration of an idea! The idealists immortalize the soul. Its experience should not suffer the violent cleavage it does were merely an idea affected, and there should be neither birth nor death. Imagine our unfolding a chain of ideas about the career of Adolf Hitler and hating them! In effect, we are angry at our own fantasies. To combat them, imagine that other minds are stricken with the same mania and join us to overthrow the idea of the dictator. Playing with shadows is apt to lead to the asylum.

If I do not give credence to external reality, I cannot logically hold that anything exists, save my mind, as my knowledge of other minds is obtained from my perception of their bodies; and if these do not exist, I can hardly maintain that there is a whole world of souls. Nor, to be consistent, can I have faith in an eternal mind, seeing that God is to me only an idea. If it is true that this can resemble only another idea, then it can't be related to an external mind, which is by no means idea itself. In truth, I alone exist. My memory does not go back far, so my mind must have had a definite beginning. From where did it spring? Presumably from nothingness; how this could happen is unintelligible. As it did not exist before, it is possible that it will disappear into the void in the future; moreover, I have ideas of a host of minds arising and disappearing, and these testify that I myself shall vanish. Is it credible that there should be an absolute void disturbed by a tiny momentary ripple of consciousness without cause, effect, or meaning? If matter exists, the universe is intelligible; if it doesn't, mystery piles upon mystery. All reason points to its reality, and only too much preoccupation with the ego disregards external truth.

However, the conception of matter must be revised: the notion of an unknowable substance conjoined with some qualities is untenable. What is material substance? It is incomprehensible how qualities, by their nature absolutely dissimilar, are attached to it; neither by perception nor reason do we have any idea of it. It is a *deus ex machina*, postulated from a false notion of necessity; the independent existence of objects does not require it, and it makes the mutual influence of mind and matter inexplicable.

Matter is the name given to one of the principal divisions of the universe, an entity distinguished by its occupancy of space; it has the dimensions of length, breadth, and depth. It is the extended or spatial entity. It is broken up into masses of various sizes, endowed with changeable qualities, and governed by regular laws. A material object is a distinct portion of matter, big or small, displaying the physical constituents. It is composed of detachable parts and may break up into a number of objects and coalesce with others to form a new object. Matter is lifeless, without consciousness. Science, its proper investigator, finds that it is composed of atoms and, ultimately, electrons. Its constituents include existence, behavior, transformation, space, time, quantity, number, finiteness, extension, mass, force, size, shape, solidity, motion, light, color, sound, smell, taste, texture, heat, harmony, value, and meaning.

Material qualities are known through sensation, though they may not be identical to sense data. Sense data are not the simple products of an object but are affected by physical factors, such as light and the receptive organs, and external conditions, such as distance. The distinction between primary and secondary qualities is unjustifiable: sound and taste reside in objects as much as shape and size. If they are mental properties, they are not erratic, and their variations are explicable in terms of attendant factors. If sound is intimately associated with wavelength, it does not mean that this is its cause and that it is nonexistent; the phenomenon can be likened to the relationship between light and perceptible quality.

Science has made the laws of nature very prominent. What exactly are they? Are they entities like shape and color, or are they mere words describing the behavior of objects? Consider as an illustration one of Kepler's laws of planetary motion, which states that in completing its orbit, a planet takes a periodic time whose square is proportional to the cube of its mean distance from the sun. Why should this be the case? What makes the heavenly body follow such a rule? Is it obeying a law imposed from outside, as individuals submit to governmental decrees for fear of punishment? Nobody would believe this for one moment. The law cannot be outside the object, suspended by itself, for there can be no legitimate relationship between an inanimate world and an assemblage of laws. Neither can the law be nothing, a descriptive expression framed by humans for their own convenience, as it is independent of thought. It must be an entity within the object—and what can this mean but a constituent? As there is not one but many laws governing matter, we conclude that it possesses a constituent that we may call the *Behavior Principle*, and the diverse laws are its forms. The Behavior Principle imparts order to the physical universe: nothing happens by accident. The law of cause and effect is rigorous. Some supposed it to have been destroyed by the unpredictability of the movements of individual electrons, but this is ludicrous. It would be more rational to suppose that the physicist is not equipped to solve this problem than that one or two exceptional instances can nullify a general truth vindicated by innumerable other events.

Change is a familiar phenomenon: it is one of the themes of poetic lament. Youth in all its shimmering beauty soon gives way to haggard age; the water of the ocean streams into fleecy clouds, which coalesce into amorphous masses, change their color from burnished gold into grim gray, and drop rain. Though an object's quality is not discarded altogether, its forms continually alter. How does this come about? Why do the constituents not remain static? They have nothing in themselves to promote transformation. An internal force modifying them is a *sine qua non*; entity is endowed with a transforming principle that acts on the various qualities. The principle is not outside the object but within; through it, the mutual influence between entities is intelligible. When a roller passes over a field, the grass bends and is crushed, but there is no reason why weight should produce motion. When a heavier weight comes into contact with a lighter, one acts on the other, but the transforming principle must be called into play before shape and motion could be affected. When two gases, hydrogen and oxygen, blend in the atomic proportion of two to one, they interact with the help of the principle, and water is the result; how do we account otherwise for the phenomenon? Matter is subject to ceaseless change; no object remains definite. The transforming principle is ever active, each type of action being a form. Nevertheless, the total quantity of matter persists with neither augmentation nor diminution: this is the Law of Conservation of Matter. Evolution is but another name for transformation, and this shows an upward trend; matter proceeds from chaos to harmony.

Time and space are external to objects and do not appertain to any particular one: they form the framework in which matter moves. Nevertheless, they could not exist by themselves; they are real constituents and are not mere nothing. Space has dimensions, and what has properties must be positive. Again, mind does not need space; what is peculiar to a single substance must be its constituent. Nothingness is the negation of existence and cannot appertain to only one particular entity. Time is a continuous line, and it is impossible to imagine how change could take place without it. Moreover, it is capable of remarkably exact measurement, while nothingness could not be subjected to such treatment. Neither can the two constituents be subjective categories. In such a case matter cannot occupy space and would consequently not be matter; nor could it really flow in time, and change would be deceptive. It would be impossible to account for the succession of sense data from a collection of static objects.

All the constituents of an individual object are finite: size, however large, is limited, and so are shape, color, and so on. We cannot talk of infinite sweetness or loudness, save in hyperbole. Infinite elements cannot be conjoined with the finite, and, as size is finite, other elements present in the same entity must likewise be so. What does infinite divisibility mean? A definite quantity cannot be infinitely divisible; mathematical infinities must be regarded as mere words to express ideal concepts, not actual realities. The more difficult problem is the extent of the totality of matter. What we know is only a part, and we have no ground for believing in its illimitability. All the material qualities we know are finite, but this does not preclude the possibility of an infinite quantity. There is no infinite redness, but there may be an infinite amount of color. What this means is that only quantity among all the constituents may be infinite; but is it likely that an infinite element should be associated with a number of finite ones? To say the least, it is improbable; the material universe is finite. If this is the case, then space and time, being constituents, are also finite. The material universe had a definite beginning and will have an end. The sky, which is space, appears to be a hemispherical dome, and the stars, the largest aggregates of matter, are spherical: it would seem that space is a sphere.

Chapter 7
Mind

A cursory consideration of mind is enough to reveal the immense difference from matter, the dissimilarity of their properties. Mind does not possess extension, shape, size, or color, and it has what are denied to matter: consciousness, sensation, and ideas. Though forming a comparatively smaller portion of the universe, mind displays deeper significance: a single unit can contain an entire world. The two substances are so unlike that thinkers have found it hard to reconcile them. In order to circumvent the intricate puzzle of their apparent coexistence and interaction in human beings, thinkers have either suppressed one or the other as nonexistent or deemed them absolutely disparate, explaining their mutual influence as an illusion. This problem has led to the principal modern philosophies.

The actuality of mind is as debatable as that of matter; from a commonsense point of view, even more so. The theory of materialism, the antithesis of idealism, upholds the sole existence of matter and has naturally received a preponderant share of science's blessing. It denies the distinct substantiality of mind, making thought the secretion of the brain. Its great stumbling block is that animate matter has never yet been shown to proceed from the inanimate. If this were true, then all physical objects should be able to think, just as they possess size and shape—thought being manifestly a quality.

Thought does not behave the same way as shape; inconstant, it appears and vanishes mysteriously. Objectively, it is recognized only through physical qualities. It is not transmitted to our consciousness directly through our mental apparatus; we know and guess it through noises and facial expressions that we have learned to associate with it. Subjectively, it is present in our consciousness with remarkable immediacy.

Mind must be regarded as a separate substance, distinct from matter. What is it? It is an entity endowed with the possibility of life and thought. It may be termed the *organic entity*, for it functions only in an organism. An organism is an intimate union of mind and matter behaving as a single entity; the functional association, effected through the property of life, terminates at death. It may also be described as the thinking entity, in contradistinction from matter. Among its constituents are existence, life, behavior, transformation, finiteness, quantity, consciousness, sensation, memory, intuition, reason, imagination, will, feeling, emotion, time, harmony, value, and meaning.

What is the basis of mind? A substance is commonly postulated—quite enigmatical—with its relationship to thought inexplicable. It is distinguished from material substance without a single point of resemblance; explaining how two utterly dissimilar substances could be so closely conjoined in an organism is tough. The Existential Principle offers a solution: the mind is of the same nature as matter, though bearing another form. It is logical to maintain that when associated with unlike qualities, it should undergo modification, for there is no reason why it should not bear a number of forms, as is the case with every other constituent, material or mental. The divergence of form does not alter its essential character, just as shape remains the same type of constituent whether it is round or square. Divergence of form accounts for the mutual influence of mind and matter and explains the possibility of the separate reality of mind, for it endows mind with inevitable existence. It is the basis that binds the various mental constituents together, giving the impression of a single entity.

Life is a strange phenomenon: it makes a lump of inert matter grow and move. Is it unconnected with mind? Plainly, it is not matter, as whatever militates against the concept of mind as a material product is equally applicable to life. If it is not mind either, then it must be a third substance, a highly improbable hypothesis, for if it is hard to understand the association of two substances, it must be even more so regarding three. As life bears close resemblance to mental properties, thought existing only in conjunction with it and fading from our observation altogether at the same time, it must be a property of mind. It is distinct from the Existential Principle, for it is not eternal or universal, does not serve as a base or a binding power, and has a different function, which is to make matter self-acting. Unlike thought, life is not located in any particular part of the body but fills every cell.

Mind is no less governed than matter by innate laws, though these appear vague; that they exist is beyond doubt, however, as psychology attests. As the comparatively new subject advances, the laws of mental behavior are more clearly enunciated; if they were not in control, behavior would be extremely erratic. Only regarding the human mind is their force doubtful; the animal mind is not presumed to act arbitrarily.

Individual minds do not alter in the facile way of matter; they do not drastically change the forms of their constituents. They do not blend themselves as sodium and chlorine do to make a new unit with dissimilar properties, but they retain their identity imprisoned in their organisms. Nevertheless, they are also subject to transformation; their constituents develop and, less often, degenerate, while the expressions are even more numerous than those of a material object and arise easily. They assimilate into their systems particles from the environment and reject their own; at death, their transformation is enormous, breaking into fragments and losing all activity.

Quantity is as applicable to mind as it is to matter. Because of its necessary existence, mind must always persist, though this does not imply that it must always remain the same: its quantity is constant, and this refers to its total aggregate of constituents, not merely the basic constituent. Even a thought does not vanish completely; it either has a consequent or lies quiescent. Though it would be rash to assume that mind exists throughout the universe, it would be rasher to imagine that it is limited to the existing organisms on the earth. As matter and mind exist together, one substance is not likely to have been produced in such comparatively small quantities. There must be a vast amount in the universe beyond the earth. Even on the earth, the major portion must have remained inert until now. That in other parts of the universe there is also active mind is probable, though the organisms may vary from what we know, since it is hardly credible that only a tiny planet contains it. Nevertheless, mind is of lesser extent than matter; this is naturally the case in view of the fact that it is found only where there is matter, which, on the other hand, can maintain itself alone. That the major portion of matter contains no mind is indubitable; the amount of organic matter on the earth is little compared to pure matter.

Whatever we choose to doubt, we never hesitate to believe in our consciousness, for we are directly aware of our ideas. What distinguishes mental properties from material qualities is their sudden appearance when wanted and seemingly complete disappearance when not functioning, a fact suggestive of another mode of connection to their base. In sleep, they lie quiescent, for all practical purposes nonexistent. That they can dissolve into nothingness is impossible, since they must exist. It follows that they have an active and a passive condition.

The faculties of sensation, memory, intuition, understanding, judgment, reason, and imagination are concerned with thought and ideas; and they give mind its peculiar significance, its special function, making it transcend the limits imposed by physical conditions. In respect to them, minds show a clear evolution from the lower to the higher types. Instinct, supreme in animals and, though powerful, not paramount in human beings, makes behavior spontaneous; associated with self-preservation, its efficacy is undoubted. To live and propagate are its commands, which cannot be obnoxious, it being natural that mind endeavors to preserve its ability to exercise its functions. Though it is not derogatory to human dignity to listen to its voice, the emergence of reason is plain evidence that instinct should yield to a higher sway.

We are aware that we possess a will. What is it? It is the power of conscious determination as to whether an action shall be pursued. How does a deed originate? It may occur spontaneously, but when we are conscious of it, we find it is actuated by a motive. From motive to action is not one simple step, for we are aware of choice. Motive acts on will, an intermediary between it and action, the will producing the action. Motive inclines the will one way or the other, motive being the cause and action the effect. The intervention of the will introduces a complication and makes the connection of cause and effect less simple than in matter. Motive acts through the resistance of the will, which can vary from strong to weak; the same motive may not issue in the same action. Choice applies only to alternative possibilities; we are equipped to run, and whether we do so depends on our will, but no amount of will can make our bodies float toward the stars. A motive, however potent, cannot issue in action if it encounters a will whose resistance can override it; like the faculties, the strength of the will depends on nature and habit.

Feelings and emotions are the forces that direct action and are the wellsprings of creative energy; they make a person active, urging him to realize his aims, and without them, existence would be pallid, devoid of vitality. To deracinate them is to lose valuable ingredients of the mind, but they must be elevated by reason to give only beneficial effects.

Mind does not occupy space, but it undoubtedly dwells in the flow of time, identical to that surrounding the material realm, a conclusion enforced by events. Here is a remarkable phenomenon—the same constituent for two substances; only in that it is external is the fact intelligible. Time is baffling, not to be likened to other qualities; each of its moments is common to the entire material and mental universe.

The harmony, value, and meaning principles are found in mind as in matter, but with other forms. Harmony confers beauty on the artistic products of the human mind. Value applied to the emotions bears the name of *ethical good*, which, as far as we are concerned, is the chief variety. Likewise, the meaning of mind, including destiny or goal, is of paramount significance.

The constituents of entity may be classified descriptively. The Existential Principle is the basic constituent, the base for the others. Behavior and transformation are the controlling constituents, directing activity. Space and time are the *external constituents*, endowing entity with significance. The rest may be called *descriptive constituents*. Constituents found in more than one division of entity, such as behavior and finiteness, are called *common constituents;* those peculiar to only one division, such as shape and emotion, are *specific constituents.*

Mind has often been contradistinguished from life and soul. It is preposterous to regard the body as containing three distinct substances with inscrutable relationships. Life is no more than a constituent of mind, its connecting link with matter, while the soul is a fiction if it means something above mind; this postulate is unnecessary, as whatever properties it is supposed to have may equally well be ascribed to mind.

According to the usual conception of mind, it is made of indivisible wholes; a material object has parts but not thus with a mind, which is said to be simple. That it has no parts cannot be true in view of the circumstance that thought is located in the brain and emotion in the heart—its properties are concentrated in diverse places. Mind fills the entire body, as it has being wherever there is life, which every cell contains. That it is indivisible cannot be upheld either, for if a man's arm is cut off, what happens to the mind in it? Isn't it severed from the main portion? That it can be simple is ludicrous, considering its complex array of qualities. It is divisible—to what extent? It is not necessary to suppose that it consists of discrete particles like atoms; today, not even matter need be thus conceived. Yet a finite mass cannot be infinitely divisible, the phrase *infinitely small* being a mathematical fiction. It may be divided into particles to a certain extent, but there will come a point when the process cannot be carried out after a certain size is reached. The particles do not represent discrete atoms, for they may flow together again; on redividing the mass, the same particles may not be obtained. What is meant is this: a certain size is stipulated, but the particles are not ultimate units. A mind is a continuous expanse, not made up of perennially distinct particles. An analogy may be made with space, which, though it is indivisible into parts, is not a collection of ultimate units.

Mind is a dependent substance, always associated with matter; this is an obnoxious idea to those who deem mind sacrosanct, immeasurably superior to lowly matter. This feeling must have been chiefly responsible for the rise of idealist theories, of opposition to the notion of evolution, of the conception of God as a supreme mind, of the doctrine of the soul's immortality. It is mere prejudice due to the easily intelligible desire of human beings to think of ourselves as unique. We would doubtless have liked to regard our bodies as invaluable, had the unfortunate fact of death not rendered this inadvisable. From observation, we find that mind blooms only in organisms; as a body is largely composed of carbon, it appears to have a special affinity for this element. If it did exist separately, we should be aware of it, considering that it should be easier for mind to come into direct contact with mind than with matter; it must be because mind can only function through matter that we do not enjoy this experience. Ghosts, spirits, and angels are mere products of superstition.

In spite of its lesser extent and its parasitic condition relative to matter, mind is of considerably greater importance in the scheme of things. It possesses its own highly developed *raison d'être*, while the purpose of material objects regarded as self-sufficing is vague. Its units are capable of holding the totality of entities within their tiny realms; it aspires to a position of control and molds matter to suit it. Though it is too much to say that deprived of it the universe is meaningless, it is certain that in such a case, the universe would be robbed of an immense part of its meaning. There is no need to descant over its glory, which is indubitable; it sounds ludicrous to remark that thought excels extension, but nothing need be taken for granted.

One point about mind that requires elucidation concerns the problem of creation. In what sense can it be said to create? We often hear of the creative activities of poets, painters, and musicians. All these persons do is think certain thoughts, feel certain emotions and then express them through words, colors, and sounds, which are not produced by mind—only ideas of them are. The hand is the immediate instrument responsible for what we see and hear, for the books, pictures, and tunes. Mind, in fact, can create only ideas, not matter, which is directly molded only by itself.

Before the first organisms arose, mind must have already been in existence, slowly evolving with matter to produce the organisms; it could not have suddenly sprung up and entered into them full-fledged, for this is not how evolution works. Moreover, even on earth, its quantity must be greater than what exists in living things. How then does it exist outside organisms? It must be associated with inorganic matter, which shows no sign of its activity. It must then be quiescent; in this state, we will call it *inert mind* to distinguish it from the active mind of organic beings. Inert mind is still mind, possessing its constituents in latency; only when it becomes associated with matter in an organic fashion does it become active.

Egoism has led us to ascribe mind only to human beings, though every organism possesses it, since life is a mental constituent. From our experience, we can classify active mind, in ascending order of importance and complexity, into three types: the vegetable, the animal, and the human. The distinctive property of the first is life, of the second sensation, and of the last reason; but the higher also exhibits those of the lower. The vegetable lives and grows; the animal lives, grows, moves, and sees; the human lives, grows, moves, sees, judges, and reasons. Vegetables display only one active trait characteristic of mind—life; the others are latent. In addition to life, animals possess sensation and feeling; in humans, all the constituents are developed, of which the crown is reason.

Mind is one, and out of the original mass must have come the multitudinous units. Logically, the complex proceeds from the simple; humans have evolved from animals, which grew out of vegetables. The known facts of evolution confirm the first half of the statement, though they have not yet produced an indubitable conclusion for the second half. It would be preposterous to aver that only the physical organism of the human being has evolved from the animal, while our mind originated from another source. How could this be? How could evolution take place with only one part affected? An organism is a whole. As the animal does not materially differ from the human in bodily structure, so it exhibits many identical mental phenomena.

Though mind and matter are endowed with the same basic constituent, they are distinct entities, their properties being largely dissimilar. As experience demonstrates, they are so formed that one cannot be derived from the other. The Law of Conservation of Energy implies that an individual mind must emerge from another; this is effected through the phenomenon of birth, a plant coming from a plant, an animal from an animal, and a human from a human. An embryo results from the secretions of its parents, of their matter and mind: a portion of their organisms thus separates to make a new being. In the growth process, a baby absorbs material nutriment, which is converted into part of its body; its mind must develop in the same way, absorbing the mind from the air it breathes, the water it drinks, and the food it eats. This sounds incredible, yet how could we otherwise explain the larger quantity of mind in an adult organism, with its multitude of cells, compared with an embryo? Mind must be renewable, though not to such an extent as matter; its structure not being atomic, the cohesive power between its parts must be comparatively much greater. A human mind contains a hard core, little subject to change, a truth attested by the persistent unity of the self as manifested in consciousness.

It is likewise impossible for a mind to pass into nothingness. At death, the body disintegrates, but the quantity of matter remains the same; this is also so with mind, which ceases to be active, but its quantity does not diminish. In what form does it exist? It is no longer part of an organism and ceases to function; it becomes inert. Being a dependent substance, it cannot maintain a separate existence and breaks into parts that cling to diverse portions of matter. Mind is divisible, and after passing into an inert state, an individual unit does not necessarily continue to persist as a single whole—in fact, it rarely does; its former abode, the body, has dissolved into bits, taking with them fractions of mind. There is no question here of disembodied spirits or ghosts, since these are imagined to be active and represent the departed souls in *toto*. Active units of mind, moving freely about outside of matter, cannot exist; there is no proof of the reality of such phenomena, the number of supposed visitors from the world of spirits and angels notwithstanding.

Chapter 8
The Primary Entity

The Law of Conservation of Energy, which states that entity remains constant in total quantity, neither increasing nor decreasing, neither capable of arising from nothing nor of destruction, is universal, with no exception. A particular entity may go through the strangest transformations, a veritable Proteus, but its aggregate of constituents does not vanish—including not only the Existential Principle but the others as well. This does not imply that any constituent is unalterable or even that a principal division of the universe, such as mind or matter, must always preserve its identity. It means only that whatever exists will continue to do so under some guise or other.

The idea of the continuity of entity is a logical necessity, and it is difficult to see how its opposite could be true. If objects could every now and then spring from nothingness or suddenly vanish, then anything might happen. The universe would be a chaos, and all our knowledge would be a hopeless tangle of confusion. The ancient dictum, *ex nihilo nihil fit* —nothing can come out of nothing—is axiomatic; it is more self-evident than the truth that when equals are added to equals, the sums are equal. The Law of Conservation is intimately associated with the Existential Principle. If an entity must exist by virtue of its nature, then it cannot disappear into, nor can it ever arise from, nothingness. Experience confirms the Law of Conservation. In the world of science, there is no instance of generation or destruction of matter from or into nothing; a quantity never alters, whatever the changes may be.

In the days of superstition and casual observation, it was easy to believe that objects arose spontaneously or disappeared mysteriously, but the laws discovered by science show that what really happens is only transformation; even an intangible property like energy remains constant in quantity. Nature's capacity for metamorphosis is amazingly subtle, and it is at the bottom of the naïve belief in absolute creation and destruction. It is only in reference to mind that experience does not conclusively demonstrate the truth of mind's conservation, since mind is directly knowable only through its manifestations in matter, and after death its behavior is no longer observable. But the manner of its generation supports the theory of conservation—an organism embodying mind always being born of another.

The doctrine of psycho-physical interaction regards the mutual influence of mind and matter as a fact, and ordinary experience brings it home with force. Prick the flesh with a pin, and pain is immediately felt: an operation on matter has produced an effect on mind. Will yourself to lift up an arm, and without any hesitation the movement is performed: a mental phenomenon has caused a physical act. Anger suffuses the face with blood, joy makes the lips stretch, and bravery makes a man jump into the water to rescue a drowning person. Sensations, phenomena of the mind, are products of material objects. The perfect coordination between the mind and the body, which appear to act as one, is palpable.

A more profound investigation initiated by psychology confirms the view. The nervous system, a collection of matter, transmits the impacts of material objects to the mind. A defect in an organ engenders a catastrophic mental result; an injury to the brain can turn an intelligent person into an imbecile; an unusually intense degree of worry can make the hair turn gray; the act of lying inhibits the action of the salivary glands; the pressure of a pillow or a physical stimulation induces a dream in a slumbering individual.

It is ridiculous to suppose that the observed interaction is pure illusion. The Theory of Psycho-Physical Parallelism is one of the most far-fetched imaginable. That the complete synchronization of physical and mental events is explainable by the analogy of two miraculous clocks that keep perfect time is too ludicrous for words, and an element of the supernatural creeps uneasily into view. Coincidence is eschewed even in fiction—how could it be upheld as occurring every minute in real life? There is not the slightest necessity in such a view for body and mind to function together, and they might as well stay apart. The eyes become superfluous for receiving images, while the hands might wield pens or swords without any directing intelligence. As there is no connection whatsoever, the mind might leave the body for a long journey, and the mouth would still eat and the legs walk. One astonishing inconsistency is the belief that the soul continues to exist in the same way when the body perishes; the faultless synchronization appears to be at fault here, seeing that the physical event is not accompanied by a corresponding mental change. Events may occur in the body and not in the mind and vice versa: the hand may make involuntary movements with the mind an absolute blank, and one may indulge in a daydream without any noticeable bodily action. Where then is the correspondence? Could one clock temporarily cease to function and, on restarting, immediately pick up the synchronization again?

The interaction of mind and matter is indubitable. How is it possible that two substances that appear dissimilar exert mutual influence? The only logical explanation is a common origin; that is, they must have evolved from one original substance and thus possess a common bond. If this is the case, then they must have similar points, a fact to which their common constituents attest. If they are totally different with no point of contact, then they could not evoke mutual response. When a heavy individual sits down on a rickety chair, it collapses, the lamentable result being attributable to weight, a greater acting on a lesser. It is improbable that entities could enjoy similarities and hence interact if they did not trace their descent from a common ancestry.

The two substances must either be eternal or come from an eternal substance, for the Law of Conservation of Energy makes it impossible for them to have arisen from nothing. Science shows that matter has been evolving slowly for eons from a chaotic mass to its present state as a complex variety of objects. Mind has been evolving through the stages of vegetable, animal, and human, from simplicity to complexity. When did the process begin? The date, though long ago, was definite, as change could not have commenced from eternity. If we trace the process backward, we must eventually reach a point of extreme simplicity, beyond which we can go no further, and this point has a beginning, while eternity has none. Yet it is impossible that they should have existed from eternity in a simple, unchanging state and then started to evolve; if the cause was external, it would logically have preceded their existence, and they would then have had a beginning. If the cause was internal, then the process should have commenced from eternity, as it is unintelligible how the cause could have lain in abeyance and suddenly started to operate; a cause to account for the behavior of this cause would then be necessary and so on *ad infinitum*. It follows that evolution, which implies a beginning, could not be applied to substances without a beginning but is coeval with them. Being subject to evolution, matter and mind must have had a definite commencement; they are not eternal and therefore must have issued from a third substance.

What is the nature of their production? They could not have arisen from nothing and hence could not be, as usually conceived, created at the behest of a god. Believing that a divine being called them out of the deep is believing that they were made from nothing—an impossibility. This notion contradicts the theory of the Existential Principle, which states that an entity exists because it must. If an entity must exist, then it could not have been nonexistent once upon a time. Matter and mind could have evolved only from another entity—made of its stuff. We will make the idea clearer by citing the analogy of a flower growing from a plant. A common origin, naturally producing the mutual interaction of the two substances, can mean only this. Divine creation is arbitrary and does not explain the behavior of the substances; it could be called in to advance any theory. The idea of evolution precludes a cataclysmic creation, and whims are not in the natural order of things.

What is the original substance? I will call it the *Primary Substance* or the *Primary Entity*, which cannot be either matter or mind. If it were matter, it could not be the source of mind, which in our experience, though it is conjoined with matter, is not its product. If it were mind, it could not generate matter, for the specific character of mind is thought—the production of ideas, not external objects. A supreme mind is still a mind with powers greater in degree but not different in kind, or else it could not appropriately be termed *mind*. It is obvious that if it were either matter or mind, then one of these is eternal, and it has been shown that this is impossible.

It must then be another substance. I use the term *substance*, not in the old-fashioned sense of a concrete entity to which qualities are stuck or in which ideas arise, but to denote a main division of entity composed of an aggregate of constituents. One substance differs from another in a number of constituents but has others in common. The most fundamental constituent of both matter and mind is the Existential Principle, the basic constituent that makes an entity exist. The Primary Substance exists and must therefore possess the principle, which, as it forms the base of an entity, is therefore similar to that of matter and mind. As it is a third substance with some peculiar constituents, the principle must differ in form to suit them. It is self-evident that the base could not be thoroughly different, or matter and mind could not have proceeded from the Primary Substance. the Theory of Psycho-Physical Parallelism has arisen from postulating two absolutely dissimilar substances; inconsistently enough, matter has been held to come from a supreme mind. When two substances cannot even exert mutual influence, one can create the other!

The Primary Entity is eternal. Being the first cause, it could have no beginning, and, possessing necessary existence, it could have no end. This means that it does not move in time. It is infinite, which implies that all its constituents are so. If it were finite, then, with the production of matter and mind, it would have vanished. To do so, it would have to possess the constituent of disappearance, which as a constituent would have operated from the beginning; this means that it would have vanished the very moment it existed—an absurdity. Supposing it did not vanish instantaneously; then it would have undergone a process of diminution. This means that it possesses the constituent of diminution, which, as it must continue to operate, would ultimately reduce it to nothingness; then what has no beginning has an end. Termination and eternity are incompatible terms. If the Primary Entity is infinite, then the production of matter and mind does not affect its character; subtract a finite quantity from an infinite, and the remainder is still infinite. It does not occupy space, for, if it did, then even though space is infinite, it would entirely fill it, and none would be left for matter.

The Primary Entity is composed of constituents that may be termed *attributes*, comprising existence, eternity, infinity, production, homogeneity, perfection, wisdom, harmony, value, and meaning. Each of these is infinite in extent to suit the infinite nature of the first cause. As eternity signifies changelessness, the attributes are fixed in character; they do not vary like material and mental constituents. This entity does not consist of a collection of objects but is a single continuous expanse, like a vast ocean, not a number of lakes; were it otherwise, its character would not be infinity but an array of finite qualities. The existential attribute is the base that unites the others.

The most remarkable attribute is production, the emergence of fresh entities. Matter and mind issued forth with laws that determined the trend of their evolution. Henceforth, they pursued their career from their inner necessity, without any interference from their originating substance. This accords with what we know of their behavior, with the concept of naturalism. Miracles and supernatural influences are unmitigated fiction. How could other substances proceed from the Primary Substance? This is possible if we remember that they are similar in that they all possess the Existential Principle. The other constituents arise because they exist in potentiality and flower as a result of the activity or the productive attribute. Even within the realm of matter, an object produces another with dissimilar qualities: a chicken bears no resemblance to an egg, in which, however, it is potential. The productive attribute cannot be exercised just once, or it would scarcely be a real attribute. The idea that the divine power created the world and then ceased the work altogether means that production was not an essential characteristic but an accident.

The Primary Entity is homogeneous, exactly similar throughout its expanse. It cannot be composed of different parts, for it would then be divisible and would cease to be infinite. The intervals between the discrete quantities would nullify the notion of absolute infinity, and in reality there would be just a collection of finite objects. All the attributes are infinite, and it is difficult to see how one like wisdom could have parts. How would the attributes of infinity and eternity be associated with the parts? Besides, if there are parts, with production some might be diminished more than others or disappear altogether, and then the entity would have undergone a change of nature, and its eternal constancy would be affected, when, as a matter of fact, it cannot possibly suffer change that can take place only in time.

The Primary Entity is perfect! How is it perfect? Every attribute is infinite and eternal, constant, not subject to change, which cannot exist without time. If it were imperfect, it could never remain constant, for it would tend to evolve to realize its harmony, value, and meaning. Imperfection and infinity are incompatible. Mind and matter could not be evolving toward perfection if their source were not perfect.

The Primary Entity is suffused with wisdom, which must not be confounded with the quality characterizing mind, which is what we mean when we say God or a person is wise. The attribute does not possess the same implications as its human counterpart; it has nothing to do with thought, which consists of a succession of ideas. I use the word to suggest the character of rightness appertaining to the nature and action of the entity; the word *behavior* may be used, as in the case of matter and mind, but this is not really appropriate, as it does not suggest the notion of correctness. The attribute of wisdom is postulated from a consideration of the nature of the universe, which could not be the work of folly. If the Primary Entity were stupid, there would be a force tending to destroy the existential attribute, which could hardly maintain itself in perpetual subjection to unfavorable conditions. As it is inconceivable that existence can vanish, the conflict must be absent.

Like wisdom, harmony is interwoven into the being of the first cause. It is deduced from the order prevailing among the emergent products, matter and mind. Without the principle of harmony, we would not find it in the material universe, and a substance would be deprived of much of its glory: its importance cannot be overrated.

Value is an attribute and may be referred to as the *good*, signifying whatever constitutes genuine worth. As harmony, value, and meaning are constituents of both matter and mind, it is to be expected that they should be present in the original source. As the good is infinite, it follows that it is not admixed with the bad.

Existence is inconceivable without meaning: the idea of an entity that is eternal and infinite yet possesses no meaning is difficult to swallow. Its meaning is interwoven with all its other attributes, expressed in them; it is constant, not embodied in an ultimate goal. If existence is the basic constituent, then meaning is the most sublime. Without it, existence might as well not be; the Primary Entity—and therefore the emergent universe—would be a colossal blunder! How could this be said of an entity that could produce a harmonious universe and rational mind?

As the various attributes are fixed, there are no forms; there could not be a form at one moment and another at the next. As there are no forms, there are no expressions. The attributes are constant, not susceptible to modification.

Chapter 9
The Determinate Entity

The Primary Entity is characterized by the attribute of production. What does it produce? Matter and mind are known to us, but these could not be the only substances it has evolved. Considering their evolution from the simple to the complex, the productive attribute must have been in operation prior to their emergence. Their existing quantity is not increasing; the constancy regarding matter is an acknowledged scientific fact, while, as mind must exist in conjunction with matter, its amount is definite. They emerged long ago and thereafter saw no addition. It follows that the permanent productivity of the Primary Entity is infinite. Perpetual production can never exhaust it; it remains infinite.

This substance, which is forever being produced, I am calling the *Determinate Entity*. Its constituents include existence, determinacy, variety, comprehension, permanence, homogeneity, perfection, harmony, value, and meaning. It goes without saying that it must possess the existential constituent to allow it to maintain its being; it thus has the same base as the other substances. This is natural, for the three secondary substances are all equally derived from one primary substance.

The Determinate Entity does not exist in space, as it would then be matter and we could perceive it; neither does it exist in time, or we should find it in our familiar universe, for time is akin to space, and mind, which flows in it, is associated with matter. As it is timeless, it cannot change; therefore, it does not emerge in a chaotic, amorphous stream, which would require evolution toward a goal, but issues in definite units, each a distinct and complete whole. The units are changeless. They are determinate, hence the name adopted for the substance. They are unlike material objects, which change the form of their constituents, and mental units, whose constituents have expressions that come and go. They are fixed, unalterable from the moment of their emergence. Each unit is known as a *Determinate Unit* or *Determinate Object*. The attribute of determinacy is what distinguishes the substance from the others, for mind and matter are subject to ceaseless transformation, while the Primary Entity is not completely determinate because of its productive activity. Perfect determinacy implies finiteness, infinity being vague. The units are finite, and their constituents are therefore all finite; an infinite constituent coexisting with a finite is incomprehensible and impossible. Determinacy conveys more than the idea of changelessness; it implies definiteness. The Primary Entity is changeless, but it is not definite because products issue from it.

There is no reason why the units should be identical; material and mental phenomena are various, and the Primary Entity is wise and could not narrow down its activity to endless repetition. They must have variety, which is thus a constituent. This constituent endows each unit with its specific character. The constituents have diverse forms, and the forms are fixed for each unit, but every unit does not contain identical forms.

The units possess the constituent of comprehension, by which is meant a pervasive awareness of the universe: that is, an ineffable relationship to the Primary Entity and the world of Determinate Objects. This is not the same as mental consciousness. Like the wisdom of the first cause, it does not consist of a stream of ideas, nor does it advance and retreat. The constituent is postulated as the universe must form a unity, and a certain relationship must exist to bind together the units, all of which proceed from one substance.

As the Determinate Entity does not exist in time, it is permanent. It cannot vanish into nothing, and, as it does not change, it cannot transform itself into something else; permanence is thus a constituent. A Determinate Unit surpasses in importance a material or mental object that is transitory, easily changing its character or dissolving into parts and losing its identity. Note that permanence is desirable only in conjunction with perfection; it would be productive of stupendous tragedy were it associated with wrong. Artificial stationariness in human institutions has bred a hideous amount of woe. Progress is valuable only because there is room for it; were perfection already in being, it would be ridiculous to yearn for advance, to say nothing of the fact that that would be impossible. A Determinate Object is a perfect whole and is unalterable for all eternity.

As there is no possibility of change and therefore of subdivision into discrete entities, it is to be expected that a Determinate Unit would not be built up of smaller pieces, as a material object is of atoms. It is a homogenous mass, all the portions absolutely similar. This is different from a material object like a cup, where one part may be white and smooth and another brown and rough. Perfect unity requires homogeneity, which means that every constituent is equally diffused through the object.

Determinate Units are perfect. They must be so because, were it otherwise, they would remain eternally faulty, as they are not subject to evolution—an untenable supposition; the Primary Entity, which is perfect and wise, would be belying its character to produce a perennially imperfect substance. This perfection is finite, which must be distinguished from infinite perfection. Perfection can be finite in the sense that there is a definite limit. Within the bounds of a unit, the constituents have no fault; but being restricted in extent, their perfection is limited. The infinite perfection of the Primary Entity is due to its infinite extent. The Determinate Entity may be designated the *Perfect Entity*, as it is produced perfect in contradistinction to mind and matter.

The interpretive constituents common to matter and mind and present in infinite form in the Primary Entity reside in the Determinate Entity also. Determinate harmony shines with a constant, unwavering light and, without discord, transcends the harmony of material nature. It weaves all the constituents of an object into a harmonious whole and flushes it with a superb glow of glory; if it did not exist, the different constituents might be mutually discordant, which is incompatible with the concept of perfect unity.

Unlike the material and mental, determinate value is absolute, complete in itself, not contributory to another. It is not utility that is good *per se*; it is not moral good; but it is a quality that makes for right existence. Good or evil in the moral sense is inapplicable to the objects, which are not endowed with will or the other specific properties of mind. *Good* in reference to them means that they are proper modes of existence; they are desirable even from the point of view of humankind.

Determinate meaning has nothing to do with a goal or ultimate aim, as the units do not change, but is meaning in itself, the meaning of existence. It is not yet unrealized purpose, but it already implies the absence of evolution. Meaning must necessarily be: a meaningless permanent object is impossible to visualize.

A passing reference may be made to Plato's ideas, the most distinguished feature of a sublime philosophy. They are conceived of as eternal and perfect; however, beyond the one point of perfection, they bear no resemblance to the Determinate Objects. Not produced by another entity, they have existed from the beginning of eternity. They are arranged in a graduated scale of importance and are dominated by the idea of the good; they are connected with the sublunary world—the archetypes of terrestrial phenomena, the models that concrete individual objects imitate. The Determinate Units are none of these things; they bear no relationship to material and mental entities, which are no less real in their own right. Like other Greek thinkers, Plato was not concerned with the nature of substance, which he did not define. Though the ideas are neither material nor mental, he did not say they were made of another substance; in fact, they are mere abstractions in contradistinction to matter, which he regarded as concrete. He believed in gods and self-existing souls. The ideas, though real, appear to exist not in their own right with their own meaning but as visions to bring satisfaction and rapture to souls. The notion that universals must lead an independent existence in order to explain the similarity between particulars is untenable. The similarity is due to natural laws of behavior and change. In what sense can an object without volition be said to imitate another? Is it conceivable that a horse sets out to imitate horsiness? It cannot do this itself, for it already exists, and by no stretch of the imagination can it be supposed to know the idea of the horse. If it is created by an almighty being, then he could do it to accord with an idea in his mind. Note that only organic beings and artificial objects comprise the majority of clearly distinct units, bearing close resemblance if they belong to the same class. A swallow engenders almost identical offspring; can this not be explained by a law of reproduction? A chair can be made indistinguishable from another; its creator, man, does this with a particular specimen before him and not in terms of an idea of chairiness. As for inanimate nature, things tend to merge into an amorphous mass, and the separate units are little alike. How much of the earth is water, which is not a collection of wholes like oranges? If you take rocks as discrete objects, do they resemble one another? They are variable in composition and are of diverse colors, shapes, and sizes.

The conception of the Determinate Units may lead to the wrong impression that they are playful products of fancy. The ideas of Plato have made posterity rashly assume that he was a dreamer devoted to exercises of the imagination. He wished to eliminate poets from his Republic and was humorously dubbed a poet himself by Milton. I do not subscribe to the Platonic ideas, but not on the grounds that they are fantastic. The ordinary nature of our experience is extremely strange, but we do not commonly think so, because habitual contact has blunted our sense of wonder. The human mind is so constituted that whatever it is accustomed to seems true and right, while what is unfamiliar seems ludicrous. If one is to engage in a dispassionate inquiry into truth, one must learn to take nothing for granted, to divest oneself of prejudice, to believe that anything is possible in this strange universe. Truth can be settled only by reason. Throughout history, the most curious theories and practices have obtained currency. No doubt they were regarded as fantastic at first, but, with their spread and establishment, they were swallowed unquestioningly by the generations who inherited them. People continue to believe in religions thousands of years old, made up of absurd fancies that, were they uttered for the first time today, might make psychiatrists consign their announcers to the asylum. The theories of present-day science are odder than any poet's vision. Strangeness must not be made an objection to an idea; life itself is incredibly odd.

Chapter 10
Permanent Existence

Matter and the Determinate Entity can exist in a solitary state, apart from other substances. Mind alone is dependent, always linked to matter. As this is the case, it must have been forged as an intermediate entity between the other two; in its essence, it is more shadowy and less stable than either. It is not dependent on the Determinate Entity; it is intermediate in the sense that with its peculiar function of understanding, it relates to both.

Mind and matter were not created perfect, full-fledged, and changeless; they have been undergoing a process of ceaseless evolution from chaos to order, from simplicity to complexity. If they are already perfect, then any change would be for the worse, an idea belied by observation and experience; yet as wise and perfect emanations of the Primary Entity, they should contain the germ of perfection. It is inconceivable that from perfection should flow eternal imperfection. Their known history is one of progress. How unlike are an orderly array of stars and an amorphous nebula, a bunch of beautiful flowers and a miscellaneous assortment of carbon compounds! How superior is human to animal mind and rational thought to superstition! Progress is an undoubted fact. Mind was born ages after matter, yet even now it is more impressive, nearer perfection: its evolution is faster. As it is a dependent substance, being unable to remain without its ally, matter, it would have to disappear at an earlier date.

In what sense could mind come to an end? According to the Law of Conservation of Energy, it is indestructible and will not vanish into nothing; yet being a finite substance subject to change, it could not maintain itself forever and be infinite. What involves change moves in time, which is different from eternity. Once its perfectibility has achieved fruition, it would remain immutable, there being nothing beyond perfection. But change is of the essence, and, though becoming perfect, it would still live in time, which connotes change. Hence, once perfect, it cannot remain in time but acquires the quality of permanence. Yet one of its constituents is time; to be able to shed it, it must therefore alter its nature and transform into another substance that has perpetual existence for its intrinsic character.

The Perfect Entity is permanent: it does not move in time. Its constituents are perfection and determinateness or immutability. Hence, for mind to become permanent, perfect, and immutable, it must transform itself into the Determinate Entity. This transformation is its ultimate goal, the meaning of its evolution. The need for perfection is contained in the transformation constituent: imperfect at first, mind brings its seed of perfection to full flower through toil. Nothing is more natural than such transformation. Within the region of matter itself, an object can change its character easily: water may be heated into steam or congealed into ice, while, chemically combined in equal proportions, sodium and chlorine turn into ordinary table salt, so divergent in its properties from either. It may be argued that the substance itself does not undergo transmutation, for what is matter remains matter. Quite true! The instances are merely intended to indicate transformation on a lesser scale. Mind and the Determinate Entity are not totally opposite in nature but possess the same basic constituent. The transformation is only a more drastic change than that of water into steam.

Under what circumstances does the transformation of mind occur? The condition is that it should reach perfection, which in this connection denotes a strong will, wisdom, harmony, and virtue. Portions of mind are caged within distinct bodies that are not all on the same level. Animal and vegetable minds are in a rudimentary stage; even within the realm of humanity, individuals differ in their mental development. A particular mind will transform itself without reference to others, as each is a distinct unit undergoing its own process of development and attaining perfection by itself. As the stream of time flows onward and humanity becomes wiser, more and more minds will transform themselves; ultimately, all minds will disappear.

Each mind transforms itself into a single Determinate Entity. The act occurs at death, when the mind is no longer organically associated with the body, which decomposes; its constituent atoms are scattered, some lost in the lifeless sea, some entering into the composition of flowers, some helping to produce new human bodies. The mind, if imperfect, dissolves into parts, clinging to pieces of matter, all its qualities inert, showing no signs of life. The dispersed bits will eventually help form new minds in new bodies, though not all the parts of a dead mind will come together again in a fresh body; a new mind is composed of fragments of a number of old or inert minds. This differentiates it from mere metempsychosis, the Buddhist doctrine of reincarnation, in which each individual soul is reborn entire. The dissolution of mind is a phenomenon that is still happening and has happened for untold ages. But there is another story to tell—a lofty destiny awaits humanity! Our minds may attain transformation soon. Cultivate the will and make it strong; contemplate the Primary Entity and the universe; live a noble life—and instead of dissolution when the body perishes, the mind will experience metamorphosis into a Perfect Object.

As a Determinate Unit, a mind possesses permanent existence, and this is the only kind of immortality preached by theistic religions, which say that a soul departs a dead body, retaining the same identity and all its memories, and sets out on a journey to heaven or hell, according to the good or evil committed by its owner. I deny that there is a soul in a human body apart from its mind; I deny that there are specific abodes of bliss and misery where it finally takes up its residence. I affirm that for permanent existence, a mind ceases to be a mind and becomes another thing altogether. This is the great hope, this promise of ultimate perfection and imperishable being. It is salvation, sublime, satisfying—much more so than ordinary immortality. The distinguishing characteristic of a transformed mind is that it is capable of direct, immediate relationship to or awareness of the Primary Entity and the world of Perfect Objects.

When a mind transmutes itself into a Perfect Object, it ceases to possess the mental characteristics of sensation, thought, and emotion. Its constituents will be those appropriate to its new state, such as determinacy, variety, comprehension, permanence, and homogeneity. Naturally, it will not be identical to the Perfect Objects directly emanating from the Primary Entity, for not even these exactly resemble one another; there is variety in unity. Nor will all the transformed minds be absolutely similar, since everyone is different; in the transformation process, the consequent is conditioned by the antecedent. There will not even be the type of consciousness peculiar to mind; there will exist in its stead awareness pertaining to the Perfect Object, though this will be closer to consciousness, seeing that the new entity has evolved from mind and therefore resembles it more than the Perfect Object radiating from the Primary Entity.

Transformation is achieved by attaining perfection, whose cultivation constitutes a duty. Perfection is sublime, and whatever is conducive to sublimity makes for perfection. Nothing could be more sublime than the contemplation of the universe, and nothing induces perfection so much as concentrated devotion to perfection and reflection on the Primary Entity and the world of perfect units. To elevate the mind, adore the Primary Entity; this does not entail serene contemplation, as is the case with religions with their attitude of lazy somnolence, but active thought. Dynamic contemplation accords with the nature of the cosmos. What is this species of contemplation? It is severe thought, charged with emotion and enthusiasm. The will must be made strong: there must arise the will to perfection. The will is not given to humanity in vain, for, as far as mind's immediate functions are concerned, it is the medium through which thought issues in action. In its transcendental purpose, it is the agent of transformation. The will to perfection operating in the mind concentrates its force and overcomes all obstacles, working toward the great goal; it resembles a catalyst that accelerates chemical reaction in matter.

The immortality of the soul as advocated by theistic religions is far from the satisfying fulfillment of desire that is commonly supposed. Mere prolongation of earthly life, even with the elimination of its pains, is not to be regarded as the last word of hope. Aside from the fact that the wish is a vain illusion, there are many objections to eternal life, which is a mere sublimation of terrestrial experience. If memories were retained, the bitter would persist along with the sweet. As the soul is not necessarily perfect, save perhaps in the matter of virtue, when it enters heaven, it is to be expected that if foolish, it will remain so. Unless the saints develop a peculiar and revolting callousness, how is it possible for them to live in bliss when there are hordes of others stewing in misery? A universe that contains an eternal hell must be eternally defective.

Existence as a Perfect Object is glorious, for perfection is glorious. Worldly dross is completely shed. The existence is not shadowy; its peculiar type of awareness gives the Perfect Object a link to the universe more comprehensive and more real than thought gives a mind. Sublime is such permanence and absolutely satisfactory! How wonderful is a universe that is freed from the slightest fault! Perfection is the acme of desire, and nothing can be greater. That the universe should ultimately become perfect is not incredible; on the other hand, it would be astonishing if it were to be eternally defective, for its existence would then be inexplicable. It would be incomprehensible how a universe could exist yet remain forever riddled with faults, as existence itself is so strange that perfection is not much more so. Hope accords with logic, feeling with reality.

The total disappearance of mind is a long process, requiring eons for its consummation. On earth, humans possess the most developed mind, and any further evolution must be through us. Animal and vegetable minds cannot transform without having gone through the stage of human mind. There is nothing shocking or impossible in this; is not the human body composed of what originally might have been filth? The prejudice in favor of the peculiar nobility of mind must be discarded. It is not probable that mind should be confined only to the earth, out of the entire extensive universe; and there is no reason why it must live under conditions that are familiar to us. The mind in other parts of the cosmos will transform itself into the Determinate Entity.

Chapter 11
Beginning and End

Mind and matter arose out of the Primary Entity in an imperfect state, in amorphous masses: they sprang forth in rude simplicity as inert mind and electric streams. Inert mind became the active, living principle of vegetables; animals evolved from vegetables, and human beings from animals. Humanity will ultimately achieve perfection, and mind will have transformed itself bit by bit into the Determinate Entity. Evolution is as much the law of mind as it is of matter, which is also developing toward perfection. Nature is already ineffably sweet, though mixed with jarring deformities. The combination of electrons into atoms, of the atoms of a hundred elements or so into the molecules of an innumerable host of compounds, of molecules into the stupendous array of objects forming the glorious domain of nature, is a masterly scheme. But progress is still treading its course; the colossal spiral nebulae, rotating masses of gas, still have to settle down into galaxies, of which the Milky Way with its billions of stars is but one.

What is the fate of the material world? When it has climbed to its peak of perfection myriads of years hence, like mind, matter neither will be able to maintain itself in a changeless state—perfection implies immutability—nor will it be capable of passing into nothingness. Change is one of its qualities, yet it is destined to reach a state when no further change is practicable. As eternal repose contradicts its essential character, it follows that it must transform its nature. Its evolution demonstrates that it has a purpose that must eventually be fulfilled and can be no other than permanent perfection. It will have to undergo transmutation into the Perfect Substance, and the visible world will then cease to exist.

As formulated by Kelvin and Clausius, the Second Law of Thermodynamics declares that heat cannot pass from a body of lower temperature to one of higher, or that entropy tends to increase. Heat that flows from a warmer to a colder body can perform useful work, and, as the process is irreversible, energy gradually dissipates. A state of equilibrium is reached when there is no temperature difference, when entropy is at a maximum; all energy will have been converted into heat at a uniform temperature, and the universe will be dead. What does this mean? The time will come when the universe is changeless, when matter ceases to exercise its present functions. For matter to persist to eternity in this aimless state is to belie the meaning of evolution. It is far more credible that by then it would have consummated its inherent goal. The Second Law states only that if the process continues, a state of equilibrium will be attained; it does not prove that this state must endure forever. Energy is essential to matter for its evolution and naturally decreases as the goal comes nearer; when the goal is realized, energy will no longer be needed, as the universe will transform itself into the Perfect Entity and will disappear. Thus, the dissipation of energy proves the necessity for the eventual transformation of matter.

That matter can change into the Determinate Entity is due to the fact that they are not absolutely dissimilar; the most important of their constituents, the Existential Principle, is common to both. Only some of their other characteristics differ, and it is possible for the transformation constituent to manipulate matter. In nature, a quality easily assumes a new form, a round object becoming elliptical or square or amorphous, or a green leaf turning yellow. Change of constituent is more drastic than that of form, but there is no reason why it should not be feasible.

Individual minds are not strictly bound together by stern laws, each an inevitable complement of the rest, hence they can transform themselves at any point. But material objects are so interlinked, forming a systematic scheme, that their transformation individually is impossible. Nature must be perfect as a whole before the process can take place; only then will the material realm metamorphose into a collection of Determinate Entities. This tangible world will vanish, and it will be as if it had not been. It will change, not into one continuous expanse of Perfect Substance, but into an array of distinct Perfect Objects, because a huge, undefined mass will not possess the kind of determinacy associated with the substance. Besides, it is unlikely that matter could have been evolved for the purpose of terminating in only one object. Matter as we know it consists of discrete entities, and, though they blend and separate, it is beyond expectation that they would ultimately coalesce into a single entity.

Being a dependent substance unable to exist alone, mind can certainly not outlive matter but will have transformed before the time comes for its ally to do so. There will then be an interval during which the world will contain no life, no vegetables, animals, or human beings, when matter will not have mind in association, whether of the inert or active kind.

A sharp distinction must be made between the cessation of the material and mental universe in terms of transformation and the end of the world as conceived in some creeds. That the world will vanish in a conflagration or in some catastrophic manner is impossible, for it will be a case of disappearance into nothingness, nullifying the Law of Conservation of Energy. It is not uncommon for philosophers, who follow the irrational tradition of despising matter as basically vile, to dream of the universe one day consisting wholly of mind, or returning to this enviable condition, as matter is supposed to have been brought forth by mind. The minds now imprisoned in bodies will either continue to live as separate units or lose their distinct identities by dropping into the infinite ocean of mind. Unfortunate matter somehow sinks into the void. That mind cannot create matter is evident from their disparate powers; that matter can vanish without a trace is unaccountable. Only those who are prepared to involve themselves in contradiction can believe that their god is wise when he creates a meaningless substance in order to exterminate it in the end.

Mind arose after matter, the order of production of the three Emergent Substances being the Determinate Entity, matter, and mind. This is obvious from the fact that mind is a dependent substance and hence could not have been generated prior to matter, with which its existence is necessarily associated. Where no matter is, it cannot be. In the beginning, matter arose and evolved; only after a certain stage was reached, when the ground had been sufficiently prepared, did mind shoot forth and cling to matter. Portions of mind entered into intimate union with physical bodies, and the first organisms came into being. Simple, unicellular life forms developed, and, as we know from the theory of natural evolution, there emerged higher and higher species until human beings arrived, in whom mind accelerated its evolution so that it has now traversed farther along its upward journey than its predecessor. The later emergence of mind can also be proven from what we know of evolution. The stars arose eons ago; though science has told us nothing of life on other planets, life on Earth certainly came into being long after matter, when the world was fit to receive it. We may say that mind might have existed in an inert state prior to matter, but this is not probable, seeing that it would have had to persist for a tremendous length of time for no apparent reason while it waited for matter to adapt to its needs. Its progress is comparatively rapid, so the idea that it should have issued only after matter had advanced considerably is more rational.

As mind arose after matter, so it will disappear before it from the same causes—its dependent nature and its swifter progress. When every bit of it has been transformed, there will come a period when the proximate world—that is, the world of matter and mind, which are nearer to our awareness than the other two substances—will contain only matter. Then all at once matter will metamorphose as a whole, and the proximate world will cease to exist.

There were definite periods of production of matter and mind. Matter issued in a continuous stream, and the process was completed before; mind emerged after an interval. On the cessation of the flow of mind, the amount of substance in the proximate world no longer increased.

The proximate world moves according to laws implanted in it from the beginning. It arose in amorphous masses and slowly evolved toward order and an array of harmonious units, strengthening in beauty and growing toward its teleological consummation. Its purpose is perfection, and it is fraught with meaning. It is not a fortuitous concourse of atoms, and it is destined neither to be consumed in a gigantic conflagration nor to settle down to pallid death as a result of the inexorable dissipation of energy. It had a commencement and must have a termination, but it need not encounter inglorious annihilation; it would be curious if at the end of its progressive career it were to meet with nothingness. It is more logical that its continual advance would spell final perfection, which it will achieve as a collection of Determinate Units, imperishable, sublime.

Chapter 12
Cosmos

I have now given the metaphysical doctrines of the Entitarian system of philosophy. We have seen that the universe contains four entities or substances: the Primary Entity, which knew no beginning and was the source from which the others flowed; and the Determinate Entity, matter, and mind, which may be called *Emergent Entities*, for they emerged from another substance. Matter and mind are also designated the *Proximate Entities*, being immediately known to us, while the other two are the *Transcendental Entities*, for they transcend our everyday experience. The Primary Entity had no beginning and will have no end, while, after emergence, the Determinate Units maintain their existence forever. The Proximate Entities, on the other hand, had a definite beginning and will come to an end after they have fulfilled their evolutionary career. Ultimately, the universe will contain only the two Transcendental Entities, with the world of Determinate Objects augmented by the new collection of transformations.

Progress is the principle of the Proximate Universe. Progress—the past has revealed its operation, and there are no grounds for doubt concerning its effectiveness in the future. True, its course is not straight, and not the shortest distance between two points; rather, it may be likened to a sinuous river, travelling directly forward at times, bending backward at others, flowing into stagnant marshes too often, and winding along as it goes. It has to do with imperfect substances, and toil is its inseparable companion. Humanity will reach a lofty balance, whole in itself, an integral part of the universe, partaking of its character and resting on natural laws; nature itself will attain a pinnacle of ethereal beauty and sublime glory. When perfection comes, matter and mind will metamorphose and exist perennially as a collection of Perfect Objects. Perfection is the glory of the universe; the Transcendental Realm is already steeped in it, while the Proximate is evolving in that direction.

The universe is rational, possessing supreme order and behaving in accordance with specific rules, with no room for miracles or other infringements of natural law. Miracles are impossibilities, as they imply a lack of rigorous order; nothing would then be predictable, rendering the quest for knowledge futile. Determinism rules the sum of things, every event having a cause, and even in the realms of mind, it holds good in the sense that every action must be initiated by a force. The universe works out its destiny after its own inherent tendencies.

Entitarianism denies the validity of deism and theism; there is no personal God, from whom the Primary Entity must be carefully distinguished. God is a mind, and mind cannot create another substance; still less can any being call the universe out of the void. The notions of God are contradictory. If he were infinite, how could he have a finite form resembling a human being? If he were omniscient, how did he create vile matter for no other purpose than to destroy it in a fit of rage? If the devil and evil could wreak havoc, then God is either not omnipotent or not all good. He should be able to annihilate them, and if he did not but instead condemned his weak creatures to eternal hell for succumbing to them, could he not be accused of taking cruel delight in laying snares for us? God is conceived of as a superman with human passions and emotions, such as anger and mercy; he created the world for his own glory in order that he might exist in an atmosphere of servile flattery. As the conception of God was made in the days of monarchy, it is no wonder that he resembles an emperor. He has a strange weakness for adoration and apparently cannot endure solitude. He is a linguist, able to understand the many languages used by his benighted earthlings. He is a marriage broker, arranging for destined couples to meet and mate, but, as in so many of his labors, he does not seem to be very efficient if you consider the number of disastrous unions. In his tremendous justice, he makes one person inherit wealth so that by giving the superfluous portion of it in charity he may enter heaven, and another born to such penury that he may turn thief and be condemned to hell. He demands faith and displays his wrath if it is not forthcoming but forgets to provide a touchstone for it; considering the diversity of creeds, all of which can elicit unbounded faith, one can find oneself in tribulation for obstinacy in allegiance to what one considers his genuine desire. In his infinite wisdom, he chose certain races to receive his message first, while others remained ignorant until they found themselves conquered by the favored, thus receiving both spiritual joy and material misery. But enough of this: the ways of God are inscrutable, as his adherents declare when they find themselves driven into a corner, the same persons being quite ready to make a goodly number of affirmations about him, betokening an amount of knowledge that does not square with their unfortunate ignorance. The Primary Entity is not a glorified human being: it does not interfere with the workings of the Proximate Realm and does not act in the character of a Providence supervising human affairs. What is the use of natural rules if they cannot function of their own accord? Matter and mind arose, and their innate character is sufficient to make them run their destined course. Prayers, sacrifices, and the paraphernalia of popular religion designed to propitiate the Divine Power and avert calamity constitute superstition. The curious thing is that, though their efficacy has never been demonstrated, they persist obstinately from force of habit.

There are no specific places called *heaven* and *hell*, abodes of bliss and woe, in which human imagination has attempted to reproduce earthly hopes and fears. The universe of Perfect Objects surrounds the Primary Entity, but it is not a specific place, which implies a corner of space. Note that the Primary Entity is infinite and that the Determinate Entity tends toward infinity, but, unconcerned with space, they can coexist. If space were infinite and contained an infinite substance, there would be no room for another entity that also existed in space, but it would not be the case with substances that do not occupy space. Mind does not occupy space and can therefore coexist with matter in the same organism. Permanent existence is not the immortality of the soul, which is an inherently indivisible unit and must go either to heaven or hell. There is no soul over and above the mind, which is divisible and may be scattered, like matter, in fragments after death. As mind cannot exist apart from matter, there can be no ghosts, spirits, or angels. If its units continue whole after death and attain permanent existence, they do so on condition of transformation into objects of another substance.

Entitarianism is scarcely to be described as a system of pantheism, which identifies nature with God and usually conceives of him as a total mind. Matter is not mind and is not part of it. Mind is not a continuous single entity; it is inconceivable how, if it were fundamentally a vast expanse like an ocean, units could exist apart from it, enclosed in bodies. In Entitarianism, there is a distinction between Primary and Emergent Substances; though the latter evolved from the former, the separation is complete and will last unto eternity. In one form or another, pantheism is popular among thinkers, due, apparently, to their curious contempt for matter. In Entitarianism's identification of God with the totality of things, individual units cease to have any separate reality, a view difficult to entertain in light of the fact that each person is, by virtue of the nature of knowledge, more certain of his particular consciousness than of anything else. Spinoza did not make God a mind, but he regarded matter and mind as mere attributes, with no independent existence, and explained their interaction by the fanciful, albeit ingenious, concept of parallelism.

Agnosticism and skepticism are not tenable attitudes toward truth: ultimate reality is not unknowable, nor is it necessarily dubious. It may be granted that knowledge is difficult to acquire, but it does not follow that it is unattainable. The fact that various doctrines exist that are doubtful or wrong does not preclude the possibility of the human mind eventually arriving at truth. I repudiate skepticism in the sense of doubt concerning the possibility of acquiring knowledge of ultimate reality; if the word merely means doubt of the truth of existing religions, then I endorse skepticism; in fact, I go further and categorically deny their validity. The agnostic does not uphold his ignorance in the way that a simple-minded peasant would do but proudly affirms his position with some theory about the nature of knowledge. He knows for certain that he cannot know! But humankind is not likely to rest content with such an anomalous attitude.

Entitarianism may be described as partaking of atheism in the strict sense of disbelief in the existence of a personal God. Reason cannot prove the actuality of God, who is merely a sublimation of the comprehensible tendency of human beings to magnify themselves and a relic of ancient animism. However, there is no peculiar necessity for an atheist to be a materialist, as the conventionally religious imagine. The trouble is that it is customary to think only of two substances, and if one denies mind, then only matter remains. Similarly, permanent existence is conceived of in terms of inevitable immortality of the soul as an indivisible unit, and if, as usually happens, the atheist does not subscribe to this, he concerns himself only with our present existence and is stigmatized as worldly. Entitarianism offers other substances and another version of permanent existence. Nothing is wrong with genuine atheism, which has been entertained by many thinkers, though some, through the desire not to incur the opprobrium and persecution that might follow, or through contempt of popular opinion concerning their doctrines, have not unequivocally avowed it. Others inconsistently acquiesce in the prevalent theology, though it conflicts with their ideas, maybe because they think it useful for the masses but chiefly because they are not militant reformers. By using the word *God* to describe their peculiar conceptions, many philosophers, notably the pantheists, have given rise to confusion. Indeed, in an age of prejudice, Shelley boldly proclaimed the necessity of atheism, thereby showing that he had no desire for any misapprehension concerning his conception of the spirit's being coeval with the universe. It is a Western prejudice that religion is synonymous with theism: Buddha and Lao-tze had no place for an anthropomorphic God in their scheme of ultimate values.

It is trite to aver that the universe presents a picture of sublime order; it is wise to remember that the order is, at present, incomplete. It has as yet performed only part of its journey and has yet to reach perfect harmony. It would be absurd to declare that this world is the best of all possible worlds in the sense that none can conceivably be better. The theory of perfectibility does not mean that the world is already perfect, still less that it has always been perfect; what is asserted is that it will eventually attain perfection through an inherent principle. The theory postulates dynamic progress and has more regard to the "what will be" than the "what is."

The essence of the Entitarian theory is the idea of perfection. The Primary Entity is perfect; the Determinate Units are perfect; matter and mind are evolving toward perfection. Without ultimate perfection, the universe must be a colossal blunder and would have no meaning. Existence *per se* is strange; that it should have a meaning to explain it is more credible than that it hasn't. The riddle of the universe is great, but it would be even more perplexing if there were no meaning in the scheme of things.

Chapter 13
Ethical System

Every religion is associated with a moral system: ethics is the natural ally of metaphysics, and a way of life implies a set of rules. But for a system to be truly integrated, all the doctrines must be linked to one another like flower petals; moreover, if an ethic and a metaphysic form part of a creed, the former must be directly derived from the latter. In some religions, the moral code consists of arbitrary commands without mutual relationship, each standing alone. In accordance with the Spherical Method, there will be a central principle from which flow other doctrines: the ethical system will be a unified whole that is coordinated with the metaphysical system.

All ethical systems can be divided into two classes: the self-abnegatory and the hedonistic. The former, by far the more numerous and specially allied with religion, preaches the cultivation of virtue, while the latter advocates giving free rein to the instinctive desire for happiness. Some particular virtue is usually stressed, such as filial piety in Confucianism, inactivity in Taoism, or the suppression of passion in Stoicism. The mere fact that we exist could only mean that we are meant to live, and happiness often denotes no more than the easiest and most assured way of maintaining life. To revile the love of personal welfare, as saints do, is irrational; on the other hand, an unmitigated struggle for existence can never lead to the formation of a stable society, nor even of a small unit like a family. The desire for one's own good must be tempered by the dictates of duty. Virtue is a prerequisite of the higher life: civilization and the loftiest individual good demand the renunciation of many pleasures. The reconciliation of virtue and happiness is not easy, yet this is essential for true good, based on natural laws. Their opposition is stressed in theory, though in principle people manage to effect a compromise of a minimum of virtue and a maximum of enjoyment. Thus, even in a society dominated by a rigorous saintly creed, civilization could display its secular plumes. Life has been rendered unwholesome and bitter by the discrepancy between the instinct for pleasure and the teachings of morality.

Before proceeding any further, we must define the object of ethical inquiry. Every branch of knowledge is concerned with a particular aspect of reality: chemistry deals with the constitution of matter; astronomy surveys the stars; esthetics aspires to discover the character of artistic beauty. The problem of ethics is the good. What is meant by this term? In an extended sense, it signifies every variety of worth—it is synonymous with *value*; but the investigation of value as a whole should be the province of another subject.

Value can be looked at from two points of view: the universal and the human. Universal or absolute value exists independently of humanity. It is not variable but is a quality inherent in all the four entities; in the scheme of things, the stars possess a particular value that many may disregard but that they cannot alter, for it has to do with the universe. Human or utilitarian value depends on human needs and rises or falls with our estimation. The goods economists ponder are of this type; a loaf of bread may possess more value or less than a piece of cloth to an individual, depending on his requirements at the time, their absolute value being unaffected. Ironically, an object of greater absolute value is generally regarded as being of lesser value by the ordinary person. How many men would not prefer a pipe of tobacco over a peony or would feel deeply inclined to watch the rippling sea rather than sit down to a banquet?

It is evident that ethics does not concern itself impartially with all value and that its interest is more concentrated on a certain species: wisdom and beauty undoubtedly possess the highest value, but it is not its business to scrutinize their nature. It deals with a particular type of good, whose problems revolve around happiness and the ego.

This may be termed *ethical good*, in contradistinction from *total good*, which denotes all value in the universe. Ethical good relates to the interest of humanity, to our ends and aims, and it takes into account our emotions, will, and actions. It is an aspect of absolute value having to do with the individual mind, its glory and aspirations; but it also refers to utilitarian value and must have it since it is preeminently a human concern.

Ethical good should be derived, not divorced, from total good. Metaphysics is a subject with its own special interests, attempting to solve the general nature of the universe; but, for its purposes, it touches on psychology and the physical sciences. In order to possess real significance, ethics must be related to the universe, to metaphysics; it must not stand isolated but must be based on total good, which is an integral aspect of the cosmos. The universe is brimming with value displayed in beauty, harmony, and rationality, its most sublime characteristic being perfection. The Proximate Realm is not yet perfect, but it contains an irresistible tendency toward perfection, and humanity as well as nature have this for their goal. Hence, to love the good is to love perfection; perfection is the good. This is not to say that the two terms are synonymous; they are merely intimately interrelated. When a hedonist avers that pleasure is the good, it is impossible to suppose that pleasure and good have the same meaning, and the only implication should be that pleasure is endowed with good. When a physicist states that heat is molecular motion, it would be unwarrantable to conclude that there is no difference between them, and the only rational belief is that they are associated. For two terms with different significations to be regarded as synonymous is absurd.

As perfection is the good, ethical perfection should constitute ethical good. What is ethical perfection? It is the perfection of human aim and life, of attitude toward the universe and its realization in action. What can be more perfect than a life that has for its interest the entire scheme of things? Since human beings are part of the universe, it is natural for our lives to revolve around it. Cultivate a comprehensive life, a life that comprehends the universe: this is the basic tenet of the Entitarian ethical system, from which more detailed rules of conduct may be deduced. It is the test of the validity of an ethical rule, and it is objective, unlike pleasure or the conscience with its disjointed deliverances. This doctrine relates ethical good to total good and, with the universe conceived of in the Entitarian light, ethics to metaphysics.

"Love pleasure!" shout the hedonists. "Love virtue!" exclaim the moralists. Both these rules are narrow in scope, pleasure and virtue being only parts of the sum of things. The antithesis between pleasure and virtue is consequent on preoccupation with a restricted province of experience: the former centers itself mainly on artificial products, such as wine and raiment, while the latter would renounce the world. A life whose base is the universe as a whole includes wisdom, virtue, and happiness: wisdom, because it rests on truth and knowledge; virtue, because it shuns absorption in the interests for which humans struggle; and happiness, because it revels in the glories of nature. No longer will the good person be thought a simpleton with misery for his dower: one can bless the earth, enjoying oneself every day without being filled with the pangs of conscience and fits of agonized self-recrimination. Desire and action will go hand in hand, and an individual will cease to be his own inveterate enemy, yearning for one kind of deed yet finding himself performing the opposite.

The term *ethical* needs to be distinguished from the term *moral*, which has a more restricted meaning, in that an ethical good connotes any value that we pursue, while a moral good is only that species that we ought to cultivate as a duty, even though we may be reluctant to do so. Pleasure is an ethical good, and so is virtue, but only the latter is a moral good. Pleasure is instinctively sought, and, if it were not, no blame could be attached to the sufferer, as it concerns only his personal welfare. Virtue is primarily cultivated for the fulfillment of a cosmic or social purpose, and, though it is not detrimental to our ultimate good, it may constitute an immediate loss or run counter to our desire; nevertheless, it should not be violated, as we exist as part and parcel of the scheme of things.

Pleasure or pain is a sensation found to accompany all mental states in greater or lesser degree. Unlike all others, pleasure constitutes an end in itself, and it is not therefore any cause for wonder that it should have been identified with the good by many thinkers—and instinctively by the ordinary person as well. That it is the sole determinant of human action is false, but that it is in actual life the chief determinant is indubitable. John Stuart Mill introduced into Bentham's dictum of maximum pleasure a distinction between one's pleasure and the pleasure of others and a further distinction between higher and lower pleasures. Whether individuals ought to or not, facts prove that they do, to a certain extent, promote others' pleasure at their own expense and deliberately pursue pleasure of lesser intensity; they must be singularly obtuse to do so if they do not recognize that there are other considerations besides pleasure. The criterion of pleasure subserves purely a human desire, having nothing to do with the cosmic purpose. It pays no attention to the destiny of humanity, segregates us from nature, and, in fact, creates an artificial little world in the stupendous expanse of the universe. Carried to its logical ends, it is antagonistic to progress, social good, and knowledge and ultimately destroys itself. Progress entails labor, which is a pain for the normal human constitution; pleasure is personal, and the individual's pursuit of it is hampered by consideration of others' rights. It is idle to suppose that intellectual development gives more vivid intensity of enjoyment than physical experience; a maximum of pleasurable sensation terminates in revulsion and exhaustion. Because of these difficulties, Epicurus and Bentham inconsistently pictured the happy life as a serene attitude and promotion of public welfare, respectively. Most individuals would consider the absence of sensual delights a grievous affliction and would not imagine that if they lost a million dollars in taxation, their happiness would be increased.

Virtue is largely a negative characteristic; it is an eschewal of pleasure. It is passive rather than active, and it owes its prominence to the fact that so many types of pleasure are deleterious in their effects. What is onerous to attain tends to be regarded as valuable, and, as human beings are constitutionally inclined toward pleasure, the suppression of this desire is deemed a triumph of the will and an indication of superiority. However, since the good as an entity denotes what has actual being, not what is nonexistent, virtue, insofar as it is merely the absence of certain traits, cannot be the good: ultimate good must be positive. The Stoic, who regards suppression of passion as the aim of life, is not actually demonstrating that virtue is the good but that life contains no good. There is, of course, the positive virtue associated with altruism that needs analysis. Altruism cannot be the good, for it must revolve around some entity; it would probably be defined as the pursuit of the happiness of others, in which case happiness is the good. If the happiness of others is good, then why not the happiness of oneself? This sounds cynical, but it is necessary to face facts clearly. What it all boils down to is that virtue is not the ultimate good, though it is an aim contributing to it, a legitimate pursuit, a necessity, whether in its positive or negative aspect; and evil must be destroyed, its existence being worse than its absence. Virtue would scarcely arise as a necessity if individuals did not engage in conflict in pursuit of their respective pleasures; that is, it is preeminently a social problem. Had it not been for the fact that the masses were desperately poor, saintliness would not have been an object of veneration as a counterblast to unattainable luxury, a way of indicting the wealthy; now that socialism provides a method of allowing the disinherited to partake of material enjoyments, asceticism incurs popular ridicule as symptomatic of insanity.

Virtue and happiness have always formed the themes of ethics; but, in reality, the latter is the theme, the former being merely its negation, though it is that with which most moral systems are concerned. The explanation lies in the fact that there is no particular need for any treatise on the desirability of happiness, as everyone instinctively courts it: the hedonist is the most unoriginal of thinkers, uttering the greatest of platitudes, which every person knows. Virtue contradicts instinct, hence the difficulty of attaining it; of all types of value, it alone bears this singular distinction—everyone is more anxious to have it cultivated by others than to arrogate it to oneself! This is irrefutable proof that possessing it is considered a loss, and thus there arises that strange discrepancy between theory and practice, so little in evidence in other provinces of life. Why, then, should virtue be advocated? Because unbridled pleasure is damaging to social stability and the cosmic purpose.

The ego is a principal interest of ethics: it is the self, and it is natural that an individual should be concerned with what is his most intimate possession. Moral codes generally condemn preoccupation with it, and some, like Buddhism, preach its utter extinction. Egoism is opposed to altruism; it would not be an evil if its dictates were not commonly of the wrong category and had not led to the infliction of injury by one person on another. It is clear that it cannot be totally annihilated, because, if a person didn't care for himself at all, he would soon be dead, as he would not eat or do anything to preserve his life. A celebrated dictum of Kant claims that a moral action is one that, when made universal, does not nullify itself. Lying is wrong for, if everyone perpetually resorted to fibbing, then nobody would believe anybody else, and the object of lying would be defeated. This test is objective and attempts to unify all moral rules, thus setting the Kantian ethical system apart from other puritanical codes with their arbitrary dogmas. Unfortunately, it is inapplicable to many virtues, while, on the other hand, it satisfies many vices. It would be difficult to deem cowardice a virtue, yet if everyone were endowed with a faint heart, nobody would engage in an encounter with anybody else, and safety, the object of cowardice, would be attained; if everybody ran away from a battlefield, all life would be preserved, and war, an evil, would vanish! The aim of drunkenness is pleasure: if everybody got drunk, there would still be pleasure. If everybody were charitable, there would be nobody left on whom to exercise charity; if everybody were uncharitable, everybody would retain what they had! The test fails as a sure mode of distinguishing virtue from evil, but it is useful in showing that universal practicability is desirable for a good. In respect to altruism, if everybody unstintingly cared only for others and neglected himself, it would become unable to function, as nobody would consent to receive anything. This clearly demonstrates that a certain measure of egoism is a prerequisite for life to maintain itself. If everybody were egoistical, everybody would sustain his being, and this is a possibility, though society would be in chaos. It seems then that a combination of egoism and altruism works for maximum good. Egoism is the core, and no one who absolutely does not consider his own welfare can possibly look after another's: altruism is necessary for a harmonious society. Both must be conditioned by a right ideal or they go astray, especially egoism, though altruism is not immune from it, as an individual who admires and pursues an evil pleasure may be unselfish when he desires another to share it with him.

The ultimate objective of conduct is the good, which has been defined as perfection and which is attained by a life that comprehends, comprises, or revolves around the universe or the totality of entity. A specific action conducive to the good is termed a *right*. The good and the right are related to each other, the former bearing a general meaning and the latter detailed in application; the two terms are to be understood in their ethical sense only. By the good is meant perfection of character and conduct, and by the right traits like enjoyment of nature, kindness, and chastity.

What is the criterion of a right? How do we know that a particular course of action merits approbation? The utilitarian makes the test objective: what engenders happiness is right, and what produces pain is wrong. This rule confers on the test an air of certitude and simplicity, and it is mainly easy to apply. The intuitionist has recourse to a special sense, usually the conscience, to distinguish right from wrong, the test being subjective. That the moral deliverances differ from race to race and from age to age proves the fallibility of this mode of judgment. Conscience is conditioned by habit or prejudice; through training, one comes to regard certain actions as right or wrong, and the strength of one's conscience depends partly on one's character and partly on one's receptivity to external influences. In any case, people do not feel identical pangs of conscience.

A valid criterion must be objective if all the rules are to be harmonized and flow from a single principle. Perfection is the good: whatever tends to perfection is right, and whatever impairs it is wrong. This test is even more objective and universal than the pleasure principle, for pleasure is a sensation varying from person to person and not strictly capable of being evaluated. Ethical perfection is based on the perfection of the universe, and, though opinions may differ as to what perfection is, there can be only one perfection that characterizes the universe. A diversity of views is attributable to the human liability to err, in the same way that there are various concepts concerning the nature of the ultimate substance—dualism, monism, materialism, idealism—that do not prove that the universe is not real or that its nature is not definite. Ethical perfection is defined as a comprehensive life: whatever promotes this is right, and whatever hinders it is wrong.

Pleasure, the good of the utilitarian, is humanity's ultimate objective; but virtue to the moralist is seldom an end in itself but a passport to heaven, social stability, mental peace, and so on. Ethical perfection is an intrinsic part of universal perfection, and its attainment is an end in itself as a component of the cosmic purpose. It does not resemble pleasure, a transitory aim important only to humans, but is a constituent of the abiding nature of the universe, while, unlike virtue, it is not wholly dissimilar from its ultimate objective but is its own objective.

One problem, an eternal bone of contention, concerns the freedom of the will, which is of paramount significance in connection with ethics. One school, the free-willists, maintains that a person can do anything he chooses, and if he transgresses the moral law, he has done so with deliberate intent, for he can refrain from such behavior. The other school, the determinists, contends that every deed is the product of inexorable forces, and, given the conditions, there is no possible alternative to the line of conduct taken. Is it possible that an individual can freely will an action and thereby execute it, or is he an automaton, his acts determined by causes over which he has no control?

As has been pointed out, the will does exist, but it is only an intermediary between motive and action. One cannot will at random, but a certain motive produced in the course of one's inner experience or embodying a reaction to an external event acts on one's will, which engenders the action. Before the deed can materialize, three conditions are essential: the motive must be adequate, the will must be responsive, and there must be the capacity for performance. There must, in fact, be cooperation among the three factors; action is the joint product of ability, motive, and will. A stronger motive may fail against a weaker if the will refuses to function, and both motive and will can avail nothing if an individual is suffering from some bodily infirmity that compels him to a particular course of conduct. An evil deed may ensue if a good intention is overwhelmed by a motive that, though not so much desired if there is complete freedom of choice, is compelling by force of circumstances. The view advocated is not strictly one of free will or determinism; the will is not free, as it alone cannot beget an act, while behavior is not deterministic, as a deed is not the simple, direct outcome of forces outside a person's control. An action is not erratic, without explanation, but is the product of motive, will, and ability and is determined by them. It may be called voluntary if there is an element of will in it; there is, of course, the other type of action, which is automatic, created by a force without reference to conscious will or motive. Determinism is the correct view in the sense that conduct is conditioned by causes, including the will, which itself is a natural entity not functioning arbitrarily. The universe is an interrelated system of strict order that would be upset if an errant factor could alter it *ad lib*. If everything behaves according to natural law, it would be preposterous to presume that humanity alone is exempt from its control; will is not free if this means it can do anything without cause, but it possesses a determining power.

If an individual cannot do whatever he likes, is it feasible to speak of duty, to hold him morally responsible for his deeds? Certainly, he cannot be condemned with moralists' customary self-righteous anger and hatred, but it would be fantastic to presume that evil ceases to be evil if it cannot be helped, any more than folly is to be deemed desirable. Virtue is still admirable and must be cultivated just as health or beauty is pursued. Though not erratic and arbitrary, the will is a real entity, and it can decide to adopt a certain course of behavior; the power of choice is genuine, even if it is not omnipotent. But altering character cannot be done by enunciating moral dogmas and expecting them to be practiced via mere volition. A suitable ground needs to be prepared: the mind must be trained to the right ideas and diligently cultivated; circumstances should be propitious. Duty itself is a trait of the mind and acts as a powerful motive. Responsibility means no more than that a person has the duty to realize the good, for his conduct and the fact that his character compels him to it do not release him from its consequences, which may redound to his benefit or his detriment and which will provoke others to behavior deemed appropriate. However, as the will is not absolute but is molded by diverse factors acting in accordance with mental laws, it would not do to react to a breach of duty with irrational violence.

Is human nature inherently good, bad, or neutral? Some maintain that every human being is born virtuous and explain away his evil actions by saying that he went wrong or that society corrupted him; others have it that he is born wicked and that only drastic law can restrain his passions, or that the infinite grace of God alone can save him. It is obvious that if a person is innately moral, his delinquencies must be accidental and cannot triumph over him; yet the chronic evil manifested by generation after generation demonstrates that, if existent, our native goodness must be extremely fragile. On the other hand, if we are born evil, then it is inexplicable how we come to possess a desire for good, a desire shining through all history and entwined with popular religion. What are good and evil? When it is asserted that a person is good or bad, what is really signified is that he conforms to or violates the standard of conduct currently prevailing. Human beings are born with passions, desires, and inclinations, among which cannot be found a principle of conventional good and evil; it is fantastic to suppose that we possess an inherent spirit of agreement or disagreement with any particular ethical system. Moral rules are instilled only by training, and, in the natural state, an individual knows nothing of them. All emotions and actions can be classified according to a particular theory, and if it turns out that the majority are deemed good, then human nature is dubbed moral; but if they are evil, then it is vilified as immoral. It is best to examine the purpose of human existence. Why is there life? No special intelligence is needed to know that the aim of life is not death but its maintenance. We are endowed with the instinct to live, the strongest of all instincts, a very natural phenomenon, consonant with the mere fact of our existence. Humanity struggles to survive; we naturally pursue what promotes our objective and shun what militates against it. This ultimate purpose is changeless, but the actions resorted to are conditioned by environment. Some of these happen to be good, and some bad. Judged by any moral system, they are, on the whole, often wrong; without providing the means for practicing the good, the moral system seeks to limit or prohibit the pursuit of those actions that an individual deems necessary to promote his welfare. Human nature then is basically nonmoral but is judged as evil by moral systems. There is no predilection for either morality or immorality, but, impelled by conditions prevalent thus far, the practice of the conventionally evil has triumphed.

I do not deny that human beings are born with an ethical sense, just as we enjoy an esthetic sense; however, this must be distinguished from the moral sense, which is the ethical sense conventionalized in a certain form. The moral sense is purely an artificial product, the result of belief and training in a specific moral system, while the ethical sense informs a person of what is good, what is desirable, and what he should cultivate. This good may have nothing to do with virtue; it may indeed be vice. Natural ingredients of the good as instinctively felt are the preservation of life and the cultivation of happiness. These two are the chief and most universal of all emotions, though every feeling and action may be judged in this sense to be good or bad. Like the esthetic sense, the ethical sense is influenced by environment and training, its instinctive tendencies altering with surprising results; hence, in any particular society, ideas of the good and beautiful are stereotyped and may differ from those of another. When it is said that human beings are nonmoral, what is meant is that we do not naturally set out to follow or violate the usual concepts of virtue and vice. This does not contradict the doctrine that we are endowed with an ethical sense through which we feel right and wrong; these two terms merely connote the desirable and the undesirable and do not necessarily have any connection with moral good and moral evil.

Chapter 14
Moral Code

Lead a life that comprehends the universe: this is the fundamental principle that must be elaborated. From it flow three major rules, around which gather the three divisions of the Entitarian moral code. The comprehensive life relates to the universe in *toto*; hence it is imperative to consider the scheme of things in its natural sections. As has been pointed out, there are four substances. For the moral scheme, the Primary and Determinate Entities, which are both perfect and eternal and form our ultimate interest, are thought of together as constituting the Transcendental Realm. The material realm is of paramount concern in ordinary life, and what is commonly designated *nature* is equivalent to it; the mental realm in its highest development means humanity. The moral system, then, must extend its interest over the transcendental, material, and mental realms, forming a harmonious life involving profound concern with all three.

Morality comprises three types: religious, personal, and social; but one of these is apt to be disproportionately emphasized to the neglect of the others. Religion pays scant respect to personal morality and in its mystic forms is exclusively preoccupied with its relationship to the first cause; this kind of conduct is designated *holiness*. Personal morality, or the attainment of one's own good, of realizing one's own *raison d'être*, is generally deprecated save in hedonism. It directly concerns the immediate welfare of the individual, who is composed of a mind and a body and whose first prerequisite is the maintenance of his life. This welfare is bound up with material phenomena; one does not take an interest in matter for its purposes but for one's own happiness, whereas one's interest in the Primary Entity and humanity is primarily for their ends and only secondarily for one's own. Hence, personal morality that deals with the self is said to correspond to the material realm. In the present day, social morality is of special import and is implied in political speculation and social reform and partially embodied in law. Morality has indeed been often discussed as though it were concerned solely with the preservation of society. The Entitarian ethical system is equally preoccupied with all three types of morality. By religious, personal, and social morality I mean the individual's attitude and conduct regarding the Transcendental Entities, the self, and humanity, respectively. The three divisions of the universe correspond to the three divisions of morality.

Love and contemplate the Primary Entity—this is the foundation of religious morality. The Primary Entity is the basic reality, the highest being. It is infinity, and contemplation of it will ennoble the mind, which, achieving perfection through the best of ways, will not disintegrate but transform itself into a Perfect Object and exist permanently. It is also imperative to reflect over the realm of Determinate Objects, which are perfect and increase in number toward infinity and of which a person can hope to be part after death. Especially in solitude and at night, though it can be done at any time or place, let us endeavor to apprehend the Transcendental Realm, to experience a vision of the source engirdled by the radiant collection of Perfect Objects. Intuition, which is unreliable when it ventures into the province of reason, displays its utility here as the faculty *par excellence* for beholding the invisible world at a single glance. Unlike the cumbrous process of reason, its method is direct and its action instantaneous. The universe drops into the small cage of the mind, or, alternatively, the mind may be said to expand to the infinite size of the universe. So miraculous is mind, though having only a comparatively shadowy existence in the scheme of things. Contemplation should not be quiet or lifelessly serene but should be concentrated and forceful. As the Primary Entity is dynamic, and the process of transformation of mind is dynamic, contemplation of such a substance and with such a purpose must be dynamic. Devotion to the Transcendental Realm is a joy and a duty: interest in perfection and sublimity must be the purest joy, while the duty is involved in the fulfillment of the cosmic purpose, in preparing our minds for attaining the objective, transformation.

Love and enjoy nature—pure and genuine happiness proceeds therefrom. Personal morality has this for its basis, as its immediate goal is happiness, which could best be found in the extensive domain of nature. No more abundant gratification is conceivable; the pleasure is undiluted and does not conflict with the two other divisions of morality. It is manifest that if morality is to be integrated, one department should complement another. Nature should be admired in all its aspects, from the gentle glories it exhibits, such as the limpid moon sailing over the vaulted heavens, shimmering stars, elfish clouds, and gorgeous flowers swaying softly on their slender stalks; to the stormy forms it assumes, no less splendid—raging seas and jagged lightning. Its evolution does not flow peacefully; the heart of nature holds a hurricane. Force is its essence, and majesty is more to its taste than softness. Love connotes much more than poetic enjoyment of its visible, concrete phenomena, as knowledge of nature's laws yields equal good. Live a temperate life, and happiness will coexist with virtue: rational happiness is the ideal. There is no harm in what are often designated *material pleasures*, provided they are restrained. However, when indulged in excessively, they become vices, which should be eschewed as sedulously as needless pain. The material realm should not be disdained, as an entire division of the universe should not have been brought into existence for a vile objective. The products of humanity consist only of modifications of a tiny fraction of phenomena yet, strangely enough, constitute almost the exclusive interest of the average person. They are not inherently wrong but, on the contrary, are useful and even necessary and should be accorded their due attention. They are made for happiness, which is a legitimate desire; but the trouble is that they tend to engender excessive interest, destroy the universal life, and breed conflict. The remedy is not, however, to discard them altogether but to utilize them moderately, be their master and not their slave; though the mind should be cultivated most, the body need not be neglected.

Love humanity and promote its progress—on this doctrine is reared the structure of social morality. Human beings live in communities for mutual advantage, for the interchange of benefits; consequently, antisocial conduct is not conducive to the good even of the perpetrator. The individual is an integral unit of humankind and must therefore endeavor to promote its goals; anything that contributes to the advance of civilization, be it an idea, a work of art, a scientific invention, or a good deed, is desirable, and whatever retards social development is reprehensible. Not only society but individuals should have their welfare promoted, and a person should do what he can to lighten another's lot, to help him to a better, happier life, to abstain from the commission of any act that will inflict injury on him. Envy is the root of evil; it is the most common of human failings, and it impedes the fruition of altruism. It breeds malice, hatred, cruelty, and war. Eradicate it and a benevolent, peaceful community results. Progress, which is to be taken in the sense of advancement toward perfection, is to humanity the most momentous of endeavors, whereby we realize our *raison d'être* and subserve the ultimate goal of the universe, of which we are a part. In spite of its predominant position, the human mind is still only a portion of total mind but, as it is not possible to influence the progress of other types of mind, all that can be done is to take an interest in them and, in the case of animals, to treat them with as much kindness as is practicable.

Morality, which revolves around the entire universe, comprises the three sublime responses—toward the Transcendental Entities, nature, and humankind, their collective aim being the fulfillment of humanity's destiny as an integral part of the scheme of things. A life based on these precepts is signaled by wisdom, virtue, and happiness, which form a genuine combination and are not opposed to one another. Folly is contemptible; vice is odious; pain is undesirable.

Every action will be tested by these three rules and ultimately by its exemplification of the principle of a life in harmony with the universe: all moral injunctions will be derived from them. Thus, the ethical system is an integrated whole—not a thing of shreds and patches, arbitrary dogmas, conventions, or disjointed deliverances of a supposed authority. An action that promotes the comprehensive life is right, while one that violates it is wrong: this objective criterion is not difficult to apply. To illustrate: drunkenness is reprehensible—why? Test it by the fundamental principle. An individual who is devoted to wine is overwhelmed by an infinitesimal fraction of the sum of things; his attention is distracted from the Transcendental Realm, from nature, from humankind; he is a slave to a trifle. His mania, in a word, is condemned because he allows one passion to run away with him. Note that the argument does not necessarily apply to a person who drinks in moderation; his indulgence is permissible, though the less he quaffs, the better, as his will for sublimity may be impaired. The comprehensive life does not signify enjoyment of every trifle but devotion to the universe as a whole—quite a different concept. The test is applicable to every physical pleasure. One whose interest revolves around the universe does not engage in an intense struggle with one's fellows for the realization of any personal triumph, thus avoiding evils like cruelty and robbery. Contemplating cosmic harmony prevents a person from impairing his sublimity of mind with injustice and thinking up tricks for increasing his wealth. A modicum of concern with sublunary convenience is not harmful; indeed, it is an absolute necessity, for hunger and penury would reduce one's capacity for roaming over the wide scheme of things. Preoccupation with sexual love, whether it is absorption in one person or involvement in multiple affairs, is to be shunned; it is as damaging as any pleasure and should be replaced by a reasonable affection. By leading a comprehensive life, a due balance is preserved between ordinary interests. The multifarious affairs of the world constitute a mere fraction of the totality of things and should not occupy an undue share of attention.

A comprehensive life, in harmony with the universe, is naturally conducive to virtue and happiness; it is the ideal, and all actions should be tested by it. In opposition to it is the limited life, concerned with a fraction of the sum of things, as, for example, with material pleasures; it is wrong, against truth, and though it may be consonant with virtue, which one may pursue for a variety of reasons or causes, it will not lead to the realization of the cosmic purpose. On the other hand, devotion to the universe may unnaturally and illogically coexist with vice, but insofar as vice operates, it detracts from mental harmony and injures the cosmic purpose, which will not culminate in triumphant fulfillment if it is strong.

Actions may be grouped into the moral, or those subject to the distinction between moral right and moral wrong, and the nonmoral, or those outside the scope of such judgment. The moral are classified under the terms *virtue* and *evil* and the nonmoral under *happiness* and *pain*; hence, there are four classes. All actions are capable of giving either pleasure or pain, and we naturally pursue pleasure and eschew pain; to the two terms are attached two others, *right* and *wrong*. A pleasure that is right is a nonmoral pleasure; its attainment is purely a personal problem, involving no question of duty, hence its nonmoral character. A wrong pain sustained by the agent himself is a loss to the sufferer and is thus nonmoral. A pleasure that is wrong is an evil, for it implies the duty of abstention. A pain that is right is a virtue in that it implies the duty of cultivation; however, a virtue is not necessarily a pain, as it may be just the absence of direct personal pleasure. Virtues are of two types: *altruistic* and *stoical,* the former denoting a good done to others and the latter an absence of pleasure or endurance of pain. Evils are likewise of two kinds: *egoistic* and *vicious,* the former signifying a wrong committed against others and the latter an indulgence in pleasure or an avoidance of pain.

An action possesses different degrees of desirability or condemnation. A nonmoral pleasure may be cultivated as much as possible, and a nonmoral pain is worse in proportion to its intensity. The greater the height it attains, the more praiseworthy a virtue becomes, while an evil may be so slight as to be pardonable.

There exists a conflict between virtue and pleasure, for virtue is mainly negative; that is, it is mere abstention from pleasure. This discordance can be resolved only as a whole; certain pleasures and virtues are pursued so that one can be said to be both happy and virtuous. Moreover, if we direct the will into the right channels, what is ordinarily a pain or absence of pleasure may be made to yield happiness; for instance, benevolence can confer joy, though this is indirect. Virtues and nonmoral pleasures can exist side by side, and through such a combination one attains the harmonious life, for neither is in itself everything, while wisdom must rule both.

A table of ethical actions is given. In it only the positive are listed, while the negative are to be understood as their opposites. If one is recorded as a virtue, then its corresponding negative is to be deemed an evil and vice versa. For example: kindness is put down as a virtue, and therefore its negative opposite, callousness, which is not specifically mentioned, is to be viewed as falling into the category of the evil. Sensuality is listed as a vice, so its negative, chastity, will be deemed a virtue. Every positive quality, by which is meant an active quality, has a corresponding negative quality, which simply denotes abstention from action. A positive quality may also have a positive opposite, which is tabulated. Two positive opposites are extremes, the negative coming in the middle, equidistant from them. It follows that there may be two negatives that denote the same quality, one being ostensibly a virtue and the other an evil. As one quality cannot be both good and bad, it is neither good nor bad but indifferent; according to circumstances, however, it may be good or bad. To illustrate: the negative opposites of the two positive opposites, love and hate, are both indifference, which, conveying the idea of neutrality, is neither good nor bad, being regarded from the point of view of lack of love as an evil and from the point of view of lack of hate as a virtue. The list is not exhaustive; it is intended merely to serve as a guide to the more common qualities. Variations of a quality, such as those implied in the synonyms *pride, vanity, arrogance, impudence,* and *conceit,* are not enumerated. Some words are names of things, not of qualities or actions, and are to be understood as signifying association with the things; for example, *art* connotes *love of art,* and *food, possession of food.*

I.	**Nonmoral qualities**	
	1.	Happiness Food, material convenience, beauty of person, health, hope, art, knowledge, nature
	2.	Pain Anger, despair, fear, slavery, starvation, disease, suicide, death

II.	**Moral qualities**	
	1.	Stoical virtue Bravery, work, endurance
	2.	Vice Avarice, gluttony, drunkenness, narcotics, sensuality, excessive indulgence
	3.	Altruistic virtue Honesty, sincerity, gratitude, charity, self-sacrifice, kindness, kindness to animals, faithfulness, benevolence, parental love, conjugal love, filial love, love, devotion to the Transcendental Entities
	4.	Egoistic evil Envy, malice, dishonesty, flattery, hypocrisy, treachery, pugnacity, thievery, hate, cruelty to animals, cruelty, murder

No virtue or evil is categorical; that is, no virtue or evil can be regarded as such under all conditions. When a quality is listed under a certain heading, it means only that, as a rule, it possesses the character attributed to it. Some are more flexible than others, their judgment being more apt to depend on circumstances. An evil can seldom become a good, but frequently it can lose its edge. When it is a necessity in order to attain a blameless end, it may be admirable or at least excusable, provided it is borne in mind that it is of genuine urgency and is not a tremendous horror. The case of the man who must choose between telling a potential murderer where his prey has fled, thus allowing him to be butchered, and lying in order to save a life illustrates this. No one could hesitate to resort to falsehood under such circumstances. The man in the dilemma did not manufacture the situation; he is confronted with it, his intention is to avert a major evil by a minor, and he is properly credited with a performance of the right, especially if he should incur personal danger from the frustrated fury of the homicidal maniac!

Motive and effect enter largely into the judgment of an action's merit. The same kind of deed does not bear the same value when affected by contrary motives or attended by dissimilar effects. Flattery is but gentle speech, save for its reprehensible motive of private gain through deception. Drunkenness is only the copious imbibing of a beverage, unexceptionable if it did not make a person obnoxious to others and injure his own mind and body.

A person's character must be evaluated by the sum total of his traits: if the majority are virtues, then he is good; if the reverse holds true, then he is bad. It is improbable that anybody possesses all the virtues and no vice, or all the evils and not a single good. However, because every individual is a compound of good and bad, it does not follow that no distinction is valid; the proportions of constituents vary from individual to individual. No work of art is perfect, but none can be absolutely vile; nevertheless, there exists a world of difference between a cheap romance and a classic. It is not merely a matter of comparison, for if one person is less evil than another, he does not thereby become good; rather, it is a matter of the preponderance of fine traits over the ill and vice versa. The problem is complicated. A host of minor delinquencies may be insignificant compared to a single tremendous atrocity. In fact, no exact standard of measurement can be applied to the determination of character, nor is it necessary either: a general estimate suffices.

Like virtue and vice, pleasure and pain are not susceptible to accurate determination. It is a truism to say that one man's meat is another man's poison. The curious fact is that anything can give joy. It is impossible to aver that such and such a thing is sure to be pleasurable; at most, all we are entitled to state is that it is welcome to the generality of humanity. Some of the finest pleasures are appreciated by only a few persons. Pleasure is distinguished not only by quantity but also by quality. Even measuring quantity is not easy, for account must be taken of several factors, such as intensity, duration, presence or absence of pain, and immediacy or otherwise of production. Quality is more important than quantity, and its test is the contribution of the pleasure to the comprehensive life. What is universal and perpetual is to be cultivated; hence, love of nature constitutes the highest bliss. The general rule is to avoid needless pain and lead a life that is on the whole pleasurable, eschewing whatever conflicts with virtue and the higher life.

The question of duty is real—the *ought* is not to be disregarded. It needs no inculcation to tell an individual to pursue an ordinary enjoyment, for he is instinctively prone to do so, fully aware that pleasure is pleasant. Duty applies chiefly to virtue—chiefly and not solely, for there is also the duty of cultivating sublime happiness, which, together with virtue, forms the comprehensive life, enabling the realization of the cosmic aim of existence. The universal life includes wisdom, virtue, and happiness, and it is a natural duty. Duty is not the unnatural, hypocritical brand preached by moralists and despots to make a person pursue the interests of the evil; on the contrary, it spells the fruition of the cosmic purpose. It is a personal duty, a duty one has to oneself to make the best of one's life.

The *ought* rests on the right. The unlucky truth is that human beings are prone to pursue the wrong. How is it possible to explain this? Human evolution is not smooth; the fact that we have a thinking mind proves that we are instrumental in working out our destiny. Even in the realm of matter, progress does not flow uninterruptedly in one direction but meanders. In the case of mind, it has certainly advanced and will continue to do so, but the process is tortuous. Only at a certain level of development does it become aware of its destiny or try to understand it and consciously strive toward its realization. If it does not do what is right, it is because its attainment is as yet low; it hinders its own evolution. This is not surprising, seeing that evolution does not travel straight. Even when one does not pursue the absolute right, it does not mean that wrong triumphs, for one may be advancing from a greater to a lesser wrong. Individual or general retrogression at certain periods does not preclude the eventual advance of humanity as a whole, and absolute right will finally become universal—pursued with natural eagerness.

The existence of evil is attributable to the originally faulty nature of the Proximate Substances and their evolutionary career. If a thing is not perfect, it follows that it contains what is not good, an element of the evil. In the upward course of evolution, evil tends to be overcome, but good is sometimes submerged by it, as evolution leads a zigzag course.

When perfection is reached, all evil will vanish. Evil is often explained away as though it did not exist, which is fantastic, or as a necessary element for bringing out the good, which must be very unwholesome if it could only subsist thus. One explanation says that evil would not be regarded as such if we considered the universe as a whole instead of its parts; witness the Leibnitsian theory of the best of all possible worlds—a delusive explanation, for genuine perfection and good must refer to details as well—the evils still remain evils. Even if the whole is good, it is marred and not completely good.

Chapter 15
Way of Life

The religious philosophy of Entitarianism is intended to serve as a way of life, which to be satisfactory must be intelligent, based on universal reality, on the truth and the right; hence, the need for a metaphysic. This does not mean that knowledge is valueless in itself; the intention is merely to stress the importance of practice. Theory and practice are correlated, for theory alone wears a sickly hue, while practice standing by itself spells misdirected energy.

Entitarianism combines a metaphysic and an ethic, and it rests on science; it is a rational system, all its elements cohering consistently. Its theory is a product of cold logic, and it has none of the imaginative dogmatism of superstitious religion; but to be efficacious, it must be realized emotionally in practice. Feeling is the motivating force of action, which without it is languid, pale, and of no moment. Once the truths are grasped intellectually, they must elicit passionate belief, evoke intense enthusiasm, and be put into practice with ardor. Then the philosophy becomes a religion.

All ways of life are not to be courted impartially. Surely the most significant and valuable is the way that is in harmony with the inner purpose of the universe and that forms part of its teleological nature. This is the cosmic way of life, which is of incomparable value. It is different on the one hand from the dogmatic darkness of superstitious religion and on the other from the vacuous skepticism and unsatisfying worldliness of an economic age.

The universe is a harmonious whole. Our life on earth should not be mere preparation for the next world; still less should it be concerned with the present alone. No doubt this life is only transitory, but it has its own good and immediate needs and is part of the scheme of things, to which it contributes its intrinsic value. Whatever good it possesses must be cultivated, as it can have no value for the universe if it has none in itself. Its present needs are undeniable, and merely neglecting them makes it sordid and miserable; a life of penury must have its ultimate value severely hampered. It is ridiculous to suppose that the perfection of the mind could be achieved without adequate facilities; in any case, there is no rhyme or reason in making conditions unnecessarily difficult. But the present life must not be accorded too emphatic an importance: ultimate destiny is surely the major consideration, as eternity is superior to a point in time.

A genuine way of life embraces the past, present, and future not in equal proportions but in ascending order of significance. Out of the past has emerged the present, from which will grow the future. Whatever is of value in the past may be retained, and whatever is good now may be cultivated, but a vision of the future is the most desirable. Sole reliance on the past is superstition; sole reliance on the present is convention; and sole reliance on the future breeds vague misery.

The earth is but a speck in space, but we have our being on it, so it is bound to occupy the major portion of our interest. It goes without saying, however, that the universe is the greater, and an effort must be made to apprehend it, nothing being more essential to perfection than reflection on the entire scheme of things.

A comprehensive life, then, revolves around this world and the next; the past, present, and future; the earth and the universe. The universe is evolving toward the ideal, and humanity, as part and parcel thereof, evolves along with it. The future of the race teems with hope: human beings have evolved from the ape, and the superhuman will come sooner or later.

Ordinary religion is preoccupied with sorrow and death, with frightful mummeries and arcane ceremonies, as valueless as they are unesthetic. A true religion is one of happiness, hope, and life; it is one of knowledge, not ignorance; of reason, not faith. It is a gross mistake, an unmitigated prejudice, to assume that a new religion must be defined in terms of the traditional religions; progress is eminently natural.

Religion is primarily concerned with the individual and his good, its effect on society being the sum of its effects on the component units. As society is made of a collection of individuals, it will be sound if all its members or even the majority are so.

Life should be simple, and complexities that could be eliminated should never be coddled. Nothing is more lamentable than the human tendency to associate profundity with intricacy, though there is no special value in elaboration as such. What can be acquired only in a lifetime is venerated, and what easily becomes the property of everyone is despised. Simplicity must also avoid the other extreme of bareness or the casting away of all useful paraphernalia; saintliness is inconsistent with progress.

Life should be natural. What is in accord with nature is what is rational, what agrees with reality, not necessarily what is primitive, seeing that nature changes and advances. A human invention derived from natural laws is right. What is objectionable is a product or practice not sanctioned by truth, pandering to a distorted sense of value or beauty; one who pierces one's cheeks or tattoos one's body is not acting according to nature.

Ritual is one of the most noxious acquisitions imaginable, useless, fantastic, irrational, and in direct contravention to simplicity and naturalness. Every popular religion is loaded with ludicrous ceremonies and stilted rules of conduct; nothing is more calculated to kill reason, freedom, and real desire for truth. That ritual could ever do any good is doubtful; that it is the guardian *par excellence* of conservatism is undeniable. The supreme promoter of hypocrisy and smugness, it is often claimed to be picturesque, appealing to the esthetic sense, when in truth it is revolting, its weirdness only dulled by familiarity. Like all conventions, it possesses some force as a social bond and may on this account find a shadow of excuse, but the stability of society can be maintained by more natural methods. A few simple rites may be indulged in for social purposes and as symbols of mass expression, but a great number is intolerable. In any case, ritual has no value for personal religion, whatever it may have for social cohesion. Its development is attributable to an organized priesthood that, bankrupt of all sense, seeks to retain the letter of a religion after having lost its spirit and endeavors to capture the masses by inane fatuities.

Superstition must be rigorously raked off, though it possesses a strange capacity for survival in spite of scientific advances. Legend and folklore are by no means dead; fortune telling, whether in the form of astrology, palmistry, geomancy, or whatnot, is still popular. It is astonishing how many people can vouch for the truth of the ghost stories they tell; miracles or arbitrary infractions of natural order still elicit belief; preposterous accounts of everyday phenomena handed down from antiquity have not yet been relegated to oblivion. Religious superstitions are the hardest to obliterate; there are, however, others connected with ordinary life, more childish and taken less seriously but just as revolting, such as beliefs about lucky and unlucky days, fears of misfortune linked to certain acts, and so on.

Life cannot be completely satisfactory if it does not enjoy a sound material basis and a noble spiritual objective. It is false to predicate that penury or fearsome dearth of material necessities and convenience is good for the mind. The effect of such benighted fanaticism is colossal misery, and life is rendered ugly and sordid. Is it more spiritual for an individual with sufficient wherewithal to make his daily existence secure and serene so he can devote his energies to contemplating the universe, or for him to perpetually worry about his next meal and the problem of staying alive? Ugliness is not part of truth. It is not advisable that the noble and those who have done most to benefit humanity should be condemned to a niggardly existence while the evil and the tricksters should wallow in luxury and control society. The fact is that human beings are composed of body and mind, and the former cannot be neglected without detriment to the latter. However, the warning not to disdain physical wants need not be stressed, only a few persons being likely to do so. As the majority of people are almost exclusively materialistic, the importance of a spiritual life must be emphasized. The real value of a person is his mind; although known in theory, this fact is often overlooked in practice. Mental cultivation is naturally the paramount human aim.

An ideal way of life is not easily pursued but is nevertheless a necessity; whatever is good can be obtained only through a considerable exertion of will, and to strive toward the best is consonant with human nature.

The Entitarian way of life is both ideal and practical. Ideality without practicality is futile; practicality without ideality is worthless. Both must be properly harmonized. Since the universe is essentially ideal and also exists, it is not strange that a way of life founded on its inner reality should be both right and attainable; aspiration can issue in fruition. Perfectibility is the keynote: perfection is the end and aim of life. A practical ideal that combines the realization of the good in the world with ultimate human destiny in terms of eternity forms the best mode of life. Sublime is the meaning of existence, and humanity has its part to play in the scheme of things.

SECTION 3

STATE

Chapter 1
Society

When a number of human beings live in close proximity, they develop various relationships, such as those of behavior, trade, and so on. Rules to control their activities are formulated. A society is an organized collection of people: it is inevitable for common usages to arise to constitute the bases of intercourse. Over time, it grows in extent—from a single group of people living in one place to a great many groups dispersed over a goodly area of territory. The various communities feel that they all belong to one organization, though they may be separated by mountains and rivers and may have little direct association.

Social phenomena are multifarious. All or almost all human products are consequent on social organization; they react to it and stimulate its further development. A study of social organization would therefore include subjects ranging from religion to language and from art to science. However, every branch of inquiry has narrower limits; what is to be investigated is social organization itself, in connection with which only themes bearing directly on it need be considered.

The subjects to be addressed include political theory and economics; the first concerns the nature of the state, and the second concerns the production, distribution, and consumption of wealth. In addition, various problems relating to the consolidation of society are studied. The topics are closely interlinked and can be viewed together under the name *social philosophy* or the theory of the organization of society. The term *sociology* could be used, provided it is understood without its acquired limitations; it commonly looks at society from a historical point of view, is particularly concerned with tracing its growth, and does not set out to enunciate new political or economic theories. If it were made to mean the study of society without any qualifications, comprising philosophical speculation as well as scientific accumulation of facts, it would be an appropriate term under which to include all the subsidiary social sciences, such as political science and economics. The nature of social development as known from the past cannot be neglected in a study of present society or speculation over a new; the aspect of sociology that treats of the growth of society is necessary. Similarly, history or the record of the deeds and events in the past career of the human race has a bearing on our theme, which is the formulation of a new social system.

When a community is bound together in a single unit by the varied ties of race, culture, government, and so on, it forms a nation. The land it inhabits is its country, which consists of an expanse of territory on the surface of the earth. The organization, including a government and laws, is the state.

Society should be founded on natural truth; it is absurd to allow it to run along haphazardly, the sport of villainous politicians. Nothing is more indefensible than the plea of the conservative and the lazy that, being a delicate organism existing through the ages, society must not be changed by theory: vested interests heartily applaud this view. Society is a human-made institution, and the mere fact that it has grown not in accordance with a deliberate plan but in shreds and patches does not make it any less a human product than pots and pans. Society is in chaos; mere reforms do not effect any real cure. When the tree is rotten, cut it down and plant a new tree. When the basic principles of a society are erroneous, the details cannot be correct. A comprehensive plan, founded on the truth and the right, is essential.

A political, economic, and social philosophy completely integrated as a harmonious unit is a necessity. Together with certain other institutions, the state and the economy are the instrumentalities of social organization, and they must be coordinated if a perfect whole is the aim. The word *philosophy* connotes a rational system; it does not mean that this need be divorced from the facts of experience.

Actual conditions bequeathed by the centuries are tough propositions, but considering them final and incapable of change according to a systematic plan is compatible with indolence but not with progress.

A sound system is based on a general principle from which the political, economic, and social organization is derived. Details are worthless if the foundation is false: they are senseless if it does not exist. Only in comparatively recent times have thinkers have taken the trouble to examine the bases of society and formulated theories aimed at its drastic transformation. When the French Revolution arose, the universal reaction was not rooted in whether its principles were right or wrong but in the audacity that a deliberate attempt should be impiously undertaken to alter the fundamental institutions of a state: amazement and horror were evoked. But as bad as the September Massacres and the Reign of Terror were, a dispassionate judgment refuses to see why they should have generated such loathing as infernal atrocities when history could show more frightful carnages and cruelties, when wars were commonplace ever since peoples existed; the bitter emotions were, in fact, associated with the unprecedented phenomenon of an ideological revolution. The outrage could have been easily swallowed if it had been connected with the existing familiar life. A revolution is always less frightful than a war; the customary inversion of feeling, of taking a war calmly and regarding a revolution as a horror, is nothing but prejudice attributable to age-old habit.

The fear the idea of revolution engenders is curious, but this has abated considerably in modern times. People should know and feel the value and rightness of methodical transformation. Vested interests are naturally the staunchest opponents; they dread an internal reform more than war, though if their country were invaded and occupied, they are more likely to lose not merely their fortunes but their lives as well. How many aristocracies have been swept away by foreign conquerors?

The origin of society is lost in antiquity: when and where the first community arose is little more than conjecture. There may have been a period when the denizens of an area, few in number, skulking in the gloom of jungles and eating raw meat, lived each to himself, though based on the nature of the continuation of the species, complete solitude could not have been. A man may not have formed a perpetual or even lengthy union with a particular mate, but the dependence of a child on its mother made absolute solitude impossible. The first rude society must have grown from the expansion of the family, which in itself is a miniature society.

That other factors also came into play is probable. Force, never absent in any known society, must have played its part in the formation of the first communities: the strong subjugated the weak and made them their slaves. Another factor was mutual aid: in the bitter struggle for existence, even the earliest humans must have discovered that survival was easier if one had allies.

Society did not leap into being all at once; everything pertaining to humanity evolved very slowly in ancient times. This was inevitable, as every phenomenon was in a sense adventitious, that is, not due to forethought; rationality could come only with higher intellectual development. Instinctive reaction to environment and chance discoveries explains the conditions of primitive life: society grew in response to needs.

The elementary form of society was the clan, whose members claimed kinship; it was the family grown large. Then arrived the tribe, which is conceived of as not being associated with any definite area of territory. With the nation, society assumed a settled aspect; a legal code was in force to weld its members into a cohesive unity, a specific country was its habitation, civilization was in clear evidence, and the arts developed apace.

The economic organization of society experienced several stages. The first was the venatorial, when early humans foraged, hunted, and fought with wild animals. The second was the pastoral, when nomads drove their cattle from pasture to pasture. With the agricultural, cereals were planted and garnered, and life took on the form that it was to maintain from the earliest stages of civilization until recent times. Lastly came the industrial stage, inaugurated by the mechanical triumphs of science, such as the steam engine. The Industrial Revolution arose in the eighteenth century, and from then onward, the world transformed itself into a humming factory, producing goods on a previously unimaginable scale.

When existence grew more stable with application to the land, population increased considerably, bringing new problems; as Malthus pointed out, its rate was one of geometrical progression. That the earth is not more crowded than it already is, is due to the numerous wars, famines, droughts, and pestilence that afflicted the diverse peoples. As it is, some regions of the world are overpopulated, though others, only comparatively recently reclaimed from barbarism, are still sparsely inhabited.

The difficulties in the study of social affairs are of a sort not found in pure science. The trouble is that, whereas the scientist is actuated by a dispassionate search for truth and succeeds only in proportion to the amount he discovers, the politician has an ax to grind. His aim is power, and he seeks any means to acquire it. In ruder times, force needed no camouflage; today, a theoretical façade is indispensable. Parties flaunt programs and slogans without regard to the truth; propaganda is a tissue of lies. Anyone with a pocketful of money or a desire to rise from the ranks can enter the arena as a politician and, in spite of his abysmal ignorance, talk solemnly of public affairs; a soldier or adventurer takes hold of a government and feels himself competent to settle the destinies of a race. Thinkers who give serious thought to intricate problems are seldom in a position to practice their plans.

Nevertheless, a proper society must be reared on truth. It has become a platitude to declare that social advancement lags behind material progress; there is no need for this lamentable fact to endure forever. Nature cries against an evil society, while the human conscience writhes under it. The day will come when the ship of state will be guided intelligently and honestly, when politics is not a synonym for bungling and knavery. Even now, the fact that governments and parties feel constrained to explain their policies and argue in their favor clearly demonstrates that the people want to know the why and wherefore of what is being done. From such a welter of ideas and apologies, it is not too much to hope that in the course of time truth and right will prevail.

Chapter 2
Method

Before devising any system of philosophy, whether a metaphysic or a political theory, it is best to consider the method of reasoning used to support it. Methodology has been in vogue more in metaphysical systems than in the political. It is common for a writer to plunge into an exposition of his political beliefs without paying any heed to the necessity of a method of reasoning. Jumbled citations of alleged facts, illogical arguments, violent rhetoric, appeals to the emotions and prejudices, the curious taking of popular fads as established truths that need no further examination—all these constitute the writer's idea of the irrefutability of his theory. The natural consequence is that it is rare to find a real system of principles that are harmonized, complete, and based on sufficient reason. If a theory is muddled, it is no wonder that its practice is worse. Parties and factions formulate programs containing a few points selected at random from varied sources and depend on vociferation, reiteration, and self-interest to get them accepted. The strength of a doctrine appears to be counted in terms of its numerical following: if history is any guide, every fancy, however monstrous or ludicrous, can win adherents.

But if the state is to be founded on the truth and the right, a proper system is a *sine qua non*. Such a system must be complete and consistent, its doctrines established by reason applied to facts—emotion and bias are out of place. The aim is not partisanship but the creation of the best society; politics must be studied as a science with pure disinterestedness. How long is the world going to totter along in a muddle?

The moment one talks of a good state, one immediately has a vision—not of the good state, but of the jejune scorn directed at utopia. This word is unfortunate. When Sir Thomas More delineated it in *Nowhere*, he unwittingly conferred strength on the smug and evil, who sneered that only in *Nowhere* could life be properly organized. A certain derogatory significance is attached to the term. Plato, who was deadly serious about his Republic, which he deemed should replace the corrupt Athenian democracy of his day, is regarded as the patron saint of all dreamers. His ideal state did not materialize, as no effort was made by posterity; he discussed it as a metaphysic's reverie, the two being inseparable, and thereby invested it with a pathetic air of unreality. However, to say that the plans of Plato and More were completely unrealizable means only that humanity was not prepared to execute them; it does not mean that they were actually empty dreams and completely impracticable.

Nothing is more vexatious than the complacency of the person who prides himself on being practical. What is this boasted virtue of practicality? As used in politics, it appears to be a euphemism for villainy. The practical person does not have the sense to think of a desirable society; is so stupid that all he is capable of doing is continuing the same old game of hopelessly prolonging the status quo; regards trickery, corruption, and murder as his *forté* and peculiar genius. The pathology of the "practical person" is curious, and it is even more curious that humanity in general has come to accept this definition of the word *practical*. Only in politics is one who performs bad work fulsomely praised and given the epithet. A musician who composes an excruciating symphony is not called practical, nor is a writer thus labeled for scribbling ungrammatical balderdash. The practical musician is one who produces good music, and the practical author is one who pens a good book. Only the statesman who bungles his work, perpetuating a bad society, is dubbed practical. I say *perpetuate* advisedly, for he has not even the brains to create anything original, whether good or bad. He relies on what he self importantly pronounces experience, by which he implies that there is nothing new under the sun. The erroneous significance of the word *practical* must be deracinated; it must be given its proper connotation. The practical statesman creates a good society, just as the practical sculptor carves a good statue and the practical tailor cuts a good suit. A vigorous protest is needed against the misapplication of the attribute, a falsity peculiar to the politician.

In order to avoid unsystematic thinking and prejudiced polemics, a method of inquiry is necessary for the attainment of truth. The method explained here is concrete—its essence is its preoccupation with reality. Actual facts are its tools; falsehoods, distortions, fond imaginings, and unwarranted assumptions must be eschewed. Wishful thinking is kept within bounds and not confounded with actuality; only possibilities and probabilities can be seriously considered in estimates of the future, while abstractions without any connection to facts are avoided.

The aim is the ideal society within practical limits. A worthless, mischievous, or sorrow-laden society can never satisfy any sensible aspirations, and to remain content with it or resigned to it on the grounds that it is inevitable is the hallmark of stupidity. Society is the product of human beings, and if we do not change it, this means only that we either will not or cannot. If we will not, when we know it to be bad, we must be villainous; if we cannot, then it must be the only one of our products that we cannot control, and it is difficult to see why this should be the case. A good society is a necessity; it is in our nature to strive toward the realization of the best that is potentially ours.

What is the ideal society? It is that which completely fulfills its *raison d'être*: society exists for a definite purpose, and insofar as it fails in this achievement, it is defective. A perfect society realizes all the aspirations associated with it. It follows nature: this does not mean that it is directly created by nature as stars and flowers are, but that it is based on natural laws and eschews the perversions of human fancy. Nothing divorced from truth should be retained.

Nature is never stationary but evolves. A society based on nature should follow nature's phenomena as they currently exist and change as they change, keeping *pari passu* with reality. Nature is not yet perfect but is progressing toward perfection: society, then, cannot be made perfect immediately in accordance with ideal concepts. There are bounds to ideality in practice: this explains the principle of the ideal society within practical limits. The right society, the society of serious import, is a combination of ideality and practicality.

Recourse must be had to psychology, history, geography, and science in order to determine the limits of the possible. Through psychology, natural human tendencies are understood, and it is imperative to grapple with them. The fault of utopias does not lie in the fact that they are impracticable but that they rest on an appeal to universal human goodness. As has actually been the case, the adequate response is not forthcoming, and they fail to be realized. It is useless to base an organization on the postulate that human beings are born good: first, because we find that they act more evilly than otherwise; second, because there is the possibility that a minority may be evil, for it cannot be seriously supposed that each and every person is good—and a few of the active evil can overpower or vitiate the majority. A theory that can succeed only when human goodness is present is built on shifting sand and, as history shows, is bound to fail. On the other hand, the postulate of innate evil leads nowhere; it only breeds cynicism and acquiescence in whatever is. The truth is that good and evil are mere terms for classifying human traits: we are born with a bundle of passions and tendencies, some of which are good and some bad, according to the particular system of classification. Actions satisfy aspirations, and the same passions can find expression in diametrically opposite behaviors. Socially, we are not concerned with motive, which rightly appertains to the province of religion or ethics, but are more interested in deeds. A murderer may be impelled by a lofty motive, while a peaceful citizen may be actuated by an ignoble one, such as cowardice or smug addiction to his pleasures; but insofar as the preservation of society is in question, the homicide is a menace. Practically beneficial conduct is required, whatever the motive may be. That human beings can change their behavior according to circumstance is undoubted: civilized people are not cannibals, and most are not thieves, as they can satisfy their desires in other ways. Alter the circumstances, and behavior follows suit. Hence, in order for a good society to function in practice, human tendencies must be gratified, regulated, or diverted into proper channels; the study of human nature is essential for the formulation of a practical state.

History is a record of past events. Strictly speaking, everything that affects the human race, every achievement, should be included. Commonly, it refers only to political history, with the preponderant space devoted to the lives and deeds of rulers. If it were a record of nothing but the truth, it would be more valuable than it is; unfortunately, a great many facts are obscured, not having been recorded at the time. Moreover, accounts have usually been composed by partisans who embellished and distorted at will. History can serve only as a guide, since no laws can be deduced with certitude as they can, say, in physics. Social phenomena are complex; it would be rash for a person to predict the outcome of events by comparing them with previous specimens. No two events are identical; causes and effects being manifold, it is imprudent to say what will follow a single event. But the general trend of history can be fairly understood, and therefore the future can be gauged. The advantage to be extracted from history is not that it repeats itself, as an attitude of mere reminiscence leads to stagnation: the proper use is to grasp causes and effects and to produce new results by manipulating existing circumstances. Only thus can progress be assured, because instead of history repeating itself, it is made to yield fresh forms. Scientists study their subject, be it physics or chemistry, and acquire knowledge of laws and phenomena. To make it fruitful, they experiment with their material and invent what is not found in nature. These products are valid as they are derived from natural laws. The social thinker must do the same.

We live on the surface of the earth, and it is true to state that our lives are conditioned by our environment. Geography, the character of the environment, affects our existence. Before we learned to use our brains, our species was at the mercy of external forces; but we gradually surmounted obstacles and modified our natural surroundings, so that by now we are considerably independent of them. Environment cannot be overcome by disregarding it and doing things incompatible with it but can be subdued only by cooperating with it, by modifying it where possible, and by adapting life to it in other respects. As geography varies from one region of the earth to another, it may be argued that every country needs a different constitution. However, this is not the case, as the variation in the conditions is not very great and tends to be lessened by intelligent modification. Moreover, environment is only one factor in the determination of a polity; others must be taken into consideration, and they reduce its influence. Hence a society may differ in details owing to environment but need not differ in its general outlines.

The place of science in social organization will be increasingly great; of comparatively recent growth, it exercised little influence in the past. The discoveries and inventions of physics, chemistry, and biology must be used not merely to increase human comfort but to constitute data for the organization of the state. A modern society has to incorporate technology, though this does not imply a technocracy, for nothing is worse than the type of state founded on a predominant vocation, such as the theocracy, pedantocracy, military, or commercial state. It would be as fearsome for the government to be composed mainly of technologists as of priests or soldiers, because it would be imbued with the prejudices of their profession, with their peculiar techniques inappropriate to social problems, and with narrow-mindedness. For the sake of office, a noble profession fills with the incompetent, while other equally good professions are neglected and despised. The evil of rule by priests and soldiers cannot be overemphasized: in the one case, pious fraud becomes rampant, while in the other, arbitrary violence is the normal state of affairs. A band of technologists would turn life into a machine, devoid of beauty, grace, and spiritual values: technocracy is not the ideal. Like everything else, science constitutes but one element of society; it must be accorded its due place, for it forms the material foundation of society and should rightly discharge little more than this function. So far, however, technologists have not enjoyed direct control of the shape of society, while priests, soldiers, lawyers, and merchants have been allowed to mishandle the destinies of nations.

The Concrete Method of inquiry is based on reason, for irrationality can never attain truth. In politics, reason is seldom violated in the name of mystic faith as in religion, but it is all too common to find it crushed on behalf of such excuses as practicality, authority, force, order, the organic nature of society, nationalism, and other nonrational or pseudorational grounds. That reason is the only way to attain truth applies to social theory as well as to metaphysics and science, for only reason can distinguish between right and wrong. The most appropriate type of reason may be called *Practical Reason*, which does not aim at knowledge for its own sake but at the creation of a society that can function in practice. Deduction and induction are requisite: logic and science are needed. When arriving at a conclusion, we must be able to see that each step is logically deduced; an inductive doctrine must be based on real facts. If deliberately concocted, sophisms, *non sequitur* arguments, and misrepresentations are no more pardonable than in ontology and are, in fact, far more pernicious because of their effect on real life. Unfortunately, they abound in politics as they do not in pure thought, and are even admired, so accustomed are we to corruption as evidence of cleverness. Sedulously cultivate honest reason.

The Concrete Method is systematic. An odd assemblage of doctrines does not constitute a system. A systematic method has for its goal the construction of a complete whole, standing by itself, coherent, each doctrine pertinent to the rest. Linking all ideas in a pattern, the Connective Method is the most compatible with reason and is applicable to every branch of knowledge. The Concrete Method must use connection: the political, economic, and social doctrines are interwoven into a balanced system. Truth is not attained by dialectics, by opposing one concept with another, but by harmony, by associating the ideas: for proper integration, a central doctrine is the prime source of the rest.

The Concrete Method is practical. Its aim is not to solve mysteries for the sake of knowledge but to elaborate a workable theory. Therefore, the method must take into account practical difficulties and mold theories to suit them. In accordance with strict logic, it may arrive at a concept that, were it to ride roughshod over actualities, may produce undesirable results; so the concept has to be modified. It must be borne in mind, however, that this does not vitiate the truth of the doctrine, since what is wanted is the best society practicable, not the best society in itself. The fact that absolute perfection is not attainable under the conditions of existence does not mean that any society will do. Even if there is no absolute right or absolute wrong, there is nevertheless a greater right and a greater wrong—and the greater right must be pursued. Practicality must always be kept in view and coordinated with ideality. The logic of theory is the base, and the logic of practice is the modifier. The two are not incompatible, for the Concrete Method specifies Practical Reason as the instrument.

The Concrete Method aims at a natural society—that is, one based on the laws of nature—for fanciful creations are inappropriate. Society is the framework in which humanity lives; and though it does not exist by nature, it must be devised to harmonize with natural needs. An electronic instrument is an artificial invention, but it is constructed through knowledge of the laws of nature. A natural society rests on truth and enables its denizens to work toward the fulfillment of their ultimate destiny.

The Concrete Method aims at a simple society, simple in the sense that unnecessary complexities are avoided. Of two ways, the simpler is the better; elaborate forms and usages, ceremonies and rituals, labyrinthine laws and difficult formulas are a burden. Complexity is not synonymous with profundity, and red tape does not spell efficiency. The fewer the rules of life, the better; roundabout processes are to be deprecated.

Chapter 3
Exchange

Why do human beings live in society? Why don't we exist in solitude? The dictum that we are social animals implies that instinct is accountable for the phenomenon, that by nature we espouse the collective life. This may explain how we came to be gregarious but not necessarily why we should be so, seeing that it is possible for us to suppress an instinct and act counter to it. That we can lead a lonely existence is exemplified by hermits; in any case, if reason says that solitude is preferable to society, then it must be allowed to direct an instinctive tendency into a better channel. Besides, it is doubtful whether we, as a species, actually possess a social temperament, for if we did, we would not be so pugnacious. Although early human beings could not have lived in unmitigated isolation, away from their kind altogether, they could hardly be said to have lived in society, if this means a sizable community where members are bound by common principles.

However we came to exist in society, it is imperative to know why we should continue to do so. Society must serve a purpose that cannot be attained by solitude, and it must be proved to be a necessity. Humanity lives: the indubitable corollary is that we are meant to live. It is obvious that life by its mere existence is, *ipso facto*, intended to exist: this truth cannot be refuted. The desire to live is paramount; nobody wants to die. Humanity has always endured extreme misery, while the number of suicides has been comparatively negligible; no one willingly kills oneself, and if one does so, it is only under some powerful urge when life becomes unbearable. Even a beggar subsisting amid the most wretched conditions seeks to prolong his stay on earth. Being is a supreme fact. The primary aim of an individual is the preservation of his life. There can be nothing wrong with this; it is in accordance with nature, both an ideal and a fact.

Some conditions are conducive to existence, and some militate against it; the favorable are pursued, the hostile shunned. We yearn for being, but it may be either blessed with happiness or afflicted with pain: happiness is a sign that it is satisfactory, tends toward its conservation, strengthens the will to live, and hence is ardently cultivated, while its antithesis is dreaded. The human objective is a pleasurable existence. (Note that the phrase denotes merely personal welfare—whatever promotes this helps life—not any particular brand of enjoyment.) Each person wants the ability to maintain his existence in a manner that makes it worth having; that is, he cares for his own welfare. Stern moralists may deem this selfishness and condemn it as base. The instinct for life is egoistic, but it is natural and right, for, as we are born to live, it cannot be evil. The manifestations of this instinct may become perverse and blameworthy; but in its essence, it cannot be brushed with the odium of immorality. Nature has planted it, and the universe would be a monstrous mistake if, after engendering life, it enjoins that the desire for its perpetuation is wrong.

Life is intertwined with material needs—food, clothing, housing, and so on—one or two of which, like air, the most urgent of all, are procurable without any effort. The majority require work, which in the first place is performed by manual labor and, in its most effective forms, utilizes mental power. Brain and hand cooperate; if the product is fine, the former has an increasing share of responsibility. The primary need in which toil is involved is food, but a secure, pleasurable existence must have much more than this.

Humanity is not only meant to exist but is destined to fulfill a certain role in the scheme of things and, as an integral part of nature, is bound to evolve toward perfection, or else there is no meaning in the possession of a rational mind. The human body has hardly changed since our emergence as a distinct species, but the mind has; human evolution is, therefore, mental in character, and the meaning of our existence is to be sought in this. The mind is not passive, its own activity reacting to its evolution and working for its own destiny. Work is for humanity our instrument of preservation and progress.

The individual's capacity for production is extremely limited, and even with the best will in the world, his hands cannot make much. With the exception of the simplest and crudest work, the acquisition of the ability to perform a particular kind of work demands considerable time, which varies in proportion to its intricacy. It is beyond the bounds of possibility to acquire at best the ability to produce more than a few products, insufficient to supply the diversity of physical and mental needs. It has also been demonstrated from experience that long practice in one art breeds a superior degree of skill that would be unattainable were interest spread over several skills. Though it is not actually impossible to depend on one's efforts alone, subsistence is precarious, circumscribed, and fraught with peril and pain.

The solution to the problem of limitation is exchange—the mutual transference of articles of equivalent value. Each person specializes in one trade—by exchanging his products, he acquires the various commodities he requires for his sustenance. In this way, the difficulties attendant on total self-dependence vanish. It is much easier to pursue only one vocation than several, and the results are more effective. Through the division of labor, an astonishing diversity of goods come into being, of a quality more commensurate with the purposes they serve.

For exchange to take place, a number of individuals must dwell in propinquity and enter into habitual, peaceful interaction: they live in communities. Gregarious existence becomes indispensable. The quintessence of society is to be sought in this fact—the necessity of mutual exchange of benefits. Herein lies its justification, its *raison d'être*, which explains why individuals who are discrete units should form an aggregate. None of society's other phenomena can be regarded as its prime mover. The basis of society is exchange; people abandon solitude for society, which is more conducive to their personal welfare.

Individuals form society for the specific purpose of negotiating transactions of exchange, expecting to increase their chances of survival and enjoy a more extensive measure of welfare. Were the consequences baleful, they would be defeating their aim; they might as well seek an anchoretic retirement. Hence, in order that society might fulfill its mission, exchange must be valid and must be recognized as correct and justifiable by the participants.

The first condition is that the transaction be voluntary. The producer is *de jure* the owner. How can this truth be contradicted? If force deprives the producer of his property, he feels bound to recover it, and in this he is vindicated by moral right. Any individual who obtains possession of it without the knowledge of the producer is a thief, who uses false pretense is a cheat, who takes it by violence is a robber. A state that confiscates it is guilty of collective brigandage. The property of the producer should pass out of his hands only with his consent.

The second condition is that the transaction be equivalent. Two articles must be deemed of equal value before they change proprietorship, or else the loser is entitled to consider himself aggrieved. An element of fraud becomes apparent, and a society beset with deception fails in its primary objective—the satisfaction of its components. The quantity of products in a community is the sum total of the contributions of its members, each of whom is entitled to receive only the share he creates; if he gets more, it is at the expense of others. The advantage of social organization is to enable an individual to exchange his one type of commodity for an assortment. If all are to participate in this benefit, then exchange must be just, equality of value being emphasized.

Valid exchange is voluntary and equivalent; that is, free and equal. Any form of constraint is antipathetic to the very character of proprietary right—the producer has the natural and therefore inalienable right to dispose of his property as he pleases; where force is utilized, it begins to smack of robbery. A person owns a certain quantity of value in his possessions, and if he were dwelling alone, this could neither increase nor decrease from extraneous causes, it being able to grow only with fresh production and to diminish only with consumption. Strictly speaking, this should not change just because he is in society; he should not obtain by devious methods unequal value in exchange. To each genuinely his.

The full connotation of the term *exchange* must now be indicated. So far, it has referred to commodities, as they form its basic counters, but it must be extended to cover a wider field. Every entity capable of entering into a reciprocal transaction is included in its scope: such are service and knowledge.

Service consists of performing a task that promotes the welfare of another person: exchange applied to it indicates mutual service. In a complex society, a considerable amount of benefit is derived not from tangible products but from various types of service, and a proportion of the population is engaged in their performance. Service embodies value, which is commensurate with that of goods and can be made to bear a definite ratio in exchange.

The acquisition of knowledge is the most significant boon of social organization; it is cumulative and has grown with hard work through the centuries, the store made by the efforts of successive generations. The striking difference between knowledge and material products is that knowledge is not consumed and does not disappear but endures forever; it easily becomes common property. Its effect on life is not direct, for in its absence one does not perish, as is the case with food, but it is the motivating force of production, especially of the finer type. Above all, it spells the glory of the mind and is the agent of humanity's evolution toward its ultimate destiny. The value of knowledge is incomparable. It sounds bathetic to measure it in terms of sensible, ephemeral commodities; however, it has a value in exchange and for this purpose must be appraised along with service.

The function of society is the valid exchange of benefits, which include tangible goods, service, and knowledge. For organization purposes, justice must be the regulator: this does not conflict with the principle of benevolence, which makes an individual give more than he takes. Action that prompts such gifts is a matter for religion and ethics and should not be enforced as the governing doctrine of a practical state; it would vitiate it, producing injustice, giving rise to exploiters and exploited, leaving the unassertive at the mercy of the iniquitous. Altruism is an action whereby an individual serves his fellows without thought of return, but a polity reared on its assumption breeds hypocrisy and misery. Society should be erected on elementary rights so that, at the very least, justice reigns, while love, which appertains to private morality, could still exercise its wand if it chose. Justice is not contrary to altruism.

However society arose and however its professed aims varied according to the thought of the time, its real cementing force was the principle of exchange. Exchange did not run along the correct path, since it was not consciously and steadily kept in view as the social basis. It bore a false character, and hence human existence was involved in iniquity and calamity. Prophets fulminated against society and appealed to universal love as the remedy; philosophers descanted on public welfare as the objective of government; visionaries deemed private property an evil; passive moralists discoursed on the acceptance of one's lot. The masses were bewildered and for long ages either resigned themselves to hopeless apathy or burst into spasmodic outbreaks that brought no real or lasting relief. In the meantime, kings sat on their thrones and, with tongue in cheek, proclaimed their divine character; soldiers seized power and rested their rule on might; politicians sought office by specious rhetoric and knavish corruption; and merchants who amassed fortunes through trickery were protected by law and fulsomely praised, even by their victims, the indigent.

Exchange was perverted by bad organization and falsified by erroneous conceptions of the nature of the state. It was submerged by other forces and persisted in a mutilated condition. Like all early phenomena, it did not arise or grow through conscious direction; it zigzagged and stumbled along, loaded with errors, dispersing ruin and calamity, a blessing turned into a curse. Probably never pure at any time—certainly not in historical ages—it was never clearly recognized as the primary social fact. Even now, it is dealt with in economic treatises as merely one phenomenon among many and is of no peculiar significance.

What is the nature of value? There are three types. *Absolute value* is what an entity possesses in the scheme of things; it is inherent in or intrinsic to it and is inapplicable to economic goods, being either little or nonexistent in them and, in any case, indeterminate. *Utilitarian value*, as its name implies, denotes utility; it is the contribution to human welfare of an article, and it is this that motivates production. *Exchange value* is the price set upon an article in comparison with others; in respect to social organization, it is the most regarded of the three, though in truth it is less important than the others. It depends on a variety of factors, including utility, labor, cost, availability, and desire.

The quantity of labor expended on a product influences its exchange value but not as much as might be imagined. If value were created solely by labor, then it would vary directly as the latter, but this is not the case; most laborers work much the same number of hours a day, yet if their tasks are different, the results are apt to be variously priced. Labor is not identical in quality, notably between the intellectual and the manual; the former produces a more striking result, more valuable, though the latter involves a greater expenditure of energy and is more exhausting. *Cost* is the sum of the value of the labor expended on production and the value of the raw material. Availability greatly influences price fluctuations: scarcity increases exchange value, and abundance diminishes it, though the utilitarian value may be hardly affected. Desire is the ultimate determinant in exchange; it is, of course, conditioned by the other factors and may be influenced by idiosyncrasy and fashion. A person may want an article that the generality of his fellows slight and may also covet what has become a fad, though it serves little purpose.

Utilitarian value is strictly the actual value of an article in regard to humankind. It should properly be the sole consideration, but, as social phenomena are complex, it is not and cannot be; it is swamped by the other ingredients that go with it to form price. Different kinds of articles have different utilities. Utilitarian value can be judged under three categories: existence, pleasure, and culture. The first denotes those items serving basic needs and, being the most urgent, embodying the greatest degree of utility, such as food, clothing, and shelter. The second, comprising items like jewelry and wine, is dispensable and of the least value. Products in a developed society tend to cater to both existence and pleasure, which together determine their value; examples are rich food and gaudy apparel. The third is meant for mental development; it is not urgent, though its value is of a higher quality than what is incorporated in the others and of greater ultimate importance. Books and music are not necessities of life but aid in its struggle toward realizing its meaning. Popularly and, unfortunately, the second class are the most desired.

For products of the same kind, their value depends on quantity and quality; the more there is of an article, the more value is available. This refers only to real utility, for in practice the price of each of a million articles is less than that of one hundred, for scarcity or abundance exerts its influence. Two articles of the same type are evaluated differently according to quality, that of the higher fulfilling its purpose better.

The relationship among absolute, utilitarian, and exchange value varies; it would be good if they could be identical. But as far as artificial commodities are concerned, absolute value is of little moment and may be neglected. Utilitarian value is the important consideration. Exchange value is a purely social phenomenon, and it must approach as closely as possible to utility; this adjustment is necessary for harmonization with both reality and justice.

Commodities are not made out of nothing; their material already exists in nature. Material cannot strictly be said to belong to humanity, either individually or collectively, but is a part of nature. Labor is expended in obtaining it or converting it into a product for human use. The person who first gets possession of a natural article or who makes a commodity, transforming one thing into another, is designated the *primary owner*; he has a right to it, as nature does not forbid him to use it. He has a prior claim against others, for he has given energy to its acquisition. By a process of proper transfer, it passes into the hands of another, the *secondary owner*; it may see a succession of these, but at any one time, the person in possession is to be recognized as such. Primary and secondary owners have rightful claims and are to be regarded as legal owners. A person who acquires a commodity by fraud, thievery, or violence is an illegal owner; the right to it still belongs to the legal owner.

The political, economic, and social system reared on the fundamental principle of exchange will be entitled *Exchangism*. The principle is defined as the valid exchange of benefits: it is derived from natural truth, and every social phenomenon will be tested by it. It is a simple criterion, making for a methodical society that is rational, just, ideal within practical limits, and organized for the preservation and amelioration of life, for the welfare of its members and the individuals who represent life.

Chapter 4
Economy

An economy is an organization that produces, distributes, and consumes wealth, which refers to the aggregate amount of utilitarian goods in a community. The problem of systematic organization became acute only with the advent of socialism in the nineteenth century, and now it engages more popular attention than any other subject. We would not disregard it if we could; we could not do so if we would; it is as bound up with our welfare as the beam with the house. It is essential in the consideration of a rational society.

Two main economic systems exist, capitalism and socialism, both of which, if a narrower meaning were given to the former as referring to its present form, were of comparatively recent growth. Prior to them, all communities lived under what might be called the handicraft system, understanding by it the various forms of economy that differed in greater or lesser measure from country to country and age to age. Goods were produced by manual labor and hence were very restricted in output; the predominant occupation was agriculture. Save for a small percentage, the people were farmers, who, as in China, either owned the lands they cultivated or worked them in tenantry or, as in medieval Europe, were serfs sweating for their lords under the darkest oppression. The idle landowners obtained the preponderant share of the products. Other commodities were made by craftsmen who traded their wares; slaves performed unpaid drudgery. Merchants were on the whole not powerful, while professional men were insignificant. The world looked as if it were toiling solely for the benefit of kings and nobles, glorified robbers. Exchange was a travesty. The small class of expropriators, who gorged on the fat of the land while they maltreated the starving masses, maintained themselves by force and fraud—the force of armies of adventurers, mercenaries, and conscripts and the fraud of priesthoods. No individual was responsible for the creation of the system, which was the muddled, chaotic product of generations who had given no rational thought to the bases of society, which staggered along reacting to circumstances and being influenced by rulers and preachers. A section of the expropriators came into their possessions by chance, knavery, or cunning, but the majority simply inherited theirs. As human beings have always had a strong tendency to accept what already is, the hereditary despoilers were regarded as invested with a natural right.

With machinery came capitalism, which does not differ in essence from its predecessor, the new features consisting of the nature of the property and the mode of production. The property comprises power-driven equipment located in factories, and production is *en masse*; the result is that material life is on a higher plane than before, not only for the few but also for the masses. The owner of capital or the instruments of production is the counterpart of the feudal expropriator; the worker is fleeced, though he enjoys a better lot than the slave and the serf. Exchange is specious; it appears voluntary, with goods and services sold apparently unrestrained in the open market, and it also seems equitable, for the ratios look fair. Actually, it is neither. The relationship between capitalist and worker, employer and employee, is highly unsatisfactory: the worker is free to refuse to work—he can starve. The subtle restraint differs little from that imposed on the erstwhile slave, who was free to commit suicide. The glaring disproportion between the incomes of the employer and the employee points to the existence of an unjust exchange. The capitalist either does nothing or performs the duties of an organizer and manager. Though his work is not greater in quantity and little more in quality than that of his mechanics, his remuneration is tremendously larger. If the employer takes no part in the business, then he receives an income in return for nothing; if he is active, then he obtains much more than what he gives. How does he come to be the proprietor of the capital that endows him with his privileged position?

By heritage, trickery, or cleverness, he comes into its possession, in which he is confirmed by a legal fiction. Trickery confers no right of valid ownership; cleverness may entitle him to the property but not to exploitation, without which great accumulation is impossible. A person has the right to give to another whatever is his, and it is natural that he should do so to his children. Inheritance is unobjectionable, provided the property is genuinely the donor's; but, as the capital has been amassed by fraud and exploitation, heredity confers no right of possession. Capitalist society has engendered a large middle class performing professional services; though they receive better income than the workers, they are likewise victims of the plutocrats. Most of them are forced to be employees for the same reason as the workers, are forced to do the brainwork for their employers, and, subject to involuntary exchange, must accept what is given to them. Compared to the capitalists, they are sufferers, though to the workers, they are well enough off. Their plight is not acute, and they enjoy the inglorious privilege of being classified along with their masters as supporters of an iniquitous system; they remind one of the chief slaves of ancient society. Even in a highly industrialized community, the old types of expropriators persist—landowners, merchants, and usurers—parasites on the body politic.

Socialism, which arose as a protest against capitalism, was a product of the concentration of workers in factories. It has more factions than any other creed, ranging from mere philanthropists, who want the government to undertake some social service for the mitigation of the workers' lot, to communists, who advocate the collective ownership of property, all working together and the aggregate produce divided among them. If they have any common principle, it is that the community or its deputy, the government, nominally owns all property and should control it for the general welfare. A strong delusion exists that only socialism aims for the economic welfare of the people; this is preposterous, for every system for which an apology has ever been written pretends to it. Supporters of monarchism and capitalism did not say that only kings and plutocrats were to have their happiness considered. A vague concept of public welfare is not specific to socialism, which, if it were to differ from other ideologies, must be characterized by more distinctive traits. The theory of socialism is best seen in communism; anarchism and syndicalism also demonstrate it. The many milder forms of socialism are, at least in practice, mere illogical introductions of socialist concepts to reduce the iniquities of capitalist economies. Fascism is autocratic imperialism with a socialist tinge. In criticizing socialism, reference will be made only to its specific tenets, essentially communism.

All property is supposed to belong to the community, nation, or state. How is this? According to inherent right, an individual owns what he produces; for the state to dispossess him of it is wrongful expropriation. State operation is ineffectual. Work is not welcome to most people; if all labor is for the common pool, each might deem it a grievance to toil more than others and consequently shirk his duties. To be diligent, they have to be forced and thereby become slaves. Regarding the division of produce, one of three methods may be used: to each an equal share, to each according to his needs, or to each according to his desserts. With the first, exchange becomes unjust, as some may produce more and others less, and the loser suffers from expropriation. With the second, the same objection holds; moreover, this principle, which does well in morality, is dangerous when forcibly attempted to be put into universal practice, for the powerful and the subtle can contrive to use it to cover their demands for disproportionately greater shares for themselves. The third is theoretically right, but as the community as a whole cannot know of an ordinary person's qualities, the individual is left to the mercy of his immediate overseer, who, being human, is not above favoritism and corruption and may refuse to recognize his claims.

Socialist exchange is neither voluntary nor equivalent and is therefore contrary to nature and right. A person is not simply indirectly forced to labor and give up his products as under capitalism; he is directly compelled by state power. The individual has no alternative but to submit, as he cannot choose another job, there being no other employer or anything that he can do on his own. His labor is remunerated without consideration of equivalent value unless the method of apportioning income according to merit, hardly fashionable in communist theory, is utilized. The lure of communism is its regard for equality, which is unlikely to materialize, especially when combined with political despotism. Is it credible that rulers and ruled are equal when the latter are at the mercy of the former? Socialism came not so very long ago and hence has not yet had time to reveal fully its fallacies and evils, as it will do when its superficial moral force vanishes, when it becomes securely entrenched and taken for granted. The bureaucracy associated with it is the most powerful in the world and, when corrupt, can become the most terrible of exploiters of the masses: such a mandarinate grown old will be almost impossible to dislodge. The state is a mere abstraction; it has to function through individuals, and, if history is not completely false, total power is perilous to public welfare sooner or later.

Capitalism and socialism violate nature and are inimical to valid exchange. The first is defined as separate ownership of the instruments of production by a small class of individuals who operate them through hired labor, and the second as collective ownership and operation of the instruments of production and subsequent division of the goods. The first is freer than the second but more iniquitous in the distribution of income. A proper society must be reared on both freedom and justice. Exchangism is based on these principles—it is defined as separate ownership of property by every person who creates it through his own labor or obtains it through voluntary and equivalent exchange.

Property is produced by individuals and by right belongs to them. What a person produces is his own, and he should not be deprived of it by force; it should pass out of his hands only when he gets a product of equal value in exchange. In nature, each person must depend on his own efforts to survive and is therefore endowed with an innate capacity for production. The individual enters society primarily to obtain a more secure and abundant life, for the impact of person on person heightens the force of production. He does not therefore lose his original right to the retention of his products. The instinct of private property is strong. Goods are meant to be consumed by individuals; even in a collective state, they ultimately must be divided among individuals and become private property, thereby setting the principles of communal and private property at variance. Everyone can produce and can therefore own property. Every person is an owner: this is a fundamental principle to govern the new society. Each individual owns what he produces and what he acquires in fair exchange. When there are only a few owners, as in capitalism, it must be due to deceitful expropriation.

When a person depends on his efforts alone, the amount of property he can acquire is very limited, as all people belong to the same species and have similar physical and mental traits. The quantity of labor of each is restricted by time, as much the same number of working hours a day are available; the quality is more alike than otherwise. Hence, all workers naturally cannot make excessively disproportionate accumulations of property. A correct society will see only harmless variations of wealth and may be regarded as enjoying either equality or inequality, depending on one's standard of comparison. The most appropriate description is equality modified by merit or inequality compatible with justice.

Production is undertaken by individuals who own the tools. One is driven to work either through inclination or self-preservation, without external compulsion from others; one performs the tasks one likes and of which one is capable, knowing that the returns will be commensurate with effort. The individual is free and feels a sense of justice. He will give his best, for if he does not, he alone suffers. He is encouraged to do what he can; he is not hampered, as in capitalism, by vested interests and lack of a good start furnished by wealthy parents; nor, as in socialism, by force and cultivated extinction of individuality. Under capitalism, production is for the exploiter's profit; under communism, it is for collective confiscation; under Exchangism, it is for personal good.

Competition is an incentive to effort, and it is not injurious to public welfare if it is regulated by justice; if it is confined to developing one's own powers, success spells no loss to others. It is an evil only when wealth can be amassed by devious methods, when the mere possession of riches evokes respect, when the consequences of success and failure are artificially rendered poles apart. In a naturally egalitarian society, where differences are small compared to similarities, it is true that competition brings no great monetary rewards; but as one does not like to fall behind if one can help it, energy will not be spurned. Besides, a reward like public approbation is not slighted. It is disdained only when a fortune is available by nefarious means; even then, it is not really disregarded, as the richest are the most respected. Regulated competition is a beneficial principle.

If property could be had only through personal labor and expropriation were exterminated, then the employer/employee relationship must be sundered. There will be no employers and no employees: each employs only himself. It stands to reason that an individual who pays a fixed wage to another bound to him will resort to exploitation; he does not give from philanthropic motives. Complete dependence on an autocrat regarding livelihood is galling; who likes an employer? Ludicrous fear embitters the days of the unlucky drudge; the position is undignified to say the least, one remove from slavery. The cause of the capitalists' amassing of fortunes lies in the monstrous institution of personal employment; they secure as many hands as necessary, and, as their wealth increases, they use more, the process going on viciously. The greater their business, the more people they exploit, and the less their own share of work; thus wealth makes wealth through expropriation. Left to themselves, they could never make such accumulations. To produce a fairly egalitarian society, wages must be banished. As is ironically the case when an evil principle stalks unrecognized, an aggravation of the evil is deemed a remedy. The manufacturer who takes more people into his factory is hailed as a benefactor; a scramble is made for jobs; big unemployment figures—referring to those who can find no masters—betoken national disaster. The majority of human beings live in daily fear of losing their chances of getting exploited.

The excision of the colossal error of the employer/employee relationship will go a long way toward forming a valid society. Instead, the individual will receive his income from the general public, from individual payments for specific services. A lawyer is not regarded as the employee of his clients, each of whom is related to him only temporarily and in connection with a particular piece of work: he is not dependent on any one person. Neither is a shopkeeper the employee of his customers; he is engaged with them only in transactions of exchange. Lawyers and shopkeepers are no more the employees of their clients and customers than they are their employers; both parties give and receive on equal terms.

Chapter 5
Operation

Private production and operation are the natural mode and should be conducted either by individuals or companies. Where one person is sufficient to produce an article or to perform a service, such as a carpenter or a doctor, he will run his business alone. With machinery and certain forms of organized service, isolated effort becomes impossible; a number of people must work together, and they should do so in a company owned by its personnel, comprising all those actually engaged in its activities. This type of company may be designated the *work-and-own company*; the capitalist and the idle shareholder are eliminated. It does not belong to one person but to every one of its workers. A joint-stock company is not socialistsic; neither is the work-and-own company, for socialism implies the proprietorship of the entire community in all its property, not the existence of innumerable companies, each owned only by its staff. The company is preferably kept as small as is consistent with efficiency.

Individual operation can be extended much more than it is in capitalist society by dividing work among persons who are not in one organization. Take the example of the clerk, who never has an independent status but is always an employee and is to be found in both a firm with a large staff and one with only himself and an employer. Why can't he set up a separate clerical office? Then the lawyers, merchants, and others who need his services can pay him fees for particular work assignments, and he will not be at the mercy of one master. Take the case of domestic servants, of all employees the closest to the slave. There is no reason why they could not operate on their own: they can be engaged by a number of households for occasional services. A number of domestic workers might set up a company, and they could go to a household for definite hours in rotation. Much of the work performed by the domestic servant can be distributed: cooking, washing, and cleaning can be done by restaurants, laundries, and cleaning establishments, which can be of any size, even so small as to be operated by a single person. No household need have a servant if the necessary tasks are performed by diverse individuals and companies. The personal bond of employment must be snapped: every kind of work can be done by an individual working on his own or by a work-and-own company. If different types of workers need close cooperation, they can have their offices in the same or contiguous buildings; for example, doctors, medical assistants, and nurses can operate separately but are easily available to their patients; they can enter into some kind of arrangement for collaboration.

Regarding the work-and-own company, its members exercise joint ownership, production, and participation in the profits. They either share the income equally if they perform similar work or receive different percentages according to their diverse capacities. Each has a direct interest in its success, for his earnings vary in proportion to the total profit. The company may be of any size, depending on the nature of the work, the general rule being that it is kept as small as is consonant with efficiency. In some cases, it may have to be so large as to constitute a monopoly, as in the postal service. A company beginning in a small way may grow large, but its staff shall be limited at a point when it threatens to drive off similar concerns; it should not be permitted to have branches in other places. To fulfill public needs, new companies will be set up, run by separate staff. This limitation is needed to curb the dangers of competition, which is just an incentive to effort, not to annihilate the livelihoods of others. The more enterprising company will earn more than the less; the difference should not be allowed to reach a point where suffering is produced. This is especially true when the less prosperous does not lack energy but is handicapped by disadvantages. A big concern possesses advantages in competition that have nothing to do with the capabilities of its members, such as prestige and display.

The control of the company is vested in its members collectively. A manager performs particular duties but is no more an owner than the lowliest staff member. Disciplinary action appertains to the entire staff, who are all partners and cannot be penalized by individuals. There is no question of employer and employee. Each does his duties, and anyone who fails is responsible to all the others; such individuals may have their income reduced or may even be expelled. On the other hand, the especially good, earning the appreciation of their fellows, may be accorded extra benefits.

The work-and-own company is in accord with the principles of valid exchange, for entrance into it is voluntary and services are equitably remunerated. It is not a capitalistic joint-stock company with interest-receiving shareholders and paid employees. It is more akin but not identical to the cooperative society, for it is a profit-making enterprise, not a philanthropic endeavor; it is a mode of private exchange, not of socialization. Every kind of enterprise, whether of production or service, can be thus organized. It is permissible to create such companies as those of lawyers or architects, but, as in these cases individual operation is easy, it is unnecessary. For the same kind of work, both individual and company enterprise may be utilized, depending on circumstances and the desire of the individuals.

Human beings live on the land and off its products: to us it is of the utmost importance, but we are not the real owners, whether individually or collectively. The theoretical owner is nature; however, as humanity is part of nature, we have the right to utilize its bounties to preserve our existence. This being the case, who is to use the land? Evidently, all have an equal right: it should be divided among all. But, save as a dwelling place, its utility really lies in its products, which are procurable only through labor. Hence, though everyone has a right to land, only those who work it are entitled to the products. Its principal utility lies in agriculture. All tillable land will be divided equally among the cultivators: this agrarian principle eliminates the idle landowner. As land is rightfully everybody's, it is at the disposal of society, which, represented by the state, is the regulatory owner; that is, it distributes it for purposes of cultivation. The cultivator is the virtual owner, for ownership ultimately denotes the ability to utilize, and the individual who actually exercises this power is practically the owner. Only those who wish to and can perform the labor of cultivation are given plots of land. Each farmer tills his piece, and the produce is entirely his.

The fact of cultivation does not imply the right of transfer. Land is not for sale; the farmer keeps it as long as he can cultivate it, and on his ceasing to do so, either through death or from any other cause, it reverts to the regulatory owner, who will give it free to another cultivator. The implements and crops originally produced and acquired must be reimbursed to the farmer but not the land itself, which is not theoretically his or, in fact, anybody's. The capitalistic ownership that allows landlords to receive rent from land regarded as theirs is a falsity. In nature, it cannot possibly belong to them, unless they cultivate it themselves; thus, for them to hire labor to work it and earn an income is pure expropriation. Neither is the state, as in socialism, the theoretical owner; it can be the regulatory owner, but the person who actually produces has the right to retain the produce.

The mode of cultivation, as in other enterprises, can be by individuals or companies composed of farmers. Where the individual is sufficient, it is best to allow him to do it; where mechanical production is introduced, the company may be formed, the area given to it being equal to the total of the areas that the members would receive separately if operating alone.

Agriculture constitutes the chief activity of a population, but its number of farmers can be beneficially reduced as the food produced becomes sufficient. Industry and other services can absorb the superfluous so that existence can rise to a higher material and cultural plane. It was settled life that engendered civilization, but the more active intelligence of a varied industrial economy is necessary for greater progress.

Land to be used for other purposes, such as building, mining, growing of rubber or cotton, and so on, will be distributed by the state to individuals or companies in the same manner. It is important to note that the land itself is not for sale. Whatever is attached to the land that is produced by the virtual owner is his and may be sold by him, but the purchaser of these items attached to the land can only be the person to whom the state grants the right of succeeding him in the utilization of the land. Unless he can utilize it to advantage by his own efforts, it will not be given to him. All land not utilized for any purposes is regarded as the state's.

Industry is more various than agriculture; its essential task is the production of commodities, and, in its modern form, it uses mechanical power installed in factories. Needing cooperative effort, each factory will be operated by a company and jointly owned by the staff. Under the greed of capitalism, a number of factories scattered up and down a country are under a single control; monopolistic exploitation of the consumer is the consequence. This must be eradicated; each factory is to be under separate management. There is no loss of efficiency, for a number of branches are virtually under separate operation, though there is a certain amount of coordination, but the chief result is centralization of profits. Whatever coordination is necessary can be provided by state regulation; the competitive spirit is not quashed altogether. Capitalism may spell freedom and enterprise in its initial stages, but when it grows into a system of colossal monopolies, it means death to both and has, in addition to its own, all the evils of socialism without the benefits. Super-capitalism is a frightful curse, a product of the power of money to make money, the employer/employee relationship, the increasing augmentation of personnel.

We live in an industrial age, which would be an undiluted blessing compared to the agricultural if it were not attended by a faulty social system. With its power of producing goods for the masses, machinery is marvelous, yet when it was first introduced, it was wrecked by outraged laborers. Later, the remedy for the evils of the social system machinery created was sought by reverting to the millennia-old all-powerful state, from which the people had only recently succeeded in delivering themselves through bitter struggle, partly with the help of the wealth produced by mechanical production. Freedom and private property were blamed; surely freedom is better than slavery and private property is better than confiscation. But the new seigneurs, the capitalists, taking advantage of wrong conditions, gave rise to a new form of slavery and confiscation—is the cure then total slavery and total confiscation?

Handicrafts are still of service, and they are easily undertaken by individual operation; but as mechanical tools should replace labor wherever possible, a modified type of craftsmanship is desirable. Small machines operable by solitary effort are great aids to the craftsman. Craftsmanship has certain advantages over machine production in terms of beauty and art; it supplies the needs of places where, if the demand is small, local factories are uneconomical, while goods brought from a distance impose unnecessary burdens on transport services and utilize more middlemen, whose number should be minimized. The retention of handicrafts swells the number of individual workers, who are desirable for maintaining a balance between individual and company operation.

Of all forms of activity, trade is the least to be encouraged, being absolutely nonproductive and the service of little utilitarian value, yet it has always secured the most lucrative returns, an anomalous position that must be corrected. Unfortunately, it must be retained for its work of bringing goods from the producer to the consumer. The number of merchants should be kept low; wherever possible, the producer should sell his own goods directly to the consumer, as in the case of craftsmen, who make and sell in their shops. One means of controlling traders' profits is price fixing, which renders them unable to earn more than producers. A better mode of control is turning them into direct agents of the producers, who make arrangements with them, fix the prices for sale to the public, allow them to take away their goods, and receive the receipts at intervals, only a reasonable income being left to them. Shops may be operated by individuals or by groups of partners, each under separate control. Imports and exports are conducted by large establishments that need to be more closely supervised by the government.

There is a variety of services ranging from the professions to skilled and unskilled labor. These people do not produce any goods, but their work is important for its utilitarian value and, in the case of cultural creation, of the utmost significance. Though culture is apt to be despised, the taste for it acquired by sedulous application, a community without general culture is of little worth. Individual operation is best for the professions in general. Schools and hospitals must be run by cooperative staffs; so too must railways, airlines, and so on. Clerks are numerous and may be divided into more specialized categories according to the type of work they perform; they can work individually or in companies. Those who may be called *service workers*, such as launderers, carriers, and so on, can likewise work individually or in companies. Those who are called *domestic servants* will cease to be servants and become domestic workers, paid piecemeal and operating alone or in groups so that, if one household needs a helper frequently, a company can send any of its staff, not always the same one.

Unearned income must be abolished. Rent from land and houses, interest on capital invested in business and from money lent, dividends from joint-stock companies—these are pernicious, contrary to the principle of valid exchange, whereby only work begets value and money cannot earn money by itself. Landlords, capitalists, usurers, and shareholders will cease to exist and exercise their disastrous influence. Commercial banks will be closed, and bankers will sink into deserved oblivion. The functions of these institutions are printing money, receiving and lending money, and transmitting money; in a word, juggling with money. The issue of currency is strictly a government duty. Deposits can be made with a government department—lending for interest is iniquitous whether done by private people or the government—and transmission belongs to the postal service. Commercial banks, established for trading in money, are superfluous and objectionable.

Speculation will largely disappear when business is no longer operated with stocks and shares. Nothing dislocates an economy as much as manipulating a money market. This form of unearned income is a fruitful source of trouble and shall be eliminated from every variety of commodity. One of the eyesores of a capitalist newspaper is the financial page, with its quotations of stocks and shares and its information on foreign currency exchange rates, in both cases different for buyers and sellers. Regarding currencies, exchange should be done over a government counter, and the rate should be identical for conversion from one to the other. Gambling in any form, including lotteries, shall be prohibited. The principle to be observed is that money cannot produce money; all forms of monetary transactions shall not incur gain to either party, and where they are liable to abuse, they shall be made through the government.

All individuals will exercise a legitimate occupation, and the government will help them to do so. When a person goes wrong from an inability to make himself profitably useful, it is a matter of concern to the government. Criminals should be returned to society with possibilities for pursuing proper careers instead of being merely released with little likelihood of achieving anything, only to pick up the thread of their former delinquencies.

Chapter 6
Distribution

Goods are not produced for their own sake but for consumption by individuals. From one process to the other lies distribution, which of all economic problems is the one of most concern to the ordinary mortal. People do not judge capitalism and socialism on the merits and demerits of production but on their share of the produce; save for thinkers, a theory does not convince chiefly because of its formulas and arguments. How many members of the communist proletariat are devoted to dialectical materialism applied to the interpretation of history? And is the capitalist enchanted with the term *laissez-faire* because it sounds euphonious? The implication is not that people are wholly selfish; they are not—they can be touched by altruism and are open to reason. But it remains true that, regarding economics at any rate, personal benefit is the most convincing argument. However, if a society is to be natural and right, it must be based on reason and justice; and if it should harmonize with personal welfare, then it is both the best and the most practicable.

It has been shown that personal welfare is not wrong and that, conforming with nature, everyone has a right to it; the problem is ensuring that all attain it. It is also a point of justice that they who produce own. It has been found that the production capacities of all members of the species are much the same, and, if property is possessed in very unequal masses, it can be due only to expropriation.

Distribution, then, is a consideration of primary importance, and all attempts must be made to align it with justice.

The mode of distribution will be exchange, which actually refers to commodities. Barter is a primitive method whereby the commodities actually change hands at every transaction, a cumbrous and impracticable system in a developed society. A wants what B has, who wants what C has, who wants what D has, and the chain is indefinite. Instead of A handing his product to B and then handing B's over to C and then C's to D and so on until he comes to Z and gets what he covets, it is much easier to recognize a common medium of exchange. This medium is called *money*. A gets money from B in exchange for his goods and gives them to Z in exchange for the desired article, the intervening transactions being eliminated. The invention of money was an undoubted boon.

Unfortunately, money has produced much evil; the passport to goods, it is the principal object of desire and has served as an easy weapon of expropriation. It is easily negotiable, and by manipulating it, the unscrupulous have amassed wealth to the detriment of their fellows. It must be retained, though, on account of its usefulness in exchange and will be subjected to vigilant control so that exploitation will be unable to play its pranks.

A convenient medium of exchange is gold, a natural product that is imperishable and attractive for its ornamental value. Another medium is printed paper, which is easily destroyed, has no intrinsic worth, is an artificial product, and can be made in any quantity, thereby leading to abuse in inflation. Its advantage over gold is its greater facility in handling and carrying. Currency, whether in the form of metal or paper, shall be issued solely by the government. If metals like gold, silver, and so on were to bear identical exchange values, whether minted or unminted, dangers could arise from the difficulty of keeping them thus, especially where their import and export are allowed. The prices of unminted metals vary in regard to other goods in proportion principally to their quantities; hence, coins may be struck or melted down, as their face values are higher or lower than what their metal content can bring. Moreover, if the precious metals are abundant, an inconvenient bulk may have to be handled in transactions. It is best that the government fix the nominal values of coins as much higher than their actual value as bullion. Conversion of metal into currency must then be undertaken only by the government of the country where the currency is legal tender, private people being forbidden to do so, the crime made similar to the forgery of paper notes. The metals as currency are regarded solely as tools of exchange.

Currency is standardized; the national government creates a uniform issue, and it should not sanction local authorities and private organizations to make other issues. There is only one unit of money, and it is small enough to measure a little quantity of everyday goods serviceable in transactions. There being only one unit, the decimal system follows as a matter of course. It is desirable to issue as few varieties of coins and notes as are necessary for daily use; denominations may be made high enough to avoid the trouble of handling large quantities of separate pieces in ordinary transactions.

As monetary transactions should never be allowed to earn any profit, the government will organize a department, which may be known as the *Currency Department*, to deal with money itself. Its functions will include minting, printing, storage, reception of deposits, issue of loans, and utilization of checks to facilitate business operations and transmission. No interest is payable or receivable for deposits and loans, respectively; this is why such service can be undertaken only by the government. Currency is a peculiar government product and hence should be within its province of operation; the check system is confined to it.

Price is synonymous with exchange value; stated in terms of money, it is the sum paid by the purchaser. Both parties to a transaction are responsible: the price that rules is that at which the seller is willing to part with his article and the buyer to acquire it and is somewhere between the expectations of either. The factors determining it are utility, cost, labor, availability, and desire. The proportions of these are indeterminate. Utility should be of paramount consideration; if all articles were of equal utility and prices were based on utility alone, then their exchange ratios could be obtained simply by comparing their relative quantities. However, utility varies for each commodity, and its degree cannot be fixed; and given the erratic character of desire, arranging price by utility alone is impossible. Cost is commonly regarded as molding price, but it must be formed by the other factors. Moreover, availability and desire prevent price from being determined solely by cost. Labor brings utility to light, but it does not account for its degree; the same amount of labor expended on the production of two different commodities, such as rubber and tapioca, does not give them the same value, which is partly inherent in their nature. In comparison with the other factors, labor has the least to do with price formation. Availability has to do with quantity; price increases with scarcity and decreases with abundance. Naturally, plenty is better, as everyone can have more, but there is a limit to consumption, beyond which it is unnecessary to produce. Desire is the final arbiter of price, and in most cases it is advantageous to let it run its course; an economy is then easier to operate, and prices are arrived at without difficulty. But it must be directed when its effects are pernicious—it would be disastrous if a general thirst for alcohol were easily gratified by low price.

All these factors are not independent but exercise mutual influence. It is exceedingly difficult to arrive at a correct price; with absolute lack of control, desire will be the determinant, but this will produce results that are not in accord with social welfare. Price must be controlled by the government, and a certain measure of arbitrariness is likely to be present in the regulation, the general rule being that it should be brought as close to utilitarian value as possible. If prices cannot be accurately made, there is no cause for lament. Even in a science like physics, which prides itself on exactitude, approximations are often tabulated and considered good enough; when a number is worked out to four decimal places, it is used, though it does not spell absolute accuracy. How much more unattainable is accuracy in the formulation of social rules, where phenomena are complex and indeterminate! But a practical society is concerned with the best that can be achieved, not the best imaginable. There is no excuse for wrong when it is possible to eliminate it; hence, the plea that any wrong can be tolerated because absolute right is not procurable is ludicrous. Humanity must always strive toward the better, even though the best is not on the horizon: thus can we fulfill our destiny.

The ultimate aim of production is consumer goods. The more there are, the more there will be for everybody, if distribution is adequate. Variation in the amount of products changes the fluid price—that is, the price that would be obtained if the competition to sell and the desire to buy were to operate untrammeled—which varies according to the quantity of goods available at any one time. The regulated price is fixed by decree of the government, which acts as the intermediary between producer and consumer. Fluid price is the product of the factors that comprise exchange value, while regulated price modifies it in the direction of utilitarian value and public welfare. When production increases, price falls and consumption rises; when production decreases, price rises and consumption falls. Consumption varies inversely with price within limits only; when these are reached, there is no longer any proportional change. When consumption has reached a maximum, production may still be able to proceed, and a further fall in price will not raise production. Production should not exceed this point or else a surplus remains and the producers have less income than before, though they may have displayed no less energy and maybe more. This is manifest injustice, and the remedy is for the government to fix a minimum price. When consumption is already at a minimum, production may continue to drop and price will increase, with the consequence that the consumer suffers while the producer earns more with less effort. This exploitation is to be stopped by a maximum price.

Producers may combine to manipulate price to the detriment of the consumer. They may deliberately cut down production in order to maintain high prices, making it far below the maximum limit of consumption, in which case they are not giving the equivalent service in return for their incomes. Though maintaining normal production, they may raise prices without seeing a corresponding decrease in demand, owing to a human tendency to sacrifice some things for others or because normal production is barely more than the minimum limit of consumption; they obtain an increased income for the same work. Conspiracies like these should be defeated by price regulation and taxation. Consumers must be protected from exploitation, and production must be encouraged to rise to its maximum level of competition.

The danger of price regulation is the rise of a black market, so it cannot be indiscriminately introduced. As much as possible, the fluid price should be allowed to run its course. Price control ordinarily applies to essential services. In normal times, when the supply is sufficient, people are not tempted to incur legal punishment; only when demoralization is universal and the supply is exiguous, as in wartime, does the black market flourish. The only real remedy in these cases is the return to normal production. When goods are less, it means that the average share has fallen, and no legal device can alter this. The exchange ratio of money is bound to be unfavorable, and the price level rises. If control is applied effectively to maintain the previous prices, it means only that a portion of the currency is superfluous. If the shortage of goods is permanent, a new issue should replace the old so that exchange can still be transacted in reasonable units of currency. If it is temporary, as is more likely the case, the superfluous money should be saved, maybe compulsorily deposited with the government. If prices were allowed to run their course unchecked, the misfortunes of shortage would not be so injurious if the share of every individual were decreased by the same ratio; they would be aggravated by the wealthier people buying up most of the available goods to the detriment of the poorer. If prices are not checked, the poorer suffer; if they are controlled, the black market rears its head. In an Exchangist economy, where incomes do not differ much, the balance of distribution is not greatly disturbed by the black market; but in a capitalist society, it is otherwise. The black market is to be eliminated by strict supervision of producers and traders, rationing the amount each person is permitted to purchase, and compulsory savings. The public is taught to refuse to deal with it. If the black market cannot be suppressed, price control is lifted; it disappears as prices rise. The adjustment of exchange is then effected through taxation. The issue of additional currency leading to inflation worsens the situation and must not be undertaken. It does not cure a shortage of goods but lowers the exchange value of money and produces more unequal distribution.

Chapter 7
Income

The problem of income is of greatest importance to people, for it represents personal welfare, which is the motivating force in the establishment of society. Personal welfare stands for the preservation of existence. In the state of nature, each person works toward this end, and it is in order that he may achieve this with greater facility that society exists. Hence, everyone has a claim to a reasonable income. The difference between penury and opulence is contrary to right and means that society has gone wrong and is not fulfilling its purpose. If this state of affairs cannot be otherwise, it would be better if society were dissolved. The acquisition of wealth by the individual under capitalism is not due to natural power but is a product of legal fictions, and the plutocrat is preserved in his possessions by the force supplied by soldiers and policemen who have wrong ideas of justice. An egalitarian economy within the limits of justice is not merely a moral requirement but is strictly in accord with truth.

Income should be proportionate to service. In a proper economy, labor should be the only criterion in its assessment, attention being directed to both its quantity and quality. If earnings were judged according to the actual returns of articles produced, there would be grave injustice, as prices are based largely on factors that have nothing to do with the relative merits of the producers. Two individuals of the same skill and energy are engaged in two different occupations, one of which by its nature has a tendency to earn more than the other. Are they then to be unequal in respect to income? If they were, then one is obtaining an advantage over the other from adventitious causes. Two articles or services should be equivalent in exchange. As the service rendered in the more lucrative occupation may be no greater than that in the less, if equal service begets unequal remuneration, then the principle of exchange is violated.

It is necessary to distinguish between commodity value and service value as factors in exchange. Commodity value is what appertains to the nature of an article; the ratio of exchange of goods is rightly based on their commodity value. The price of one pound of gold is much more than that of the same amount of silver. The difference is traceable to their difference in commodity value, which is not identical to utilitarian value, being merely the value given to an article by general desire. Service value is the value of the labor expended in producing a commodity. Income should be based on service value, not commodity value, which is not created by the individual. A goldsmith who expends a full day's work at his trade is not performing any greater service than a silversmith working with the same skill for the same period. They should receive equal income, though if they sell all their products, the goldsmith would make more. Income is the price paid for a service and should be reckoned as an exchange of service and not an exchange of goods. If this were borne in mind, there would be no anomaly of a film actor earning more than an author; though as people prefer patronizing the cinema to reading books, the actor is apt to receive a disproportionately higher income.

It is the state's responsibility to adjust income to service. Unjustifiable incomes will be reduced by taxation to the appropriate scale; on the other hand, certain types of work that are not likely to earn enough to assure proper incomes will be subsidized. These modes for income distribution are supplementary to price regulation, to which there is a limit for effective operation of the economy. Prices cannot be raised high in the case of essential services, which must be available to all, nor lowered much in the case of those that are pure luxuries.

In the determination of income as in price, it may not be possible to arrive at exact estimates. This is one of those practical limits that affect the realization of ideals but do not change their truth. A society must be based on theoretically correct principles. Where the foundation is wrong, the superstructure cannot be right; where the former is right and the latter can be shaped closely to correspond, then this society is what should function. People do not quarrel over slight differences, which cannot be helped, but they do and should feel resentful over flagrant breaches of justice. In the evaluation of income, any error should lean toward equality. The inexactitude is more rational thus, as society influences the abilities of individuals who, born in the state of nature, might have a different ratio of powers. Most of the work in society is created by the people living in society. In nature, innate physical strength plays a preponderant part in humans' struggle for existence, while in society it is unimportant. In society, the accountant does more difficult work than the porter, but in nature, he would be inferior in obtaining sustenance. The power of keeping complicated ledgers may be naturally incompatible with the inherent capacity of the porter. If the accountant earns more, it is for his higher social usefulness. This is right, but as the porter has less power in the capacity of acquisition, the difference in income should be decreased rather than increased. Of course, it cannot be judged from present powers what an individual would be if he had been born in the state of nature. The power of the soldier, who is stronger than the priest, is in large measure attributable to social cultivation. If they had not entered society, the man who is now a priest might have been the stronger. However, once society is formed, judgment must be based on present capacities, as usefulness is theoretically the meaning of exchange; moreover, the test is the only practicable one. However, in consideration of unknown possibilities and the manifest truth that an individual should not become worse off in society than he could be in nature, differences of income should be reduced rather than aggravated.

People are to work either individually or cooperatively in companies. In the case of solitary operation, income is easily determined, as one's earnings are constituted by whatever is obtainable. When it comes to group effort, the profit does not belong to one person but must be divided. In theory, the share of each worker is proportionate to the amount of value he creates, but in practice it is difficult to adjudge with complete exactitude, unless all the members put in an identical quantity and quality of labor. A company specializes in one type of service, but not all workers need to be engaged in one kind of work; for example, it may include messengers, clerks, mechanics, and engineers. The problem can be tackled in two ways.

In one company, all perform the same type of labor—for example, a factory is made to have only mechanics on its staff. Messengers, engineers, and so on form separate companies whose services can be enlisted and remunerated by this factory, among others. An engineer who is part owner of his firm and has no share in the factory acts in a consulting capacity to the factory, which pays his company a fee for his services; he is comparable to the lawyer who acts as legal adviser to a number of concerns. Work like that performed by watchmen and messengers can be undertaken by the workers in rotation to save expense. As a group must have a unifying hand, the workers elect from among themselves a committee with a chairman and take turns sitting on it. Control of the factory is vested in its personnel, who determine all its major problems. Difference in quantity of work is minimized by fixing the same number of working hours per day for all. Regarding quality, only beginners learning their trade lag behind the normal skill; after a certain amount of experience extending over a variable period of time, most individuals acquire the same skill, and longer experience produces no appreciable difference. Hence, everyone should undergo a training period, including practical experience, in vocational institutions; then, on entering a factory, they are no worse than the old-timers and can make up for their lesser experience with greater enthusiasm. A factory organized in this way will divide its profits equally among its members. If some members are energetic and skillful while others are lazy and clumsy, they will have their income increased and decreased, respectively, from adjudication by their fellows.

If this type of organization is unsatisfactory, then the arrangement can be this. Take, for instance, a commercial ship and let it include a captain, officers, engineers, doctors, clerks, sailors, cooks, stewards, and so on. These categories of workers perform different kinds of work, some higher than others. Their individual percentages of the total profit will be determined by the crew. The captain has executive control, but the general policy is settled by the whole staff, as the ship does not belong to him but to all, including the lowliest members. Differences in quality and quantity of work are given dissimilar awards, and such problems are decided by the crew. In this type of organization, the power of government arbitration regarding income variation is a greater necessity.

Apportionment of income will be according to creation of utilitarian value, which implies social service and is based on the amount of knowledge required for the task. The usual test of knowledge is education, which will be used as a measure of earning capacity. All persons will be made to attend schools for general education. According to their potentialities, they will then be sent to vocational institutions of different grades of importance to learn specific types of work, and upon graduation they will undertake the jobs for which they have been trained. A scale of normal incomes may be prepared appropriate to the quality of the work category; in each, a similar remuneration accrues to the average worker, those above or below the normal gaining more and less, respectively. The different categories are classified into levels according to the grade of vocational institution producing them. There are only a few levels, and each will receive an income generally the same for all its categories.

The test of education should be easy to administer, but it is not rigid. An individual with inferior training may turn out to be a better worker than one who is given knowledge at a higher institution: nothing prevents him from earning more than the other. No one is prevented from changing his occupation or from receiving the necessary training. Even without formal training, a person is free to perform any work, whether of a different type or of a higher grade, if ability or experience qualifies him. Education is used only as a normal guide in judging ability, not as the exclusive criterion.

Income for the different levels is allocated without great disparities, for, as has been explained, the production of value does not differ much from person to person. The determination is somewhat arbitrary, but it suffices for practical purposes. The normal standard of income does not imply that the income of individuals follow it rigidly or even closely, since, as the workers are not receiving fixed wages but profits, they may earn more at certain times and less at others. But it does mean that it is not departed from widely for the average worker.

To launch any operation, especially in connection with the production of tangible commodities, capital is needed; a factory cannot function without machinery. Capital, applied to money, implies its power to obtain in exchange the requirements for conducting an enterprise. Everyone has a right to acquire capital, which is a form of property, so he can preserve his existence. How is he to get it? Initially, he has none, as it is a product of work, yet to start with, he must possess it.

Society is called into being with the express intention that every member will be able to secure his personal welfare with greater effectiveness than he could do otherwise: it is insurance against insecurity. The individual has the right to demand that society aid him in his attempt to maintain his existence. If it were an institution in which an individual incurs loss, then it is useless to him; if it were to benefit only a section of the populace, then it is nothing but an iniquitous conspiracy, a fraud depriving him of his rights. It cannot aid the individual who deliberately refuses to fulfill his part of the bargain, but it must do so against perils that are not his fault. This social insurance is what induces human beings to dwell together.

The state, representing the community, will furnish the capital; individual operators and new companies will be granted loans adequate for the normal functioning of enterprises. These are repayable in installments as soon as regular and sufficient incomes are made; the outlay has not been earned by the borrowers. As money cannot beget money, the state can take no interest on loans. In the case of a person entering an established company, no loan is necessary; he will be declared an equal owner with his colleagues, but as his share originally belonged to his co-workers, he must pay for it by a regular deduction from his income until the full sum is met. When the person retires, his share of the capital is transferred to the company, and payment for it will be effected in the form of a pension.

The same procedure holds true of farmers. The individual cultivator will be granted a piece of land and a loan to obtain the requisite implements. Those who enter a company will acquire their share and receive a pension the way that a mechanic would in a factory. Land itself is not a negotiable commodity, and no payment will be made for it but only for the accessories required for operation. When a farmer quits work, the transfer of the land and its appurtenances is effected by the state.

The instruments of production should not be hereditary, as everybody has an equal right to acquire them. If they were hereditary, and therefore in private hands, the newcomer would be acquiring them not as a right but as a favor, which would be unreliable and disastrous. The state will manage their transfer and will grant the most suitable applicant, the individual who can turn it to best advantage, the priority of acquisition.

The state has a duty to guarantee employment for every person; the right to work is part of social insurance. Everyone must exercise a regular vocation that will earn him a sufficient income; if a person does not do this, he fails to fulfill his obligations as a citizen, and he becomes a nuisance and a menace to relatives, friends, and strangers. Hence, proper training will be provided and employment found for him. Employment will depend on individual choice, on the condition that the person is able to do the work properly. The incompetent will find themselves at a disadvantage, but they will still be able to exercise some appropriate vocation. No one is to starve.

Women are to work at regular vocations in the same way as men, as all human beings possess equal rights and obligations, and they will receive similar opportunities and incomes. The men do not thereby forfeit their chances for employment; if necessary, working time is reduced to attain the objective of employment for all. Neither do men lose their incomes; it only means that instead of their first acquiring the money and then using it to maintain their families and themselves, half of what they would earn is now gained by their wives.

The practical problems presented by the employment of women revolve around their functions as mothers and keepers of households. They are incapacitated only during the short periods of child bearing, when they will receive incomes from the state, for they are performing a service to society and therefore should not incur losses. Their babies can be cared for in nurseries run by women who specialize in the work as a vocation and receive their earnings thus; of course, the mothers can and should look after their children part of the time. They cannot lose their vocations during the periods of enforced absence, whether they work individually or in companies. Regarding housekeeping, many household tasks, such as cooking, washing, and sweeping, can be undertaken by concerns set up expressly for these. Women need suffer no disadvantage in the pursuit of their careers.

Certain sections of the population really are unable to work, including children, the elderly, and the disabled, though even they are not completely helpless. They are protected by social insurance by virtue of their membership in society, as they have an inalienable right to existence, not a mere claim based on pity. Society is formed expressly for greater individual security, and these cases fall within the plan. Of course, they are not actually producing anything, but it is because they cannot, not because they will not, and social insurance means that in such eventualities, their personal welfare is guaranteed.

Children are given regular incomes from the day of their birth until they are equipped with proper vocations to start earning on their own. These payments, which are receivable by all and vary according to needs, are regarded as advances made on their future service. They are thus independent regarding their livelihoods, though their parents can do whatever else they like for them.

All persons will work until they reach the normal age of retirement; some may be incapacitated earlier, while those who are able to do so can work longer if they are willing. Payments to the elderly come under the category of pensions as part of their previous earnings returned to them. The state, which has been receiving taxes from them, makes the payments. In addition, they have saved up on their own, including the capital that they can draw out for their diurnal needs. Irrespective of their private savings, they must all be paid their pensions.

Unless their infirmities are congenital, the disabled have done service part of their lives. The incomes received from the state for their support thus constitute returned earnings to a certain extent; but, even if they have never worked, and such cases are not likely to be common, their right to maintenance is vindicated by social insurance. However, it is rare for a disabled person to be absolutely helpless; if properly trained, he can perform some appropriate work, and he will be provided with such employment. He can dwell in his own home or in an institution, depending on his circumstances; he need not rely on others for charity, for as a member of society, his natural rights cannot be forfeited.

Chapter 8
Regulation

In the state of nature, each person fends for himself, relying solely on his own powers, and no injustice can arise. Absolute freedom is, then, a blameless entity. Even when an individual covets another's possessions and uses force to acquire them, this is still not particularly reprehensible, as the struggle for existence has not yet been tempered by reason, and everyone is free to use his strength, which is the wellspring for the attainment of his welfare. However, as they are precarious and unfruitful, such conditions are unsatisfactory, and organized society is a necessity.

Society presupposes rules that must be founded on reason and must produce a better life, or else there is no meaning in its formation. Liberty is regulated by justice and is limited; this circumscription preserves its essence but eliminates its excesses. To annihilate liberty, however, is to breed a host of evils—the loss of a natural right, initiative, self-respect, energy, and happiness. As it cannot be presumed that others will devote more attention to one's personal welfare than oneself, the promotion of exploitation, if not immediate, will be eventual. Freedom must be conserved in conjunction with justice, which means respect for reciprocal rights. In fact, freedom grows more real, for unmitigated liberty of action consumes the liberty of some and brings fear that binds the sense of liberty of all.

Society must be erected on justice. The fallacy of capitalism is the introduction of restrictions that are not conducive to real liberty, though they protect an artificial liberty, under whose aegis a delusive brand of superiority is fostered. The capitalist and the heir to a fortune are not by nature superior to their employees; if it comes to unhampered struggle with personal strength and all the faculties coming into play, they would be defeated. A congeries of legal restraints embalms their artificial superiority; this false freedom accounts for the evils of capitalist society.

Society must be derived from valid exchange, which must be ensured by a central authority. The government, which does not undertake any productive function, is to fulfill the role of mediator. Freedom is not thereby violated; in its genuine essence, it breathes, coordinated with right. In the political sphere, even in a democracy, freedom is regulated to effect equal rights; why should this be less in the economic sphere? If it is rational to prevent an individual from throwing a bomb, why is it not so to hinder him from depriving another of his legitimate acquisitions? No law allows one to inflict a physical injury, so why is a violation permissible in respect to property? Robbery is no less injurious because the law punishes one form of injury and not the other.

The government's service is regulatory; it supervises exchange so that it does not deviate from the correct path. Its measures are designed so that everyone shall obtain his due, that he shall not suffer from fraud, that the principle "to each genuinely his own" is observed, that equal opportunities are given to all, and that no loopholes and erroneous laws allow an artificial superiority to flaunt ludicrous postures. Convention has a strange power of engendering blindness to truth. Were each individual to exercise only his own productive powers, there would result only inconsiderable differences of property, and a virtual equality would prevail. The frightful disparities of capitalist society would be impossible, for it is incredible that any person could produce one hundred times as much as another. With its possibilities for exploitation, the employer/employee relationship is the villain. What should be the limits of inequality? If not hampered and hindered by others, every individual is capable of producing a sufficiency for himself; therefore, the first requirements of a right society are that all should enjoy adequate incomes and have food, clothing, shelter, and a supply of the essential constituents of personal welfare. The extent of the surplus products, nonessentials over and above the minimum standard, will determine the degree of unequal distribution, which cannot make the difference between the extremes of income very much. Such variations can cause no oppression while they are just recognition of merit.

The state is to regulate private property, which is a good, not an evil; every type of property will be subjected to control to ensure equitable distribution. Money and goods should be had by all. Since it is of the utmost importance that every person should have a place to live, he will be entitled to own a house or have part ownership of one. None shall be permitted to possess more than one house, either in whole or in part—he can have only that in which he actually lives, houses being meant for habitation and not as sources of profit. Rent is unearned income and will be prohibited. Houses will be built by private enterprise and are saleable and inheritable; loans will be granted by the state to individuals for the purchase of their abodes and will be returnable in installments. Money and goods are transferable and inheritable; the principle of inheritance is not wrong if it is not associated with exploitation. Money does not increase of itself, and most goods are perishable. The person who inherits them will have some additional enjoyment bestowed on him by his parents—there is nothing unnatural in this—but he still has to work for a living, as what he inherits will never be sufficient to confer on him idleness for life.

Part of the government's regulatory technique is taxation, which is made for two purposes: first, to pay for the cost of running the government, including salaries, public office being engaged in a distinctive species of service for which payment in exchange is made as with any other company; second, to adjust incomes by subsidies to those groups whose services can be adequately remunerated only in this way and by payments to sections of the population, such as children, who have a claim on society.

Taxes are levied on commodities, services, and incomes. The categories of commodities bear duties in different ratios to their prices, higher for those less essential. The prices of services embody taxes; for example, theaters pay a tax on each ticket sold. Taxes on the incomes of different callings and persons vary, with the intention of reducing them to normal, appropriate standards and effecting equalization. Taxation is not a device for burdening the people; on the contrary, it is an instrument for distributing income and promoting public welfare. It is not a levy on capital and does not withdraw money that might be used for conducting enterprises. The money that is taken from the public is distributed in a different form among its members and provides greater good for the whole. In the feudal economy, where kings raised the taxes for their private expenditures, there was good ground for horror on the part of their subjects, to whom the abstractions from their earnings were similar to confiscation and constituted pure losses. In a good state, taxation has a different meaning.

The government does not acquire its revenue only through taxation. One source is fees or charges made for some forms of its services that are calculated per item and are payable by the individual users. As the government does not own cultivated lands and does not operate any industry, it can draw no income from them. Loans may be raised on occasion, but as they are returnable, they are merely temporary expedients. Voluntary subscriptions are gifts that are permissible, but their motivating force is morality, and they do not fall within the scope of a planned economy. Loans and subscriptions are superfluous for normal functioning. The continual issue of paper money makes for inflation, dislocates the economy, injures valid exchange, produces misery, and is little short of a fraud.

For adjustment of exchange, the counterpart of taxation is the subsidy. Payments, regular or occasional, are made to persons who, owing to their callings, cannot attain normal standards of income, though their services fully merit them, either through lack of popular appreciation or, more often, through governmental fixing of prices to make the benefits more widely available. Payments must also be made to fulfill the obligations of social insurance. Loans for commencement or continuation of business come from the revenue, though as they are returnable, they do not ultimately affect it. It cannot be overemphasized as a counterblast to capitalist practice that loans do not bear interest and do not add to or detract from income. If the government takes interest on loans, it is an exploiter; if stocks and bonds give unearned income to their holders, this is the surest road to engendering a parasitic class and ultimately a vast difference of wealth between members of the community.

In addition to taxes and subsidies, regulatory measures include price control, apportionment of the instruments of production, provision of employment, and others, the sole aim being the promotion of equitable exchange. Laws are passed, and their application is vigilantly supervised; abuses that are not corrected redound to the discredit of the government, which, if it will not or cannot fulfill its obligations, forfeits its right to function.

Price control does not imply that goods are to bear the same prices forever; they must be revised from time to time in accordance with actual conditions. Attention is paid not only to the fluid price, from which too great a departure is generally inadvisable, but also to the needs of the moment, the guiding star being utilitarian value. Actual utility, not marginal utility, is the determinant—that is, contribution to human welfare. Grain will remain grain whether it is abundant or scarce; its marginal utility shapes its exchange value and hence its fluid price, but its actual utility is given first place in the consideration of its regulated price. Left to itself, a narcotic may have a high marginal utility, but its actual utility is low; it may be outlawed or the price increased to such a height that its consumption is exiguous. In either case, the fluid price is neglected, the controlling factor being the actual value. Regulated prices may be higher or lower than the fluid, depending on the nature of the commodity and the motivating ideas.

Nothing could be more important to the proper functioning of the economy than the furnishing of capital to the workers. All the horrors and woes of the capitalist system ensue from the concentration of capital in the hands of a few, leaving the rest helplessly dependent. No one should have more capital than necessary to run the business operated by his sole labor, and if the employer/employee relationship were deracinated, any additional capital would become superfluous to its owner and would pass over to other workers. The distribution of capital is no less a prime consideration than that of income. A distinct, superior class of capitalists would not exist; capital would not be an instrument of oppression but purely what it should be: an instrument of production, accessible to all. The division of capital is a necessity and must be effected by the state. It is apportioned according to the needs of the vocation and hence is not equally divided. This, however, is harmless as long as a greater capital secures no greater personal benefit than a small; that is, when incomes are regulated. A person engaged in professional service requires little capital, but his standard of living does not suffer. Capital is not evil when it does not produce unearned increment.

The state has a duty to find employment for all. The individual first chooses a vocation and, if capable, will receive proper training, part of which could be in the company where he would like to work afterward. Save for the one limitation of capacity as tested in competition with others, he is free to select whatever calling pleases him, and he will be provided with appropriate work. If an individual elects to operate individually, he is granted a loan. No company may refuse to take in a newcomer if the government decides it is able to do so. One important point in regulation is the quota of persons admissible into a vocation; it is extremely undesirable that one should be glutted and another undermanned, hence the selection of candidates for ability. The unemployment problem in a capitalist society is attributable to employers' greed, which makes them hire as few hands as possible consistent with their volume of business in order to swell profits. In order to have everyone in regular employment, either greater production should be encouraged or working hours should be reduced. This is a step toward the good if production is already sufficient, as more leisure is available for cultural and recreational activities. Work is, for the most part, only a means to an end, though to a certain extent it is valuable in itself; and if goods are sufficient, there is no need for further toil.

The scope of regulation is to comprehend only as much as is needed for the existence of valid exchange. A law must be genuinely necessary and effect good. Idle and fussy rules are not made, and needless restraints on free enterprise are eschewed. Laws must be carefully considered by the legislators responsible and must be passed for the general welfare, not to support particular interests that are antagonistic to this. For one section of the populace to exploit another or for the state to exploit the people is to injure natural right.

The government's regulatory activities do not make the system socialistsic, the word being objectionable on account of its connotation of slavery. The promotion of the public weal is not peculiar to socialism, as every theory pretends to it. *Public welfare* is a rather vague phrase and has many interpretations, the capitalist eulogizing it in *laissez-faire* and the socialist in extinction of individuality. Socialism, if it means anything at all amid its welter of actions, signifies state operation of industry or nationalization, and it does not confine governmental activity to regulation. Neither is the system capitalistic because of the concept of private property, for capitalism signifies the employment of labor by capitalists. The sharp antithesis between capitalism and socialism on the grounds of private and communal property is no reason to suppose that private property must be associated with the noxious phenomena of capitalism. As a matter of fact, both systems can come under the common name of *Expropriationism*, because both are engaged in defying valid exchange and the natural bases of society and possess the same characteristic of unjust expropriation of the property of the producers, equally evil whether done by individuals or the state. Exchangism is opposed to both.

Chapter 9
Political Organization

Leading a free and solitary existence in nature, human beings should choose to form society only to secure advantages consequent on the mutual exchange of benefits. Every phenomenon has specific problems, and exchange can be accompanied by exploitation. Moreover, individual exchange has its limitations, and when people live in propinquity, conflicts of interest arise. To make exchange run smoothly and capably, fully developing its potentialities, a system of regulations must be instituted to which everybody subscribes. But these rules do not function by themselves and remain a dead letter unless society molds its behavior in accord with them. Made by individuals, rules can be broken by them at will unless there is an external restraining influence. A community thus needs to be organized to live in harmony; this organization is the state, whose specific function is the regulation of exchange. The organization assumes the form of a code of laws, and a government, composed of individuals, is appointed to make the organization function properly.

What is the origin of the state? Hobbes described an age when every man was the mortal enemy of every other man until they realized the impossibility of carrying on thus and agreed to surrender their individual powers to a sovereign; society was formed, and order prevailed. This myth, which he formulated in support of despotism, was adopted by Locke and Rousseau and grew into the rationalized foundation of democratic theory. No social contract is mentioned in the records of early history; if it ever was made, it must have been concluded verbally. This presupposes that its framers could understand one another through a common language. In order for a language to develop, its speakers must have had a good deal of friendly interaction, which in effect means that society has already been formed. Individuals living from the beginning in isolation, meeting only to kill one another, could not possibly have the time or opportunity to sit down and agree to make certain sounds represent certain meanings! It also bespeaks a high degree of intelligence for a host of enemies to devise a rational plan acceptable to all; that so-called savages were capable of such a feat is beyond belief.

Like all other institutions, the state must have grown gradually. A few persons, who for some reason subsisted in mutual dependence, came to recognize one of their number as their leader; these groups expanded naturally or coalesced as a result of war. The inevitable authority of parents over their children must have been a powerful factor in the formation of the state, which has largely been associated with the notion of kinship.

The state has strutted most fearfully; it is a monster of iniquity. Through inheritance, puny individuals were made masters of millions and were worshipped as gods. Artificially made strong, these wretches raved and trampled. War is the most notorious feat of the state, and war does not exist without the state. What is the use of such a state? To preserve order among individuals! Could any private crimes have wrought such misery? A good deal is to be said for the anarchist position!

Is the state necessary? And can it be made good? Its nature and purpose must be consequent on the nature and purpose of humanity, for it is nothing but a mode of human organization. The inherent purpose of every human is the preservation of his existence. This purpose is described as inherent in that it is associated with each and every one of us from the day of our birth, is ours by virtue of our humanity, and is confirmed by nature. It is equally possessed by all. Primarily referring to existence *per se*, it extends its scope with the evolution of reason and other human powers to cover whatever gives life its value. The inherent purpose must be an inherent right simply because it is a natural element.

To realize their inherent purpose more easily, human beings settled in society to effect mutual exchange of benefits. To keep this exchange pure and prevent whatever injures an individual's ability to promote his personal welfare, a community forges an organization invested with power. As all are equal in respect to their inherent purpose, which is the state's inspiring cause, they must exercise equal power to control its destiny. As they create it, they cannot be its slaves; each individual retains his freedom, relinquishing only his power to inflict injury on others.

The state is a necessity, unless all human beings are good, when it could well vanish. The greatest danger posed by its removal is not that the conflict between individuals would breed misery but that as people have come to realize the strength of organization, they will not exist as solitary units but will unite into bands, waging ceaseless conflict and destroying civilization. But the state must be purged of its evil. A cruel state is even worse than anarchy, for the maltreated cannot defend themselves but are forced to live in passive agony without the consolation of occasional triumphs over their persecutors. To ensure that the state fulfills only its proper destiny, it must be in the hands of the whole people, its tasks must be categorically defined by law and limited to what are genuinely necessary to maintain justice, and its bureaucracy must be secured against corruption.

Because of its compact organization, its position as ruler, and its ability to command force, a government is apt to degenerate into an oppressor of the people, from whom its authority is derived for a specific purpose. Being composed of human beings with all their frailties, it can misuse its power. On the one hand, it is imperative to have such an organ; on the other, it must not be allowed to deviate from its proper nature. While supervising the people, it must be supervised itself, and only the people can do this; hence, it must be an elective organ, representing the community.

Primitive peoples could not have formally instituted a social contract, but nothing prevents civilized humanity from agreeing to create a state and a condition of society based on rational principles that are recognized as acceptable. The foundations of the state must be clearly formulated and understood, and they must win general assent before they can be regarded as binding. An inherent agreement pertains to the right state, an agreement prompted by nature, subscribed to by the people, proper to the concept of the state, and embodying the principle of promotion of the fundamental purpose of the members.

Are human beings born free? The most striking fact about a baby is its helplessness; it is absolutely under its parents' control. Though the care it receives is naturally loving, its dependent condition does not suggest freedom. Then there is the inevitable subjection of humanity to nature; we cannot perform numberless things, and those we can must follow its laws. We are, however, a part of nature, and there is no question of master and slave. The helplessness of our early ancestors and the limitations imposed by natural laws show that a human being is not an independent entity. But it would be a clear travesty of facts to conclude that he might be subjected to slavery by another person or the state, for each of us is born with an inherent purpose of our own and is not meant to exist for the sole fulfillment of others' ends. Slavery is not innate in humanity but is a condition imposed from without. The relationship to nature and to parents is one of love; other than these, a human is not born with a necessary link to any person or institution and is therefore free in the sense that he ought not to be subject to the irresponsible control of others. In the state and by the law, an individual's freedom can be limited only insofar as is necessary to prevent mutual injury; he curtails his freedom to obtain security.

Are human beings born equal? One enjoys a strong physique, has a transcendent intelligence, or is graced with virtue, while another is weak, stupid, or vicious. When it comes to any quality, it is always possible to find one who excels in it more than another, for every trait has degrees. Individuals do not bear resemblance in every respect; to each quality is attached a value, and it is self-evident that dissimilarity begets a difference of value and, hence, inequality. Unless two people are born perfect twins, physically and mentally identical in every particular, they cannot be equal in all respects. Does all this inequality warrant us to categorically affirm that one person is superior to another? When we say that A is superior to B, what we normally mean to imply is that A is *higher in our estimation as a person* than is B. Such a dogmatic judgment is indefensible. Human beings are a bundle of qualities whose number is difficult to compute. It is true that no A is superior to any B in every quality: if one is wiser, he may have a weaker body; if another is stronger, he may be less stoic; if yet another has a more vivid imagination, he may be unable to conduct a practical affair successfully. Who is the best: the boxer, the statesman, or the philosopher? The first could easily knock the other two down; the second could carry through a plan for getting into power or solving a national crisis, leaving his rivals muttering or fuming; the third could penetrate the laws of the universe, and his problems would only leave the others with a premature headache.

The social criterion of superiority is due to oversimplification. Every community selects some particular trait as the test, more often than not one without any real value: ancient China prized a man for Confucian scholarship, feudal Europe for birth, the modern capitalistic country for wealth. By such exclusive tests, one individual is rated higher than another, apparently all in all; such a judgment is not in accord with truth but is a palpable fiction.

Anyone is bound to be superior to another in some respects and inferior in others. As the qualities are numerous, it is impossible to arrive at a correct decision as to the actual superiority of one person over another by considering all of them. For practical purposes, it is necessary to assume that all human beings are equal in respect to their nature. All are to be treated as equals from the point of view of society, with equal rights before the law. Individuals do not really differ much, for as we are all members of the same species, it cannot be otherwise. Our exaggerated notions of disparity are derived from the relative nature of our judgments. Within the limits of human possibilities, we notice differences, which we magnify out of all proportion to their true value. The principle of equal legal status is supported by another consideration—the equality of life. The preservation of existence is the principle of the formation of society, and if this is equal for all, then legal treatment must consequently be equal. Civil equality does not, however, imply that the natural differences will vanish, nor does it conflict with the limited range of income variation permissible, this being based on productive ability, which is not similar for all. The great danger to guard against is artificial inequality, which produces disastrous effects that natural inequality can never do.

There are different ways of classifying states, of which two are of special interest. On the basis of number of rulers, we have autocracy, aristocracy, and democracy. As the Exchangist state has an elected government representative of the people in whom is vested ultimate authority, it is a democracy. The other two types, where the one and the few rule not directly subject to popular control, sooner or later terminate in oppression and exploitation. On the basis of the qualification of the rulers, we have theocracy, stratocracy, plutocracy, and so on, members of the ruling class being bound by ties of vocation or interest. It is unwise to make one calling with all its limitations supreme over the others, as such a state is bound to be one-sided, unable to fulfill with due balance the diverse needs of its denizens. In any case, it has all the evils of an oligarchy, arrogant and corrupt. The government should be composed of individuals drawn from all walks of life.

Rule of the people does not mean that all individuals actually perform the work of government. They only exercise ultimate control and elect a few representatives to carry out their wishes; hence the distinction between the government and the people. It is impossible for all the members of a nation to be engaged in the diurnal tasks of government, as they have their specific occupations, could not be gathered in any one place, and do not possess the requisite knowledge. But they could and must perform the general work of control and election, not because the government is less efficient otherwise, but because it may deliberately go wrong in order to exploit the masses.

A state is really run by a small body of individuals; for the purpose of unification, it also requires a single person to act as the head. We label it an autocracy, aristocracy, or democracy, depending on the authority apportioned to the one, the few, or the many, respectively. A correct division of authority and function is the best, as long as it is based on capability and produces the maximum efficiency and integrity. The one can assume responsibility for the proper execution of policy and serve as the center of unification; the few can legislate, act in an advisory capacity, and perform the detailed work of administration; the many can have the decisive voice in policy and hold their representatives accountable.

A country will be a collection of towns. Villages are incompatible with the attainment of high civilization; since they are objectionable units, they will be either destroyed or extended into towns. Where they have to exist, the urban pattern of governmental organization will be adopted with the requisite amount of adaptation. The units of government are the towns, which are grouped to form progressively higher units from districts to provinces. Each town, district, or province has a local or regional government whose duties are chiefly executive, within the framework of the national laws.

Should the government be centralized or decentralized? Society is an integral whole; exchange achieves its maximum benefit when it is extended. Exaggeration of local peculiarities destroys harmony and breeds dissension. Though individual distinctions are harmless, group differences, especially when the groups are collected into separate territories, brim with mischief. The cause of war lies in the incompatible interests of territorially organized communities. It is natural for one person to differ from another, and, as no two are similar in all respects, the individual easily learns tolerance. It is artificial for a collection of individuals to overemphasize their points in common, and organization makes diverse groups work themselves into a frenzy of mutual hatred. It is ridiculous that a rule that is right in one place is wrong in another; yet that is what decentralization produces. The state should lean toward centralization, but not so much as to make a local government irresponsible to the people directly concerned.

The Exchangist state may be of any size, the principles being equally applicable to a small country as to the whole world organized into a single state. The more extensive the society, the greater the benefit of exchange. The human race is one, and there is no reason why it should be divided into an array of antagonistic camps. If it is natural for human beings to form society for mutual good, it must be just as natural for society to be of global extent. A planetary state will do away with many of the stumbling blocks to effective organization that a regional state encounters as it tries to counteract the impact of other states, especially if these are of dissimilar principles and hostilely disposed. War will be obliterated, and all the miseries of international exploitation will cease.

But until and unless the people of the world are willing to enter into a single state based on truth and right, with its component individuals equal and free, there will continue to be separate states, each of which is justifiably ruled only by its citizens; hence nationalism, the need of a people to govern itself, is proper to encourage. But nations should never wield absolute sovereignty to the point that their mutual relations are not controlled by common agreement. Imperialism, or the dictatorship of one race over another, is an unmitigated wrong, since a whole population is denied its inherent right to pursue its maximum welfare.

Chapter 10
Agent of Exchange

There have been many theories about the function of the state. The monarchist regards the king as the recipient of a divine appointment to execute God's plans; the fascist makes the state an entity having purposes of its own that are distinct from those of individual persons; the communist looks upon the state as an instrument for cultivating the interests of a class; the democrat talks of the welfare of the people. Divine Right is a religious fraud for the usurpation of the claims of the community. The state is an abstraction—what purpose can it have apart from that pertaining to living, breathing beings? It is true that any particular individual may have his interests sacrificed, but this can mean only that the people as a whole or one section of the state obtains benefit thereby. Dictators chanting state supremacy mean nothing but their own personal supremacy and are hypocrites like their prototypes, the hereditary despots. To refer to the state as representing a class is to deny its status as an organization of the whole community. The other classes owe it no allegiance; if they are totally annihilated, then, of course, it ceases to represent a class, being now *de facto* inclusive of the entire population. However, if the other classes continue to exist, then they must be subject to barbaric exploitation against their human rights. The welfare of the people is an unsatisfactory generality, which every state can arrogate to itself in theory; a more definite conception is essential.

Exchangism defines the state's primary function as the regulation of exchange, which is precise and endows it with its *raison d'être*, investing it with a character consonant with human purposes. The state pays attention to the inherent rights of all its citizens and promotes public welfare by exercising its specific work of regulation. Whatever secondary functions it possesses are derived from the primary. Exchange must be understood in a comprehensive sense as covering all benefits, not merely tangible commodities. Regulation is the function, and general welfare is the consequence. General welfare can be conceived of as the state's aim, though this is not peculiar to it, as a religious organization can profess it likewise. Only the state is invested with the authority to enforce the regulation of exchange, promoting public welfare in this way.

The government is the agent of exchange. It is not, in the delusive jargon of capitalist democracy, the servant of the people, and it certainly should not be the master. It must be looked upon as an equal with the rest of the community, performing a service for which it is paid according to the rules of exchange. Neither divine nor devilish, it exists to fulfill a need, is an institution on a par with others, and should assume no airs of arrogance, though, because of its central position, it is distinctive. It exists to regulate the affairs of the community, but, being itself human, it must be regulated so that a reciprocal tie binds it to the people, who appoint it and hold it accountable.

The government performs the service of regulation and is to confine itself to this. It should not undertake any productive enterprise or a service that can be performed by private bodies. Nothing is more inappropriate than an organization being the producer as well as the judge—if it produces an inferior product, or if it is inefficient or corrupt, what remedy is there? Surely it would not make an adverse decision against itself. Nationalization constitutes a frightful monopoly against which there is no redress. There is no court of appeal against evil management and no other source to turn to where better work might be obtained; it is a case of take it or leave it—the worst of it being that one may not even leave it. A contravention of the principle of free exchange, state ownership and operation of industry is highly undesirable. The function of administrator and producer should be separate, as the latter, easily blinded by prejudice, is not the best judge of his own work.

That socialism has been more conducive to public welfare than capitalism is a moot point. Still preaching with evangelistic fervor about the welfare of the masses, it may seem to be a lesser evil economically. It has given rise to the lamentable tendency to regard nationalization as a panacea for all ills, so that even a capitalist government operates many utilities directly—activities that may be indispensable to curb the excesses of the form of economy it seeks to maintain; though lesser evils palliate the greater, they do not cease to be wrong. The woes of capitalism are traceable to the employer/employee relationship, with its consequences in private property for the few; curiously enough, they are supposed to be due to private property. Socialism could easily be turned into exploitation by a minority. The only difference from capitalistic exploitation is that the exploiters work together instead of separately.

All production and service will be conducted privately, with the government acting in a supervisory capacity. This also applies to the post office, schools, hospitals, railways, and all those activities undertaken by governments in capitalist countries under the appellations of public utilities, public works, and social services. The amount of control needed depends on the enterprise; some are closely associated with the government, may have to be subsidized, and may be organized as single bodies instead of collections of competitive groups. But they remain the property of their personnel, who are not public functionaries. Centralized companies are few and are permissible only from the nature of the service, while the vast majority of enterprises are broken up into small units.

Regulation in the interest of mutual benefit requires that all actions prejudicial to personal welfare be eliminated. Homicide and all forms of physical crime—that is, infliction of bodily injury—must be severely suppressed, for they militate against the inherent purpose, the right of each individual to attain a satisfactory existence. Liberty is maintained, and no one is to become subject to another; all are treated with equal regard by the law, and no section of the community enjoys a privilege at the expense of the rest.

Among the government's functions and duties, the preservation of its power and prestige commonly turns into a mania. It is in the hands of a small group, so it is easy to understand its selfish desire to suppress all antagonism toward it. Political revolutionaries, often individuals of more than average goodness, have been persecuted by every government more than any prisoner guilty of a private crime. The lust for power is one of the state's supreme evils—and it must be curbed. A state is constituted by the entire population and exists to perform a specific service; its power is not an end in itself, and it is not sacred. It must pay paramount attention to its actual advantage to the people, and it may be changed or even abrogated by them if so desired.

A state may also yearn to cultivate its power *vis-à-vis* other states. It is made up of human beings and is therefore liable to deem its cause right and, when confronted with a weaker neighbor, is prone to aggression. It is proper for it to develop its strength to be able to resist ambitious foes and protect its members against foreign exploitation, but it must not use this as an excuse for demolishing the liberty of the people. It has no right to invade another nation, for all are born with the same inherent purpose of existence, and no race should live in slavery. But, as with individuals, so with states; if they do not enter into an agreement whereby coercive authority can decide their altercations with justice, they are bound to go to war sooner or later.

War is a disease of the state. Two multitudes of strangers, who have had no opportunity to indulge in any personal quarrels, fiendishly endeavor to annihilate each other. If they acknowledge the state as a useful instrument for security and order, here they find themselves engulfed in a maelstrom of horror and chaos. Those who glorify war as a test of virility should be the last to champion the institution of the state. War is good to them because it spells unrestricted struggle. Isn't it more logical, then, to have absolute anarchy, where every individual can fight with every other? After all, the soldier is a slave, with his will to power an ironical joke; he is a poltroon, hiding inside a colossal organization instead of daring to stand on his own feet.

Power is not the object of the state. The people do not obtain any benefit simply because the government is strong—in fact, they may incur losses, for it does not get its strength from itself but from them. If its power is turned into a weapon to crush their liberties and aspirations, then it is guilty of breaking the inherent agreement and of violating its proper duties. If it encompasses the enslavement of foreign nations, then it has infringed on the inherent right of their members to lead their own lives. Sufficient strength to keep internal order and resist external aggression is all a state can justify.

There is a distinction between the government and the state. The state comprises all a country's inhabitants, while the government runs the nation's affairs, with a minority of the population constituting its personnel. In a democracy, the people may decide the general policy of the government, but the state must be differentiated from government: the government is the instrument of the state, which is a coercive organization of the entire population of a territory.

Born with a consuming desire to further our welfare, human beings are by nature impatient with external restraint. Our satisfaction is more easily achieved when we follow the native bent of our minds instead of forcing our behavior to conform to the dictates of authority. The strange phenomenon of all the individuals of a community believing the same ideas and acting in a similar manner comes from training. Is it likely that, left to their own devices, they would come to regard a certain style of clothing as beautiful and all others ludicrous, or a certain fanciful version of the universe as true and all others absurd? It is difficult to introduce a change into society not because its members resist innovations that may conflict with their interests, but because they feel that their established notions are correct, a feeling that has the force of certitude induced by habit. Training is partly the result of imitation and partly of force applied physically, economically, or in the form of anger and condemnation. Force in one way or another is never absent, and freedom is very exiguous.

The government embodies direct force, usually of the worst kind—infliction of physical pain by imprisonment and execution. For long ages, it was the instrument for oppressing the masses and preserving the privileges of the few; but as monarchs were deemed inevitable entities, there was no genuine way to escape suffering. With the arrival of democracy, there grew the idea that the scope of governmental activities should be minimized, to national defense and protection of life and property. Adam Smith formulated the doctrine of *laissez-faire*, which would allow economic affairs to be run by unregulated private enterprise in the belief that free competition would be conducive to the public good. Following fast on the heels of triumphant capitalism, socialism, however, propounded the opposite concept; in its extreme and logical form, it would completely submerge the individual. In ancient times, monarchs interfered little with the management of commerce and industry; their fell work was in connection with taxation, privilege, and religion. Under capitalism, specious freedom is secured, the extortions of hereditary noblemen being transferred to unscrupulous manufacturers. Socialism made the government supreme in a new way, but, as it aims at the welfare of the whole population, its exactions may paradoxically be less unbearable than those under other regimes.

A country's government will be composed of a Legislative Council to make the laws, an Advisory Council to guide the nation along the right path, and an Executive Council, headed by the national ruler and directing a bureaucracy to perform the diurnal tasks of administration. They are all ultimately responsible to the people, by whose consent they exist. Overshadowing the government is the constitution, the set of principles approved by the people for the promotion of general welfare.

Chapter 11
The Legislative Organ

Every person has the duty to pursue the right, as he is a part of nature and is created for a universal purpose. As its units are human beings, the nation is subject to the same obligation. But to err is human, as the trite saying affirms, and an entire community, no less than an individual, can go astray. To hold that the people are infallible is absurd; *vox populi, vox Dei* is a fantastic sentiment. If each individual can do wrong, then all together they do not miraculously attain the right. Right and wrong, however, are abstractions, which humans must discover and practice and which they may not have discovered or may refuse to practice. Who then is the judge? Each person can decide only for himself.

As society is formed by a collective of individuals for certain purposes, all have the right to formulate its rules. If they do wrong, they suffer. Society has no natural authority to force an individual to do what it thinks fit if his actions do not directly injure others, for it has no monopoly of right. It can, of course, give the individual advice, just as he can reveal his ideas, but persuasion is not compulsion. A social compact is applicable only to acts that induce mutual consequences. Its terms cannot be broken by a member with impunity but can be altered or abrogated by the community, as they who originate it may also destroy it. If its terms were changeless forever, there could be no new legislation, no progress; and if it should turn out to be a Frankenstein, it would be preposterous not to effect its downfall. The fact that the social compact was originally founded by the ancestors of a community does not preclude the possibility of change, since every person is a distinct entity existing in his own right, and parents cannot bind their children.

Only the wearer knows where the shoe pinches: the right of the people to establish their rules cannot be gainsaid. How are they going to do this? The procedure is through the plebiscite and election of representatives to devise measures that they can approve. Representation is an indirect mode of attaining the desired objectives and of having the people perform the work of government, whose controlling factor is the legal system. Legislation that embodies the social compact must be undertaken by the people through their representatives.

The Legislative Council is composed of a convenient number of persons directly elected by the people; it makes laws and supervises the government's work. The delegates should be individuals of ability and probity, but it is up to the people to decide upon their qualifications; hence no restrictions shall be placed on their free election. They are its direct representatives, each of whom normally holds office for a term before a new election takes place; and, as the people can choose whomever they like, the reelection of a representative is permissible, irrespective of the number of times.

The party system in capitalist countries does not make for efficiency, only for corruption. How is it possible for two or more parties who make it their principal business to decry one another to produce anything but confusion? A party member does not get into power based on his own sterling qualities but as the agent of a group. Members feel bound to support all their party's proposals and even vote against their convictions on particular problems. Nothing is more iniquitous than the nursing of factional interests instead of paying attention to the good of the nation. Only war temporarily unites the parties of a country and makes them drop their interminable altercations.

It is preferable that a member of the Legislative Council be elected on his personal merits. Anyone can stand for election, either nominated by himself or by others with his consent. It stands to reason that an individual who has achieved nothing outstanding and is not likely to inspire respect will not put himself to the fore. The successful candidates will be those drawn from all walks of life, who have achieved distinction. In a legislature composed of individuals elected on their own account, A may not agree with B on any specific problem but may agree on another; instead of every question becoming a party affair, each is tested by itself. Differences of opinion are confined to particular themes and do not divide the members into irreconcilable camps, ardently engaged in mutual vilification.

In the party system, those who are designated independents may exist, but they are very ineffective; the strength of the organized groups is too much for them. Parties will not be abolished by law, as the right of association is one of the freedoms that should not be suppressed. The people should, however, be taught to look askance at them, and measures should be taken to make it easy for candidates to come forward on their own.

Three main systems of representation have arisen: territorial, occupational, and proportional. In the first, each district sends a deputy; in the second, each vocation chooses its representatives; and in the third, parties are accorded seats in proportion to their voting strength. Can such delegates be truly regarded as representing the nation? Each actually stands for a mere fraction of the populace and does not speak for the nation. A legislature with such ingredients is a mere cockpit for the contention of sectional interests. The proper system is one where each delegate represents the entire nation; such a system is the proposed diffuse system of election. With adequate organization, it should not be difficult to disseminate information so that the voter will be aware of the country's distinguished citizens. For this, the Media can be called into service to help.

The diffuse system of election divides the country into a number of voting divisions, each comprising towns or districts scattered over the country. A division, which consists of a representative cross-section of the general population, has a voting list of candidates for the legislature, and every elector voting in one division chooses several persons. Since each division returns a few members to the Legislative Council, the total number of divisions is only a fraction of the total number of members. As a member is not elected by a distinct section of the population with geographical or other particular ties, he can be said to constitute a true national representative standing for the people as a whole.

For elections to be held by the people themselves, there must be an organization that undertakes the task of conducting them. This organization, which will be known as the Electoral Organization, is charged with the primary duty of conducting elections and helping the people to express their voice effectively. The Electoral Organization has nothing to do with ruling the country; it acts as a link between the people and the government, and its power is limited to helping the people make democracy a success.

In a town, the population will be divided into groups, which will elect from among themselves one electoral representative each. All the representatives form the town's Electoral Assembly. Each Town Assembly sends delegates to the District Assembly, from which comes the Provincial Assembly, and from the latter, the National Assembly. Each representative holds his post for a definite number of years. As the Electoral Organization possesses little power and its function is of no particular importance, this mode of representation suffices. It has nothing to do with parties; by its services, the party system would be discouraged and the government severed from tampering with free elections.

Every candidate for the Legislative Council sends in his name to the Electoral Organization; all the names will be recorded on lists that will be published, and all citizens will easily have access to copies. Voting papers are prepared, and every citizen will vote for whomever he likes; each person should make it his duty to exercise care and judgment and select only those he appreciates. The ballots are collected by the Organization, which counts the votes, and the candidates who receive the highest number in their divisions become the legislators.

The people can exercise their will directly on any problem by means of the plebiscite, which can be launched either by them, the ruler of the state, the Advisory Council, or the Legislative Council; a fundamental constitutional principle should be decided thus. If any member of the public desires that any question be determined by popular vote, he writes to the Electoral Organization, and if within a definite interval of time the number of requests aggregates more than a minimum fixed proportion of the electorate, a plebiscite will be held. The Electoral Organization is to conduct a plebiscite when the request comes from any of the legally recognized sources. After the counting of votes by ballot, a law will be passed if more than half of the electorate so desire it. However, a plebiscite is a rare necessity; save for fundamental constitutional principles, it is not resorted to without very strong reasons, as the Legislative Council is meant to undertake legislation and ordinarily possesses the confidence of the people.

The initiative for legislation formally emanates from the state ruler, the Advisory Council as a body, any member of the Legislative Council, or a section of the people. If more than the requisite proportion of the electorate send in requests to the Electoral Organization for the passing of any law, the matter will be taken up for discussion by the Legislative Council, which will frame a bill and vote upon it. The bill may or may not be passed.

A law passed by the Legislative Council is effective from the date it fixes; one determined by a plebiscite must be adopted by the Legislative Council as soon as possible. A law thus made is binding on everybody without exception, and the Executive Organ cannot refuse to carry it out. It may, of course, by repealed by its makers.

The Legislative Council cannot be dissolved, save by the people or by itself. The former members must continue in office until the new are duly elected and take over. The Legislative Council owes allegiance to the people and nobody else. Its members should work in cooperation and consider first and foremost the nation. They may take up the cause of any section of the population in order to promote justice but not to injure the country as a whole.

Suffrage is universal; as every person is a member of society, he has a right to determine its affairs. With the exception of children, whose exercise of the franchise must be delayed, everyone is given the vote, though in practice some may not be able to use it. If a person cannot trust his own judgment, he can very well seek advice. Naturally, if an individual cannot or does not care to vote, he may abstain, but this is a purely voluntary matter.

The functions of the Legislative Council include the determination of the constitutional principles, which promote public and private security; the regulation of exchange; taxation; supervision of the executive; ratification of treaties; control of foreign affairs; and regulation of the armed forces—whatever is necessary to ensure that the state is operating properly in the interest of public welfare. The measures it approves are made into written law; its work is perforce of a general nature. The legislators are not to be passive, merely listening and approving or disapproving, but are to be actively engaged in initiating and investigating.

Corresponding to the National Legislative Council are the local Legislative Councils for the provinces, districts, and towns. Their members, successively fewer in number from the province to the town and drawn from the places to which they attach themselves by virtue of habitation, are elected in the same manner as for the National Council, the local Electoral Assemblies undertaking the task of holding the elections. These councils do not perform major legislation, as all laws emanating from the central source apply to every part of the country; they carry them out in detail, make minor laws, and supervise the work of their particular administrative bodies. They cooperate with the National Legislative Council, sending up their requests for solutions to particular problems affecting their regions. They are responsible primarily to their electorates but cannot contravene a law made by the National Council.

Chapter 12
The Advisory Organ

The objection to an aristocracy is that there is no way to ensure that it will not abuse its power. Formed of a minority with peculiar ties among the members and irresponsible to the people, if it possesses unlimited power, it soon starts to care only for its own interests. Even if its first members are good, their successors will be largely made up of persons who are hypnotized by wealth and position.

The Platonic idea of philosopher-kings, if put into practice, will soon result in a race of philosopher-exploiters. A guardian like Socrates is more likely to be succeeded by one like Alcibiades. A theocracy is an aristocracy, and it would reasonably be expected that, as its passport to superiority is based on religion and morality, it would make for a good state; yet its corruption and misrule are notorious. No tribe of philosophers has ever ruled a country, save maybe in China, where the bureaucracy was composed of scholars who had studied and absorbed the philosophy of Confucius. But the mandarins on the whole were villainous, for an aristocracy soon attracts those who care only for its privileges without its principles of rectitude.

Nevertheless, not everyone possesses the same intelligence. Left to themselves, the majority of a population might not be able to distinguish right from wrong. It goes without saying that it is more difficult to devise than to learn; all people could follow, though few could originate. Therefore, the people should be given sound advisors, whose position should ensure that their advice is easily obtainable, but who should not be endowed with power to execute their aims against the wishes of the people. The masses could learn from them voluntarily, but if they refuse to do so, it cannot be helped; converting advice into compulsion is fraught with peril.

The Legislative Council is preferably composed of individuals with superior intelligence, but as the election is perfectly free and ought to be so if the electorate is to do whatever it thinks fit, the wrong persons might be chosen. However, it is invested with power, and many of those who long to get into it are more likely to cater to whatever follies the voters want than to risk their chances of getting accepted by telling the truth.

The section of society that is more intelligent than the majority of the citizens will form a Selective Organization. Admission is through selection by the members themselves, and candidates must have above-average wisdom and a requisite amount of integrity. The members may be drawn from any walk of life. The Organization extends throughout the nation, with the unit in the town. The members in a town will form a Town Body, and higher bodies will be drawn from lower bodies; the District Body will be drawn from the Town Bodies, the Provincial Body from the District Bodies, and the National Body from the Provincial Bodies. A new person first enters a Town Body with the approval of those already in it. Membership is for life.

The Selective Organization will select, usually but not necessarily, from among its enrollment a number of individuals to constitute the National Advisory Council; they hold office for a term, but they may be chosen again and again. They are not responsible to anybody but the Organization and may be recalled by it.

The function of the council is purely advisory; it issues advice to the executive, the legislature, and the people. Its instruction may be followed or disregarded, and no ill feeling need be engendered thereby. Its members should not be selected on the basis of party; it acts as a body and publishes its resolutions for public knowledge.

As part of its advisory duties, it can do three things. First, it can nominate a ruler of the republic, using its judgment and discretion to determine ability and probity; however, the people will decide whether to follow its recommendation. It is to select its candidate from the whole population; any person is eligible for consideration. Its choice is no more than a recommendation, and the decision rests with the people. Second, it has the right of initiative: it passes a resolution and submits it to the Legislative Council for discussion, and this may be adopted or rejected. Third, it may desire to hold a plebiscite on any problem, passing on its instruction to the Electoral Organization. All its duties are solely of an advisory nature; none of its decisions are compulsory.

It cannot be dissolved by the executive or by the legislature but may be dissolved of its own accord or by the Selective Organization. It is, of course, possible for the people, who can decide anything they like, to dissolve it. But they should leave it strictly alone, for it can do no harm and is meant only to guide them.

The Selective Organization is also to oversee the forming of local Advisory Councils for local affairs, based on the pattern of the National Advisory Council, to which they stand in the same relationship as the local Legislative Councils to the National Legislative Council. The local and regional councils are formed by their respective Selective Bodies, each to have a lesser membership than the National Council, decreasing in number from the province to the town.

The Advisory Council may be viewed in the light of an aristocracy, one not of force but of persuasion. The objection to popular rule so common among thinkers is the ignorance and viciousness of the multitude. Ignorance can be removed by education; as for viciousness, it cannot be ensured that any particular section of the community is devoid of it. Nevertheless, it remains true that a select group can have more wisdom and goodness than the bulk of the populace, and it is right and necessary to have the benefit of its services. But, as it is perilous to endow any group with power that it may misuse, it should constitute only an advisory aristocracy. Should the people refuse to listen to it, it is they who would suffer, and they could not be so vicious or stupid as to not recognize their own welfare or to not understand things when these are pointed out to them. If an aristocracy wields and abuses force, it is not the perpetrators but the masses who bear the evil consequences; if history is not absolutely false, a small body of individuals can work more harm than the people as a whole.

An aristocracy is not without its merits. Its advocates conceive of it as comprising a special group of persons of peculiar wisdom and virtue, who know what is good for the nation and act with pure disinterestedness. It is said that the world of the government is for experts, not bunglers elected at random by a mob of the foolish. All this is plausible enough, and, in theory, it sounds correct. That a few sages are available is more readily believed than that all human beings are wise. An aristocracy possesses a certain dignity and refinement. Assured of its position, it can carry out a good plan in the face of the mob's ignorant opposition.

The members of a democratic assembly have gained popular favor, which has nothing to do with wisdom. The individual with an attractive manner, the hypocrite, the good mixer, the public flatterer, the dispenser of largesse, the unscrupulous manipulator, and the florid-faced laugher—these types are more to the popular taste than the crabbed philosopher, the solitary sage, and the guileless character. To win a great number of votes, one usually must spend a lot of time moving around in company, thereby leaving no time for reflection and the acquisition of real knowledge. Originality becomes a handicap, while commonplace behavior is regarded as necessarily correct.

A democracy easily turns into an arena for the competition of sectional interests. The good of the nation is forgotten, while the real aim of existence is neglected in a struggle for power. No consistent policy is pursued by the country, which is subject to periodical upheavals. The work of government is slow; innumerable debates take place before a measure is carried through. The people tend to think in terms of the present, not of the future. The rights of the minority are trampled upon; mob violence is fearsome.

In spite of all that can be advanced on behalf of aristocracy, its theoretical good is far outweighed by its practical evil. No thinker has yet formulated a reliable method for sifting the elite from the multitude. A professional test means nothing, as it fails to account for virtue; and not every wise individual takes interest in a particular calling, while a dull person, actuated by ambition, can fulfill the requirements. In practice, an aristocracy degenerates into a closed corporation with birth as the passport to its ranks and wields power for its members' benefit at the people's expense—it is arrogant and incompetent. It does not even avoid the bane of democracy, factious quarrels. If its members find that the people are not aligned against them as a race, as commonly happens when the theory of popular rule is unknown or forgotten, then they divide into camps or strive against one another individually, filling the nation with their discord and wars. Their animosities are not even enlightened by ideological differences as in a democracy but are due solely to personal ambition.

Most oligarchies have not even professed to use the criteria of wisdom and virtue, which are as much despised by them as by the mob over whom they rule. The qualifications are often birth, riches, or military prowess; they are worthless as proof of ability to rule. More often than not, the wise beget asses and villains. A hereditary aristocracy is bound to be unprogressive. As its right is derived from the past, its eyes will be turned backward. Possessing an accidental yet inexorable qualification, it looks upon its subjects as naturally inferior beings with no rights; hence its cruelty, as evidenced under feudalism, is monstrous. Wealth is a sorry test; in addition to a large element of chance, its acquisition is often due to some of the meanest qualities in the human character—avarice, unscrupulousness, and cunning. Supposing that one who has made a fortune is entitled to be a ruler makes politics the evil it is. A military government is particularly terrible. The idea that a great soldier must make a good ruler is absurd. Owing to his merciless exercise of force, he may indeed preserve order, which is by no means the most desirable constituent of a state. Living death is not an ideal; dumb misery is not welfare. A usurping army is just a gang of brigands with their mentality: mere soldiers cannot govern properly.

A democracy does the least harm. Besides the plain fact that the people are naturally the sovereign, it could not oppress itself; it will take care of its welfare. If a democracy entails general misery, it is often because it is false, the actual power being in the hands of a group: it must be made genuine.

From a consideration of the advantages and disadvantages of both democracy and aristocracy, the best state is one in which the people exercise ultimate control and possess the decisive voice. For it to function efficiently, it needs expert knowledge, which is the only good furnished by a true aristocracy. This knowledge should take the form of guidance, persuasion, and advice, hence the concept of an advisory aristocracy.

Chapter 13
The Executive Organ

The actual work of government is not performed by the Legislative Organ but by the Executive Organ, which, if it functions badly, is sure to ruin the country. Save in democratic countries, there cannot be said to be a genuine legislature, the despots and oligarchs taking over its duties. The Executive Organ wields the most power, and suffrage is peculiarly important as a control so that it does not abuse its strength.

A chief of state is needed to serve as the center of unification. It may seem strange that one person could govern a nation, for it may reasonably be supposed that a number of colleagues would have a greater quantity of ability and energy. In reality, the chief of state would only issue general instructions, and his subordinates would not refuse to carry them out. A number of equals who can do what each pleases terminates in inaction or discord. It is easier to hold one person accountable than to make many responsible; moreover, somehow people find more interest in one person than in a crowd.

Herein lies the danger of despotism: not because the single person could possibly withstand a multitude, but because of the human tendency to hero worship. Napoleon could have been knocked down without difficulty by any farmer. The truth is that a solitary tyrant is no worse than many. In fact, a tyrant could do little mischief if a section of the populace, especially the military, did not support him, partly deluded by some theory of right, partly in order to triumph over the rest of their countrymen. A single chief is needed to coordinate action but must be controlled by the people.

The Exchangist state will have a ruler to act as the Chief Executive, who would be elected by a plebiscite of the entire nation. The election would be conducted in the same manner as for the members of the Legislative Council by the Electoral Organization. As it generates far more serious consequences to have a mischievous ruler than an incompetent legislator who is only one of many, the people must choose wisely. The Advisory Council could perform a notable service by recommending a candidate to the electorate. Presumably composed of individuals who are wiser than most, it could lead the people to make a more informed choice. The party system of nomination is undesirable; the ruler is not a truly national figure if he is bound to party interests, and noxious quarrels are endlessly fomented. Under this system, instead of voting for the candidate they like best, the people must choose from among the representatives set up by the contending parties, some of whom they may not respect for their personal qualities. The Advisory Council only puts forward a recommendation; any voter is free to elect anybody from the entire nation.

The ruler holds office at the discretion of the people and cannot dissolve the legislature. If he finds himself unable to work with it altogether, he may hold a plebiscite to determine the formation of a new legislature. If the response is favorable, then a total election will be held, and not until the new Legislative Council assumes its duties can the old dissolve. If the decision of the electorate is adverse, the ruler may resign. The ruler cannot interfere with the workings of the legislature in any way. He cannot relinquish his post at the bidding of the latter, which, however, may ask for a plebiscite to replace him and, if the request is not granted, may arrange a general election and dissolve itself. These actions should be resorted to only in extreme circumstances.

The ruler is to stand only for the nation. As neither the ruler nor the Legislative Council ought to consider party distinctions, they may not agree on some problems and agree on others. These differences are natural, and no conflict should be provoked thereby; the ruler must carry out whatever the Legislative Council passes. He undertakes the executive work of the government and is responsible to the people. The ruler has the right of initiative, but any measures he proposes must be approved by the legislature before they are valid; he has the authority to inaugurate a plebiscite.

Vis-à-vis the Advisory Council, the ruler is to seek its advice, but he cannot be compelled to follow it. He cannot be recalled by the Advisory Council, though he might have been originally nominated by it, for he was actually elected by the people. The ruler can neither dissolve the Advisory Council nor interfere with its duties in any way.

The ruler heads an Executive Council consisting mostly of ministers who deal with the different departments, each with separate duties and each accountable to the ruler. To expedite the execution of state affairs and to enable the ruler to keep in constant contact with each of them, the council should be composed of only a few members. The chief authority in the council appertains to the ruler, who is to consult his opinions but is not bound to follow them. The council or each member thereof is to carry out the instructions of the ruler, save for those that are contrary to the constitution, the mandates of the people, or the decisions of the Legislative Council. The members can individually deal with the Legislative and Advisory Councils but only with the consent and in the name of the ruler. Like those of the ruler, their actions can be controlled by the Legislative Council. Whether collectively or otherwise, the members of the Executive Council cannot formally launch a plebiscite. An Executive Council has a definite term of office, ordinarily of the same duration as a ruler. It comes into being with him and dissolves when the ruler relinquishes office. The members of the Executive Council are elected by the people at the same time as the ruler, and, like him, each is chosen by the nation's entire electorate. They are not appointed by the ruler and cannot be dismissed by him.

The administration is divided into a small number of ministries, each under a minister who is an elected member of the Executive Council. The selection of a minister for a particular ministry depends on the ruler, who can shift him from one ministry to another at his discretion. The ministries deal with the major divisions of public service, all branches of which must come under one or the other of them. Each ministry comprises a number of departments under departmental chiefs. Subject to revision according to circumstances, they may include religious affairs, culture, defense, finance, justice, economy, land, works, society, and foreign affairs.

The Ministry of Religious Affairs is concerned with religion and morality. Religious thought is free, but the state should not neglect to pay attention to religion, to forms of popular worship and organization, to the impact of religion on society, to customs and manners, and to the cultivation of genuine morality. The Ministry of Culture supervises education and examinations and fosters the growth of knowledge, science, and the arts. The Ministry of Defense controls the armed forces, including the army, navy, air force, and so on, and is responsible for national defense, armaments, and whatever relates to the strength of the nation. The Ministry of Finance considers taxation, subsidies, proper distribution of income, revenue, and expenditure. The Ministry of Justice deals with the administration of law—the police, courts, and prisons come under its control. The legal measures passed by the Legislative Council are binding and must be interpreted and carried out with meticulous accuracy. The Ministry of Economy supervises the production and exchange of goods. It takes care of employment, its duties being to find work for the citizens of the state. It also controls factories and shops, industry and trade. The regulation of exchange is its most important function; the economic welfare of the people is its province. The Ministry of Land is concerned with all land, whether arable land, building sites, or forests. It divides land among the farmers and watches over their work; it pays special attention to agriculture and food production. The Ministry of Works deals with and is responsible for the structural foundation of society, technical problems, town and country planning, communications, buildings, machinery, and engineering products. The Ministry of Society addresses the problems of social life. It cultivates social services, such as recreational facilities, public health, and welfare measures; registers marriages; and keeps a census of the population. General affairs that cannot come under other ministries fall within its scope. The Ministry of Foreign Affairs is devoted to relations between the state and other countries; under it are the ambassadors and other representatives of the nation in foreign lands.

The governors of provinces, districts, and towns are elected by the people pertaining to these places in a manner similar to that for the national ruler; they may or may not be from the ranks of government officers. Each term of service is limited; however, they may be reelected over and over again. If they prove unsatisfactory while in office, they may be recalled by their particular electorates, who alone can appoint them. They are bound to carry out the laws of the land and the instructions of the national ruler within the limits of his duties and rights. If they commit crimes, they can be tried in courts of law like private citizens and suffer the ordinary penalties, though they do not automatically forfeit their posts.

The governors have Executive Councils to assist them, the members of which correspond to the members of the National Executive Council, are elected in a similar way, and head bureaus corresponding to ministries, not all of which, however, have local counterparts. For example, there is no bureau of defense or foreign affairs. The bureau chiefs do not hold office permanently. The local Executive Councils perform their work under the supervision of their respective Legislative Councils, and their members deal directly with the corresponding members of higher councils, including the national ruler and his ministers. A goodly measure of local autonomy will be assured when the administration is run by locally elected councils; there will be no undue centralization of the government's executive work. The citizens will take interest in local affairs, and local problems will be accorded the requisite consideration.

Under the direction of the national ruler is an organization performing the detailed administrative work. Designated the *Executive Service*, it is controlled by the Legislative Council and is answerable to the people. It may be regarded as a company, performing a special service; but, in order to conform to its peculiar nature, the rules are different from those of private companies. The members do not share profits but receive fixed salaries appropriate to their work, neither more nor less than the people's normal standard of income. The number of these public functionaries is kept as small as is compatible with the needs of the work. Their appointments are permanent, irrespective of changes in the personnel of the Executive Councils. They are to discharge their duties conscientiously and behave politely toward the people. They should follow the instructions pertaining to their posts and should not regard themselves as servants of their chiefs but as members of a company that is answerable to the people.

The work of the bureaucracy is divided among departments, each of which deals with a specific type. Each national ministry superintends a number of departments, which have offices of decreasing importance from the province to the town. The local departments or offices are for the most part under the control of the governors and the various bureaus among which the local Executive Councils divide their work, but some are outside such control and deal in a direct line with the national ministries according to the needs of the case.

The work of the Executive Service must be undertaken by an immense body of specialists, each versed in his particular craft; the labor is detailed and involves daily application. As it would not do to elect anybody to a post, the most appropriate person should be selected. A free election indicates popularity, not necessarily ability; the ordinary voter is in no position to understand the requirements of a specific situation. Moreover, as the jobs are numerous, it would be impracticable to resort to an election for each. An appointment to the Executive Service is a lifelong career. Selection of members should be based on rules. The selectors are those with the ability and impartiality to make sound judgments. Though it is difficult and inefficient for the public to undertake the work of administration directly or to elect all the administrators, the Executive Service must be under their general supervision. It is not beyond the powers of the average citizen to distinguish right from wrong. An executive who is irresponsible to the people is a tremendous danger, as he can pervert laws. The best, most practicable state is subject to popular supervision, is guided by the counsels of the wise, and contains an efficient administration.

The qualification of an official should be professional. It is unrealistic to set a general examination for all officers or to give them distinctive bureaucratic training and then expect them to do any work, transferring them randomly from one department to another. A few versatile persons might indeed do a number of things well, and those thus gifted should be prized. Some kinds of work require general capacity and should be undertaken by them. The ordinary person is not thus situated and should be given the task he can do. Specialization in life is a mistake; that is, it is not desirable for a person to limit his interests and activities so that he looks askance at universal culture or develops a crabbed professional character. However, specialization in vocation is a necessity for the average person, or he will not do his work well.

The appointment of a public functionary is according to ability and is made by a Service Board on the basis of rules passed by the Legislative Council. Consisting of representatives of the various groups and ranks of the Executive Service and including members of the Executive Councils, the board has powers of appointment, dismissal, reward, and punishment. It must act impartially; it must know that its actions should be determined by the good of the service and not by other considerations. Each department of the Executive Service has Service Boards, and they may be as many as are required. They are graduated in importance and are coordinated into a unified whole, the highest board headed by the national ruler as chair for making the most important appointments.

The boards will also deal with conditions of service and with department affairs. The head of a department will not be a dictator, for its members will have a voice. The representative of a group on a board will be elected by the group members.

Much of a state's welfare depends on the character of a bureaucracy. Laws do not operate themselves, and if the officials are corrupt, the state goes awry; hence, nothing is more important than making proper appointments. As human behavior is governed by circumstances, the conduct of officials largely follows the conditions of their position. If they can do anything they please, if the public is unable to indict them effectively, if they are taught to think that they are superior to the private individual and allowed to disport themselves accordingly, if they are poorly paid compared to other citizens, if opportunities for graft and peculation are abundantly available and the culprits are not easily caught and severely punished, if their employment is insecure, if favoritism is rampant, if they are capriciously maltreated by their superiors, if they obtain no special recognition if they work well and have nothing to lose if they perform badly—then they are liable to become inefficient and corrupt. The remedy is to fix the proper conditions of service. The official's power must be limited by a division of functions and a system of checks. Officers who deal with individual members of the public should transact business in open rooms in the sight of all, while business that is not immediately urgent is preferably conducted by correspondence within a specified time limit. An officer should be appointed on a definite basis, should be paid an adequate salary, and should be treated according to regulations in all matters, including rewards and penalties.

In public offices, red tape and unnecessary formalities must be abolished; every act must be sensible and practical. Rapidity of execution is cultivated, especially when a task directly concerns a member of the public. There is no need for several officers to endorse a document before a simple thing is performed, as the requisite checks can be done at leisure by examining records. Nothing is more annoying for a person than going from one officer to another before he can get what wants; the necessary steps can be taken in the office without bothering the applicant. Power is divided among officers as much as is consistent with efficiency and integrity.

A Department of Public Assistance with officers in every town helps individuals in their dealings with the government. One who is dubious about the procedure for taking on a problem or who is unable to obtain satisfaction from an office goes to this department for advice and help. A special court forms part of the judicial system to try cases arising from the work of the government offices, either between officers themselves or between officers and members of the public.

The Judicial and Police Departments are branches of the Executive Service. They carry out their functions in strict accord with the law and are like all others ultimately responsible to the people. To ensure integrity, regulations for them must be detailed and stringent.

The armed forces are part of the Executive Service and are under the national ruler's control. They deal directly with the Ministry of Defense and have nothing to do with the local authorities. They are not allowed to take part in civil administration and must not meddle with it. They must regard themselves as owing supreme allegiance to the people, not to their commanders or the national ruler. If they range themselves with these against the people, they are guilty of breach of duty. They should take no sides between the ruler and the Legislative Council, but in cases of extreme necessity, when the people cannot express their voice through a plebiscite, they are to regard the Legislative Council as representing the people and are to champion its decisions. None of their members can be appointed or dismissed, save in accordance with rules passed by the Legislative Council.

A distinction must be made between the Executive Council and the Executive Service. The Executive Council is composed only of the ruler and his ministers and is one of the three organs of state, the other two being the Legislative and Advisory Councils. Other than members of these three councils and their local counterparts, all those who work for the government are in the Executive Service.

Chapter 14
The Legal System

The formation of society is justifiable only as an institution whereby individuals can live together to intensify their ability to secure personal welfare, which they would find more difficult to attain in complete isolation. This implies their consent to its existence. Once society comes into being, however, it breeds its own evils. Human beings are not altruistic by nature, and when it is possible for them to benefit at their neighbors' expense, they do so. In this way, they destroy the value of society and make the chances of promoting their welfare precarious. It seems curious that they should do this, which amounts to a nullification of their original purpose, but they must be thought of as individuals, each of whom is not out to annihilate his own welfare but is trying to augment it in the belief that if others lose, he wins.

When they are rational, humans realize that this state of affairs will not do and formulate rules to control their actions so that each ultimately will secure the happiness he desires. They allow an authority to enforce these rules as the best way to avoid mutual conflict. The legal system is thus a product of general consent. In all this, reference is made only to the way individuals would act if they clearly appreciate the nature of the state and always bear it in mind. Historical states were formed by a variety of forces, and their laws, written or unwritten, were made by rulers with diverse motives, usually to maintain their own power.

A valid law must proceed from the sovereign—that is, from the people—and is just only insofar as it promotes a mutually beneficial relationship between the component members of a society. It is wrong when it results in the oppression of one section by another. It is commonly supposed that its aim is to maintain order, by which is meant the status quo. However, if it has no better justification than this, it can be a great evil, a mode of injury in the name of right. There is nothing sacred about it; it is the use of organized force to maintain a particular line of action, and if neither the source of the force nor the nature of the conduct required is right, then it possesses no moral authority.

Law is a social phenomenon, an instrument designed to execute the state's purposes. It is a restraint on liberty, using force to punish the individual. How can it be vindicated? Its nature is explained by the reason for the formation of the state, which should exist for the mutual exchange of benefits. All human beings have an equal right to this. They agree that in order to make their personal welfare more easily attainable, they should not molest one another and should abide by resolutions made by the entire community for their common good, and that anyone who breaks the compact is endangering the safety of all and must be punished in proportion to the crime. Only in this way can law be a necessity and a right.

Laws are not made so that as many people as possible fall into their snare; they are not made to secure profits for lawyers or to provide employment for judges and the police. Their purpose is to maintain justice; hence, they should be simple, systematic, taught in schools, discussed at public meetings, published frequently for general information, and be interpreted in the spirit rather than the letter. When it is clear that resorting to a verbal quibble or technical trifle will make for wrong, the duty of the judge is plain; he is there to give all parties their due. For a person's fate to depend on eloquence is an absurdity. Law is not an end in itself; it is a means to an end.

Law is largely negative in character because it prohibits evils rather than asking for positive performance of the good. This is inevitable, seeing that it is far more difficult to enforce positive good than to prevent positive evil. Moreover, if liberty is to be maintained, the members of a society cannot force one another to do more than abstain from committing mutual injuries. Beyond a minimum requirement to ensure the safety of society, the pursuit of the good must be left to the individual moral will.

The conduct of affairs in a state is carried out by the government, composed of individuals, each of whom, being human, has passions and prejudices. Should they administer according to their sense of right and wrong? Should they be bound by written laws determining their actions? This problem was of greatest moment in ancient China, where the Confucianists represented the theory of personal rule and the Legalists maintained the omnipotence of law. As is well known, the former triumphed, and the mandarins were allowed to follow their whims in their judgments, to the tremendous harm of the people. This system could be beneficial only if all officials were virtuous. Hoping that a regular supply of paragons can be ensured is the vainest of delusions, one by no means peculiar to Confucius and not dead yet, though nobody now would advocate the substitution of trust in personal qualities for a legal code, which in a democracy at any rate is a *sine qua non*. The embodiment of the people's will is in the law.

Is the legal sovereign to do anything he pleases? Has he the power and the right to pass any law? Being the source of authority, he doubtless has the power to carry it out. When a single person is the sovereign, his power, though made excessive by human folly, has a limit beyond which his subjects cannot endure, and revolts break out that dethrone him; but a sovereign can always count on the support of a section of the populace, who, though inferior to him, are superior to the rest and will lose their privileges with his collapse. An autocracy is virtually an oligarchy; owing to organization, the few can have the strength to keep the many in subjection. The sovereign constituted by a few can exercise unlimited power; the individual sovereign has the delusive appearance of such power.

A distinction must be made between legal and rightful sovereignty. The legal sovereign is the source of law, the law-making organ, but whether it has the right to do so is another question. By force and fraud, the few can attain this power. The rightful sovereign is the entity possessing natural authority to determine the affairs of a society. A society is composed of individuals, each of whom has a natural right to regulate the conditions of his existence. If they dwell in society, they ought to determine its rules collectively. The people is the rightful sovereign and ought to be the legal sovereign.

Does a people have the right to pass any law? *Vis-à-vis* society, which is its product, it has the right to determine its nature and can therefore do anything. But a people, meaning humankind, does not exist as an absolute entity, divorced from all relationships; it forms part of a universal scheme of things, and its duty is to promote its purposes. Its right is transcended by its duty; hence, it should not pass any law that conflicts with truth. Human law must follow natural law. If human law conflicts with natural law, then it is wrong even when passed by a rightful sovereign. A people has the right and the power to make any law, but it must voluntarily fulfill its duty to nature. The duty of a people cannot, of course, be enforced by only one of its groups, which cannot be the rightful sovereign.

When it is said that a people has the right to pass any law, it is implied that all its members assent to the law; this, however, is never the case. A collective noun like *people* is apt to give a misleading impression of unity. A people is composed of a multitude of units, each a concrete being. It is not a united entity with one voice. When a law is under deliberation, some persons support it, while others oppose it. But the majority come closer to constituting a people than the minority; hence, in practice, a law approved by the majority can be regarded as being made by the people, though this is not strictly the case. As no human being has the right to oppress another, the majority ought not to injure the minority; so only those laws that prevent mutual injuries between individuals are rightful, while those that prevent a person from doing what does not directly affect others are not.

The doctrine that all human beings are equal in their rights is applicable to groups. One state has no right to oppress another; aggressive war in unjustifiable. The state's need is traceable to human selfishness. An unorganized number of states come to loggerheads for the same reason. It is also necessary to have at least a central authority to arbitrate between the states with a system of international law. The ideal is for all nations to merge into a single state with all persons equal and free. Then sectional interests will completely disappear, and humanity will derive its fullest benefit from society. This conception is the antithesis of the principle of the subjection of one people to another. Nothing is worse than this; it is more evil than the existence of an array of mutually antagonistic nations, for no form of exploitation can be more drastic, more subversive of human rights, than the racial.

Under what conditions should the state punish criminals? They are its members, party to its formation; if they break its rules, they must be punished. But by infringing one law, they should not lose all its privileges; they remain members of society and should not be deprived of their vote. Punishment of criminals must be commensurate with their crime. What is the idea of punishment? One reason lies in retribution: felons receive what they deserve for the wrongs they commit. The proper requital is productive labor. Another is prevention, for as they have shown themselves to be a menace to their fellows, they must be deterred from repeating their crime: by making them feel the consequences of a departure from it, they realize the desirability of keeping to the straight path. But it is useless for them to realize this if they find it difficult to maintain themselves by acting legally. Criminals are therefore to be given adequate opportunities for rehabilitation—upon reentering normal society, they must be able to lead a useful existence.

Justice is derived from the concept of equal exchange; it pertains to equivalent treatment, giving the individual his due. A just state is one where everyone obtains his desserts; a just person treats others according to their rights; a just court arbitrates between people with impartiality; a just legal system is erected on the basis of recognition of reciprocal duties. A law for the preservation of unilateral privileges is a product of injustice. A law made for no other purpose than to maintain state authority is a clear misuse of power and a palpable misunderstanding of the position of the government.

It must be realized that the criminal is a human being whose human qualities do not vanish with the infringement of a law. He must not be treated as an outcast or outlaw. He must not be treated as though nothing were too bad for him, as though he has lost all his ordinary rights. He still has his human dignity, and his judges and jailers are far from being his superiors. In fact, he is still an equal, as he is required only to make a compulsory retribution appropriate to his crime. A criminal must be presumed innocent until he is definitely convicted. The police must not be allowed to regard society as their hunting ground for beasts. They must behave politely and should not use more force than is required for self-defense.

The legal system is not primarily based on moral considerations; its aim is not the promotion of virtue. It must follow from the nature of the state, in whose organization it is the principal element. The state is not founded primarily to enforce moral good but to ensure that personal welfare can be more effectively cultivated. It stresses rights, not duties, and is a guarantee against insecurity. The higher life, the attainment of greater virtue, is a voluntary achievement of the individual. Basing the state on moral grounds is irrational. If it assumes that human nature is good, it is not logical to use coercion, for people will naturally behave well, and the state is a superfluity. If it assumes that human nature is bad, it is preposterous to imagine that it could be made good by delegating authority to some individuals who presumably possess the same tendency toward evil and would now have more opportunity to exercise it than before. The state is made to secure the minimum conditions necessary for society to function. Whether people are good or evil, they can recognize that the best way to secure their welfare is to have security and avoid eternal conflict; hence, a state should be formed by compelling all its components to adhere to its rules. The legal code must then confine itself to the enforcement of rights and not presume to compel an individual to be a paragon of virtue. If a section of the law cultivates negative virtues, such as abstention from cruelty, this is only incidental. It is not that cruelty is a moral evil but that it conflicts with the right to personal welfare that leads it to be restrained by force. Another section has no relationship whatsoever to morality. The payment of taxes is neither moral nor amoral: the person who pays a high tax is not a whit more virtuous than one who pays none. The tax evader is not thereby vicious, though the state indicts him and must do so to maintain its existence. A transaction for mutual convenience is not a moral affair. A criminal is not synonymous with a villain; in fact, he may even be on the side of virtue when he defies an oppressive law. There is, of course, no conflict between a right state and a genuine morality. What the state requires is not inconsistent with virtue; what it enforces incidentally produces a minimum morality, for it is surely moral for one to give another his due. What distinguishes virtue from law is that it is over and above what the state exacts.

A state has a nonmoral purpose: it is neither a moral nor an immoral entity. The word *nonmoral* must not be used in the Nietzschean sense of immoral. The universe contains a moral purpose—it is not the state's business to attain this directly, but it should not conflict with it if life is to be harmonious. Life is more than the state, and all its ingredients must be in accord. The proper province of the state is the prevention of exploitation. This objective does not constitute all life, but it does not conflict with morality. With its coercive authority, law is primarily directed toward this end.

Chapter 15
Social Cohesion

A society is a community of individuals with interests in common; a state is an organization of the community endowed with coercive authority. A society has a wider sphere than a state, which is only one of its manifestations—knowledge is another manifestation; religion is a third. Historically, no society has ever existed devoid of a coercive authority, but social phenomena are not thereby products of the state. Force cannot create an idea: civilization is a product of society but not of the state.

The state and the economy are the two greatest social forces cementing a community into a single unit and are largely accountable for its happiness or misery, but they do not stand alone. A miscellaneous assortment of problems should be treated separately in their bearing on the organization of society; they may be called *social constituents*. Social phenomena are extremely varied, the whole of civilization being a creation of communal life; but it would be outside the legitimate scope of social philosophy to investigate them, save in their social aspects.

The factors that make for social cohesion comprise whatever is practiced by all the members of a community. Language and religion can be studied in their social aspects, but their contents have a distinctive quality more important than their impact on social organization, and it is best to deal with them as separate subjects. In considering social formation, attention is concentrated on those problems that have a more intimate bearing on it, the theme being society itself rather than its phenomena.

Social solidarity has shown a singular persistence. Its forms may undergo alteration; states have come and gone. Still, a community has never broken up into a scattered number of hermits but has continued to survive through thick and thin, unless its members were completely exterminated. It could receive into its midst a horde of strangers, usually conquerors, but the two races tended to blend; and even if they did not, they could still be said to constitute a single society. This fact of social solidarity is attributable in the first place to limitations of space, as it is impossible for a population to dissolve into solitary units with no prospects of mutual contact; the territory available is insufficient for such a purpose. In the second place, there is a need for exchange. Exchange, even in the most corrupt and most oligarchic state, is unequal between masters and slaves but reasonably equal between the majority of the exploited. Under a capitalist economy, laborers are fleeced by their employers, but they exchange among themselves on a fairly equivalent basis; and exchange, of course, is not confined to commodities but is just as applicable to the multitudinous forms of mutual aid. A society is practically indissoluble, though it may change its ways.

The factors contributing to the nature of society are numerous. One is geography—the character of the environment determines the conditions of existence and molds character, and thereby the form of social organization. The earliest civilizations, such as the Egyptian, Sumerian, Babylonian, and Chinese, arose on the banks of rivers, which provided easy means of communication and rendered the surrounding territory cultivable. The inhabitants of a plain were drawn toward amalgamation into a single nation. Climate affects behavior and food supply. The influence of geography affects the very existence of society and civilization but has little role in determining the particular type of state, whether monarchic, aristocratic, or democratic.

Society is the product of human beings, and psychology must therefore be instrumental in its formation. Being the primary constituent in the makeup of humanity, egoism inevitably exerts a tremendous impact on social organization; without it, the state would not have come into existence. Egoism is not pernicious if it is of the solitary type turned inward; but in communal life, it usually expresses itself in aggression, in endeavors to dominate others and deprive them of their property, strongly propelling every society into the mire. Were egoism the only force operating, the only possible result would be perpetual savagery, with every individual warring against all others; human existence would be the presocial chaos described by Hobbes. However, in combination with altruism, fear, admiration, desire for security and happiness, and all the other traits, civilization and society could come into existence and persist in a distorted way. Every element of human nature affects the social structure, whether for good or ill. Random examples may be cited. Hope serves to bolster democratic capitalism, as it is easy to harbor the illusion that in the future one could rise to the top; fear is responsible for submission to tyranny; vainglory produces ruthless war; discontent is good for revolution; justice renders law operative; loyalty helps to maintain the hereditary monarch on his throne; prejudice makes it difficult to change existing conditions; credulity is indispensable to a theocracy's success. As the passions are multitudinous and contradictory, every social phenomenon is a possibility; hence, a community does not strictly adhere to any consistent system of principles. This largely explains the variance of practice from theory. Remember that psychology supplies only the motivation for social organization and does not determine it; indeed, psychology must combine with external factors to engender social organization. Ambition alone does not account for despotism; might is a prerequisite. Human nature is capable of being modified, though this potentiality must not be exaggerated. We must not so much appeal to voluntary will as create another mode of satisfying the quest for well-being. The compulsion of institutions alters behavior, which, grown habitual, makes it possible for them to become more enlightened. Social change influences human nature and, in its turn, partially depends on its reorientation.

Since all human beings belong to one species—a fact many appear to have forgotten, if one considers all the talk of inequality, racial inferiority, and so on—we must possess the same general characteristics. We are, however, very adaptable, and, since our lives are conditioned by external factors, our reactions can produce a variety of phenomena;

hence, national dissimilarities arise, even as to character. Racial differences are not innate but acquired and, as such, can be abolished if the formative factors vary; there is nothing eternal or necessary about them. The ancient Greeks prided themselves on their love of liberty and their intellectual activity; but before long, they lost them. It is preposterous to say that a particular race is naturally materialistic or spiritual, kindly or cruel. The ruthless Mongols of Genghis Khan produced descendants who have turned gentler under the sway of Buddhism. Alter the circumstances, and character follows accordingly. An acquired trait is, of course, strong and does not easily vanish in the individual who possesses a natural unity. A nation is a conglomeration of individuals who live and die. New individuals reacquire the same traits, though there is no need for them to do so, save that without any additional forces, their parents would train them to follow in their footsteps. This is not to say that human beings may not possess innate differences; but nations, which are products of circumstances, can do so only inappreciably. The fact that their dissimilarities are more glaring than between single persons is almost entirely due to cultivation.

History records a succession of events that are connected but are not absolutely caused by one another, if it is taken in the narrow sense as a compilation of objective social phenomena. If it is meant to refer to every thought and deed of humankind and every event of nature, then all history must be linked in a system of inevitable causes and effects. However, it is impossible to possess such information, because history cannot show that any of its facts must necessarily have come to pass as they did. Historical knowledge breeds one outstanding result: it conduces to the perpetuation of a social form. A country's people deliberately uphold what they call their tradition, which, harking back to the past, is an impediment to progress. Since it is much easier to imitate than to create, many changes labeled as innovations are in fact resurrections of extinct practices, some even dating back to barbarous ages. Irrespective of conscious effort, what has already come to light has a strong tendency to persist. The effective counterblast to the dead hand of history is reason, which sees that the universe is not static, cannot believe that the Golden Age lies in the past, and regards advance toward perfection as the ideal. History can then be studied not for the purpose of imitation but for circumvention of erstwhile errors; otherwise it would be better to cast it into oblivion.

Invention of new tools and appliances affects a society, for it is what produces the entire material structure of civilization; without innovation, life would not be what it is. Innovation does not refer only to the marvelous scientific achievements of recent centuries, though we naturally tend to invest these with an overwhelming importance, but includes everything that has emerged in the career of the human race. The plough, spear, hammer, saw, loom, sailing ship, house, wheel, cup, mirror, compass, paper, and printing were as much inventions as the steam engine, telephone, automobile, airplane, radio, atomic bomb, television, robot, computer, and cell phone. Once an invention was made, it usually remained for good or evil, and its effect singly on society was seldom momentous; but as one tended to produce another, the combined influence was great. Unlike ideas, inventions are never woven into a consistent system and consciously created according to a comprehensive plan, so their social effect is various and contradictory. A material apparatus does not by itself radically transform the structure of society, though it can be a very strong force. In the sense of a momentous influence, it can be said that agriculture gave birth to the territorial state; the cannon demolished the feudalism of medieval Europe; machinery introduced industrial capitalism; and air travel, satellites, and electronic media are making for a world organization. With the capacity to overcome the limitations of the natural environment, invention is a powerful factor in promoting a homogeneous social structure through a vast expanse of territory. Without easy means of transport and the possibility of rapid diffusion of information, democracy over an extensive state could not function successfully. Modern scientific inventions have changed the face of the world. And since only with their aid can the difficulties that accompany the shaping of society be conquered, they are important to political theory.

A moral code or a set of customs stereotypes a society, making it difficult to alter. Like most social phenomena, it is a product of society; at the same time, it determines society's subsequent course. Ethical doctrines popularly held in theory have generally been of an altruistic, puritan type, imploring individuals to sacrifice for the community and curb their appetites. Since these requests run counter to instinct, it is not surprising that practice deviates from profession. What is cause for congratulation is that these doctrines attained a considerable measure of success. The more urgent of them have been made obligatory by law and public opinion. Customs that arose casually did not form a system as moral rules tended to do, though they became even more fossilized and compulsory. They assumed strange and fantastic forms, most of them senseless, but were venerated as truth, and transgressors found themselves outcasts. Their repercussions on society were adverse, serving no useful purpose and detrimental to progress—embodiments of superstition and fancy. Morality should be reconstructed to harmonize with reason. Rules of life, which are necessary, should be useful and true and never allowed to degenerate into mere customs to be upheld at all costs because they are universal. They should be changed if they have outlived their original utility or are discovered to be false. Unless the violation of a rule is directly injurious to others, in which case the rule would become a law, one should be free to adopt or reject it. Society should not ostracize an individual who does not conform to custom, for this is even worse than legal punishment, which is definite—a certain penalty for a certain crime. Ostracism is blind, furious, and excessive and ruins a person's life; it is a variety of lynching, which is detestable.

Custom and morality have been largely associated with religion, which, as a social weapon, has exercised tremendous power. Since human beings are given to struggle for power and states are based on force, it would seem more logical that all states should have been ruled by soldiers; yet priests, who are supposed to concern themselves with spiritual interests and cultivate gentleness, have dominated ever since the most ancient ages, when humanity was admittedly more brawn than brain. This shows how contradictory and complex social phenomena are. Of course, an explanation is not difficult to find after the event, and we can say how superstitious primitive humans were and how easily duped. Nevertheless, this strange fact proves that from the dawn of communal life, thought was already more important than physical prowess. At present, religion is a questionable force, and it is ludicrous to revive its ancient forms. But religion, meaning a system of belief about the ultimate nature of the universe, is useful for giving direction to life, and it needs a new expression. It should influence society not through the instrumentality of irrational force but through voluntary acceptance.

Knowledge—philosophic, scientific, and literary—gained by formulating and spreading political theory and consciously interpreting social events is what should mold society if human beings are rational. Unfortunately, with the exception of a few periods of peculiar intellectual activity, its influence has not been extensive; owing partly to the obstacles it met when being diffused in the past and partly to the inertia of the ordinary mind, its acquisition was confined to a few. It has never been more momentous than at present and is destined to be the chief force in social organization. It is preposterous to talk of tradition, social organism, historical continuity, and so on in order to oppose deliberate progress, as we have reached a stage in our evolution when reason must be the principal instrument in controlling our destiny. Reason is a natural entity, meant for the unraveling of truth, and a society created by it and resting on right is eminently natural. Confusion in the universe is unknown; why should it be proper in human affairs? Knowledge must reign supreme.

Language is the sign manual of a nation; purely a social product, it affects social organization by acting as a bond to keep a community together. The most artificial of all things, it has been the least systematically renovated. While new religions, political theories, and scientific concepts have arisen and established themselves, no country has ever adopted a new language. The propensity to confuse casualness with naturalness and all the associations, sentimental and otherwise, linked to a tongue make for staunch opposition to its abolition.

With the exception of geography, all the foregoing ingredients of social formation are the offspring of group life. Certain problems remain that are more directly concerned with social organization itself, and as they are more pertinent to an inquiry into social principles, attention will now be directed to them.

Chapter 16
Family

Whether or not the family was the origin of society, it has always existed. In historical times, it was regarded as a sacred entity, and it was the unit of the state more often than was the individual. Punishment in ancient China was not confined to criminals; it extended to all their relatives up to nine degrees of kinship. The family system is associated with both good and evil. Its good lies in the mutual aid among its members. Where the state is not effectively organized to care for the individual, and, as was the case in antiquity, the government is an individual rather than an organization, a person needs a small unit to which he can easily turn for protection. The inherent evil in the family system is traceable to the antagonism apt to arise between groups, an antagonism much direr in its results because it is more potent than that between single human beings. An individual is restrained by moral considerations and seldom regards it as a virtue to care only for his own interests; however, he may pursue them in practice. When an individual is a member of a group, he deems group loyalty to be a point of morality; that is, he promotes the group's aims as a duty, and his feelings of selfishness are intensified by his devotion to an ideal. In some communities, feuds between families or their extensions, clans, were common. In the most civilized society, coldness toward the stranger is the rule. *Vis-à-vis* the state, the family system breeds nepotism and the institution of inheritance, severely circumscribing opportunities for exercising the talents of great masses of persons.

Should the family be retained? It is clear that in its absence, human nature being what it is, sexual license will ensue; this is extremely unwholesome. Even with the family system, far too much attention is given to sex, and it would be much more so if people were on a perpetual hunt for temporary unions! Sex is but one aspect of life and by no means the grandest or most necessary. The goal of humanity is the cultivation of the mind; the less interest paid to the sexual relationship, the better. The family system helps to regulate the amorous proclivities of the ordinary person.

Universal affection is an ideal. But it is manifestly difficult for a person to feel more than a vague regard for a multitude of human beings. The benefit of intense affection is more easily realized in a small group. Real attention is available to one in need, as general benevolence is inadequate in moments of distress. Spontaneous, lifelong affection, given and received, softens life's blows.

Mutual aid can never be more easily attained than in a family. Other associations can help their members with specific problems; in a family, every kind of service is given unstintingly. The manifold, intangible forms of mutual aid, based purely on affection, are not available anywhere else with such ease. The foundation on which the family rests is supremely natural; it should exist as a moral unit of society.

The family should not be a political unit. The state is viewed as a body of individuals, each of whom constitutes a unit. In a political and legal capacity, individuals are to be considered solely by themselves; they are not responsible for their family. Making the head of a family its legal representative is making that individual a miniature despot, and it saddles him with the burden of suffering for crimes he has not committed. It is irrational to make one person answerable for another's actions. If one can control the other, he becomes a master; if not, then he becomes a scapegoat. The natural affection that gives the family its beauty is destroyed by turning it into an organization like others and importing into it an element of coercion.

The family should not be an economic unit. All its members should earn for themselves; adults will work, and children will receive independent incomes from the state. If one person must keep an entire family, he loses his sense of enterprise, becomes fixed in a rut, and is burdened with perpetual worries. As for the dependents, their position is precarious, subject to the chances affecting a single person. At best, they are pampered subordinates; at worst, they are slaves under the dominion of a capricious tyrant. The economic relationship is unhealthy and turns the bond of affection into a bond of selfishness. It leads to the loss of equality and freedom and produces more family quarrels than any other cause.

The family is founded on marriage, which takes place when a couple agree to set up a home together. The decision must be purely voluntary; any species of compulsion, whether physical or economic, actual or threatened, is prejudicial to personal welfare. Freedom of choice must be exercised by both partners, who are not to constrain each other. Parental consent is not required.

For marriage to rest on any other basis than love is to vitiate its character; any semblance of a commercial transaction is derogatory to the essence of freedom and dignity, producing compulsory subjection of one person to another. A human being is not a saleable commodity; and it certainly partakes of the character of a purchase when a man is forced to support his wife, which is tantamount to paying to acquire a piece of property. This is the subtler element left of the full-fledged transaction of erstwhile times, when the bride's parents received a sum of money for parting with her. The woman loses her dignity, and the man incurs a burden.

The institution of marriage is purely a social arrangement for the promotion of public harmony; its primary purpose is the foundation of a family. All the maudlin sentiment and fantastic romance made fashionable in connection with it are not at its core. It is a practical need for the welfare of the average person. It cannot be made compulsory; those who are completely chaste are not following a wrong line of conduct. It is a necessity only because the ordinary person would otherwise be entangled in a whirlpool of promiscuous passion, ruining social good.

On the basis of the number of mates a person can have, there are forms of marriage known as monogamy, polyandry, and polygamy; monogamy is the desirable basis for the foundation of a family. The population of any country in any age is more or less evenly divided between the sexes, and the distribution of one to one is the most practical arrangement. As a matter of necessity, the majority of people have never been able to do otherwise than take one spouse each, and only for a few of the rich is polygamy possible. On the theory of reciprocal right, it would be unjust for one man to have a number of wives, while a woman does not have a collection of husbands. If the women also indulge in plurality of mates, then confusion would inevitably ensue, and there would not be families but sexual sets! For a woman to have more than one husband is senseless from the point of view of child bearing, as her capacity would not be augmented.

The family is meant for mutual service and, unlike others, is a natural group; hence, its dissolution spells tragedy. Marriage should be a perpetual union. If transitory, its thread of love and service is adverse to maximum benefit—not giving that character of a special association superior to all crises of life and making it a bedrock on which to rest one's hopes of compensation against the tides of fortune. But it is palpable that in practice some marriages are failures and are a perennial loadstone of sorrow. Marriage is not made by any peculiar destiny; love that initiates it can turn to aversion. It is a contract and is therefore not unbreakable. People should not be bound together against their will. Where loathing and disdain prevail, the endeavor to live together is a mistake, so divorce is a permissible solution. It is surely not conducive to social well-being that murder should be committed to get rid of a nightmare. A union should be dissolved if it is disastrous. However, it is undesirable for divorce to take place without extreme necessity. Mutual consent is sufficient grounds for divorce. Where only one of the parties desires it, it shall also be granted, but monetary compensation may be payable by one party to the other deemed as aggrieved.

Both parties have equal duties and rights; no privilege should be granted by law to one at the expense of the other. The position has changed from giving all rights to the man to conferring them on the woman. It is all very well to talk of the woman requiring special protection, but it is perilous to use the law to bind the man with diverse penalties, leaving the woman in the ascendant. The marriage contract is based on reciprocal love; an abused husband is no more a wholesome spectacle than a maltreated wife. The legal system should not consider sentiment any more than aggression. If a man enjoys unilateral advantages, he infringes on the woman's inherent right to personal welfare; if the woman is artificially given the upper hand, this does not promote social good. An unwarranted superiority enforceable by law always becomes oppressive. Witness the institutions of birth, wealth, and priestly status; no less so is the stark tyranny of physical strength. In a proper society, genuine equality and freedom must be upheld; it is always iniquitous for one person to injure another. Both partners must learn to give and take on an equal basis; whatever is reprehensible in the man is so in the woman and vice versa.

The family arises from marriage, which has its meaning in the biological necessity for the race to continue through reproduction; hence, it derives its existence from the need for children. The rearing of children is naturally a task for their parents, and it is best done by them. The only other alternative is to turn them over to the state to be cared for by unsympathetic strangers, whereby the intense affection peculiar to parents is lost—a disadvantage to both generations. The institution of the state is primarily for regulation, and the job of child rearing is a superfluous and unjustifiable extension of its rights and duties. No good can be served thereby.

The relationship between parents and children is naturally one of love. A child is not a commodity, and it has its own inherent purpose. Parents have the right to look for respect from their offspring, whom they have brought into the world and on whom they have showered their care. However, as rights must be reciprocal, parents need not expect any love in return if they are perverted enough to maltreat their children. They should be able to control them until adulthood—but this is limited to a consideration of the children's welfare. Lacking the ability to stand on their own feet, children would be liable to go astray otherwise.

Parents owe a duty to their children, who have not come into existence of their own volition; they must rear them properly and do whatever they can for them. It is evil for people to produce babies without any intention of caring for them; they must be made to bear the responsibility. Both parents are to exercise equal rights and duties.

Children are human beings and possess inherent rights. They are not saleable; they must not be treated like slaves. They have a will of their own, and their natural tendencies should not be crushed if they are not injurious to others; guidance and persuasion, not force, should play a role in their training. They should not be flogged or subjected to physical mistreatment of any sort; a slight harmless spanking is permissible if it deters them from mischief, but the best way to direct them along the correct path is to make use of rewards, such as gifts of coveted articles, and penalties in the form of temporary deprivations of their customary enjoyments. As part of their social insurance, they are provided with incomes by the state to be expended by the parents or guardians on their behalf, including the cost of education, to which they are all entitled. There is no distinction between boys and girls in respect to their privileges.

Children's duty is to obey their parents within the limits of the good. When they have reached maturity, the close tie is relaxed, and they should become masters of themselves; they should act in accordance with their conscience and should be self-dependent. It is clear, however, that throughout their lives it behooves them to revere their parents and render whatever service they could for them. Indulging in complete neglect of one's parents is rank ingratitude. However, children should not have their enterprise and their sphere of activities hampered in order to take care of their elders, who, in a proper society, should be able to be self-dependent until death and need not lean on them for support in their old age. Nevertheless, children should not cheerfully cease to care for their parents.

A family consists of more than a husband, wife, and children; it includes other relatives as well. But this does not mean that they all dwell in the same house. The members are knit together purely by ties of affection, and where this does not exist, they have nothing to do with one another. The link is wholly one of voluntary affection; there is no question of responsibility, of complex problems arising therefrom. Dislike of a noxious relative cannot be regarded as wrong, and there is no moral compulsion to maintain an unpalatable association. Society should not judge anyone based on the actions of his relations and make his standing depend on his family's position and behavior. Brothers and sisters naturally have a close tie, and the propriety of their mutual service is greater than that between more distant relations. One should make a special effort to help one's relatives but not to the detriment of the public.

A family should not develop into a clan, weaving into a unit all varieties of distant relatives; the clan spirit should be discouraged, for it is inimical to popular good. Families of reasonable size are far from being self-sufficient, and they are unlikely to cultivate rivalries injurious to public justice. Clans are artificially organized groups, and, like all such where a certain amount of strength is possible, their attitude to outsiders is one of hostility, and vendettas are fearsome possibilities. Regarding their members, individuality is crushed and sacrificed to group tyranny.

Chapter 17
Population and Race

A society presupposes a population and is large or small according to its size. A large population has good and bad points. It facilitates civilization, as forests are cut down and farms and towns spring up; in the matter of a people's survival, it is distinctly advantageous. It is a misfortune when its volume of production of food and goods is far below its requirements and general penury prevails. The desirable size of a population is such that a country's resources can be effectively utilized, with the resultant products sufficient for a reasonable standard of living for all.

Population tends to increase. This has been ordained by nature as part of its plan of evolution; at the beginning there could have emerged only a few human beings, and, if they did not augment by reproduction, there could have been no progress of the species, unique for its possession of rational mind. If the number remained stationary, it would have been bad enough; but, if it had decreased continually, it would have eventually reached zero. With a natural birth rate, a population could multiply several times in a century if the adverse phenomenon of a high death rate did not exist.

Malthus showed that population grows more rapidly than the food supply, as the former multiplies by geometrical progression while the latter increases by arithmetical progression. He believed that population is reduced to conform to the available food supply and that this law explains social misery, for population is checked either positively by starvation, pestilence, and war, or preventively by the postponement of marriage, which fosters vice. He advocated prudence for individual parents as the solitary cure for this unhappy state of affairs.

Are his pessimistic ideas tenable? That the population tends to outstrip the means of subsistence is true enough, though the increase in the food supply does not strictly follow any law. Fish and animals multiply even more rapidly than human beings and, if used as food, would seem inexhaustible; however, they themselves are dependent on their ability to procure food. The ultimate source of food is vegetable life, which, attached to the earth, is more in proportion to the amount of land available. As population grows, a greater area is cultivated, but the amount of land is not limitless. Human ingenuity and effort can, however, augment the yield per acre. The earth's resources are far from being exhausted; science may be able to solve the food problem hereafter.

In any case, population increase is not the prime cause of human misery. Pestilence and war are produced by ignorance and ambition, respectively, and not by population growth; and they are far worse than starvation. The cruelties of despotic emperors, the miseries of superstition, the chill penury of the masses groaning under feudalism—were not these more frightful than any sorrows that a mere growth of population could produce?

That population needs to be checked is nevertheless true. That it should wait for dire calamities, such as famine and war, to do the work is, of course, undesirable. The Malthusian preventive check of individual foresight, which amounts to an appeal to chastity, is useless; human nature being what it is, it can never succeed. Malthus wrote in the days before birth control, which provides the most practical of all checks. Chastity should be encouraged, not in order to limit population, but because it is good for humanity's ultimate purpose, the cultivation of the mind. However, chastity in practice is not likely to be extensive enough to limit population. Birth control produces no misery, so it is justifiable; it need not give rise to any greater immorality than its absence. The birth of unwanted children does not make passion less censurable but only brings sorrow on the innocent; and if people cannot rely on their moral will to control themselves, they are not likely to be continent through fear of consequences. When seeking a solution for a political, economic, or social problem, it is dangerous to depend on morality. The ages have demonstrated the certain failure of this method. Society should be made happy by other means. Morality, however, can still be achieved, and it adds its luster to an individual; but, if it is not, society will nevertheless remain peaceable, just, and joyous. Social security should not be endangered so that a minority may glory over their virtues and lament over or rant against the depravity of the times.

A judicious use of birth control and devoted attention to the possibilities of increasing food production should solve the problem of the impact of population on social welfare. The human race has grown continually in the course of evolution, though particular peoples have had checkered histories, some disappearing altogether. A rapidly growing population is usually, though not always, a sign of a country's prosperity. It shows that the material production has expanded considerably, but then the average share may be still the same or even less. Social prosperity must be measured by the welfare of the nation. A small country is more prosperous than a big if its per capita wealth is greater, though its total is less.

One of the disadvantages of partitioning the world into an array of sovereign states relates to population. When national strength is measured by number of citizens, every country is anxious to increase its manpower, irrespective of its material resources. At the same time, due to restriction of immigration, sparsely peopled lands are not as fully developed as they could be. When a prolific race has overstepped its means of subsistence and cannot discover an outlet through peaceful emigration, it must either be content to suffer poverty or resort to war. The encouragement of racial growth to obtain huge armies is a noxious policy.

The distribution of population even within the confines of a country is extremely unequal. This is explained by the varying productive capacity of the land in different places. In desert regions, inhabitants are scarce, while on the banks of rivers, they swarm. This is not very desirable, though unless future knowledge can triumph over the difficulties, it is inevitable. This uneven distribution is not wholly due to the productive character of the soil; an area may not originally have been opened up and continues to be neglected, as the adjunct territory is sufficient to hold the population. Wherever practicable, distribution should be balanced. Congestion and desolation in various parts do not give a country harmonious equilibrium.

There are two primary problems when considering humanity from the social standpoint: population, which has to do with number of people, and race, which deals with type of people. A people usually but does not necessarily belong to the same race. The connection of race with nation and country is apparent. If a country contains several racial groups, they tend to amalgamate into a new entity against their wishes and prejudices over time.

One of the most difficult issues relates to race. Were there any racial differences when *Homo sapiens* emerged? It is a habit among students of antiquity to fix upon some particular spot as the birthplace of the species. It is logical to assume that all the members of a species have a common origin; all human beings were of the same race at first. When they dispersed over the earth, the groups lost touch, reacted with their environments, evolved diverse ways of life, and developed physical and mental characteristics that came to constitute the racial differences of later ages.

But the races that sprang up were not settled once and for all. In the course of migrations and wars, existing races might be exterminated, might coalesce, or might break up to form new ones. The transformations of race were veritably protean in character. It would be difficult to say what is meant by a "pure" race. The arbitrary thing to do is to take an extant nation, trace its history to its legendary beginnings, and say that its race is pure from the moment of its inception, meaning that its present members are lineal descendants of its founders. Even in this narrow sense, no people could be said to be absolutely pure, as all have absorbed foreign elements.

The intellectual differences between races appear to be more profound than the physical. How great is the gulf between early societies and civilized human beings? Yet whereas physical characteristics are permanent in a race, mental phenomena are not. The products of the mind are distinguished from the quality of the mind itself. All races possess the same innate mental potentiality; only circumstances create intellectual disparity, which can be eliminated by altering them. As an example, a child who has been born into primitive or deprived conditions but who has been educated in a civilized environment and given all its advantages will grow up to be just as intelligent and knowledgeable as one who has been born into privileged circumstances. Evidently, the mind is extremely pliable. It is thus false to talk of inherent racial superiority. If the power and achievements of nations are attributable to circumstances that are not eternal, then it is easy to understand their rise and fall.

All races are to be regarded as having equal rights by virtue of the inherent purpose of all human beings. Owing to circumstances, different races may differ in their practices, but none should be subjected to another. Each race should have the power to do what it can for its welfare but, as with the individual, should not encroach on the equal rights of others. Should there be a world state, all persons will be citizens with identical privileges irrespective of race. If regional states persist, then none of their citizens should suffer any discriminatory treatment on racial grounds. There should be no ruling and subject peoples, and minorities should not be maltreated by majorities.

Chapter 18
Territory

Humanity dwells on the surface of the earth, on what may be designated as territory. We cannot be said to own what belongs to nature, but, being ourselves a product of nature, we could rightfully use it for our maintenance. One important fact is that the earth does not present the same conditions in all its parts; its diversity of phenomena is amazing. In the course of history, humanity has spread over it, each group attaching itself to some particular portion, which is termed a *country*. The individual usually stays in the locality where he was born and regards it as home.

Each person occupies a tiny area of territory. The earth does not grow in extent while the human race continues to increase in number. It would be fanciful to speculate about what would happen if the global population were to grow to such proportions that sufficient standing room were not available! As territory is not used merely for occupancy but for the provision of sustenance, the population would be incapable of further expansion long before that point, for starvation would do its fell work. Human increase should be controlled at the point where a comfortable existence for all becomes impossible.

A community is a number of people dwelling in propinquity. Should the denizens of a country be spread evenly over its entire expanse? Since the available area per person may not be small, if this were done, there would arise an array of hermits, and the benefit of social organization would vanish. If they were collected into a single spot, making a huge community, the rest of the country would cease to be of use. Since neither of these measures is practicable, the only thing to do is to have a collection of communities studding the length and breadth of a country.

Each community inhabits an area that is developed into a town. The town is the territorial unit of society. With the exception of a few that serve as capitals, the normal town should be of moderate dimensions, not too small to allow the introduction of all the benefits of civilization nor too large to render the distance between one another inconveniently great. The actual size of any town must depend on local conditions, but it should be made to approach the standard.

The small town is the ideal. In it, life can be refined yet not hectic. Its extent should be so harmonized with its population that there is adequate dwelling space and ease of movement—no overcrowded houses, no jostling in the streets, no incessant traffic. It should be a thing of beauty, regularly planned, radiant with flowers and foliage, a fit abode for a life of useful joyousness. All utilitarian conveniences should be installed, and cultural and recreational facilities should be abundantly provided.

Each town will have all those services necessary for the welfare of its citizens. It may also specialize in some particular type of production, depending on local facilities. A good proportion of its inhabitants will be devoted to agriculture: the farmers go out to the fields in the morning and return in the evening.

The town is to have definite limits and not straggle into an amorphous mass of suburbs. It will be surrounded by a belt of parkland. Running all around it is a strip of land of some width, planted with trees, alive with birds, adorned with pavilions and sculpture, dotted with fishponds—a sanctuary where the citizens may stroll and enjoy the fragrant air. Beyond the park, which defines the boundaries of the town, lies the countryside with its cultivated fields; the farmers till their farms but do not live there. Every town controls a stretch of territory within a certain radius, and thus the entire land is divided into an assemblage of small units, each with a town as the center. The space between towns should not be great, as it would be difficult for the farmers to travel far to reach their fields. Besides, the country would present a more balanced appearance if it did not consist of only a few towns amid vast expanses of lonely land. For convenience, buildings are erected at intervals over the countryside to be used as hotels called *service stations*, where the farmers take their lunches and pass their periods of rest and guards watch over the farms at night; they can also be used by casual passersby for any service that may be easily performed.

The village must be abolished—it is a relic of barbarism, a survivor from prehistoric ages when human beings first emerged from their caves, cleared the jungles, and built collections of flimsy sheds. It exists in somnolence, dragging on wearily, its inhabitants wallowing in an atmosphere of squalor—an unmitigated horror, disgusting to behold and hateful to live in. It is bare of civilization; the agricultural laborers who drag along their wretched days in it suffer the anomaly of living in civilization and not partaking of its benefits. No cultural activities or recreational facilities are available. Its denizens are stultified by toil and dullness. Dilapidated hovels and muddy lanes salute the eye; circumscribed lives flow away listlessly. Can such surroundings be consonant with progress and a tolerable mode of existence?

The village is planless. Uneconomical to develop, it struggles on as best as it can; it is difficult to introduce into a tiny community of a few hundred souls an adequate amount of amenities, if any at all. There is nothing admirable about the sordid life and ignoble dwelling places, about filth and ragged raiment and windblown shacks and muddy lanes and flickering oil lamps. The villager is no theme for lyrical eulogies, wearily plodding from dawn to dusk, dully conscious of the slow movement of time, brutish and ignorant.

Every human being has the right to enjoy civilization. The problem of the town has been sadly neglected by reformers in spite of its tremendous importance, interwoven as it is with a people's daily life. There have indeed been plans for rural development, embodying no more than some sanitary projects and slight improvements in material conveniences—palliative measures that are supposed to cure social evils by concealing them beneath a thin veneer of good intentions. The destruction of the village has not been a prominent objective. Town planning appears to be chiefly concerned with cities, mending them to be more beautiful. The glory of a country does not lie in its few cities with their striking monuments, triumphal arches, multistory buildings, and halls of amusement. It is to be judged through the whole length and breadth of the land, in the dwelling places of the majority of the inhabitants.

A country will consist of a network of beautiful towns connected by good roads. Country planning is as important as town planning. The proper locations of towns and their relationships to one another, the intervals between them, their special industries, the system of communications, the utilization of the countryside—the land should be laid out to achieve maximum beauty and utility. In the past, towns sprang up haphazardly; many cities are located on islands and some on hillsides. A city on a small island is cramped and lacking road communication with other towns. A city on a hillside is impossible to plan properly and possesses unnecessary transportation difficulties. An island should consist rather of one or more small towns; as for hills, towns should be constructed at their bases and not on their sides. A town should preferably be erected on a plain in the midst of cultivated land with roads leading in all four directions to other places. The nature of the available terrain and the actual requirements and circumstances will largely determine the choice.

For administrative purposes, the country is divided into sections. An area comprising a group of towns is a district while a number of districts form a province. Each district or province contains a large town called a *capital*, contradistinguished from the small towns, which may be called *basic towns*. The district capital, as a rule, is bigger and has a higher population than the basic town; the provincial capital is likewise greater than the district capital. Over the entire country presides a national capital, the biggest of them all.

The relative sizes, of course, are not perfectly strict. Some district capitals may be larger than their provincial capitals by virtue of their peculiar circumstances. The capitals should preferably be situated around the centers of their sections, which should be equalized as much as possible; number of towns, area of territory, and population size must be considered. Each capital can hold its inhabitants comfortably without overcrowding and is planned on the same principles as the basic towns, with engirdling parks and areas of countryside.

Town and country planning confronts obstructions arising from the difficulty of changing structures already in existence. Only in totally undeveloped territory would it be possible to build strictly according to a systematic plan. Most countries have been inhabited for untold ages and possess numbers of villages, towns, and cities. As it would require enormous labor and expense to transform them radically, in practice, the work must be undertaken slowly, consisting in great measure of adaptation. Existing towns and cities must be gradually modified, while villages can be destroyed altogether and towns built to hold new communities. The process naturally takes time.

About the Author

Born around the time of the foundation of the Republic of China, in the former English colony of British Malaya, Tan Kheng Yeang was educated in an English school. His father was from China but had emigrated to Malaya and had become a successful businessman, involved in various activities, including as a rubber merchant. From his early days the author was interested in literature and philosophy and as his interest evolved to  science, he decided to study civil engineering at the University of Hong Kong, as he felt he needed a practical career.

After the Japanese occupied Hong Kong, he went into free China where he found work in an office constructing roads and later an airfield in Guangxi Province. After the war ended in 1945, he returned to Malaya and became an engineer in the City Council of Georgetown, Penang. After his retirement, he worked as an engineering consultant. He is the author of twelve books that reflect the broad range of his interests and talents.